THE HUMAN JOURNEY SEMINARS

Great Books in the Catholic Intellectual Tradition

CIT 201

Sacred Heart University

Change the course.

ISBN 13: 978-1-50669-608-9

Second Printing

Acknowledgments:

pp. 1–9: From *Plato's Republic* translated by I. A. Richards. Copyright © 1966 by Cambridge University Press. Reprinted by permission of the publisher via the Copyright Clearance Center.
pp. 10–160: From the *New American Bible, Revised Edition*. Copyright © 1991 by the Confraternity of Christian Doctrine, Inc. Reprinted by permission.
pp. 161–247: From *The Confessions of Saint Augustine* edited by Michael Foley, Translated by F. J. Sheed. Translation copyright © 1942 and 1943 by Sheed & Ward, Inc. Assigned to Hackett Publishing Company, Inc., 1992. First Hackett edition copyright © 1993 by Hackett Publishing Company, Inc. Second Hackett edition copyright © 2006 by Hackett Publishing Company Inc. All rights reserved. Reprinted by permission.
pp. 248–257: From *Summa Contra Gentiles Book One: God* translated by Anton C. Pegis. Copyright © 1975. Originally published by University of Notre Dame Press. Reprinted by permission of Penguin Random House, LLC via the Copyright Clearance Center.
pp. 258–330: From *The Divine Comedy* translated by John Ciardi. *The Inferno* copyright © 1954 by John Ciardi *The Purgatorio* copyright © 1957, 1959, 1960, 1961 by John Ciardi. *The Paradiso* copyright © 1961, 1965, 1967, 1970 by John Ciardi. Published by The New American Library, a division of Penguin Group (USA) Inc.

Change the course.

530 Great Road
Acton, MA 01720
800-562-2147
www.xanedu.com

Contents

The Human Journey Seminars: Great Books in the Catholic Intellectual Tradition

The Catholic Intellectual Tradition

The Human Journey Seminars: Great Books in the Catholic Intellectual Tradition are Sacred Heart University's academic signature core courses. These are the only two courses which intentionally and directly engage all students in an understanding of the Catholic Intellectual Tradition— which is at the heart of the University's Mission as a Catholic institution.

We understand this Catholic Intellectual Tradition as an ongoing two thousand-year-old conversation between the great thinkers, writers, artists of this Tradition and the cultures in which they live, discussing questions about God, humanity, society and nature.

Thus, these two seminars are framed by four fundamental and enduring questions of human existence: what does it mean to be human; what does it mean to live a life of meaning and purpose; what is our relationship with the natural world; and what does it mean to form a more just society for the common good?

Why does any of this matter? First the great texts of the Catholic Intellectual Tradition which you will be reading form a major portion of the conceptual foundations of much of western civilization, and the ideas of this Tradition—ideas about faith, reason, truth, love, goodness, justice, suffering, and evil—are ideas that we still wrestle with and that continue to form the basis of our lives today.

We understand this Tradition to be a living, developing Tradition which engages all of us in conversation, and we invite you to enter this conversation by carefully reading, thinking about, and discussing these great books and the important ideas expressed in them. Some of this reading will be challenging, but these texts are challenging us to think seriously about important, enduring, even vexing questions and if we are serious about who we are, the purpose of our lives, and the condition of our world and society, then our task is to accept this challenge and enter the conversation.

The Journey to God

In CIT 201, the first seminar, we will be reading some early texts. We begin with Plato's "The Allegory of the Cave." Plato (428–347 B.C.) was a Greek philosopher who is one of the most important thinkers of western culture. "The Allegory of the Cave" is a powerful metaphor for the human striving toward transcendence and Ultimate Good. Plato's work, which comes well before Christianity, asks us to think about important questions: what is the meaning and purpose of our life; what is the difference between appearance (what seems real) and true reality—that which is Ultimate Good and Truth.

The Hebrew Bible, or what Christians call "The Old Testament," is a sacred book of both Judaism and Christianity. The first book of the Old Testament is Genesis. The section of Genesis 1–3 that we will read tells the story (really two stories) about the creation of the world and of human beings by a Divine Creator. Genesis also tells about the alienation of human beings from their Creator. Some of the questions these chapters ask not only have to do with: if we are made in the image of God, then who are we and why are we here, but they also raise vexing questions about suffering, evil, and death. The book of Exodus tells the story of the Jews deliverance from slavery in Egypt. In Exodus 20, which we read, we learn about the covenant of the Law given by God to Moses to establish God's relationship with his people.

The Gospel of Matthew is found in The New Testament of the Christian Bible. The Gospel story is the fundamental text of the Christian Tradition. It tells the story of the life, crucifixion, death, and resurrection of Jesus of Nazareth. The Gospel proclaims Jesus as Son of God and Redeemer of humankind. The Gospel, or "Good News" is a story of love, forgiveness, and redemption.

St. Augustine (A.D. 354–430) was an early Christian theologian and philosopher whose writings influenced the development of western philosophy and western Christianity. *The Confessions* is his personal journey which reveals to us the anguish of struggling with our human frailty, our proclivity to wrongdoing, and the importance of our relationship with God. Augustine reminds us of our origin and destiny: "You have made us for yourself, and our heart is restless until it rests in you."

Dante Alighieri (A.D. 1265–1321) was an Italian poet, prose writer, moral philosopher, and a literary theorist. Dante's monumental epic, *The Divine Comedy*, is a masterpiece of world literature. In *The Divine Comedy*, Dante portrays the human journey to God as a journey of discovery: a descent into the darkness of hell to learn the nature of sin, evil, and suffering, and an ascent to discover Divine Love and God's Grace. On this journey with Dante, we are asked to consider who we are, what our relationship is with others, and most important of all, what is our relationship with God.

St. Thomas Aquinas (1225–1274) was an Italian Dominican Friar and Catholic Priest. He was a philosopher, theologian, and jurist and he is considered one of the most influential thinkers of western culture and thought. In his work he synthesizes Aristotelian philosophy with Christian theology. His most influential works are *Summa Theologica* and *Summa contra Gentiles*. In our selection from *Summa contra Gentiles*, St. Thomas uses his formidable wisdom, knowledge and intelligence to make the case for the compatibility of faith and reason which is a cornerstone claim of The Catholic Intellectual Tradition.

The Journey to the World

In CIT 202, the second seminar, we read works that take us right up to the contemporary world. We will begin with *Nostra Aetate* (*In Our Time*) which is a document from the Second Vatican Council in 1965. The document is the Declaration on the Relationship of the Church with Non-Christian Religions. This document affirms the unity of the origin of all people by God, and it asks the fundamental questions of human existence which we discuss in this course. The document explains how different religions respond to these enduring questions and it also shows The Catholic Intellectual Tradition's ongoing conversation with and openness to all religions and cultures.

Caritas In Veritate is a Papal encyclical written by Benedict XVI in 2009. This encyclical asserts the central claim that "Charity in Truth, to which Jesus Christ bore witness, is the principal driving force behind the authentic development of every human person and all humanity." The encyclical brings us to the root of Christianity which is Divine Love as the basis for the dignity of every human being and for our work to form a more just society.

Cardinal John Henry Newman (1801–1890) was an academic, an intellectual, and originally, he was an Anglican until he converted to Roman Catholicism. "The Uses of Knowledge" which we are reading comes from Newman's landmark work, *The Idea of a University*. In this latter work Newman discusses the place of religion and moral values in the University setting and the competing claims of liberal and professional education. In our selections, Newman discusses the importance of knowledge as a value in and of itself, in its relationship to professional skills, and to religion. The relationship between knowledge, learning, and faith is the basis of the Catholic Intellectual Tradition.

Gerard Manley Hopkins, S.J. (1844–1889) was an English poet, a Roman Catholic convert, and a Jesuit priest whose innovative poetic style (sprung rhythm) and his unique poetic concept of "inscape" express the sacramental principle of God's presence in nature and reality.

Thomas Merton (1915–1968), arguably one of the greatest spiritual thinkers of the twentieth century, became a Catholic and a Trappist Monk, after he had led a rather rambunctious and wild life. While he was studying at Columbia University he read the great philosophical and theological thinkers of the Catholic Intellectual Tradition and he converted to Roman Catholicism. In the 1960s, Merton was very active in the Civil Rights and Peace Movements. He claimed that race and peace were the two most urgent issues of our time. For Merton, to be a saint meant to be yourself, and according to him, that meant discovering your authentic self. Often compared to St. Augustine's journey in *The Confessions*, Merton's work, *The Seven Storey Mountain*, tells about the struggles he went through to find his true self. For both these men, that journey leads to God.

Dorothy Day (1897–1980) was a journalist, a social activist, and after living a rather bohemian life, she became a Catholic convert. She established The Catholic Worker Movement, which was a pacifist, nonviolent movement on behalf of the poor and homeless. Her activism for social justice and her dedication to non-violence were recognized by the U.S. Conference of Catholic Bishops as having a profound impact on the Catholic Church in America. Her essays in this reader illustrate her thinking about working for justice for the poor and vulnerable.

Martin Luther King Jr. (1929–1968) was an American Baptist Minister, a social activist, the martyred leader of the Civil Rights Movement in America. He organized and led the Selma to Montgomery Civil Rights marches, and his advocacy for civil rights was based upon using nonviolent civil disobedience and Christian belief. His "Letter from a Birmingham Jail" defends the use of non-violent protest to fight racism, and based upon Christian beliefs and natural law, he explains why people have a moral responsibility to break unjust laws. He received the Nobel Peace Prize in 1964 and he was assassinated in 1968.

Gustavo Gutierrez (1928–present) is a Dominican Priest and a Peruvian theologian. He is recognized as the founder of Liberation Theology which sees poverty as the result of unjust social structures. Gutierrez's article emphasizes the dignity of the poor and he locates the basis for the preferential option for the poor in the Christian Gospel.

The Fundamental Claims of the Catholic Intellectual Tradition

Embedded in all of these writings we will discern the fundamental claims of The Catholic Intellectual Tradition. As we read these works we will focus on four of these claims. So what are these claims and how can we understand a little bit about each one?

— The first claim of the Catholic Intellectual Tradition is that human beings exist in relation to a Triune God, the Trinity. The belief in the Trinity is the great dividing line between the Christian and Jewish and Muslim conceptions of God. In the Catholic Tradition, the doctrine of the Trinity is a mystery of faith and cannot be known by natural reason, but human reason can help us to have some understanding of this Mystery. The Trinity is understood as One: there is only one God and the three Divine persons of the Trinity—Father, Son, and Holy Spirit—are distinct persons within this one Divine Unity.

Human beings have wrestled with the idea of ultimate reality forever (see Plato). Does reality have an ultimate good and absolute truth that grounds all the diverse and partial truths we experience in life? The Trinity offers a way of understanding the relationship between Ultimate Unity—God—and plurality: a relationship of three persons forms the One God. God is Love and the three persons of the Trinity are united in a relationship of Divine Love. In the Catholic Tradition, being fully human and living a life of meaning and purpose means joining in this relationship of love.

◄ The second claim states: God's presence in the world is mediated through nature and reality. Another name for this idea is called the sacramental principle. Basically this idea means that God is present in the nature and reality. The defining feature of Christianity is the Incarnation: God enters the world as the human person, Jesus of Nazareth. Further, the Holy Spirit infuses the world with the Divine. This, then, is the sacramental principle: because God is present in reality, human beings and nature have innate value and meaning. As Gerard Manley Hopkins writes: "The world is charged with the grandeur of God."

➤ The third claim asserts that faith and reason (science) are compatible. Our short selection from St. Thomas Aquinas explains that faith and reason are compatible. Aquinas asserts this claim because God, the source of Grace and Revelation is also the source of nature and human mind, and so the human mind's desire to understand and know what is true is compatible with an inquiring faith whose search is for understanding and Truth.

➤ The last claim states that the dignity of the human being is inviolable and therefore the commitment to justice for the common good is necessary. A central conviction of Christianity has always been that human beings, created in the image of God, endowed with a soul, and redeemed by Christ are sacred. When the Catholic Intellectual Tradition reflects on "what does it mean to be human," it is based upon this conviction. That means all human beings—regardless of their race, gender, religion, class, ethnicity, or sexual orientation—have innate dignity and it is our responsibility to respect that dignity, in ourselves and in others. Further, because of the Divine Love which has created us and which is at the center of all Christian thought, and informed by the Gospel injunction to love God with our whole heart and soul and to love our neighbor as ourselves, it is our responsibility and obligation to work toward justice for the common good.

Seminar Pedagogy

At its heart, seminar pedagogy respects the experience and understanding that students bring to a careful and thoughtful reading of a text, and it relies on their willingness to engage with other students in discussion of the texts. Seminar pedagogy assumes that students want to be active in their own learning and that they have something to contribute to the learning experience that takes place in the seminar. These CIT Seminars are purposefully employing the seminar pedagogy to cultivate in students an ability to read great texts and to wrestle with the BIG questions that these texts address and that are fundamental to every student becoming a knowledgeable and educated person.

Book VII: Allegory of the Cave

Plato

Book VII begins with another unforgettable image, the allegory of the Cave, which fits together with the Sun and Line (517b) and which illustrates the effects of education on the soul (514a). It leads to a brief but important discussion of education (518b–519b) in which Sacrum makes it clear that the aim of education is to turn the soul around by changing its desires.

The next topic is the education of the philosopher-kings. (1) Their initial education is in music and poetry, physical training, and elementary mathematics (535a–537b). (2) This is followed by two or three years of compulsory physical training, rather like the military service that some countries still require (537b–c). (3) Those who are most successful in these studies next receive ten years of education in mathematical science (537c–d, 522c–531d). (4) Those who are again most successful receive five years of training in dialectic (537d–540a, 531e–535a). (5) Those who are still most successful receive fifteen years of practical political training (539e–540a). Finally, (6) those who are also successful in practical politics are "compelled to lift up the radiant light of their souls" to the good itself (540a) and are equipped to be philosopher-kings.

The centrality of mathematics in the philosopher's education is somewhat surprising, as is the restriction of dialectic to mature people who have mastered science. But the fact that the largest component of this education consists of practical political training should reassure those who think that philosopher-kings would not even begin to know how to rule a city. It is an interesting question as to why this training must take place before they can see the good itself. Plato's discussion of users, makers, and imitators in Book X (601d–602b) is surely relevant to this question, for it suggests that only those who use an entire city (see 428c–d) could know what a good city is.

The city that contains philosopher-kings and the educational institutions necessary to produce them is the third and final stage in Plato's construction of the kallipolis (535a–536d, 543c–544a).

Next, I said, compare the effect of education and of the lack of it on our nature to an experience like this: Imagine human beings living 514 in an underground, cavelike dwelling, with an entrance a long way up, which is both open to the light and as wide as the cave itself. They've been there since childhood, fixed in the same place, with their necks and legs fettered, able to see only in front of them, because their bonds prevent them from turning their heads around. Light is *b*   provided by a fire burning far above and behind them. Also behind them, but on higher ground, there is a path stretching between them and the fire. Imagine that along this path a low wall has been built, like the screen in front of puppeteers above which they show their puppets.

I'm imagining it.

Then also imagine that there are people along the wall, carrying all kinds of artifacts that project above it—statues of people and other

c   animals, made out of stone, wood, and every material. And, as you'd

515   expect, some of the carriers are talking, and some are silent.

It's a strange image you're describing, and strange prisoners.

They're like us. Do you suppose, first of all, that these prisoners see anything of themselves and one another besides the shadows that the fire casts on the wall in front of them?

How could they, if they have to keep their heads motionless

b   throughout life?

What about the things being carried along the wall? Isn't the same true of them?

Of course.

And if they could talk to one another, don't you think they'd suppose that the names they used applied to the things they see passing before them?[1]

They'd have to.

And what if their prison also had an echo from the wall facing them? Don't you think they'd believe that the shadows passing in front of them were talking whenever one of the carriers passing along the wall was doing so?

I certainly do.

c   Then the prisoners would in every way believe that the truth is nothing other than the shadows of those artifacts.

They must surely believe that.

Consider, then, what being released from their bonds and cured of their ignorance would naturally be like if something like this came to pass. When one of them was freed and suddenly compelled to stand up, turn his head, walk, and look up toward the light, he'd be pained and dazzled and unable to see the things whose shadows he'd

d   seen before. What do you think he'd say, if we told him that what he'd seen before was inconsequential, but that now—because he is a bit closer to the things that are and is turned towards things that are more—he sees more correctly? Or, to put it another way, if we pointed to each of the things passing by, asked him what each of them is, and compelled him to answer, don't you think he'd be at a loss and that he'd believe that the things he saw earlier were truer than the ones he was now being shown?

Much truer.

And if someone compelled him to look at the light itself, wouldn't his eyes hurt, and wouldn't he turn around and flee towards the *e* things he's able to see, believing that they're really clearer than the ones he's being shown?

He would.

And if someone dragged him away from there by force, up the rough, steep path, and didn't let him go until he had dragged him into the sunlight, wouldn't he be pained and irritated at being treated that way? And when he came into the light, with the sun filling his *516* eyes, wouldn't he be unable to see a single one of the things now said to be true?

He would be unable to see them, at least at first.

I suppose, then, that he'd need time to get adjusted before he could see things in the world above. At first, he'd see shadows most easily, then images of men and other things in water, then the things themselves. Of these, he'd be able to study the things in the sky and the sky itself more easily at night, looking at the light of the stars and the moon, than during the day; looking at the sun and the light of the *b* sun.

Of course.

Finally, I suppose, he'd be able to see the sun, not images of it in water or some alien place, but the sun itself, in its own place, and be able to study it.

Necessarily so.

And at this point he would infer and conclude that the sun provides the seasons and the years, governs everything in the visible world, and is in some way the cause of all the things that he used to *c* see.

It's clear that would be his next step.

What about when he reminds himself of his first dwelling place, his fellow prisoners, and what passed for wisdom there? Don't you think that he'd count himself happy for the change and pity the others?

Certainly.

And if there had been any honors, praises, or prizes among them for the one who was sharpest at identifying the shadows as they passed by and who best remembered which usually came earlier, which later, and which simultaneously, and who could thus best divine the future, *d* do you think that our man would desire these rewards or envy those among the prisoners who were honored and held power? Instead, wouldn't he feel, with Homer, that he'd much prefer to "work the earth as a serf to another, one without possessions,"[2] and go through any sufferings, rather than share their opinions and live as they do?

e   I suppose he would rather suffer anything than live like that.

Consider this too. If this man went down into the cave again and sat down in his same seat, wouldn't his eyes—coming suddenly out of the sun like that—be filled with darkness?

They certainly would.

And before his eyes had recovered—and the adjustment would not be quick—while his vision was still dim, if he had to compete again with the perpetual prisoners in recognizing the shadows, *517* wouldn't he invite ridicule? Wouldn't it be said of him that he'd returned from his upward journey with his eyesight ruined and that it isn't worthwhile even to try to travel upward? And, as for anyone who tried to free them and lead them upward, if they could somehow get their hands on him, wouldn't they kill him?

They certainly would.

b   This whole image, Glaucon, must be fitted together with what we said before. The visible realm should be likened to the prison dwelling, and the light of the fire inside it to the power of the sun. And if you interpret the upward journey and the study of things above as the upward journey of the soul to the intelligible realm, you'll grasp what I hope to convey, since that is what you wanted to hear about. Whether it's true or not, only the god knows. But this is how I see it: In the knowable realm, the form of the good is the last thing to be seen, and it is reached only with difficulty. Once one has seen it, however, one must conclude that it is the cause of all that is correct *c* and beautiful in anything, that it produces both light and its source in the visible realm, and that in the intelligible realm it controls and provides truth, and understanding, so that anyone who is to act sensibly in private or public must see it.

I have the same thought, at least as far as I'm able.

Come, then, share with me this thought also: It isn't surprising that the ones who get to this point are unwilling to occupy themselves with human affairs and that their souls are always pressing upwards, eager to spend their time above, for, after all, this is surely *d* what we'd expect, if indeed things fit the image I described before.

It is.

What about what happens when someone turns from divine study to the evils of human life? Do you think it's surprising, since his sight is still dim, and he hasn't yet become accustomed to the darkness around him, that he behaves awkwardly and appears completely ridiculous if he's compelled, either in the courts or elsewhere, to contend about the shadows of justice or the statues of which they are the shadows and to dispute about the way these things are understood by people who have never seen justice itself?　　*e*

That's not surprising at all.

No, it isn't. But anyone with any understanding would remem-　*518* ber that the eyes may be confused in two ways and from two causes, namely, when they've come from the light into the darkness and when they've come from the darkness into the light. Realizing that the same applies to the soul, when someone sees a soul disturbed and unable to see something, he won't laugh mindlessly, but he'll take into consideration whether it has come from a brighter life and is dimmed through not having yet become accustomed to the dark or whether it has come from greater ignorance into greater light and is dazzled by the increased brilliance. Then he'll declare the first soul happy in its experience and life, and he'll pity the latter—but even if　*b* he chose to make fun of it, at least he'd be less ridiculous than if he laughed at a soul that has come from the light above.

What you say is very reasonable.

If that's true, then here's what we must think about these matters: Education isn't what some people declare it to be, namely, putting knowledge into souls that lack it, like putting sight into blind eyes.　*c*

They do say that.

But our present discussion, on the other hand, shows that the power to learn is present in everyone's soul and that the instrument with which each learns is like an eye that cannot be turned around from darkness to light without turning the whole body. This instrument cannot be turned around from that which is coming into being without turning the whole soul until it is able to study that which is and the brightest thing that is, namely, the one we call the good. Isn't　*d* that right?

Yes.

Then education is the craft concerned with doing this very thing, this turning around, and with how the soul can most easily and effectively be made to do it. It isn't the craft of putting sight into the soul. Education takes for granted that sight is there but that it isn't turned the right way or looking where it ought to look, and it tries to redirect it appropriately.

So it seems.

Now, it looks as though the other so-called virtues of the soul are akin to those of the body, for they really aren't there beforehand but are added later by habit and practice. However, the virtue of　*e* reason seems to belong above all to something more divine,[3] which never loses its power but is either useful and beneficial or useless

and harmful, depending on the way it is turned. Or have you never
519 noticed this about people who are said to be vicious but clever, how
keen the vision of their little souls is and how sharply it distinguishes
the things it is turned towards? This shows that its sight isn't inferior
but rather is forced to serve evil ends, so that the sharper it sees, the
more evil it accomplishes.

Absolutely.

However, if a nature of this sort had been hammered at from
childhood and freed from the bonds of kinship with becoming, which
have been fastened to it by feasting, greed, and other such pleasures
b and which, like leaden weights, pull its vision downwards—if, being
rid of these, it turned to look at true things, then I say that the same
soul of the same person would see these most sharply, just as it now
does the things it is presently turned towards.

Probably so.

And what about the uneducated who have no experience of
truth? Isn't it likely—indeed, doesn't it follow necessarily from what
was said before—that they will never adequately govern a city? But
neither would those who've been allowed to spend their whole lives
c being educated. The former would fail because they don't have a single goal at which all their actions, public and private, inevitably aim;
the latter would fail because they'd refuse to act, thinking that they
had settled while still alive in the faraway Isles of the Blessed.[4]

That's true.

It is our task as founders, then, to compel the best natures to reach
the study we said before is the most important, namely, to make the
ascent and see the good. But when they've made it and looked suf-
d ficiently, we mustn't allow them to do what they're allowed to do
today.

What's that?

To stay there and refuse to go down again to the prisoners in the
cave and share their labors and honors, whether they are of less worth
or of greater.

Then are we to do them an injustice by making them live a worse
life when they could live a better one?

e You are forgetting again that it isn't the law's concern to make any
one class in the city outstandingly happy but to contrive to spread
happiness throughout the city by bringing the citizens into harmony
with each other through persuasion or compulsion and by making
them share with each other the benefits that each class can confer
520 on the community.[5] The law produces such people in the city, not in
order to allow them to turn in whatever direction they want, but to
make use of them to bind the city together.

That's true, I had forgotten.

Observe, then, Glaucon, that we won't be doing an injustice to those who've become philosophers in our city and that what we'll say to them, when we compel them to guard and care for the others, will be just. We'll say: "When people like you come to be in other cities, they're justified in not sharing in their city's labors, for they've *b* grown there spontaneously, against the will of the constitution. And what grows of its own accord and owes no debt for its upbringing has justice on its side when it isn't keen to pay anyone for that upbringing. But we've made you kings in our city and leaders of the swarm, as it were, both for yourselves and for the rest of the city. You're better and more completely educated than the others and are better able to share in both types of life.[6] Therefore each of you in turn must go *c* down to live in the common dwelling place of the others and grow accustomed to seeing in the dark. When you are used to it, you'll see vastly better than the people there. And because you've seen the truth about fine, just, and good things, you'll know each image for what it is and also that of which it is the image. Thus, for you and for us, the city will be governed, not like the majority of cities nowadays, by people who fight over shadows and struggle against one another in order to rule—as if that were a great good—but by people who are awake rather than dreaming,[7] for the truth is surely this: A *d* city whose prospective rulers are least eager to rule must of necessity be most free from civil war, whereas a city with the opposite kind of rulers is governed in the opposite way."

Absolutely.

Then do you think that those we've nurtured will disobey us and refuse to share the labors of the city, each in turn, while living the greater part of their time with one another in the pure realm?

It isn't possible, for we'll be giving just orders to just people. Each *e* of them will certainly go to rule as to something compulsory, however, which is exactly the opposite of what's done by those who now rule in each city. This is how it is. If you can find a way of life that's better than ruling for the prospective rulers, your well-governed city will become a possibility, for only in it will the truly rich rule—not *521* those who are rich in gold but those who are rich in the wealth that the happy must have, namely, a good and rational life. But if beggars hungry for private goods go into public life, thinking that the good is there for the seizing, then the well-governed city is impossible, for then ruling is something fought over, and this civil and domestic war destroys these people and the rest of the city as well.

That's very true.

b   Can you name any life that despises political rule besides that of
the true philosopher?

No, by god, I can't.

But surely it is those who are not lovers of ruling who must rule,
for if they don't, the lovers of it, who are rivals, will fight over it.

Of course.

Then who will you compel to become guardians of the city, if not
those who have the best understanding of what matters for good government and who have other honors than political ones, and a better
life as well?

No one.

Do you want us to consider now how such people will come to
be in our city and how—just as some are said to have gone up from
c   Hades to the gods—we'll lead them up to the light?

Of course I do.

This isn't, it seems, a matter of spinning a potsherd,[8] but of turning a soul from a day that is a kind of night to the true day—-the
ascent to what is, which we say is true philosophy.

Indeed.

Then mustn't we try to discover the subjects that have the power
d   to bring this about?

Of course.

So what subject is it, Glaucon, that draws the soul from the realm
of becoming to the realm of what is? And it occurs to me as I'm speaking that we said, didn't we, that it is necessary for the prospective
rulers to be athletes in war when they're young?

Yes, we did.

Then the subject we're looking for must also have this characteristic in addition to the former one.

Notes

1. Reading *parionta autous nomizein onomazein*. E.g. they would think that the
   name "human being" applied to the shadow of a statue of a human being.

2. *Odyssey* 11.489–90. The shade of the dead Achilles speaks these words
   to Odysseus, who is visiting Hades. Plato is, therefore, likening the cave
   dwellers to the dead.

3. See 589d, 590d, 611b ff.

4. A place where good people are said to live in eternal happiness, normally
   after death.

5. See 420b–421c, 462a–466c.

6. I.e. the practical life of ruling the city and the theoretical life of studying
   the good itself.

7. See 476c–d.

8. A proverbial expression, referring to a children's game. The players were divided into two groups. A shell or potsherd, white on one side and black on the other, was thrown into the space between them to the cry of "night or day" (note the reference to night and day which follows). According as the white or black fell uppermost, one group ran away, pursued by the other. The meaning here is much the same as that of our expression "tossing a coin."

from **The New American Bible, Revised Edition**

NEON

The Book of Genesis

Genesis is the first book of the Pentateuch (Genesis, Exodus, Leviticus, Numbers, Deuteronomy), the first section of the Jewish and the Christian Scriptures. Its title in English, "Genesis," comes from the Greek of Gn 2:4, literally, "the book of the generation (genesis) of the heavens and earth." Its title in the Jewish Scriptures is the opening Hebrew word, Bereshit, "in the beginning."

The book has two major sections—the creation and expansion of the human race (2:4–11:9), and the story of Abraham and his descendants (11:10–50:26). The first section deals with God and the nations, and the second deals with God and a particular nation, Israel. The opening creation account (1:1–2:3) lifts up two themes that play major roles in each section—the divine command to the first couple (standing for the whole race) to produce offspring and to possess land (1:28). In the first section, progeny and land appear in the form of births and genealogies (chaps. 2–9) and allotment of land (chaps. 10–11), and in the second, progeny and land appear in the form of promises of descendants and land to the ancestors. Another indication of editing is the formulaic introduction, "this is the story; these are the descendants" (Hebrew tōledôt), which occurs five times in Section I (2:4; 5:1; 6:9; 10:1; 10:31) and five times in Section II (11:10; 25:12, 19; 36:1 [v. 9 is an addition]; 37:2).

The Composition of the Book. *For the literary sources of Genesis, see Introduction to the Pentateuch. As far as the sources of Genesis are concerned, contemporary readers can reasonably assume that ancient traditions (J and E) were edited in the sixth or fifth century B.C. for a Jewish audience that had suffered the effects of the exile and was now largely living outside of Palestine. The editor highlighted themes of vital concern to this audience: God intends that every nation have posterity and land; the ancestors of Israel are models for their descendants who also live in hope rather than in full possession of what has been promised; the ancient covenant with God is eternal, remaining valid even when the human party has been unfaithful. By highlighting such concerns, the editor addressed the worries of exiled Israel and indeed of contemporary Jews and Christians.*

Genesis 1–11. *The seven-day creation account in Gn 1:1–2:3 tells of a God whose mere word creates a beautiful universe in which human beings are an integral and important part. Though Gn 2:4–3:24 is often regarded as "the second creation story," the text suggests that the whole of 2:4–11:9 tells one story. The plot of Gn 2–11 (creation, the flood, renewed creation) has been borrowed from creation-flood stories attested in Mesopotamian literature of the second and early*

10

first millennia. In the Mesopotamian creation-flood stories, the gods created the human race as slaves whose task it was to manage the universe for them—giving them food, clothing, and honor in temple ceremonies. In an unforeseen development, however, the human race grew so numerous and noisy that the gods could not sleep. Deeply angered, the gods decided to destroy the race by a universal flood. One man and his family, however, secretly warned of the flood by his patron god, built a boat and survived. Soon regretting their impetuous decision, the gods created a revised version of humankind. The new race was created mortal so they would never again grow numerous and bother the gods. The authors of Genesis adapted the creation-flood story in accord with their views of God and humanity. For example, they attributed the fault to human sin rather than to divine miscalculation (6:5–7) and had God reaffirm without change the original creation (9:1–7). In the biblical version God is just, powerful, and not needy.

How should modern readers interpret the creation-flood story in Gn 2–11? The stories are neither history nor myth. "Myth" is an unsuitable term, for it has several different meanings and connotes untruth in popular English. "History" is equally misleading, for it suggests that the events actually took place. The best term is creation-flood story. Ancient Near Eastern thinkers did not have our methods of exploring serious questions. Instead, they used narratives for issues that we would call philosophical and theological. They added and subtracted narrative details and varied the plot as they sought meaning in the ancient stories. Their stories reveal a privileged time, when divine decisions were made that determined the future of the human race. The origin of something was thought to explain its present meaning, e.g., how God acts with justice and generosity, why human beings are rebellious, the nature of sexual attraction and marriage, why there are many peoples and languages. Though the stories may initially strike us as primitive and naive, they are in fact told with skill, compression, and subtlety. They provide profound answers to perennial questions about God and human beings.

__Genesis 11–50.__ One Jewish tradition suggests that God, having been rebuffed in the attempt to forge a relationship with the nations, decided to concentrate on one nation in the hope that it would eventually bring in all the nations. The migration of Abraham's family (11:26–31) is part of the general movement of the human race to take possession of their lands (see 10:32–11:9). Abraham, however, must come into possession of his land in a manner different from the nations, for he will not immediately possess it nor will he have descendants in the manner of the nations, for he is old and his wife is childless (12:1–9). Abraham and Sarah have to live with their God in trust and obedience until at last Isaac is born to them and they manage to buy a sliver of the land (the burial cave at Machpelah, chap. 23). Abraham's humanity and faith offer a wonderful example to the exilic generation.

The historicity of the ancestral stories has been much discussed. Scholars have traditionally dated them sometime in the first half of the second millennium, though a few regard them as late (sixth or fifth century B.C.) and purely fictional.

There is unfortunately no direct extra-biblical evidence confirming (or disproving) the stories. The ancestral stories have affinities, however, to late second-millennium stories of childless ancestors, and their proper names fit linguistic patterns attested in the second millennium. Given the lack of decisive evidence, it is reasonable to accept the Bible's own chronology that the patriarchs were the ancestors of Israel and that they lived well before the exodus that is generally dated in the thirteenth century.

Gn 25:19–35:43 are about Jacob and his twelve sons. The stories are united by a geographical frame: Jacob lives in Canaan until his theft of the right of the firstborn from his brother Esau forces him to flee to Paddan-Aram (alternately Aram-Naharaim). There his uncle Laban tricks him as he earlier tricked his brother. But Jacob is blessed with wealth and sons. He returns to Canaan to receive the final blessing, land, and on the way is reconciled with his brother Esau. As the sons have reached the number of twelve, the patriarch can be given the name Israel (32:28; 35:10). The blessings given to Abraham are reaffirmed to Isaac and to Jacob.

The last cycle of ancestor stories is about Jacob's son Joseph (37:1–50:26, though in chaps. 48–49 the focus swings back to Jacob). The Joseph stories are sophisticated in theme, deftly plotted, and show keen interest in the psychology of the characters. Jacob's favoring of Joseph, the son of his beloved wife Rachel, provokes his brothers to kill him. Joseph escapes death through the intercession of Reuben, the eldest, and of Judah, but is sold into slavery in Egypt. In the immediately following chap. 38, Judah undergoes experiences similar to Joseph's. Joseph, endowed by God with wisdom, becomes second only to Pharaoh in Egypt. From that powerful position, he encounters his unsuspecting brothers who have come to Egypt because of the famine, and tests them to see if they have repented. Joseph learns that they have given up their hatred because of their love for Israel, their father. Judah, who seems to have inherited the mantle of the failed oldest brother Reuben, expresses the brothers' new and profound appreciation of their father and Joseph (chap. 44). At the end of Genesis, the entire family of Jacob/Israel is in Egypt, which prepares for the events in the Book of Exodus.

Genesis in Later Biblical Books. *The historical and prophetic books constantly refer to the covenant with the ancestors Abraham, Isaac, and Jacob. Hos 10 sees the traits of Jacob in the behavior of the Israel of his own day. Is 51:2 cites Abraham and Sarah as a model for his dispirited community, for though only a couple, they became a great nation. Jn 1, "In the beginning was the word," alludes to Gn 1:1 (and Prv 8:22) to show that Jesus is creating a new world. St. Paul interprets Jesus as the New Adam in Rom 5:14 and 1 Cor 15:22, 24, whose obedience brings life just as the Old Adam's disobedience brought death. In Rom 4, Paul cites Abraham as someone who was righteous in God's eyes centuries before the Law was given at Sinai.*

Preamble. The Creation of the World

Chapter 1

The Story of Creation.[a] **1** In the beginning, when God created the heavens and the earth— **2** [b]and the earth was without form or shape, with darkness over the abyss and a mighty wind sweeping over the waters—**3** Then God said: Let there be light, and there was light. **4** God saw that the light was good. God then separated the light from the darkness. **5** God called the light "day," and the darkness he called "night." Evening came, and morning followed—the first day.[c]

6 Then God said: Let there be a dome in the middle of the waters, to separate one body of water from the other. **7** God made the dome,[d] and it separated the water below the dome from the water above the dome. And so it happened. **8** God called the dome "sky." Evening came, and morning followed—the second day.

9 Then God said: Let the water under the sky be gathered into a single basin, so that the dry land may appear. And so it happened: the water under the sky was gathered into its basin, and the dry land appeared. **10** God called the dry land "earth," and the basin of water he called "sea." God saw that it was good. **11** Then God said: Let the earth bring forth vegetation: every kind of plant that bears seed and every kind of fruit tree on earth that bears fruit with its seed in it. And so it happened: **12** the earth brought forth vegetation: every kind of plant that bears seed and every kind of fruit tree that bears fruit with its seed in it. God saw that it was good. **13** Evening came, and morning followed—the third day.

14 Then God said: Let there be lights in the dome of the sky, to separate day from night. Let them mark the seasons, the days and the years, **15** and serve as lights in the dome of the sky, to illuminate the earth. And so it happened: **16** God made the two great lights, the greater one to govern the day, and the lesser one to govern the night, and the stars. **17** God set them in the dome of the sky, to illuminate the earth, **18** to govern the day and the night, and to separate the light from the darkness. God saw that it was good. **19** Evening came, and morning followed—the fourth day.

20 Then God said: Let the water teem with an abundance of living creatures, and on the earth let birds fly beneath the dome of the sky. **21** God created the great sea monsters and all kinds of crawling living creatures with which the water teems, and all kinds of winged birds. God saw that it was good, **22** and God blessed them, saying: Be fertile, multiply, and fill the water of the seas; and let the birds multiply on the earth. **23** Evening came, and morning followed—the fifth day.

24 Then God said: Let the earth bring forth every kind of living creature: tame animals, crawling things, and every kind of wild animal. And so it happened: **25** God made every kind of wild animal, every kind of tame animal, and every kind of thing that crawls on the ground. God saw that it was good. **26** Then God said: Let us make^e human beings in our image, after our likeness. Let them have dominion over the fish of the sea, the birds of the air, the tame animals, all the wild animals, and all the creatures that crawl on the earth.

> **27**   God created mankind in his image
>   in the image of God he created them;
>   male and female^f he created them

28 God blessed them and God said to them: Be fertile and multiply; fill the earth and subdue it.^{g} Have dominion over the fish of the sea, the birds of the air, and all the living things that crawl on the earth. **29** ^{h}God also said: See, I give you every seed-bearing plant on all the earth and every tree that has seed-bearing fruit on it to be your food; **30** and to all the wild animals, all the birds of the air, and all the living creatures that crawl on the earth, I give all the green plants for food. And so it happened. **31** God looked at everything he had made, and found it very good. Evening came, and morning followed—the sixth day.

Notes

a. **1:1–2:3** This section, from the Priestly source, functions as an introduction, stories of the origin of the world (cosmogonies) often did. It introduces the primordial story (2:4–11:26), the stories of the ancestors (11:27–50:26), and indeed the whole Pentateuch. The chapter highlights the goodness of creation and the divine desire that human beings share in that goodness. God brings an orderly universe out of primordial chaos merely by uttering a word. In the literary structure of six days, the creation events in the first three days are related to those in the second three.

1. light (day)/darkness (night)   =   4. sun/moon
2. arrangement of water   =   5. fish + birds from waters
3. a) dry land   =   6. a) animals
   b) vegetation   b) human beings: male/female

The seventh day, on which God rests, the climax of the account, falls outside the six-day structure. Until modern times the first line was always translated, "In the beginning God created the heavens and the earth." Several comparable ancient cosmogonies, discovered in recent times, have a "when . . . then" construction, confirming the translation "when . . . then" here as well. "When" introduces the pre-creation state and "then" introduces the creative act affecting that state. The traditional translation, "In the beginning," does not reflect the Hebrew syntax of the clause.

b. **1:2** This verse is parenthetical, describing in three phases the pre-creation state symbolized by the chaos out of which God brings order: "earth," hidden beneath the encompassing cosmic waters, could not be seen, and thus had no "form"; there was only darkness; turbulent wind swept over the waters. Commencing with the last-named elements (darkness and water), vv. 3–10 describe the rearrangement of this chaos: light is made (first day) and the water is divided into water above and water below the earth so that the earth appears and is no longer "without outline." **The abyss:** the primordial ocean according to the ancient Semitic cosmogony. After God's creative activity, part of this vast body forms the salt-water seas (vv. 9–10); part of it is the fresh water under the earth (Ps 33:7; Ez 31:4), which wells forth on the earth as springs and fountains (Gn 7:11; 8:2; Prv 3:20). Part of it, "the upper water" (Ps 148:4; Dn 3:60), is held up by the dome of the sky (vv. 6–7), from which rain descends on the earth (Gn 7:11; 2 Kgs 7:2, 19; Ps 104:13). **A mighty wind:** literally, "spirit or breath [*ruah*] of God"; cf. Gn 8:1.

c. **1:5** In ancient Israel a day was considered to begin at sunset.

d. **1:7 The dome:** the Hebrew word suggests a gigantic metal dome. It was inserted into the middle of the single body of water to form dry space within which the earth could emerge. The Latin Vulgate translation *firmamentum*, "means of support (for the upper waters); firmament," provided the traditional English rendering.

e. **1:26 Let us make:** in the ancient Near East, and sometimes in the Bible, God was imagined as presiding over an assembly of heavenly beings who deliberated and decided about matters on earth (1 Kgs 22:19–22; Is 6:8; Ps 29:1–2; 82; 89:6–7; Jb 1:6; 2:1; 38:7). This scene accounts for the plural form here and in Gn 11:7 ("Let us then go down . . . "). Israel's God was always considered "Most High" over the heavenly beings. **Human beings:** Hebrew '*ādām* is here the generic term for humankind; in the first five chapters of Genesis it is the proper name Adam only at 4:25 and 5:1–5. **In our image, after our likeness:** "image" and "likeness" (virtually synonyms) express the worth of human beings who have value in themselves (human blood may not be shed in 9:6 because of this image of God) and in their task, dominion (1:28), which promotes the rule of God over the universe.

f. **1:27 Male and female:** as God provided the plants with seeds (vv. 11, 12) and commanded the animals to be fertile and multiply (v. 22), so God gives sexuality to human beings as their means to continue in existence.

g. **1:28 Fill the earth and subdue it:** the object of the verb "subdue" may be not the earth as such but earth as the territory each nation must take for itself (chaps. 10–11), just as Israel will later do (see Nm 32:22, 29; Jos 18:1). The two divine commands define the basic tasks of the human race—to continue in existence through generation and to take possession of one's God-given territory. The dual command would have had special meaning when Israel was in exile and deeply anxious about whether they would continue as a nation and return to their ancient territory. **Have dominion:** the whole human race is made in the "image" and "likeness" of God and has "dominion." Comparable literature of the time used these words of kings rather than of human beings in general; human beings were invariably thought of as slaves of the gods created to provide menial service for the divine world. The royal language here does not, however, give human beings unlimited power, for kings in the Bible had limited dominion and were subject to prophetic critique.

h. **1:29** According to the Priestly tradition, the human race was originally intended to live on plants and fruits as were the animals (see v. 30), an arrangement that God will later change (9:3) in view of the human inclination to violence.

Chapter 2

1 Thus the heavens and the earth and all their array were completed. 2 ᵃOn the seventh day God completed the work he had been doing; he rested on the seventh day from all the work he had undertaken. 3 God blessed the seventh day and made it holy, because on it he rested from all the work he had done in creation.

I. The Story of the Nations

The Garden of Eden. 4 This is the storyᵇ of the heavens and the earth at their creation. When the Lord God made the earth and the heavens— 5 there was no field shrub on earth and no grass of the field had sprouted, for the Lord God had sent no rain upon the earth and there was no manᶜ to till the ground, 6 but a streamᵈ was welling up out of the earth and watering all the surface of the ground— 7 then the Lord God formed the manᵉ out of the dust of the ground and blew into his nostrils the breath of life, and the man became a living being.

8 The Lord God planted a garden in Eden, in the east,ᶠ and placed there the man whom he had formed. 9 ᵍOut of the ground the Lord God made grow every tree that was delightful to look at and good for food, with the tree of life in the middle of the garden and the tree of the knowledge of good and evil.

10 A river rises in Edenʰ to water the garden; beyond there it divides and becomes four branches. 11 The name of the first is the Pishon; it is the one that winds through the whole land of Havilah, where there is gold. 12 The gold of that land is good; bdellium and lapis lazuli are also there. 13 The name of the second river is the Gihon; it is the one that winds all through the land of Cush. 14 The name of the third river is the Tigris; it is the one that flows east of Asshur. The fourth river is the Euphrates.

15 The Lord God then took the man and settled him in the garden of Eden, to cultivate and care for it. 16 The Lord God gave the man this order: You are free to eat from any of the trees of the garden 17 except the tree of knowledge of good and evil. From that tree you shall not eat; when you eat from it you shall die.ⁱ

18 The Lord God said: It is not good for the man to be alone. I will make a helper suited to him.ʲ 19 So the Lord God formed out of the ground all the wild animals and all the birds of the air, and he brought them to the man to see what he would call them; whatever the man called each living creature was then its name. 20 The man gave names to all the tame animals, all the birds of the air, and all the wild animals; but none proved to be a helper suited to the man.

21 So the Lord God cast a deep sleep on the man, and while he was asleep, he took out one of his ribs and closed up its place with flesh. 22 The

LORD God then built the rib that he had taken from the man into a woman. When he brought her to the man, **23** the man said:

> "This one, at last, is bone of my bones
> and flesh of my flesh
> This one shall be called 'woman,'
> for out of man this one has been taken."ᵏ

24 That is why a man leaves his father and mother and clings to his wife, and the two of them become one body.ˡ

25 The man and his wife were both naked, yet they felt no shame.ᵐ

Notes

a. **2:2** The mention of the seventh day, repeated in v. 3, is outside the series of six days and is thus the climax of the account. The focus of the account is God. The text does not actually institute the practice of keeping the Sabbath, for it would have been anachronistic to establish at this point a custom that was distinctively Israelite (Ex 31:13, 16, 17), but it lays the foundation for the later practice. Similarly, ancient creation accounts often ended with the construction of a temple where the newly created human race provided service to the gods who created them, but no temple is mentioned in this account. As was the case with the Sabbath, it would have been anachronistic to institute the temple at this point, for Israel did not yet exist. In Ex 25–31 and 35–40, Israel builds the tabernacle, which is the precursor of the Temple of Solomon.

b. **2:4 This is the story:** the distinctive Priestly formula introduces older traditions, belonging to the tradition called Yahwist, and gives them a new setting. In the first part of Genesis, the formula "this is the story" (or a similar phrase) occurs five times (2:4; 5:1; 6:9; 10:1; 11:10), which corresponds to the five occurrences of the formula in the second part of the book (11:27; 25:12, 19; 36:1[9]; 37:2). Some interpret the formula here as retrospective ("Such is the story"), referring back to chap. 1, but all its other occurrences introduce rather than summarize. It is introductory here; the Priestly source would hardly use the formula to introduce its own material in chap. 1.

   The cosmogony that begins in v. 4 is concerned with the nature of human beings, narrating the story of the essential institutions and limits of the human race through their first ancestors. This cosmogony, like 1:1–3 (see note there), uses the "when . . . then" construction common in ancient cosmogonies. The account is generally attributed to the Yahwist, who prefers the divine name "Yhwh" (here rendered LORD) for God. God in this story is called "the Lord God" (except in 3:1–5); "LORD" is to be expected in a Yahwist account but the additional word "God" is puzzling.

c. **2:5 Man:** the Hebrew word *'adam* is a generic term meaning "human being." In chaps. 2–3, however, the archetypal human being is understood to be male (Adam), so the word *'adam* is translated "man" here.

d. **2:6 Stream:** the water wells up from the vast flood below the earth. The account seems to presuppose that only the garden of God was irrigated at this point. From this one source of all the fertilizing water on the earth, water will be channeled through the garden of God over the entire earth. It is the source of the four rivers mentioned in vv. 10–14. Later, with rain and cultivation, the fertility of the garden of God will appear in all parts of the world.

e. **2:7** God is portrayed as a potter molding the human body out of earth. There is a play on words in Hebrew between *'adam* ("human being," "man") and *'adama* ("ground"). It is not enough to make the body from earth; God must also breathe into the man's nostrils. A similar picture of divine breath imparted to human beings in order for them to live is found in Ez 37:5, 9–10; Jn 20:22. The Israelites did not think in the (Greek) categories of body and soul.

f. **2:8 Eden, in the east:** the place names in vv. 8–14 are mostly derived from Mesopotamian geography (see note on vv. 10–14). Eden may be the name of a region in southern Mesopotamia (modern Iraq), the term derived from the Sumerian word *eden*, "fertile plain." A similar-sounding Hebrew word means "delight," which may lie behind the Greek translation, "The Lord God planted a paradise [= pleasure park] in Eden." It should be noted, however, that the garden was not intended as a paradise for the human race, but as a pleasure park for God; the man tended it for God. The story is not about "paradise lost."

The garden in the precincts of Solomon's Temple in Jerusalem seems to symbolize the garden of God (like gardens in other temples); it is apparently alluded to in Ps 1:3; 80:10; 92:14; Ez 47:7–12; Rev 22:1–2.

g. **2:9** The second tree, the tree of life, is mentioned here and at the end of the story (3:22, 24). It is identified with Wisdom in Prv 3:18; 11:30; 13:12; 15:4, where the pursuit of wisdom gives back to human beings the life that is made inaccessible to them in Gn 3:24. In the new creation described in the Book of Revelation, the tree of life is once again made available to human beings (Rev 2:7; 22:2, 14, 19). **Knowledge of good and evil:** the meaning is disputed. According to some, it signifies moral autonomy, control over morality (symbolized by "good and evil"), which would be inappropriate for mere human beings; the phrase would thus mean refusal to accept the human condition and finite freedom that God gives them. According to others, it is more broadly the knowledge of what is helpful and harmful to humankind, suggesting that the attainment of adult experience and responsibility inevitably means the loss of a life of simple subordination to God.

h. **2:10–14 A river rises in Eden:** the stream of water mentioned in v. 6, the source of all water upon earth, comes to the surface in the garden of God and from there flows out over the entire earth. In comparable religious literature, the dwelling of god is the source of fertilizing waters. The four rivers represent universality, as in the phrase "the four quarters of the earth." In Ez 47:1–12; Zec 14:8; Rev 22:1–2, the waters that irrigate the earth arise in the temple or city of God. The place names in vv. 11–14 are mainly from southern Mesopotamia (modern Iraq), where Mesopotamian literature placed the original garden of God. The Tigris and the Euphrates, the two great rivers in that part of the world, both emptied into the Persian Gulf. Gihon is the modest stream issuing from Jerusalem (2 Sm 5:8; 1 Kgs 1:9–10; 2 Chr 32:4), but is here regarded as one of the four great world rivers and linked to Mesopotamia, for Cush here seems to be the territory of the Kassites (a people of Mesopotamia) as in Gn 10:8.

The word Pishon is otherwise unknown but is probably formed in imitation of Gihon. Havilah seems, according to Gn 10:7 and 1 Chr 1:9, to be in Cush in southern Mesopotamia though other locations have been suggested.

i. **2:17 You shall die:** since they do not die as soon as they eat from the forbidden tree, the meaning seems to be that human beings have become mortal, destined to die by virtue of being human.

j. **2:18 Helper suited to him:** lit., "a helper in accord with him." "Helper" need not imply subordination, for God is called a helper (Dt 33:7; Ps 46:2). The language suggests a profound affinity between the man and the woman and a relationship that is supportive and nurturing.

k. **2:23** The man recognizes an affinity with the woman God has brought him. Unlike the animals who were made from the ground, she is made from his very self. There is a play on the similar-sounding Hebrew words *'ishsha* ("woman," "wife") and *'ish* ("man," "husband").

l. **2:24 One body:** lit., "one flesh." The covenant of marriage establishes kinship bonds of the first rank between the partners.

m. **2:25 They felt no shame:** marks a new stage in the drama, for the reader knows that only young children know no shame. This draws the reader into the next episode, where the couple's disobedience results in their loss of innocence.

Chapter 3

Expulsion from Eden. **1** Now the snake was the most cunning[a] of all the wild animals that the LORD God had made. He asked the woman, "Did God really say, 'You shall not eat from any of the trees in the garden'?" **2** The woman answered the snake: "We may eat of the fruit of the trees in the garden; **3** it is only about the fruit of the tree in the middle of the garden that God said, 'You shall not eat it or even touch it, or else you will die.'" **4** But the snake said to the woman: "You certainly will not die! **5** God knows well that when you eat of it your eyes will be opened and you will be like gods, who know[b] good and evil." **6** The woman saw that the tree was good for food and pleasing to the eyes, and the tree was desirable for gaining wisdom. So she took some of its fruit and ate it; and she also gave some to her husband, who was with her, and he ate it. **7** Then the eyes of both of them were opened, and they knew that they were naked; so they sewed fig leaves together and made loincloths for themselves.

8 When they heard the sound of the LORD God walking about in the garden at the breezy time of the day,[c] the man and his wife hid themselves from the LORD God among the trees of the garden. **9** The LORD God then called to the man and asked him: Where are you? **10** He answered, "I heard you in the garden; but I was afraid, because I was naked, so I hid." **11** Then God asked: Who told you that you were naked? Have you eaten from the tree of which I had forbidden you to eat? **12** The man replied, "The woman whom you put here with me—she gave me fruit from the tree, so I ate it." **13** The LORD God then asked the woman: What is this you have done? The woman answered, "The snake tricked me, so I ate it."

14 Then the LORD God said to the snake:

> Because you have done this,
>> cursed are you
>> among all the animals, tame or wild;
> On your belly you shall crawl,
>> and dust you shall eat all the days of your life.[d]

15 I will put enmity between you and the woman,
>> and between your offspring and hers;
> They will strike at your head,
>> while you strike at their heel.[e]

16 To the woman he said:

> I will intensify your toil in childbearing;
>> in pain[f] you shall bring forth children.
> Yet your urge shall be for your husband,
>> and he shall rule over you.

17 To the man he said: Because you listened to your wife and ate from the tree about which I commanded you, You shall not eat from it,

> Cursed is the ground[g] because of you!
>> In toil you shall eat its yield
>> all the days of your life.
> **18** Thorns and thistles it shall bear for you,
>> and you shall eat the grass of the field.
> **19** By the sweat of your brow
>> you shall eat bread,
> Until you return to the ground,
>> from which you were taken;
> For you are dust,
>> and to dust you shall return.

20 The man gave his wife the name "Eve," because she was the mother of all the living.[h]

21 The Lord God made for the man and his wife garments of skin, with which he clothed them. **22** Then the Lord God said: See! The man has become like one of us, knowing good and evil! Now, what if he also reaches out his hand to take fruit from the tree of life, and eats of it and lives forever? **23** The Lord God therefore banished him from the garden of Eden, to till the ground from which he had been taken. **24** He expelled the man, stationing the cherubim and the fiery revolving sword east of the garden of Eden, to guard the way to the tree of life.

Notes

a. **3:1 Cunning:** there is a play on the words for "naked" (2:25) and "cunning/ wise" (Heb. 'arum). The couple seek to be "wise" but end up knowing that they are "naked."

b. **3:5 Like gods, who know:** or "like God who knows."

c. **3:8 The breezy time of the day:** lit., "the wind of the day." Probably shortly before sunset.

d. **3:14** Each of the three punishments (the snake, the woman, the man) has a double aspect, one affecting the individual and the other affecting a basic relationship. The snake previously stood upright, enjoyed a reputation for being shrewder than other creatures, and could converse with human beings as in vv. 1–5. It must now move on its belly, is more cursed than any creature, and inspires revulsion in human beings (v. 15).

e. **3:15 They will strike . . . at their heel:** the antecedent for "they" and "their" is the collective noun "offspring," i.e., all the descendants of the woman. Christian tradition has seen in this passage, however, more than unending hostility between snakes and human beings. The snake was identified with the devil (Wis 2:24; Jn 8:44; Rev 12:9; 20:2), whose eventual defeat seemed implied in the verse. Because "the Son of God was revealed to destroy the works of the devil" (1 Jn 3:8), the passage was understood as the first promise of a redeemer for fallen humankind, the protoevangelium. Irenaeus of Lyons (ca. A.D. 130– 200), in his *Against Heresies* 5.21.1, followed by several other Fathers of the

Church, interpreted the verse as referring to Christ, and cited Gal 3:19 and 4:4 to support the reference. Another interpretive translation is *ipsa*, "she," and is reflected in Jerome's Vulgate. "She" was thought to refer to Mary, the mother of the messiah. In Christian art Mary is sometimes depicted with her foot on the head of the serpent.

f. **3:16 Toil . . . pain:** the punishment affects the woman directly by increasing the toil and pain of having children. **He shall rule over you:** the punishment also affects the woman's relationship with her husband. A tension is set up in which her urge (either sexual urge or, more generally, dependence for sustenance) is for her husband but he rules over her. But see Sg 7:11.

g. **3:17–19 Cursed is the ground:** the punishment affects the man's relationship to the ground (*'adam* and *'adamah*). **You are dust:** the punishment also affects the man directly insofar as he is now mortal.

h. **3:20** The man gives his wife a more specific name than "woman" (2:23). The Hebrew name *hawwa* ("Eve") is related to the Hebrew word *hay* ("living"); "mother of all the living" points forward to the next episode involving her sons Cain and Abel.

The Book of Exodus

The second book of the Pentateuch is called Exodus, from the Greek word for "departure," because its central event was understood by the Septuagint's translators to be the departure of the Israelites from Egypt. Its Hebrew title, Shemoth *("Names"), is from the book's opening phrase, "These are the names . . . ." Continuing the history of Israel from the point where the Book of Genesis leaves off, Exodus recounts the Egyptian oppression of Jacob's ever-increasing descendants and their miraculous deliverance by God through Moses, who led them across the Red Sea to Mount Sinai where they entered into a covenant with the Lord. Covenantal laws and detailed prescriptions for the tabernacle (a portable sanctuary foreshadowing the Jerusalem Temple) and its service are followed by a dramatic episode of rebellion, repentance, and divine mercy. After the broken covenant is renewed, the tabernacle is constructed, and the cloud signifying God's glorious presence descends to cover it.*

These events made Israel a nation and confirmed their unique relationship with God. The "law" (Hebrew torah*) given by God through Moses to the Israelites at Mount Sinai constitutes the moral, civil, and ritual legislation by which they were to become a holy people. Many elements of it were fundamental to the teaching of Jesus (Mt 5:21–30; 15:4) as well as to New Testament and Christian moral teaching (Rom 13:8–10; 1 Cor 10:1–5; 1 Pt 2:9).*

The principal divisions of Exodus are:

 I. *Introduction: The Oppression of the Israelites in Egypt (1:1–2:22)*
 II. *The Call and Commission of Moses (2:23–7:7)*
 III. *The Contest with Pharaoh (7:8–13:16)*
 IV. *The Deliverance of the Israelites from Pharaoh and Victory at the Sea (13:17–15:21)*
 V. *The Journey in the Wilderness to Sinai (15:22–18:27)*
 VI. *Covenant and Legislation at Mount Sinai (19:1–31:18)*
 VII. *Israel's Apostasy and God's Renewal of the Covenant (32:1–34:35)*
 VIII. *The Building of the Tabernacle and the Descent of God's Glory upon It (35:1–40:38)*

VI. Covenant and Legislation at Mount Sinai

Chapter 19

Arrival at Sinai. 1 In the third month after the Israelites' departure from the land of Egypt, on the first day, they came to the wilderness of Sinai. **2** After they made the journey from Rephidim and entered the wilderness of Sinai, they then pitched camp in the wilderness.[a]

While Israel was encamped there in front of the mountain, **3** Moses went up to the mountain of God. Then the LORD called to him from the mountain, saying: This is what you will say to the house of Jacob; tell the Israelites: **4** You have seen how I treated the Egyptians and how I bore you up on eagles' wings and brought you to myself. **5** Now, if you obey me completely and keep my covenant,[b] you will be my treasured possession among all peoples, though all the earth is mine. **6** You will be to me a kingdom of priests,[c] a holy nation. That is what you must tell the Israelites. **7** So Moses went and summoned the elders of the people. When he set before them all that the LORD had ordered him to tell them, **8** all the people answered together, "Everything the LORD has said, we will do." Then Moses brought back to the LORD the response of the people.

9 The LORD said to Moses: I am coming to you now in a dense cloud, so that when the people hear me speaking with you, they will also remain faithful to you.

When Moses, then, had reported the response of the people to the LORD, **10** the LORD said to Moses: Go to the people and have them sanctify themselves today and tomorrow. Have them wash their garments **11** and be ready for the third day; for on the third day the LORD will come down on Mount Sinai in the sight of all the people. **12** Set limits for the people all around, saying: Take care not to go up the mountain, or even to touch its edge. All who touch the mountain must be put to death. **13** No hand shall touch them, but they must be stoned to death or killed with arrows. Whether human being or beast, they must not be allowed to live. Only when the ram's horn sounds may they go up on the mountain.[d] **14** Then Moses came down from the mountain to the people and had them sanctify themselves, and they washed their garments. **15** He said to the people, "Be ready for the third day. Do not approach a woman."

The Great Theophany. 16 On the morning of the third day there were peals of thunder and lightning, and a heavy cloud over the mountain, and a very loud blast of the shofar,[e] so that all the people in the camp trembled. **17** But Moses led the people out of the camp to meet God, and they stationed themselves at the foot of the mountain. **18** Now Mount Sinai was completely enveloped in smoke, because the LORD had come down upon it in fire. The smoke rose from it as though from a kiln, and the whole mountain trembled violently. **19** The blast of the shofar grew louder and louder, while Moses was speaking and God was answering him with thunder.

20 [f]When the LORD came down upon Mount Sinai, to the top of the mountain, the LORD summoned Moses to the top of the mountain, and Moses went up. **21** Then the LORD told Moses: Go down and warn the people not to break through to the LORD in order to see him; otherwise many of them will be struck down. **22** For their part, the priests, who approach the LORD must sanctify themselves; else the LORD will break out in anger against them. **23** But Moses said to the LORD, "The people cannot go up to Mount Sinai, for you yourself warned us, saying: Set limits around the mountain to make it sacred." **24** So the LORD said to him: Go down and come up along with Aaron. But do not let the priests and the people break through to come up to the LORD; else he will break out against them." 25 So Moses went down to the people and spoke to them.

Notes

a. **19:2** Apparently from a different source (P) than v. 1, which notes the date, v. 2 from the J source includes a second notice of the arrival in the wilderness of Sinai. The Israelites now will be camped at Sinai from this point on all the way to Nm 10:10. This is a striking indication of the centrality and importance of the Sinai narrative in the overall composition of the Pentateuch.

b. **19:5 Covenant:** while covenants between individuals and between nations are ubiquitous in the ancient Near East, the adaptation of this concept to express the relationship that will henceforth characterize God's relationship to Israel represents an important innovation of biblical faith. Other gods might "choose" nations to fulfill a special destiny or role in the world; but only Israel's God is bound to a people by covenant. Thereby Israel's identity as a people is put upon a foundation that does not depend upon the vicissitudes of Israelite statehood or the normal trappings of national existence. Israel will be a covenant people.

c. **19:6 Kingdom of priests:** inasmuch as this phrase is parallel to "holy nation," it most likely means that the whole Israelite nation is set apart from other nations and so consecrated to God, or holy, in the way priests are among the people (cf. Is 61:6; 1 Pt 2:5, 9).

d. **19:13 May they go up on the mountain:** in vv. 12–13a, a later Priestly reshaping of an earlier version of the instructions governing how the people are to prepare for the encounter with God (vv. 10–11, 13b), the people are to be restrained from ascending the mountain, which is suffused with the holiness of God and too dangerous for their approach. In the earlier version, as v. 13b suggests, the sanctified people must come near, in order to hear God speaking with Moses (v. 9) and in this way receive confirmation of his special relationship with God.

e. **19:16 Shofar:** a ram's horn used like a trumpet for signaling both for liturgical and military purposes.

f. **19:20–25** At this point the Priestly additions of vv. 12–13a are elaborated with further Priestly instructions, which include the priests' sanctifying themselves apart from the people (v. 22) and Aaron accompanying Moses to the top of the mountain (v. 24).

Chapter 20

The Ten Commandments.[a] **1** Then God spoke all these words:

2 I am the LORD your God, who brought you out of the land of Egypt, out of the house of slavery. **3** You shall not have other gods beside me.[b] **4** You shall not make for yourself an idol or a likeness of anything[c] in the heavens above or on the earth below or in the waters beneath the earth; **5** you shall not bow down before them or serve them. For I, the LORD, your God, am a jealous God, inflicting punishment for their ancestors' wickedness on the children of those who hate me, down to the third and fourth generation[d]; **6** but showing love down to the thousandth generation of those who love me and keep my commandments.

7 You shall not invoke the name of the LORD, your God, in vain.[e] For the LORD will not leave unpunished anyone who invokes his name in vain.

8 Remember the sabbath day—keep it holy.[f] **9** Six days you may labor and do all your work, **10** but the seventh day is a sabbath of the LORD your God. You shall not do any work, either you, your son or your daughter, your male or female slave, your work animal, or the resident alien within your gates. **11** For in six days the LORD made the heavens and the earth, the sea and all that is in them; but on the seventh day he rested. That is why the LORD has blessed the sabbath day and made it holy.[g]

12 [h]Honor your father and your mother, that you may have a long life in the land the LORD your God is giving you.

13 You shall not kill.[i]

14 You shall not commit adultery.

15 You shall not steal.

16 You shall not bear false witness against your neighbor.

17 You shall not covet your neighbor's house. You shall not covet your neighbor's wife, his male or female slave, his ox or donkey, or anything that belongs to your neighbor.

Moses Accepted as Mediator. 18 Now as all the people witnessed the thunder and lightning, the blast of the shofar and the mountain smoking, they became afraid and trembled. So they took up a position farther away **19** and said to Moses, "You speak to us, and we will listen; but do not let God speak to us, or we shall die." **20** Moses answered the people, "Do not be afraid, for God has come only to test you and put the fear of him upon you so you do not sin." **21** So the people remained at a distance, while Moses approached the dark cloud where God was.

The Covenant Code. 22 [j]The LORD said to Moses: This is what you will say to the Israelites: You have seen for yourselves that I have spoken to you from heaven. **23** You shall not make alongside of me gods of silver, nor shall you make for yourselves gods of gold. **24** An altar of earth make for me, and sacrifice upon it your burnt offerings and communion sacrifices, your sheep and your oxen. In every place where I cause my name to be invoked[k] I will come to you and bless you. **25** But if you make an altar of stone for me, do not build it of cut stone, for by putting a chisel to it you profane it. **26** You shall not ascend to my altar by steps, lest your nakedness be exposed.

Notes

a. **20:1–17** The precise numbering and division of these precepts into "ten commandments" is somewhat uncertain. Traditionally among Catholics and Lutherans vv. 1–6 are considered as only one commandment, and v. 17 as two. The Anglican, Greek Orthodox, and Reformed churches count vv. 1–6 as two, and v. 17 as one. Cf. Dt 5:6–21. The traditional designation as "ten" is not found here but in 34:28 (and also Dt 4:13 and 10:4), where these precepts are alluded to literally as "the ten words." That they were originally written on two tablets appears in Ex 32:15–16; 34:28–29; Dt 4:13; 10:2–4.

   The present form of the commands is a product of a long development, as is clear from the fact that the individual precepts vary considerably in length and from the slightly different formulation of Dt 5:6–21 (see especially vv. 12–15 and 21). Indeed they represent a mature formulation of a traditional morality. Why this specific selection of commands should be set apart is not entirely clear. None of them is unique in the Old Testament and all of the laws which follow are also from God and equally binding on the Israelites. Even so, this collection represents a privileged expression of God's moral demands on Israel and is here set apart from the others as a direct, unmediated communication of God to the Israelites and the basis of the covenant being concluded on Sinai.

b. **20:3 Beside me:** this commandment is traditionally understood as an outright denial of the existence of other gods except the God of Israel; however, in the context of the more general prohibitions in vv. 4–5, v. 3 is, more precisely, God's demand for Israel's exclusive worship and allegiance.

   The Hebrew phrase underlying the translation "beside me" is, nonetheless, problematic and has been variously translated, e.g., "except me," "in addition to me," "in preference to me," "in defiance of me," and "in front of me" or "before my face." The latter translation, with its concrete, spatial nuances, has suggested to some that the prohibition once sought to exclude from the Lord's sanctuary the cult images or idols of other gods, such as the asherah, or stylized sacred tree of life, associated with the Canaanite goddess Asherah (34:13). Over the course of time, as vv. 4–5 suggest, the original scope of v. 3 was expanded.

c. **20:4 Or a likeness of anything:** compare this formulation to that found in Dt 5:8, which understands this phrase and the following phrases as specifications of the prohibited idol (Hebrew *pesel*), which usually refers to an image that is carved or hewn rather than cast.

d. **20:5 Jealous:** demanding exclusive allegiance. **Inflicting punishment . . . the third and fourth generation:** the intended emphasis is on God's mercy by the contrast between punishment and mercy ("to the thousandth generation"—v. 6). Other Old Testament texts repudiate the idea of punishment devolving on later generations (cf. Dt 24:16; Jer 31:29–30; Ez 18:2–4). Yet it is known that later generations may suffer the punishing effects of sins of earlier generations, but not the guilt.

e. **20:7 In vain:** i.e., to no good purpose, a general framing of the prohibition which includes swearing falsely, especially in the context of a legal proceeding, but also goes beyond it (cf. Lv 24:16; Prv 30:8–9).

f. **20:8 Keep it holy:** i.e., to set it apart from the other days of the week, in part, as the following verse explains, by not doing work that is ordinarily done in the course of a week. The special importance of this command can be seen in the fact that, together with vv. 9–11, it represents the longest of the Decalogue's precepts.

g. **20:11** Here, in a formulation which reflects Priestly theology, the veneration of the sabbath is grounded in God's own hallowing of the sabbath in creation. Compare 31:13; Dt 5:15.

h. **20:12–17** The Decalogue falls into two parts: the preceding precepts refer to God, the following refer primarily to one's fellow Israelites.

i. **20:13 Kill:** as frequent instances of killing in the context of war or certain crimes (see vv. 12–18) demonstrate in the Old Testament, not all killing comes within the scope of the commandment. For this reason, the Hebrew verb translated here as "kill" is often understood as "murder," although it is in fact used in the Old Testament at times for unintentional acts of killing (e.g., Dt 4:41; Jos 20:3) and for legally sanctioned killing (Nm 35:30). The term may originally have designated any killing of another Israelite, including acts of manslaughter, for which the victim's kin could exact vengeance. In the present context, it denotes the killing of one Israelite by another, motivated by hatred or the like (Nm 35:20; cf. Hos 6:9).

j. **20:22–23:33** This collection consists of the civil and religious laws, both apodictic (absolute) and casuistic (conditional), which were given to the people through the mediation of Moses. They will be written down by Moses in 24:4.

k. **20:24 Where I cause my name to be invoked:** i.e., at the sacred site where God wishes to be worshiped. Dt 12 will demand the centralization of all sacrificial worship in one place chosen by God.

The Gospels

The collection of writings that constitutes the New Testament begins with four gospels. Next comes the Acts of the Apostles, followed by twenty-one letters that are attributed to Paul, James, Peter, John, and Jude. Finally, at the end of the early church's scriptures stands the Revelation to John. Virtually all Christians agree that these twenty-seven books constitute the "canon," a term that means "rule" and designates the list of writings that are regarded as authoritative for Christian faith and life.

It is the purpose of this Introduction to describe those features that are common to the four gospels. A similar treatment of the letters of the New Testament is provided in the two Introductions that appear before the Letter to the Romans and before the Letter of James, respectively. The Acts of the Apostles, a work that is both historical and theological, and Revelation, an apocalyptic work, have no counterparts in the New Testament; the special Introductions prefixed to these books treat of the literary characteristics proper to each of them.

While the New Testament contains four writings called "gospels," there is in reality only one gospel running through all of the Christian scriptures, the gospel of and about Jesus Christ. Our English word "gospel" translates the Greek term euangelion, meaning "good news." This noun was used in the plural by the Greek translators of the Old Testament to render the Hebrew term for "good news" (2 Sm 4:10; possibly also 2 Sm 18:20, 25). But it is the corresponding verb euangelizomai, "to proclaim good news," that was especially significant in preparing for the New Testament idea of "gospel," since this term is used by Deutero-Isaiah of announcing the great victory of God that was to establish his universal kingship and inaugurate the new age (Is 40:9; 52:7; 61:1).

Paul used the word euangelion *to designate the message that he and the other apostles proclaimed, the "gospel of God" (Rom 1:1; 15:16; 2 Cor 11:7; 1 Thes 2:2, 8, 9). He often referred to it simply as "the gospel" (Rom 1:16; 10:16; 11:28; etc) or, because of its content and origin, as "the gospel of Christ" (Rom 15:19; 1 Cor 9:12; 1 Thes 3:2; etc). Because of its personal meaning for him and his own particular manner of telling the story about Jesus Christ and of explaining the significance of his cross and resurrection, Paul also referred to this message as "my gospel" (Rom 2:16; cf. Gal 1:11; 2:2) or "our gospel" (2 Cor 4:3; 1 Thes 1:5; 2 Thes 2:14).*

It was Mark, as far as we know, who first applied the term "gospel" to a book telling the story of Jesus; see Mk 1:1 and the note there. This form of presenting Jesus' life, works, teachings, passion, and resurrection was developed further by the other evangelists; see the Introduction to each gospel. The first three of the canonical gospels, Matthew, Mark, and Luke, are so similar at many points when viewed together, particularly when arranged in parallel columns or lines, that they are called "synoptic" gospels, from the Greek word for such a general view. The fourth gospel, John, often differs significantly from the synoptics in outline and approach. This work never uses the word "gospel" or its corresponding verb; nevertheless, its message concerns the same Jesus, and the reader is urged to believe in him as the Messiah, "that through this belief you may have life in his name" (Jn 20:31).

From the second century onward, the practice arose of designating each of these four books as a "gospel," understood as a title, and of adding a phrase with a name that identified the traditional author, e.g., "The Gospel according to Matthew." The arrangement of the canon that was adopted, with the four gospels grouped together at the beginning followed by Acts, provides a massive focus upon Jesus and allows Acts to serve as a framework for the letters of the New Testament. This order, however, conceals the fact that Luke's two volumes, a gospel and Acts, were intended by their author to go together. It further obscures the point that Paul's letters were written before any of our gospels, though the sayings and deeds of Jesus stand behind all the New Testament writings.

The Gospel According to Matthew

The position of the Gospel according to Matthew as the first of the four gospels in the New Testament reflects both the view that it was the first to be written, a view that goes back to the late second century A.D., and the esteem in which it was held by the church; no other was so frequently quoted in the noncanonical literature of earliest Christianity. Although the majority of scholars now reject the opinion about the time of its composition, the high estimation of this work remains. The reason for that becomes clear upon study of the way in which Matthew presents his story of Jesus, the demands of Christian discipleship, and the breaking-in of the new and final age through the ministry but particularly through the death and resurrection of Jesus.

The gospel begins with a narrative prologue (Mt 1:1–2:23), the first part of which is a genealogy of Jesus starting with Abraham, the father of Israel (Mt 1:1–17). Yet at the beginning of that genealogy Jesus is designated as "the son of David, the son of Abraham" (Mt 1:1). The kingly ancestor who lived about a thousand years after Abraham is named first, for this is the genealogy of Jesus Christ, the Messiah, the royal anointed one (Mt 1:16). In the first of the episodes of the infancy narrative that follow the genealogy, the mystery of Jesus' person is declared. He is conceived of a virgin by the power of the Spirit of God (Mt 1:18–25). The first of the gospel's fulfillment citations, whose purpose it is to show that he was the one to whom the prophecies of Israel were pointing, occurs here (Mt 1:23): he shall be named Emmanuel, for in him God is with us.

The announcement of the birth of this newborn king of the Jews greatly troubles not only King Herod but all Jerusalem (Mt 2:1–3), yet the Gentile magi are overjoyed to find him and offer him their homage and their gifts (Mt 2:10–11). Thus his ultimate rejection by the mass of his own people and his acceptance by the Gentile nations is foreshadowed. He must be taken to Egypt to escape the murderous plan of Herod. By his sojourn there and his subsequent return after the king's death he relives the Exodus experience of Israel. The words of the LORD spoken through the prophet Hosea, "Out of Egypt I called my son," are fulfilled in him (Mt 2:15); if Israel was God's son, Jesus is so in a way far surpassing the dignity of that nation, as his marvelous birth and the unfolding of his story show (see Mt 3:17; 4:1–11; 11:27; 14:33; 16:16; 27:54). Back in the land of Israel, he must be taken to Nazareth in Galilee because of the danger to his life in Judea, where Herod's son Archelaus is now ruling (Mt 2:22–23). The sufferings of Jesus in the infancy narrative anticipate those of his passion, and if his life is spared in spite of the dangers, it is because his destiny is finally to give it on the cross as "a ransom for many" (Mt 20:28). Thus the word of the angel will be fulfilled, " . . . he will save his people from their sins" (Mt 1:21; cf. Mt 26:28).

In Mt 4:12 Matthew begins his account of the ministry of Jesus, introducing it by the preparatory preaching of John the Baptist (Mt 3:1–12), the baptism of Jesus that culminates in God's proclaiming him his "beloved Son" (Mt 3:13–17), and the temptation in which he proves his true sonship by his victory over the devil's attempt to deflect him from the way of obedience to the Father (Mt 4:1–11). The central message of Jesus' preaching is the coming of the kingdom of heaven and the need for repentance, a complete change of heart and conduct, on the part of those who are to receive this great gift of God (Mt 4:17). Galilee is the setting for most of his ministry; he leaves there for Judea only in Mt 19:1, and his ministry in Jerusalem, the goal of his journey, is limited to a few days (Mt 21:1–25:46).

In this extensive material there are five great discourses of Jesus, each concluding with the formula "When Jesus finished these words" or one closely similar (Mt 7:28; 11:1; 13:53; 19:1; 26:1). These are an important structure of the gospel. In every case the discourse is preceded by a narrative section, each narrative and discourse together constituting a "book" of the gospel. The discourses are, respectively, the "Sermon on the Mount" (Mt 5:3–7:27), the missionary discourse (Mt 10:5–42), the parable discourse (Mt 13:3–52), the "church order" discourse (Mt 18:3–35), and the eschatological discourse (Mt 24:4–25:46). In large measure the material of these discourses came to Matthew from his tradition, but his work in modifying and adding to what he had received is abundantly evident. No other evangelist gives the teaching of Jesus with such elegance and order as he.

In the "Sermon on the Mount" the theme of righteousness is prominent, and even at this early stage of the ministry the note of opposition is struck between Jesus and the Pharisees, who are designated as "the hypocrites" (Mt 6:2, 5, 16). The righteousness of his disciples must surpass that of the scribes and Pharisees; otherwise, in spite of their alleged following of Jesus, they will not enter into the kingdom of heaven (Mt 5:20). Righteousness means doing the will of the heavenly Father (Mt 7:21), and his will is proclaimed in a manner that is startling to all who have identified it with the law of Moses. The antitheses of the Sermon (Mt 5:21–48) both accept (Mt 5:21–30, 43–48) and reject (Mt 5:31–42) elements of that law, and in the former case the understanding of the law's demands is deepened and extended. The antitheses are the best commentary on the meaning of Jesus' claim that he has come not to abolish but to fulfill the law (Mt 5:17). What is meant by fulfillment of the law is not the demand to keep it exactly as it stood before the coming of Jesus, but rather his bringing the law to be a lasting expression of the will of God, and in that fulfillment there is much that will pass away. Should this appear contradictory to his saying that "until heaven and earth pass away" not even the smallest part of the law will pass (Mt 5:18), that time of fulfillment is not the dissolution of the universe but the coming of the new age, which will occur with Jesus' death and resurrection. While righteousness in the new age will continue to mean conduct that is in accordance with the law, it will be conduct in accordance with the law as expounded and interpreted by Jesus (cf. Mt 28:20, " . . . all that I have commanded you").

Though Jesus speaks harshly about the Pharisees in the Sermon, his judgment is not solely a condemnation of them. The Pharisees are portrayed as a negative example for his disciples, and his condemnation of those who claim to belong to him while disobeying his word is no less severe (Mt 7:21–23, 26–27).

In Mt 4:23 a summary statement of Jesus' activity speaks not only of his teaching and proclaiming the gospel but of his "curing every disease and illness among the people"; this is repeated almost verbatim in Mt 9:35. The narrative section that follows the Sermon on the Mount (Mt 8:1–9:38) is composed principally of accounts of those merciful deeds of Jesus, but it is far from being simply a collection of stories about miraculous cures. The nature of the community that Jesus will establish is shown; it will always be under the protection of him whose power can deal with all dangers (Mt 8:23–27), but it is only for those who are prepared to follow him at whatever cost (Mt 8:16–22), not only believing Israelites but Gentiles who have come to faith in him (Mt 8:10–12). The disciples begin to have some insight, however imperfect, into the mystery of Jesus' person. They wonder about him whom "the winds and the sea obey" (Mt 8:27), and they witness his bold declaration of the forgiveness of the paralytic's sins (Mt 9:2). That episode of the narrative moves on two levels. When the crowd sees the cure that testifies to the authority of Jesus, the Son of Man, to forgive sins (Mt 9:6), they glorify God "who had given such authority to human beings" (Mt 9:8). The forgiveness of sins is now not the prerogative of Jesus alone but of "human beings," that is, of the disciples who constitute the community of Jesus, the church. The ecclesial character of this narrative section could hardly be more plainly indicated.

The end of the section prepares for the discourse on the church's mission (Mt 10:5–42). Jesus is moved to pity at the sight of the crowds who are like sheep without a shepherd (Mt 9:36), and he sends out the twelve disciples to make the proclamation with which his own ministry began, "The kingdom of heaven is at hand" (Mt 10:7; cf. Mt 4:17), and to drive out demons and cure the sick as he has done (Mt 10:1). Their mission is limited to Israel (Mt 10:5–6) as Jesus' own was (Mt 15:24), yet in Mt 15:16 that perspective broadens and the discourse begins to speak of the mission that the disciples will have after the resurrection and of the severe persecution that will attend it (Mt 10:18). Again, the discourse moves on two levels: that of the time of Jesus and that of the time of the church.

The narrative section of the third book (Mt 11:2–12:50) deals with the growing opposition to Jesus. Hostility toward him has already been manifested (Mt 8:10; 9:3, 10–13, 34), but here it becomes more intense. The rejection of Jesus comes, as before, from Pharisees, who take "counsel against him to put him to death" (Mt 12:14) and repeat their earlier accusation that he drives out demons because he is in league with demonic power (Mt 12:22–24). But they are not alone in their rejection. Jesus complains of the lack of faith of "this generation" of Israelites (Mt 11:16–19) and reproaches the towns "where most of his mighty deeds had been done" for not heeding his call to repentance (Mt 11:20–24). This dark picture is relieved by Jesus' praise of the Father who has enabled "the childlike" to accept him (Mt 11:25–27), but on the whole the story is one of opposition to his word and blindness to the meaning of his deeds. The whole section ends with his declaring that not even the most intimate blood relationship with him counts for anything; his only true relatives are those who do the will of his heavenly Father (Mt 12:48–50).

The narrative of rejection leads up to the parable discourse (Mt 13:3–52). The reason given for Jesus' speaking to the crowds in parables is that they have hardened themselves against his clear teaching, unlike the disciples to whom knowledge of "the mysteries of the kingdom has been granted" (Mt 13:10–16). In Mt 13:36 he dismisses the crowds and continues the discourse to his disciples alone, who claim, at the end, to have understood all that he has said (Mt 13:51). But, lest the impression be given that the church of Jesus is made up only of true disciples, the explanation of the parable of the weeds among the wheat (Mt 13:37–43), as well as the parable of the net thrown into the sea "which collects fish of every kind" (Mt 13:47–49), shows that it is composed of both the righteous and the wicked, and that separation between the two will be made only at the time of the final judgment.

In the narrative that constitutes the first part of the fourth book of the gospel (Mt 13:54–17:27), Jesus is shown preparing for the establishment of his church with its teaching authority that will supplant the blind guidance of the Pharisees (Mt 15:13–14), whose teaching, curiously said to be that of the Sadducees also, is repudiated by Jesus as the norm for his disciples (Mt 16:6, 11–12). The church of Jesus will be built on Peter (Mt 16:18), who will be given authority to bind and loose on earth, an authority whose exercise will be confirmed in heaven (Mt 16:19). The metaphor of binding and loosing has a variety of meanings, among them that of giving authoritative teaching. This promise is made to Peter directly after he has confessed Jesus to be the Messiah, the Son of the living God (Mt 16:16), a confession that he has made as the result of revelation given to him by the heavenly Father (Mt 16:17); Matthew's ecclesiology is based on his high christology.

Directly after that confession Jesus begins to instruct his disciples about how he must go the way of suffering and death (Mt 16:21). Peter, who has been praised for his confession, protests against this and receives from Jesus the sharpest of rebukes for attempting to deflect Jesus from his God-appointed destiny. The future rock upon whom the church will be built is still a man of "little faith" (see Mt 14:31). Both he and the other disciples must know not only that Jesus will have to suffer and die but that they too will have to follow him on the way of the cross if they are truly to be his disciples (Mt 16:24–25).

The discourse following this narrative (Mt 18:1–35) is often called the "church order" discourse, although that title is perhaps misleading since the emphasis is not on the structure of the church but on the care that the disciples must have for one another in respect to guarding each other's faith in Jesus (Mt 18:6–7), to seeking out those who have wandered from the fold (Mt 18:10–14), and to repeated forgiving of their fellow disciples who have offended them (Mt 18:21–35). But there is also the obligation to correct the sinful fellow Christian and, should one refuse to be corrected, separation from the community is demanded (Mt 18:15–18).

The narrative of the fifth book (Mt 19:1–23:39) begins with the departure of Jesus and his disciples from Galilee for Jerusalem. In the course of their journey Jesus for the third time predicts the passion that awaits him at Jerusalem and also his resurrection (Mt 20:17–19). At his entrance into the city he is hailed as the Son of David by the crowds accompanying him (Mt 21:9). He cleanses the temple (Mt 21:12–17), and in the few days of his Jerusalem ministry he engages in a series of controversies with the Jewish religious leaders (Mt 21:23–27; 22:15–22, 23–33, 34–40, 41–46), meanwhile speaking parables against them (Mt 21:28–32, 33–46), against all those Israelites who have rejected God's invitation to the messianic banquet (Mt 22:1–10), and against all, Jew and Gentile, who have accepted but have shown themselves unworthy of it (Mt 22:11–14). Once again, the perspective of the evangelist includes not only the time of Jesus' ministry but that of the preaching of the gospel after his resurrection. The narrative culminates in Jesus' denunciation of the scribes and Pharisees, reflecting not only his own opposition to them but that of Matthew's church (Mt 23:1–36), and in Jesus' lament over Jerusalem (Mt 23:37–39).

In the discourse of the fifth book (Mt 24:1–25:46), the last of the great structural discourses of the gospel, Jesus predicts the destruction of the temple and his own final coming. The time of the latter is unknown (Mt 24:36, 44), and the disciples are exhorted in various parables to live in readiness for it, a readiness that entails faithful attention to the duties of the interim period (Mt 24:45–25:30). The coming of Jesus will bring with it the great judgment by which the everlasting destiny of all will be determined (Mt 25:31–46).

The story of Jesus' passion and resurrection (Mt 26:1–28:20), the climax of the gospel, throws light on all that has preceded. In Matthew "righteousness" means both the faithful response to the will of God demanded of all to whom *that will is announced and also the saving activity of God for his people (see Mt 3:15; 5:6; 6:33). The passion supremely exemplifies both meanings of that central Matthean word. In Jesus' absolute faithfulness to the Father's will that he drink the cup of suffering (Mt 26:39), the incomparable model for Christian obedience is given; in his death "for the forgiveness of sins" (Mt 26:28), the saving power of God is manifested as never before.*

Matthew's portrayal of Jesus in his passion combines both the majestic seren- ity of the obedient Son who goes his destined way in fulfillment of the scriptures (Mt 26:52–54), confident of his ultimate vindication by God, and the depths of fear and abandonment that he feels in face of death (Mt 26:38–39; 27:46). These two aspects are expressed by an Old Testament theme that occurs often in the narrative, i.e., the portrait of the suffering Righteous One who complains to God in his misery, but is certain of eventual deliverance from his terrible ordeal.

The passion-resurrection of God's Son means nothing less than the turn of the ages, a new stage of history, the coming of the Son of Man in his kingdom (Mt 28:18; cf. Mt 16:28). That is the sense of the apocalyptic signs that accompany Jesus' death (Mt 27:51–53) and resurrection (Mt 28:2). Although the old age continues, as it will until the manifestation of Jesus' triumph at his parousia, the final age has now begun. This is known only to those who have seen the Risen One and to those, both Jews and Gentiles, who have believed in their announcement of Jesus' triumph and have themselves become his disciples (cf. Mt 28:19). To them he is constantly, though invisibly, present (Mt 28:20), verifying the name Emmanuel, "God is with us" (cf. Mt 1:23).

The questions of authorship, sources, and the time of composition of this gos- pel have received many answers, none of which can claim more than a greater or lesser degree of probability. The one now favored by the majority of scholars is the following.

The ancient tradition that the author was the disciple and apostle of Jesus named Matthew (see Mt 10:3) is untenable because the gospel is based, in large part, on the Gospel according to Mark (almost all the verses of that gospel have been utilized in this), and it is hardly likely that a companion of Jesus would have followed so extensively an account that came from one who admittedly never had such an association rather than rely on his own memories. The attribution of the gospel to the disciple Matthew may have been due to his having been responsible for some of the traditions found in it, but that is far from certain.

The unknown author, whom we shall continue to call Matthew for the sake of convenience, drew not only upon the Gospel according to Mark but upon a large body of material (principally, sayings of Jesus) not found in Mark that cor- responds, sometimes exactly, to material found also in the Gospel according to Luke. This material, called "Q" (probably from the first letter of the German word Quelle, meaning "source"), represents traditions, written and oral, used by both Matthew and Luke. Mark and Q are sources common to the two other synoptic gospels; hence the name the "Two-Source Theory" given to this explanation of the relation among the synoptics.

In addition to what Matthew drew from Mark and Q, his gospel contains material that is found only there. This is often designated "M," written or oral tradition that was available to the author. Since Mark was written shortly before or shortly after A.D. 70 (see Introduction to Mark), Matthew was composed certainly after that date, which marks the fall of Jerusalem to the Romans at the time of the First Jewish Revolt (A.D. 66–70), and probably at least a decade later since Matthew's use of Mark presupposes a wide diffusion of that gospel. The post-A.D. 70 date is confirmed within the text by Mt 22:7, which refers to the destruction of Jerusalem.

As for the place where the gospel was composed, a plausible suggestion is that it was Antioch, the capital of the Roman province of Syria. That large and important city had a mixed population of Greek-speaking Gentiles and Jews. The tensions between Jewish and Gentile Christians there in the time of Paul (see Gal 2:1–14) in respect to Christian obligation to observe Mosaic law are partially similar to tensions that can be seen between the two groups in Matthew's gospel. The church of Matthew, originally strongly Jewish Christian, had become one in which Gentile Christians were predominant. His gospel answers the question how obedience to the will of God is to be expressed by those who live after the "turn of the ages," the death and resurrection of Jesus.

The principal divisions of the Gospel according to Matthew are the following:

I.   The Infancy Narrative (1:1–2:23)
II.   The Proclamation of the Kingdom (3:1–7:29)
III. Ministry and Mission in Galilee (8:1–11:1)
IV.   Opposition from Israel (11:2–13:53)
V.   Jesus, the Kingdom, and the Church (13:54–18:35)
VI.   Ministry in Judea and Jerusalem (19:1–25:46)
VII. The Passion and Resurrection (26:1–28:20)

I. The Infancy Narrative

Chapter 1

The Genealogy of Jesus.[a] **1** The book of the genealogy of Jesus Christ, the son of David, the son of Abraham.[b]

2 Abraham became the father of Isaac, Isaac the father of Jacob, Jacob the father of Judah and his brothers. **3** Judah became the father of Perez and Zerah, whose mother was Tamar. Perez became the father of Hezron, Hezron the father of Ram, **4** Ram the father of Amminadab. Amminadab became the father of Nahshon, Nahshon the father of Salmon, **5** Salmon the father of Boaz, whose mother was Rahab. Boaz became the father of Obed, whose mother was Ruth. Obed became the father of Jesse, **6** Jesse the father of David the king.

David became the father of Solomon, whose mother had been the wife of Uriah. **7** ᶜSolomon became the father of Rehoboam, Rehoboam the father of Abijah, Abijah the father of Asaph. **8** Asaph became the father of Jehoshaphat, Jehoshaphat the father of Joram, Joram the father of Uzziah. **9** Uzziah became the father of Jotham, Jotham the father of Ahaz, Ahaz the father of Hezekiah. **10** Hezekiah became the father of Manasseh, Manasseh the father of Amos,ᵈ Amos the father of Josiah. **11** Josiah became the father of Jechoniah and his brothers at the time of the Babylonian exile.

12 After the Babylonian exile, Jechoniah became the father of Shealtiel, Shealtiel the father of Zerubbabel, **13** Zerubbabel the father of Abiud. Abiud became the father of Eliakim, Eliakim the father of Azor, **14** Azor the father of Zadok. Zadok became the father of Achim, Achim the father of Eliud, **15** Eliud the father of Eleazar. Eleazar became the father of Matthan, Matthan the father of Jacob, **16** Jacob the father of Joseph, the husband of Mary. Of her was born Jesus who is called the Messiah.

17 Thus the total number of generations from Abraham to David is fourteen generations; from David to the Babylonian exile, fourteen generations; from the Babylonian exile to the Messiah, fourteen generations.ᵉ

The Birth of Jesus.ᶠ **18** Now this is how the birth of Jesus Christ came about. When his mother Mary was betrothed to Joseph,ᵍ but before they lived together, she was found with child through the holy Spirit. **19** Joseph her husband, since he was a righteous man,ʰ yet unwilling to expose her to shame, decided to divorce her quietly. **20** Such was his intention when, behold, the angel of the Lᴏʀᴅⁱ appeared to him in a dream and said, "Joseph, son of David, do not be afraid to take Mary your wife into your home. For it is through the holy Spirit that this child has been conceived in her. **21** She will bear a son and you are to name him Jesus,ʲ because he will save his people from their sins." **22** All this took place to fulfill what the Lord had said through the prophet:

23   ᵏ"Behold, the virgin shall be with child and bear a son,
           and they shall name him Emmanuel,"

which means "God is with us." **24** When Joseph awoke, he did as the angel of the Lord had commanded him and took his wife into his home. **25** He had no relations with her until she bore a son,ˡ and he named him Jesus.

Notes

a. **1:1–2:23** The infancy narrative forms the prologue of the gospel. Consisting of a genealogy and five stories, it presents the coming of Jesus as the climax of Israel's history, and the events of his conception, birth, and early childhood as the fulfillment of Old Testament prophecy. The genealogy is probably traditional material that Matthew edited. In its first two sections (Mt 1:2–11) it was drawn from Ru 4:18–22; 1 Chr 1–3. Except for Jechoniah, Shealtiel, and Zerubbabel, none of the names in the third section (Mt 1:12–16) is found in any Old Testament genealogy. While the genealogy shows the continuity of God's providential plan from Abraham on, discontinuity is also present. The women

Tamar (Mt 1:3), Rahab and Ruth (Mt 1:5), and the wife of Uriah, Bathsheba (Mt 1:6), bore their sons through unions that were in varying degrees strange and unexpected. These "irregularities" culminate in the supreme "irregularity" of the Messiah's birth of a virgin mother; the age of fulfillment is inaugurated by a creative act of God.

Drawing upon both biblical tradition and Jewish stories, Matthew portrays Jesus as reliving the Exodus experience of Israel and the persecutions of Moses. His rejection by his own people and his passion are foreshadowed by the troubled reaction of "all Jerusalem" to the question of the magi who are seeking the "newborn king of the Jews" (Mt 2:2–3), and by Herod's attempt to have him killed. The magi who do him homage prefigure the Gentiles who will accept the preaching of the gospel. The infancy narrative proclaims who Jesus is, the savior of his people from their sins (Mt 1:21), Emmanuel in whom "God is with us" (Mt 1:23), and the Son of God (Mt 2:15).

b. **1:1 The Son of David, the son of Abraham:** two links of the genealogical chain are singled out. Although the later, David is placed first in order to emphasize that Jesus is the royal Messiah. The mention of Abraham may be due not only to his being the father of the nation Israel but to Matthew's interest in the universal scope of Jesus' mission; cf. Gn 22:18 ". . . . in your descendants all the nations of the earth shall find blessing."

c. 1:7 The successor of Abijah was not Asaph but Asa (see 1 Chr 3:10). Some textual witnesses read the latter name; however, **Asaph** is better attested. Matthew may have deliberately introduced the psalmist Asaph into the genealogy (and in Mt 1:10 the prophet Amos) in order to show that Jesus is the fulfillment not only of the promises made to David (see 2 Sm 7) but of all the Old Testament.

d. **1:10 Amos:** some textual witnesses read **Amon**, who was the actual successor of Manasseh (see 1 Chr 3:14).

e. **1:17** Matthew is concerned with fourteen generations, probably because fourteen is the numerical value of the Hebrew letters forming the name of David. In the second section of the genealogy (Mt 1:6b–11), three kings of Judah, Ahaziah, Joash, and Amaziah, have been omitted (see 1 Chr 3:11–12), so that there are fourteen generations in that section. Yet the third (Mt 1:12–16) apparently has only thirteen. Since Matthew here emphasizes that each section has fourteen, it is unlikely that the thirteen of the last was due to his oversight. Some scholars suggest that **Jesus who is called the Messiah** (Mt 1:16b) doubles the final member of the chain: **Jesus,** born within the family of David, opens up the new age as **Messiah,** so that in fact there are fourteen generations in the third section. This is perhaps too subtle, and the hypothesis of a slip not on the part of Matthew but of a later scribe seems likely. On **Messiah,** see note on Lk 2:11.

f. **1:18–25** This first story of the infancy narrative spells out what is summarily indicated in Mt 1:16. The virginal conception of Jesus is the work of the Spirit of God. Joseph's decision to divorce Mary is overcome by the heavenly command that he take her into his home and accept the child as his own. The natural genealogical line is broken but the promises to David are fulfilled; through Joseph's adoption the child belongs to the family of David. Matthew sees the virginal conception as the fulfillment of Is 7:14.

g. **1:18 Betrothed to Joseph:** betrothal was the first part of the marriage, constituting a man and woman as husband and wife. Subsequent infidelity was considered adultery. The betrothal was followed some months later by the husband's taking his wife into his home, at which time normal married life began.

h. **1:19 A righteous man:** as a devout observer of the Mosaic law, Joseph wished to break his union with someone whom he suspected of gross violation of the law. It is commonly said that the law required him to do so, but the texts usually given in support of that view, e.g., Dt 22:20–21 do not clearly pertain to Joseph's situation. **Unwilling to expose her to shame:** the penalty for proved adultery was death by stoning; cf. Dt 22:21–23.

i. **1:20 The angel of the LORD:** in the Old Testament a common designation of God in communication with a human being. **In a dream:** see Mt 2:13, 19, 22. These dreams may be meant to recall the dreams of Joseph, son of Jacob the patriarch (Gn 37:5–11, 19). A closer parallel is the dream of Amram, father of Moses, related by Josephus (*Antiquities* 2:212, 215–16).

j. **1:21 Jesus:** in first-century Judaism the Hebrew name Joshua (Greek *Iēsous*) meaning "Yahweh helps" was interpreted as "Yahweh saves."

k. **1:23 God is with us:** God's promise of deliverance to Judah in Isaiah's time is seen by Matthew as fulfilled in the birth of Jesus, in whom God is with his people. The name Emmanuel is alluded to at the end of the gospel where the risen Jesus assures his disciples of his continued presence, ". . . . I am with you always, until the end of the age" (Mt 28:20).

l. **1:25 Until she bore a son:** the evangelist is concerned to emphasize that Joseph was not responsible for the conception of Jesus. The Greek word translated "until" does not imply normal marital conduct after Jesus' birth, nor does it exclude it.

Chapter 2

The Visit of the Magi.[a] **1** When Jesus was born in Bethlehem of Judea, in the days of King Herod,[b] behold, magi from the east arrived in Jerusalem, **2** saying, "Where is the newborn king of the Jews? We saw his star[c] at its rising and have come to do him homage." **3** When King Herod heard this, he was greatly troubled, and all Jerusalem with him. **4** Assembling all the chief priests and the scribes of the people, he inquired of them where the Messiah was to be born.[d] **5** They said to him, "In Bethlehem of Judea, for thus it has been written through the prophet:

6 'And you, Bethlehem, land of Judah,
      are by no means least among the rulers of Judah;
    since from you shall come a ruler,
      who is to shepherd my people Israel.'"

7 Then Herod called the magi secretly and ascertained from them the time of the star's appearance. **8** He sent them to Bethlehem and said, "Go and search diligently for the child. When you have found him, bring me word, that I too may go and do him homage." **9** After their audience with the king they set out. And behold, the star that they had seen at its rising preceded them, until it came and stopped over the place where the child was. **10** They were overjoyed at seeing the star, **11** [e]and on entering the house they saw the child with Mary his mother. They prostrated themselves and did him homage. Then they opened their treasures and offered him gifts of gold, frankincense, and myrrh. **12** And having been warned in a dream not to return to Herod, they departed for their country by another way.

The Flight to Egypt. 13 [f]When they had departed, behold, the angel of the Lord appeared to Joseph in a dream and said, "Rise, take the child and his mother, flee to Egypt,[g] and stay there until I tell you. Herod is going to search for the child to destroy him." **14** Joseph rose and took the child and his mother by night and departed for Egypt. **15** [h]He stayed there until the death of Herod, that what the Lord had said through the prophet might be fulfilled, "Out of Egypt I called my son."

The Massacre of the Infants. 16 When Herod realized that he had been deceived by the magi, he became furious. He ordered the massacre of all the boys in Bethlehem and its vicinity two years old and under, in accordance with the time he had ascertained from the magi. **17** Then was fulfilled what had been said through Jeremiah the prophet:

18   [i]"A voice was heard in Ramah,
      sobbing and loud lamentation;
    Rachel weeping for her children,
      and she would not be consoled,
      since they were no more."

The Return from Egypt. 19 When Herod had died, behold, the angel of the Lord appeared in a dream to Joseph in Egypt **20** and said, "Rise, take the child and his mother and go to the land of Israel, for those who sought the child's life are dead."ʲ **21** He rose, took the child and his mother, and went to the land of Israel. **22** But when he heard that Archelaus was ruling over Judea in place of his father Herod,ᵏ he was afraid to go back there. And because he had been warned in a dream, he departed for the region of Galilee. **23** ˡHe went and dwelt in a town called Nazareth, so that what had been spoken through the prophets might be fulfilled, "He shall be called a Nazorean."

Notes

a. **2:1–12** The future rejection of Jesus by Israel and his acceptance by the Gentiles are retrojected into this scene of the narrative.

b. **2:1 In the days of King Herod:** Herod reigned from 37 to 4 B.C. **Magi:** originally a designation of the Persian priestly caste, the word became used of those who were regarded as having more than human knowledge. Matthew's magi are astrologers.

c. **2:2 We saw his star:** it was a common ancient belief that a new star appeared at the time of a ruler's birth. Matthew also draws upon the Old Testament story of Balaam, who had prophesied that "A star shall advance from Jacob" (Nm 24:17), though there the star means not an astral phenomenon but the king himself.

d. **2:4** Herod's consultation with the chief priests and scribes has some similarity to a Jewish legend about the child Moses in which the "sacred scribes" warn Pharaoh about the imminent birth of one who will deliver Israel from Egypt and the king makes plans to destroy him.

e. **2:11** Cf. Ps 72:10, 15; Is 60:6. These Old Testament texts led to the interpretation of the magi as kings.

f. **2:13–23** Biblical and nonbiblical traditions about Moses are here applied to the child Jesus, though the dominant Old Testament type is not Moses but Israel (Mt 2:15).

g. **2:13 Flee to Egypt:** Egypt was a traditional place of refuge for those fleeing from danger in Palestine (see 1 Kgs 11:40; Jer 26:21), but the main reason why the child is to be taken to Egypt is that he may relive the Exodus experience of Israel.

h. **2:15** The fulfillment citation is taken from Hos 11:1. Israel, God's son, was called out of Egypt at the time of the Exodus; Jesus, the Son of God, will similarly be called out of that land in a new exodus. The father-son relationship between God and the nation is set in a higher key. Here the son is not a group adopted as "son of God," but the child who, as conceived by the holy Spirit, stands in unique relation to God. He is son of David and of Abraham, of Mary and of Joseph, but, above all, of God.

i. **2:18** Jer 31:15 portrays Rachel, wife of the patriarch Jacob, weeping for her children taken into exile at the time of the Assyrian invasion of the northern kingdom (722–21 B.C.). Bethlehem was traditionally identified with Ephrath, the place near which Rachel was buried (see Gn 35:19; 48:7), and the mourning of Rachel is here applied to her lost children of a later age. **Ramah:** about six miles north of Jerusalem. The lamentation of Rachel is so great as to be heard at a far distance.

j. **2:20 For those who sought the child's life are dead:** Moses, who had fled from Egypt because the Pharaoh sought to kill him (see Ex 2:15), was told to return there, "for all the men who sought your life are dead" (Ex 4:19).

k. **2:22** With the agreement of the emperor Augustus, Archelaus received half of his father's kingdom, including Judea, after Herod's death. He had the title "ethnarch" (i.e., "ruler of a nation") and reigned from 4 B.C. to A.D. 6.

l. **2:23 Nazareth . . . he shall be called a Nazorean:** the tradition of Jesus' residence in Nazareth was firmly established, and Matthew sees it as being in accordance with the foreannounced plan of God. The town of Nazareth is not mentioned in the Old Testament, and no such prophecy can be found there. The vague expression "through the prophets" may be due to Matthew's seeing a connection between Nazareth and certain texts in which there are words with a remote similarity to the name of that town. Some such Old Testament texts are Is 11:1 where the Davidic king of the future is called "a bud" (*nēser*) that shall blossom from the roots of Jesse, and Jgs 13:5, 7 where Samson, the future deliverer of Israel from the Philistines, is called one who shall be consecrated (a *nāzîr*) to God.

II. The Proclamation of the Kingdom

Chapter 3

The Preaching of John the Baptist.[a] **1** In those days John the Baptist appeared, preaching in the desert of Judea[b] **2** [and] saying, "Repent,[c] for the kingdom of heaven is at hand!" **3** [d]It was of him that the prophet Isaiah had spoken when he said:

> "A voice of one crying out in the desert,
> 'Prepare the way of the LORD,
>   make straight his paths.'"

4 [e]John wore clothing made of camel's hair and had a leather belt around his waist. His food was locusts and wild honey. **5** At that time Jerusalem, all Judea, and the whole region around the Jordan were going out to him **6** and were being baptized by him in the Jordan River as they acknowledged their sins.[f]

7 When he saw many of the Pharisees and Sadducees[g] coming to his baptism, he said to them, "You brood of vipers! Who warned you to flee from the coming wrath? **8** Produce good fruit as evidence of your repentance. **9** And do not presume to say to yourselves, 'We have Abraham as our father.' For I tell you, God can raise up children to Abraham from these stones. **10** Even now the ax lies at the root of the trees. Therefore every tree that does not bear good fruit will be cut down and thrown into the fire. **11** I am baptizing you with water, for repentance, but the one who is coming after me is mightier than I. I am not worthy to carry his sandals. He will baptize you with the holy Spirit and fire.[h] **12** [i]His winnowing fan is in his hand. He will clear his threshing floor and gather his wheat into his barn, but the chaff he will burn with unquenchable fire."

Trinity — **The Baptism of Jesus.**[j] **13** Then Jesus came from Galilee to John at the Jordan to be baptized by him. **14** [k]John tried to prevent him, saying, "I need to be baptized by you, and yet you are coming to me?" **15** Jesus said to him in reply, "Allow it now, for thus it is fitting for us to fulfill all righteousness." Then he allowed him. **16** [l]After Jesus was baptized, he came up from the water and behold, the heavens were opened [for him], and he saw the Spirit of God descending like a dove [and] coming upon him. **17** And a voice came from the heavens, saying, "This is my beloved Son,[m] with whom I am well pleased."

Notes

a. **3:1–12** Here Matthew takes up the order of Jesus' ministry found in the gospel of Mark, beginning with the preparatory preaching of John the Baptist.

b. **3:1** Unlike Luke, Matthew says nothing of the Baptist's origins and does not make him a relative of Jesus. **The desert of Judea:** the barren region west of the Dead Sea extending up the Jordan valley.

c. **3:2 Repent:** the Baptist calls for a change of heart and conduct, a turning of one's life from rebellion to obedience towards God. **The kingdom of heaven is at hand:** "heaven" (lit., "the heavens") is a substitute for the name "God" that was avoided by devout Jews of the time out of reverence. The expression "the kingdom of heaven" occurs only in the gospel of Matthew. It means the effective rule of God over his people. In its fullness it includes not only human obedience to God's word, but the triumph of God over physical evils, supremely over death. In the expectation found in Jewish apocalyptic, the kingdom was to be ushered in by a judgment in which sinners would be condemned and perish, an expectation shared by the Baptist. This was modified in Christian understanding where the kingdom was seen as being established in stages, culminating with the parousia of Jesus.

d. **3:3** See note on Jn 1:23.

e. **3:4** The clothing of John recalls the austere dress of the prophet Elijah (2 Kgs 1:8). The expectation of the return of Elijah from heaven to prepare Israel for the final manifestation of God's kingdom was widespread, and according to Matthew this expectation was fulfilled in the Baptist's ministry (Mt 11:14; 17:11–13).

f. **3:6** Ritual washing was practiced by various groups in Palestine between 150 B.C. and A.D. 250. John's baptism may have been related to the purificatory washings of the Essenes at Qumran.

g. **3:7 Pharisees and Sadducees:** the former were marked by devotion to the law, written and oral, and the scribes, experts in the law, belonged predominantly to this group. The Sadducees were the priestly aristocratic party, centered in Jerusalem. They accepted as scripture only the first five books of the Old Testament, followed only the letter of the law, rejected the oral legal traditions, and were opposed to teachings not found in the Pentateuch, such as the resurrection of the dead. Matthew links both of these groups together as enemies of Jesus (Mt 16:1, 6, 11, 12; cf. Mk 8:11–13, 15). The threatening words that follow are addressed to them rather than to "the crowds" as in Lk 3:7. **The coming wrath:** the judgment that will bring about the destruction of unrepentant sinners.

h. **3:11 Baptize you with the holy Spirit and fire:** the water baptism of John will be followed by an "immersion" of the repentant in the cleansing power of the Spirit of God, and of the unrepentant in the destroying power of God's judgment. However, some see **the holy Spirit** and **fire** as synonymous, and the effect of this "baptism" as either purification or destruction. See note on Lk 3:16.

i. **3:12** The discrimination between the good and the bad is compared to the procedure by which a farmer separates wheat and chaff. The **winnowing fan** was a forklike shovel with which the threshed wheat was thrown into the air. The kernels fell to the ground; the light chaff, blown off by the wind, was gathered and burned up.

j. **3:13–17** The baptism of Jesus is the occasion on which he is equipped for his ministry by the holy Spirit and proclaimed to be the Son of God.

k. **3:14–15** This dialogue, peculiar to Matthew, reveals John's awareness of Jesus' superiority to him as the mightier one who is coming and who will baptize with the holy Spirit (Mt 3:11). His reluctance to admit Jesus among the sinners whom he is baptizing with water is overcome by Jesus' response. **To fulfill all righteousness:** in this gospel to **fulfill** usually refers to fulfillment of prophecy, and **righteousness** to moral conduct in conformity with God's will. Here, however, as in Mt 5:6; 6:33, **righteousness** seems to mean the saving activity of God. **To fulfill all righteousness** is to submit to the plan of God for the salvation of the human race. This involves Jesus' identification with sinners; hence the propriety of his accepting John's baptism.

l. **3:16 The Spirit . . . coming upon him:** cf. Is 42:1.

m. **3:17 This is my beloved Son:** the Marcan address to Jesus (Mk 1:11) is changed into a proclamation. The Father's voice speaks in terms that reflect Is 42:1; Ps 2:7; Gn 22:2.

Chapter 4

The Temptation of Jesus. 1 [a]Then Jesus was led by the Spirit into the desert to be tempted by the devil. **2** He fasted for forty days and forty nights,[b] and afterwards he was hungry. **3** The tempter approached and said to him, "If you are the Son of God, command that these stones become loaves of bread." **4** [c]He said in reply, "It is written:

> 'One does not live by bread alone,
> but by every word that comes forth from the mouth of God.'"

5 [d]Then the devil took him to the holy city, and made him stand on the parapet of the temple, **6** and said to him, "If you are the Son of God, throw yourself down. For it is written:

'He will command his angels concerning you' and 'with their hands they will support you,lest you dash your foot against a stone.'"

7 Jesus answered him, "Again it is written, 'You shall not put the Lord, your God, to the test.'" **8** Then the devil took him up to a very high mountain, and showed him all the kingdoms of the world in their magnificence, **9** and he said to him, "All these I shall give to you, if you will prostrate yourself and worship me."[e] **10** At this, Jesus said to him, "Get away, Satan! It is written:

> 'The Lord, your God, shall you worship
> and him alone shall you serve.'"

11 Then the devil left him and, behold, angels came and ministered to him.

The Beginning of the Galilean Ministry.[f] **12** When he heard that John had been arrested, he withdrew to Galilee. **13** He left Nazareth and went to live in Capernaum by the sea, in the region of Zebulun and Naphtali, **14** that what had been said through Isaiah the prophet might be fulfilled:

15 "Land of Zebulun and land of Naphtali,
>   the way to the sea, beyond the Jordan,
>   Galilee of the Gentiles,
16   the people who sit in darkness
>   have seen a great light,
>   on those dwelling in a land overshadowed by death
>   light has arisen."

17 [g]From that time on, Jesus began to preach and say, "Repent, for the kingdom of heaven is at hand."

The Call of the First Disciples.[h] **18** As he was walking by the Sea of Galilee, he saw two brothers, Simon who is called Peter, and his brother Andrew, casting a net into the sea; they were fishermen. **19** He said to them, "Come after me, and I will make you fishers of men." **20** [i]At once they left their nets and followed him. **21** He walked along from there and saw two other brothers, James, the son of Zebedee, and his brother John. They were in a boat, with their father Zebedee, mending their nets. He called them, **22** and immediately they left their boat and their father and followed him.

Ministering to a Great Multitude.ʲ **23** He went around all of Galilee, teaching in their synagogues,ᵏ proclaiming the gospel of the kingdom, and curing every disease and illness among the people. **24** ˡHis fame spread to all of Syria, and they brought to him all who were sick with various diseases and racked with pain, those who were possessed, lunatics, and paralytics, and he cured them. **25** And great crowds from Galilee, the Decapolis,ᵐ Jerusalem, and Judea, and from beyond the Jordan followed him.

Notes

a. **4:1–11** Jesus, proclaimed Son of God at his baptism, is subjected to a triple temptation. Obedience to the Father is a characteristic of true sonship, and Jesus is tempted by the devil to rebel against God, overtly in the third case, more subtly in the first two. Each refusal of Jesus is expressed in language taken from the Book of Deuteronomy (Dt 8:3; 6:13, 16). The testings of Jesus resemble those of Israel during the wandering in the desert and later in Canaan, and the victory of Jesus, the true Israel and the true Son, contrasts with the failure of the ancient and disobedient "son," the old Israel. In the temptation account Matthew is almost identical with Luke; both seem to have drawn upon the same source.

b. **4:2 Forty days and forty nights:** the same time as that during which Moses remained on Sinai (Ex 24:18). The time reference, however, seems primarily intended to recall the forty years during which Israel was tempted in the desert (Dt 8:2).

c. **4:4** Cf. Dt 8:3. Jesus refuses to use his power for his own benefit and accepts whatever God wills.

d. **4:5–7** The devil supports his proposal by an appeal to the scriptures, Ps 91:11a, 12. Unlike Israel (Dt 6:16), Jesus refuses to "test" God by demanding from him an extraordinary show of power.

e. **4:9** The worship of Satan to which Jesus is tempted is probably intended to recall Israel's worship of false gods. His refusal is expressed in the words of Dt 6:13.

f. **4:12–17** Isaiah's prophecy of the light rising upon Zebulun and Naphtali (Is 8:22–9:1) is fulfilled in Jesus' residence at Capernaum. The territory of these two tribes was the first to be devastated (733–32 B.C.) at the time of the Assyrian invasion. In order to accommodate Jesus' move to Capernaum to the prophecy, Matthew speaks of that town as being "in the region of Zebulun and Naphtali" (Mt 4:13), whereas it was only in the territory of the latter, and he understands the sea of the prophecy, the Mediterranean, as the sea of Galilee.

g. **4:17** At the beginning of his preaching Jesus takes up the words of John the Baptist (Mt 3:2) although with a different meaning; in his ministry the kingdom of heaven has already begun to be present (Mt 12:28).

h. **4:18–22** The call of the first disciples promises them a share in Jesus' work and entails abandonment of family and former way of life. Three of the four, Simon, James, and John, are distinguished among the disciples by a closer relation with Jesus (Mt 17:1; 26:37).

i. **4:20** Here and in Mt 4:22, as in Mark (Mk 1:16–20) and unlike the Lucan account (Lk 5:1–11), the disciples' response is motivated only by Jesus' invitation, an element that emphasizes his mysterious power.

j. **4:23–25** This summary of Jesus' ministry concludes the narrative part of the first book of Matthew's gospel (Mt 3–4). The activities of his ministry are teaching, proclaiming the gospel, and healing; cf. Mt 9:35.

k. **4:23 Their synagogues:** Matthew usually designates the Jewish synagogues as **their synagogue(s)** (Mt 9:35; 10:17; 12:9; 13:54) or, in address to Jews, **your synagogues** (Mt 23:34), an indication that he wrote after the break between church and synagogue.

l. **4:24 Syria:** the Roman province to which Palestine belonged.

m. **4:25 The Decapolis:** a federation of Greek cities in Palestine, originally ten in number, all but one east of the Jordan.

Chapter 5

The Sermon on the Mount. 1 [a]When he saw the crowds,[b] he went up the mountain, and after he had sat down, his disciples came to him. **2** He began to teach them, saying:

The Beatitudes[c]

3   "Blessed are the poor in spirit,[d]
    for theirs is the kingdom of heaven

4   [e]Blessed are they who mourn,
    for they will be comforted.

5   [f]Blessed are the meek,
    for they will inherit the land.

6   Blessed are they who hunger and thirst for righteousness,[g]
    for they will be satisfied.

7   Blessed are the merciful,
    for they will be shown mercy.

8   [h]Blessed are the clean of heart,
    for they will see God.

9   Blessed are the peacemakers,
    for they will be called children of God.

10 Blessed are they who are persecuted for the sake of righteousness,[i]
    for theirs is the kingdom of heaven.

11 Blessed are you when they insult you and persecute you and utter every kind of evil against you [falsely] because of me. **12** [j]Rejoice and be glad, for your reward will be great in heaven. Thus they persecuted the prophets who were before you.

The Similes of Salt and Light.[k] **13** "You are the salt of the earth. But if salt loses its taste, with what can it be seasoned? It is no longer good for anything but to be thrown out and trampled underfoot.[l] **14** You are the light of the world. A city set on a mountain cannot be hidden. **15** Nor do they light a lamp and then put it under a bushel basket; it is set on a lampstand, where it gives light to all in the house. **16** Just so, your light must shine before others, that they may see your good deeds and glorify your heavenly Father.

Teaching About the Law. 17 [m]"Do not think that I have come to abolish the law or the prophets. I have come not to abolish but to fulfill. **18** Amen, I say to you, until heaven and earth pass away, not the smallest letter or the smallest part of a letter will pass from the law, until all things have taken place. **19** Therefore, whoever breaks one of the least of these commandments and teaches others to do so will be called least in the kingdom of heaven. But whoever obeys and teaches these commandments will be called greatest in the kingdom of heaven.[n] **20** I tell you, unless your righteousness surpasses that of the scribes and Pharisees, you will not enter into the kingdom of heaven.

Teaching About Anger.[o] **21** "You have heard that it was said to your ancestors, 'You shall not kill; and whoever kills will be liable to judgment.'[p] **22** [q]But I say to you, whoever is angry[r] with his brother will be liable to judgment, and whoever says to his brother, 'Raqa,' will be answerable to the Sanhedrin, and whoever says, 'You fool,' will be liable to fiery Gehenna. **23** Therefore, if you bring your gift to the altar, and there recall that your brother has anything against you, **24** leave your gift there at the altar, go first and be reconciled with your brother, and then come and offer your gift. **25** Settle with your opponent quickly while on the way to court with him. Otherwise your opponent will hand you over to the judge, and the judge will hand you over to the guard, and you will be thrown into prison. **26** Amen, I say to you, you will not be released until you have paid the last penny.

Teaching About Adultery. 27 [s]"You have heard that it was said, 'You shall not commit adultery.' **28** But I say to you, everyone who looks at a woman with lust has already committed adultery with her in his heart. **29** [t]If your right eye causes you to sin, tear it out and throw it away. It is better for you to lose one of your members than to have your whole body thrown into Gehenna. **30** And if your right hand causes you to sin, cut it off and throw it away. It is better for you to lose one of your members than to have your whole body go into Gehenna.

Teaching About Divorce. 31 [u]"It was also said, 'Whoever divorces his wife must give her a bill of divorce.' **32** But I say to you, whoever divorces his wife (unless the marriage is unlawful) causes her to commit adultery, and whoever marries a divorced woman commits adultery.

Teaching About Oaths. 33 [v]"Again you have heard that it was said to your ancestors, 'Do not take a false oath, but make good to the LORD all that you vow.' **34** But I say to you, do not swear at all;[w] not by heaven, for it is God's throne; **35** nor by the earth, for it is his footstool; nor by Jerusalem, for it is the city of the great King. **36** Do not swear by your head, for you cannot make a single hair white or black. **37** [x]Let your 'Yes' mean 'Yes,' and your 'No' mean 'No.' Anything more is from the evil one.

Teaching About Retaliation. 38 [y]"You have heard that it was said, 'An eye for an eye and a tooth for a tooth.' **39** But I say to you, offer no resistance to one who is evil. When someone strikes you on [your] right cheek, turn the other one to him as well. **40** If anyone wants to go to law with you over your tunic, hand him your cloak as well. **41** Should anyone press you into service for one mile,[z] go with him for two miles. **42** Give to the one who asks of you, and do not turn your back on one who wants to borrow.

Love of Enemies.[aa] **43** "You have heard that it was said, 'You shall love your neighbor and hate your enemy.' **44** But I say to you, love your enemies, and pray for those who persecute you, **45** that you may be children of your heavenly Father, for he makes his sun rise on the bad and the good, and causes rain to fall on the just and the unjust. **46** For if you love those who love you, what recompense will you have? Do not the tax collectors[ab] do the same? **47** And if you greet your brothers only, what is unusual about that? Do not the pagans do the same?[ac] **48** So be perfect,[ad] just as your heavenly Father is perfect.

Notes

a. **5:1–7:29** The first of the five discourses that are a central part of the structure of this gospel. It is the discourse section of the first book and contains sayings of Jesus derived from Q and from M. The Lucan parallel is in that gospel's "Sermon on the Plain" (Lk 6:20–49), although some of the sayings in Matthew's "Sermon on the Mount" have their parallels in other parts of Luke. The careful topical arrangement of the sermon is probably not due only to Matthew's editing; he seems to have had a structured discourse of Jesus as one of his sources. The form of that source may have been as follows: four beatitudes (Mt 5:3–4, 6, 11–12), a section on the new righteousness with illustrations (Mt 5:17, 20–24, 27–28, 33–48), a section on good works (Mt 6:1–6, 16–18), and three warnings (Mt 7:1–2, 15–21, 24–27).

b. **5:1–2** Unlike Luke's sermon, this is addressed not only to the disciples but to the crowds (see Mt 7:28).

c. **5:3–12** The form **Blessed are (is)** occurs frequently in the Old Testament in the Wisdom literature and in the psalms. Although modified by Matthew, the first, second, fourth, and ninth beatitudes have Lucan parallels (Mt 5:3 // Lk 6:20; Mt 5:4 // Lk 6:21b; Mt 5:6 // Lk 6:21a; Mt 5:11–12 // Lk 5:22–23). The others were added by the evangelist and are probably his own composition. A few manuscripts, Western and Alexandrian, and many versions and patristic quotations give the second and third beatitudes in inverted order.

d. **5:3 The poor in spirit:** in the Old Testament, the poor (*'anāwîm*) are those who are without material possessions and whose confidence is in God (see Is 61:1; Zep 2:3; in the NAB the word is translated **lowly** and **humble**, respectively, in those texts). Matthew added **in spirit** in order either to indicate that only the devout poor were meant or to extend the beatitude to all, of whatever social rank, who recognized their complete dependence on God. The same phrase **poor in spirit** is found in the Qumran literature (1QM 14:7).

e. **5:4** Cf. Is 61:2, "(The Lord has sent me) . . . to comfort all who mourn." **They will be comforted:** here the passive is a "theological passive" equivalent to the active "God will comfort them"; so also in Mt 5:6, 7.

f. **5:5** Cf. Ps 37:11, " . . . the meek shall possess the land." In the psalm "the land" means the land of Palestine; here it means the kingdom.

g. **5:6 For righteousness:** a Matthean addition. For the meaning of **righteousness** here, see note on Mt 3:14–15.

h. **5:8** Cf. Ps 24:4. Only one "whose heart is clean" can take part in the temple worship. To be with God in the temple is described in Ps 42:3 as "beholding his face," but here the promise to **the clean of heart** is that they will **see God** not in the temple but in the coming kingdom.

i. **5:10 Righteousness** here, as usually in Matthew, means conduct in conformity with God's will.

j. **5:12 The prophets who were before you:** the disciples of Jesus stand in the line of the persecuted prophets of Israel. Some would see the expression as indicating also that Matthew considered all Christian disciples as prophets.

k. **5:13–16** By their deeds the disciples are to influence the world for good. They can no more escape notice than **a city set on a mountain.** If they fail in good works, they are as useless as flavorless salt or as a lamp whose light is concealed.

l. **5:13** The unusual supposition of salt losing its flavor has led some to suppose that the saying refers to the salt of the Dead Sea that, because chemically impure, could lose its taste.

m. **5:17–20** This statement of Jesus' position concerning the Mosaic law is composed of traditional material from Matthew's sermon documentation (see note on Mt 5:1–7:29), other Q material (cf. Mt 18; Lk 16:17), and the evangelist's own editorial touches. **To fulfill** the law appears at first to mean a literal enforcement of the law in the least detail: **until heaven and earth pass away** nothing of the law **will pass** (Mt 5:18). Yet the "passing away" of heaven and earth is not necessarily the end of the world understood, as in much apocalyptic literature, as the dissolution of the existing universe. The "turning of the ages" comes with the apocalyptic event of Jesus' death and resurrection, and those to whom this gospel is addressed are living in the new and final age, prophesied by Isaiah as the time of "new heavens and a new earth" (Is 65:17; 66:22). Meanwhile, during Jesus' ministry when the kingdom is already breaking in, his mission remains within the framework of the law, though with significant anticipation of the age to come, as the following antitheses (Mt 5:21–48) show.

n. **5:19** Probably **these commandments** means those of the Mosaic law. But this is an interim ethic "until heaven and earth pass away."

o. **5:21–48** Six examples of the conduct demanded of the Christian disciple. Each deals with a commandment of the law, introduced by **You have heard that it was said to your ancestors** or an equivalent formula, followed by Jesus' teaching in respect to that commandment, **But I say to you**; thus their designation as "antitheses." Three of them accept the Mosaic law but extend or deepen it (Mt 5:21–22; 27–28; 43–44); three reject it as a standard of conduct for the disciples (Mt 5:31–32; 33–37; 38–39).

p. **5:21** Cf. Ex 20:13; Dt 5:17. The second part of the verse is not an exact quotation from the Old Testament, but cf. Ex 21:12.

q. **5:22–26** Reconciliation with an offended brother is urged in the admonition of Mt 5:23–24 and the parable of Mt 5:25–26 (// Lk 12:58–59). The severity of the judge in the parable is a warning of the fate of unrepentant sinners in the coming judgment by God.

r. **5:22** Anger is the motive behind murder, as the insulting epithets are steps that may lead to it. They, as well as the deed, are all forbidden. **Raqa:** an Aramaic word *rēqā'* or *rēqâ* probably meaning "imbecile," "blockhead," a term of abuse. The ascending order of punishment, **judgment** (by a local council?), trial before **the Sanhedrin**, condemnation to **Gehenna**, points to a higher degree of seriousness in each of the offenses. **Sanhedrin:** the highest judicial body of Judaism. **Gehenna:** in Hebrew *gê-hinnōm*, "Valley of Hinnom," or *gê ben-hinnōm*, "Valley of the son of Hinnom," southwest of Jerusalem, the center of an idolatrous cult during the monarchy in which children were offered in sacrifice (see 2 Kgs 23:10; Jer 7:31). In Jos 18:16 (Septuagint, Codex Vaticanus) the Hebrew is transliterated into Greek as *gaienna*, which appears in the New Testament as geenna. The concept of punishment of sinners by fire either after death or after the final judgment is found in Jewish apocalyptic literature (e.g., Enoch 90:26) but the name *geenna* is first given to the place of punishment in the New Testament.

s. **5:27** See Ex 20:14; Dt 5:18.

t. **5:29**–30 No sacrifice is too great to avoid total destruction in **Gehenna**.

u. **5:31**–**32** See Dt 24:1–5. The Old Testament commandment that a bill of divorce be given to the woman assumes the legitimacy of divorce itself. It is this that Jesus denies. **(Unless the marriage is unlawful):** this "exceptive clause," as it is often called, occurs also in Mt 19:9, where the Greek is slightly different. There are other sayings of Jesus about divorce that prohibit it absolutely (see Mk 10:11–12; Lk 16:18; cf. 1 Cor 7:10, 11b), and most scholars agree that they represent the stand of Jesus. Matthew's "exceptive clauses" are understood by some as a modification of the absolute prohibition. It seems, however, that the unlawfulness that Matthew gives as a reason why a marriage must be broken refers to a situation peculiar to his community: the violation of Mosaic law forbidding marriage between persons of certain blood and/or legal relationship (Lv 18:6–18). Marriages of that sort were regarded as incest (*porneia*), but some rabbis allowed Gentile converts to Judaism who had contracted such marriages to remain in them. Matthew's "exceptive clause" is against such permissiveness for Gentile converts to Christianity; cf. the similar prohibition of *porneia* in Acts 15:20, 29. In this interpretation, the clause constitutes no exception to the absolute prohibition of divorce when the marriage is lawful.

v. **5:33** This is not an exact quotation of any Old Testament text, but see Ex 20:7; Dt 5:11; Lv 19:12. The purpose of an oath was to guarantee truthfulness by one's calling on God as witness.

w. **5:34**–**36** The use of these oath formularies that avoid the divine name is in fact equivalent to swearing by it, for all the things sworn by are related to God.

x. **5:37 Let your 'Yes' mean 'Yes,' and your 'No' mean 'No':** literally, "let your speech be 'Yes, yes,' 'No, no.'" Some have understood this as a milder form of oath, permitted by Jesus. In view of Mt 5:34, "Do not swear at all," that is unlikely. **From the evil one:** i.e., from the devil. Oath-taking presupposes a sinful weakness of the human race, namely, the tendency to lie. Jesus demands of his disciples a truthfulness that makes oaths unnecessary.

y. **5:38–42** See Lv 24:20. The Old Testament commandment was meant to moderate vengeance; the punishment should not exceed the injury done. Jesus forbids even this proportionate retaliation. Of the five examples that follow, only the first deals directly with retaliation for evil; the others speak of liberality.

z. **5:41** Roman garrisons in Palestine had the right to requisition the property and services of the native population.

aa. **5:43–48** See Lv 19:18. There is no Old Testament commandment demanding hatred of one's enemy, but the "neighbor" of the love commandment was understood as one's fellow countryman. Both in the Old Testament (Ps 139:19–22) and at Qumran (1QS 9:21) hatred of evil persons is assumed to be right. Jesus extends the love commandment to the enemy and the persecutor. His disciples, as children of God, must imitate the example of their Father, who grants his gifts of sun and rain to both the good and the bad.

ab. **5:46 Tax collectors:** Jews who were engaged in the collection of indirect taxes such as tolls and customs. See note on Mk 2:14.

ac. **5:47** Jesus' disciples must not be content with merely usual standards of conduct; see Mt 5:20 where the verb "surpass" (Greek *perisseuō*) is cognate with the **unusual** (*perisson*) of this verse.

ad. **5:48 Perfect:** in the gospels this word occurs only in Matthew, here and in Mt 19:21. The Lucan parallel (Lk 6:36) demands that the disciples be **merciful**.

Chapter 6

Teaching About Almsgiving.[a] **1** "[But] take care not to perform righteous deeds in order that people may see them; otherwise, you will have no recompense from your heavenly Father. **2** When you give alms, do not blow a trumpet before you, as the hypocrites[b] do in the synagogues and in the streets to win the praise of others. Amen, I say to you, they have received their reward. **3** But when you give alms, do not let your left hand know what your right is doing, **4** so that your almsgiving may be secret. And your Father who sees in secret will repay you.

Teaching About Prayer. **5** "When you pray, do not be like the hypocrites, who love to stand and pray in the synagogues and on street corners so that others may see them. Amen, I say to you, they have received their reward. **6** But when you pray, go to your inner room, close the door, and pray to your Father in secret. And your Father who sees in secret will repay you. **7** [c]In praying, do not babble like the pagans, who think that they will be heard because of their many words.[d] **8** Do not be like them. Your Father knows what you need before you ask him.

The Lord's Prayer. **9** [e]"This is how you are to pray:

> Our Father in heaven,[f]
> hallowed be your name,
> **10** your kingdom come,[g]
> your will be done,
> on earth as in heaven.
> **11** [h]Give us today our daily bread;
> **12** and forgive us our debts,[i]
> as we forgive our debtors;
> **13** and do not subject us to the final test,[j]
> but deliver us from the evil one.

14 [k]If you forgive others their transgressions, your heavenly Father will forgive you. **15** But if you do not forgive others, neither will your Father forgive your transgressions.

Teaching About Fasting. **16** "When you fast,[l] do not look gloomy like the hypocrites. They neglect their appearance, so that they may appear to others to be fasting. Amen, I say to you, they have received their reward. **17** But when you fast, anoint your head and wash your face, **18** so that you may not appear to others to be fasting, except to your Father who is hidden. And your Father who sees what is hidden will repay you.

Treasure in Heaven. **19** [m]"Do not store up for yourselves treasures on earth, where moth and decay destroy, and thieves break in and steal. **20** But store up treasures in heaven, where neither moth nor decay destroys, nor thieves break in and steal. **21** For where your treasure is, there also will your heart be.

The Light of the Body.[n] **22** "The lamp of the body is the eye. If your eye is sound, your whole body will be filled with light; **23** but if your eye is bad, your whole body will be in darkness. And if the light in you is darkness, how great will the darkness be.

God and Money. 24 [o]"No one can serve two masters. He will either hate one and love the other, or be devoted to one and despise the other. You cannot serve God and mammon.

Dependence on God.[p] **25** "Therefore I tell you, do not worry about your life, what you will eat [or drink], or about your body, what you will wear. Is not life more than food and the body more than clothing? **26** Look at the birds in the sky; they do not sow or reap, they gather nothing into barns, yet your heavenly Father feeds them. Are not you more important than they? **27** Can any of you by worrying add a single moment to your life-span?[q] **28** Why are you anxious about clothes? Learn from the way the wild flowers grow. They do not work or spin. **29** But I tell you that not even Solomon in all his splendor was clothed like one of them. **30** [r]If God so clothes the grass of the field, which grows today and is thrown into the oven tomorrow, will he not much more provide for you, O you of little faith? **31** So do not worry and say, 'What are we to eat?' or 'What are we to drink?' or 'What are we to wear?' **32** All these things the pagans seek. Your heavenly Father knows that you need them all. **33** But seek first the kingdom [of God] and his righteousness,[s] and all these things will be given you besides. **34** Do not worry about tomorrow; tomorrow will take care of itself. Sufficient for a day is its own evil.

Notes

a. **6:1–18** The sermon continues with a warning against doing good in order to be seen and gives three examples, almsgiving (Mt 6:2–4), prayer (Mt 6:5–15), and fasting (Mt 6:16–18). In each, the conduct of the hypocrites (Mt 6:2) is contrasted with that demanded of the disciples. The sayings about reward found here and elsewhere (Mt 5:12, 46; 10:41–42) show that this is a genuine element of Christian moral exhortation. Possibly to underline the difference between the Christian idea of reward and that of the hypocrites, the evangelist uses two different Greek verbs to express the rewarding of the disciples and that of the hypocrites; in the latter case it is the verb apechō, a commercial term for giving a receipt for what has been paid in full (Mt 6:2, 5, 16).

b. **6:2 The hypocrites:** the scribes and Pharisees, see Mt 23:13, 15, 23, 25, 27, 29. The designation reflects an attitude resulting not only from the controversies at the time of Jesus' ministry but from the opposition between Pharisaic Judaism and the church of Matthew. **They have received their reward:** they desire praise and have received what they were looking for.

c. **6:7–15** Matthew inserts into his basic traditional material an expansion of the material on prayer that includes the model prayer, the "Our Father." That prayer is found in Lk 11:2–4 in a different context and in a different form.

d. **6:7** The example of what Christian prayer should be like contrasts it now not with the prayer of the hypocrites but with that of **the pagans**. Their babbling probably means their reciting a long list of divine names, hoping that one of them will force a response from the deity.

e. **6:9–13** Matthew's form of the "Our Father" follows the liturgical tradition of his church. Luke's less developed form also represents the liturgical tradition known to him, but it is probably closer than Matthew's to the original words of Jesus.

f. **6:9 Our Father in heaven:** this invocation is found in many rabbinic prayers of the post-New Testament period. **Hallowed be your name:** though the "hallowing" of the divine name could be understood as reverence done to God by human praise and by obedience to his will, this is more probably a petition that God hallow his own name, i.e., that he manifest his glory by an act of power (cf. Ez 36:23), in this case, by the establishment of his kingdom in its fullness.

g. **6:10 Your kingdom come:** this petition sets the tone of the prayer, and inclines the balance toward divine rather than human action in the petitions that immediately precede and follow it. **Your will be done, on earth as in heaven:** a petition that the divine purpose to establish the kingdom, a purpose present now in **heaven**, be executed on **earth**.

h. **6:11 Give us today our daily bread:** the rare Greek word *epiousios*, here **daily**, occurs in the New Testament only here and in Lk 11:3. A single occurrence of the word outside of these texts and of literature dependent on them has been claimed, but the claim is highly doubtful. The word may mean **daily** or "future" (other meanings have also been proposed). The latter would conform better to the eschatological tone of the whole prayer. So understood, the petition would be for a speedy coming of the kingdom (**today**), which is often portrayed in both the Old Testament and the New under the image of a feast (Is 25:6; Mt 8:11; 22:1–10; Lk 13:29; 14:15–24).

i. **6:12 Forgive us our debts:** the word **debts** is used metaphorically of sins, "debts" owed to God (see Lk 11:4). The request is probably for forgiveness at the final judgment.

j. **6:13** Jewish apocalyptic writings speak of a period of severe trial before the end of the age, sometimes called the "messianic woes." This petition asks that the disciples be spared that **final test**.

k. **6:14–15** These verses reflect a set pattern called "Principles of Holy Law." Human action now will be met by a corresponding action of God at the final judgment.

l. **6:16** The only fast prescribed in the Mosaic law was that of the Day of Atonement (Lv 16:31), but the practice of regular fasting was common in later Judaism; cf. *Didache* 9:1.

m. **6:19–34** The remaining material of this chapter is taken almost entirely from Q. It deals principally with worldly possessions, and the controlling thought is summed up in Mt 6:24: the disciple can serve only one master and must choose between God and wealth (**mammon**). See further the note on Lk 16:9.

n. **6:22–23** In this context the parable probably points to the need for the disciple to be enlightened by Jesus' teaching on the transitory nature of earthly riches.

o. **6:24 Mammon:** an Aramaic word meaning wealth or property.

p. **6:25–34** Jesus does not deny the reality of human needs (Mt 6:32), but forbids making them the object of anxious care and, in effect, becoming their slave.

q. **6:27 Life-span:** the Greek word can also mean "stature." If it is taken in that sense, the word here translated **moment** (literally, "cubit") must be translated literally as a unit not of time but of spatial measure. The cubit is about eighteen inches.

r. **6:30 Of little faith:** except for the parallel in Lk 12:28, the word translated **of little faith** is found in the New Testament only in Matthew. It is used by him of those who are disciples of Jesus but whose faith in him is not as deep as it should be (see Mt 8:26; 14:31; 16:8 and the cognate noun in Mt 17:20).

s. **6:33 Righteousness:** see note on Mt 3:14–15.

Chapter 7

Judging Others. 1 [a]"Stop judging,[b] that you may not be judged. **2** For as you judge, so will you be judged, and the measure with which you measure will be measured out to you. **3** Why do you notice the splinter in your brother's eye, but do not perceive the wooden beam in your own eye? **4** How can you say to your brother, 'Let me remove that splinter from your eye,' while the wooden beam is in your eye? **5** You hypocrite,[c] remove the wooden beam from your eye first; then you will see clearly to remove the splinter from your brother's eye.

Pearls Before Swine. 6 "Do not give what is holy to dogs,[d] or throw your pearls before swine, lest they trample them underfoot, and turn and tear you to pieces.

The Answer to Prayers. 7 "Ask and it will be given to you; seek and you will find; knock and the door will be opened to you. **8** For everyone who asks, receives; and the one who seeks, finds; and to the one who knocks, the door will be opened. **9** Which one of you would hand his son a stone when he asks for a loaf of bread,[e] **10** or a snake when he asks for a fish? **11** If you then, who are wicked, know how to give good gifts to your children, how much more will your heavenly Father give good things to those who ask him.

The Golden Rule. 12 [f]"Do to others whatever you would have them do to you. This is the law and the prophets.

The Narrow Gate. 13 [g]"Enter through the narrow gate;[h] for the gate is wide and the road broad that leads to destruction, and those who enter through it are many. **14** How narrow the gate and constricted the road that leads to life. And those who find it are few.

False Prophets.[i] **15** "Beware of false prophets, who come to you in sheep's clothing, but underneath are ravenous wolves. **16** By their fruits you will know them. Do people pick grapes from thornbushes, or figs from thistles? **17** Just so, every good tree bears good fruit, and a rotten tree bears bad fruit. **18** A good tree cannot bear bad fruit, nor can a rotten tree bear good fruit. **19** Every tree that does not bear good fruit will be cut down and thrown into the fire. **20** So by their fruits you will know them.

The True Disciple. 21 "Not everyone who says to me, 'Lord, Lord,' will enter the kingdom of heaven,[j] but only the one who does the will of my Father in heaven. **22** Many will say to me on that day, 'Lord, Lord, did we not prophesy in your name? Did we not drive out demons in your name? Did we not do mighty deeds in your name?' **23** Then I will declare to them solemnly, 'I never knew you.[k] Depart from me, you evildoers.'

The Two Foundations. 24 [l]"Everyone who listens to these words of mine and acts on them will be like a wise man who built his house on rock. **25** The rain fell, the floods came, and the winds blew and buffeted the house. But it did not collapse; it had been set solidly on rock. **26** And everyone who listens to these words of mine but does not act on them will be like a fool who built his house on sand. **27** The rain fell, the floods came, and the winds blew and buffeted the house. And it collapsed and was completely ruined."

28 [m]When Jesus finished these words, the crowds were astonished at his teaching, **29** [n]for he taught them as one having authority, and not as their scribes.

Notes

a. **7:1–12** In Mt 7:1 Matthew returns to the basic traditional material of the sermon (Lk 6:37–38, 41–42). The governing thought is the correspondence between conduct toward one's fellows and God's conduct toward the one so acting.

b. **7:1** This is not a prohibition against recognizing the faults of others, which would be hardly compatible with Mt 7:5, 6 but against passing judgment in a spirit of arrogance, forgetful of one's own faults.

c. **7:5 Hypocrite:** the designation previously given to the scribes and Pharisees is here given to the Christian disciple who is concerned with the faults of another and ignores his own more serious offenses.

d. **7:6 Dogs** and **swine** were Jewish terms of contempt for Gentiles. This saying may originally have derived from a Jewish Christian community opposed to preaching the gospel (**what is holy, pearls**) to Gentiles. In the light of Mt 28:19 that can hardly be Matthew's meaning. He may have taken the saying as applying to a Christian dealing with an obstinately impenitent fellow Christian (Mt 18:17).

e. **7:9–10** There is a resemblance between a stone and a round loaf of bread and between a serpent and the scaleless fish called *barbut*.

f. **7:12** See Lk 6:31. This saying, known since the eighteenth century as the "Golden Rule," is found in both positive and negative form in pagan and Jewish sources, both earlier and later than the gospel. **This is the law and the prophets** is an addition probably due to the evangelist.

g. **7:13–28** The final section of the discourse is composed of a series of antitheses, contrasting two kinds of life within the Christian community, that of those who obey the words of Jesus and that of those who do not. Most of the sayings are from Q and are found also in Luke.

h. **7:13–14** The metaphor of the "two ways" was common in pagan philosophy and in the Old Testament. In Christian literature it is found also in the *Didache* (1–6) and the *Epistle of Barnabas* (18–20).

i. **7:15–20** Christian disciples who claimed to speak in the name of God are called **prophets** (Mt 7:15) in Mt 10:41; Mt 23:34. They were presumably an important group within the church of Matthew. As in the case of the Old Testament prophets, there were both true and false ones, and for Matthew the difference could be recognized by the quality of their deeds, the **fruits** (Mt 7:16). The mention of **fruits** leads to the comparison with trees, some producing good fruit, others bad.

j. **7:21–23** The attack on the false prophets is continued, but is broadened to include those disciples who perform works of healing and exorcism in the name of Jesus (**Lord**) but live evil lives. Entrance into the kingdom is only for those who do the will of the Father. On the day of judgment (**on that day**) the morally corrupt prophets and miracle workers will be rejected by Jesus.

k. **7:23 I never knew you:** cf. Mt 10:33. **Depart from me, you evildoers:** cf. Ps 6:9.

l. **7:24–27** The conclusion of the discourse (cf. Lk 6:47–49). Here the relation is not between saying and doing as in Mt 7:15–23 but between hearing and doing, and the words of Jesus are applied to every Christian (everyone who listens).

m. **7:28–29 When Jesus finished these words:** this or a similar formula is used by Matthew to conclude each of the five great discourses of Jesus (cf. Mt 11:1; 13:53; 19:1; 26:1).

n. **7:29 Not as their scribes:** scribal instruction was a faithful handing down of the traditions of earlier teachers; Jesus' teaching is based on his own authority. **Their scribes:** for the implications of **their**, see note on Mt 4:23.

III. Ministry and Mission in Galilee[a]

Chapter 8

The Cleansing of a Leper. 1 When Jesus came down from the mountain, great crowds followed him. **2** And then a leper[b] approached, did him homage, and said, "Lord, if you wish, you can make me clean." **3** He stretched out his hand, touched him, and said, "I will do it. Be made clean." His leprosy was cleansed immediately. **4** [c]Then Jesus said to him, "See that you tell no one, but go show yourself to the priest, and offer the gift that Moses prescribed; that will be proof for them."

The Healing of a Centurion's Servant.[d] **5** When he entered Capernaum,[e] a centurion approached him and appealed to him, **6** saying, "Lord, my servant is lying at home paralyzed, suffering dreadfully." **7** He said to him, "I will come and cure him." **8** The centurion said in reply,[f] "Lord, I am not worthy to have you enter under my roof; only say the word and my servant will be healed. **9** For I too am a person subject to authority, with soldiers subject to me. And I say to one, 'Go,' and he goes; and to another, 'Come here,' and he comes; and to my slave, 'Do this,' and he does it." **10** When Jesus heard this, he was amazed and said to those following him, "Amen, I say to you, in no one in Israel[g] have I found such faith. **11** I say to you,[h] many will come from the east and the west, and will recline with Abraham, Isaac, and Jacob at the banquet in the kingdom of heaven, **12** but the children of the kingdom will be driven out into the outer darkness, where there will be wailing and grinding of teeth." **13** And Jesus said to the centurion, "You may go; as you have believed, let it be done for you." And at that very hour [his] servant was healed.

The Cure of Peter's Mother-in-Law.[i] **14** Jesus entered the house of Peter, and saw his mother-in-law lying in bed with a fever. **15** He touched her hand, the fever left her, and she rose and waited on him.

Other Healings. 16 When it was evening, they brought him many who were possessed by demons, and he drove out the spirits by a word[j] and cured all the sick, **17** to fulfill what had been said by Isaiah the prophet:[k]

> "He took away our infirmities
> and bore our diseases."

The Would-be Followers of Jesus.[l] **18** When Jesus saw a crowd around him, he gave orders to cross to the other side.[m] **19** A scribe approached and said to him, "Teacher,[n] I will follow you wherever you go." **20** Jesus answered him, "Foxes have dens and birds of the sky have nests, but the Son of Man[o] has nowhere to rest his head." **21** Another of [his] disciples said to him, "Lord, let me go first and bury my father." **22** [p]But Jesus answered him, "Follow me, and let the dead bury their dead."

The Calming of the Storm at Sea. 23 ^qHe got into a boat and his disciples followed him. **24** Suddenly a violent storm^r came up on the sea, so that the boat was being swamped by waves; but he was asleep. **25** They came and woke him, saying, "Lord, save us!^s We are perishing!" **26** He said to them, "Why are you terrified, O you of little faith?"^t Then he got up, rebuked the winds and the sea, and there was great calm. **27** The men were amazed and said, "What sort of man is this, whom even the winds and the sea obey?"

The Healing of the Gadarene Demoniacs. 28 When he came to the other side, to the territory of the Gadarenes,^u two demoniacs who were coming from the tombs met him. They were so savage that no one could travel by that road. **29** They cried out, "What have you to do with us,^v Son of God? Have you come here to torment us before the appointed time?" **30** Some distance away a herd of many swine was feeding.^w **31** The demons pleaded with him, "If you drive us out, send us into the herd of swine." **32** And he said to them, "Go then!" They came out and entered the swine, and the whole herd rushed down the steep bank into the sea where they drowned. **33** The swineherds ran away, and when they came to the town they reported everything, including what had happened to the demoniacs. **34** Thereupon the whole town came out to meet Jesus, and when they saw him they begged him to leave their district.

Notes

a. **8:1–9:38** This narrative section of the second book of the gospel is composed of nine miracle stories, most of which are found in Mark, although Matthew does not follow the Marcan order and abbreviates the stories radically. The stories are arranged in three groups of three, each group followed by a section composed principally of sayings of Jesus about discipleship. Mt 9:35 is an almost verbatim repetition of Mt 4:23. Each speaks of Jesus' teaching, preaching, and healing. The teaching and preaching form the content of Mt 5–7; the healing, that of Mt 8–9. Some scholars speak of a portrayal of Jesus as "Messiah of the Word" in Mt 5–7 and "Messiah of the Deed" in Mt 8–9. That is accurate so far as it goes, but there is also a strong emphasis on discipleship in Mt 8–9; these chapters have not only christological but ecclesiological import.

b. **8:2 A leper:** see note on Mk 1:40.

c. **8:4** Cf. Lv 14:2–9. **That will be proof for them:** the Greek can also mean "that will be proof against them." It is not clear whether **them** refers to the priests or the people.

d. **8:5–13** This story comes from Q (see Lk 7:1–10) and is also reflected in Jn 4:46–54. The similarity between the Q story and the Johannine is due to a common oral tradition, not to a common literary source. As in the later story of the daughter of the Canaanite woman (Mt 15:21–28) Jesus here breaks with his usual procedure of ministering only to Israelites and anticipates the mission to the Gentiles.

e. **8:5 A centurion:** a military officer commanding a hundred men. He was probably in the service of Herod Antipas, tetrarch of Galilee; see note on Mt 14:1.

f. **8:8–9** Acquainted by his position with the force of a command, the centurion expresses faith in the power of Jesus' mere word.

g. **8:10 In no one in Israel:** there is good textual attestation (e.g., Codex Sinaiticus) for a reading identical with that of Lk 7:9, "not even in Israel." But that seems to be due to a harmonization of Matthew with Luke.

h. **8:11–12** Matthew inserts into the story a Q saying (see Lk 13:28–29) about the entrance of Gentiles into the kingdom and the exclusion of those Israelites who, though descended from the patriarchs and members of the chosen nation (**the children of the kingdom**), refused to believe in Jesus. **There will be wailing and grinding of teeth:** the first occurrence of a phrase used frequently in this gospel to describe final condemnation (Mt 13:42, 50; 22:13; 24:51; 25:30). It is found elsewhere in the New Testament only in Lk 13:28.

i. **8:14–15** Cf. Mk 1:29–31. Unlike Mark, Matthew has no implied request by others for the woman's cure. Jesus acts on his own initiative, and the cured woman rises and waits not on "them" (Mk 1:31) but on **him**.

j. **8:16 By a word:** a Matthean addition to Mk 1:34; cf. 8:8.

k. **8:17** This fulfillment citation from Is 53:4 follows the MT, not the LXX. The prophet speaks of the Servant of the Lord who suffers vicariously for the sins ("infirmities") of others; Matthew takes the **infirmities** as physical afflictions.

l. **8:18–22** This passage between the first and second series of miracles about following Jesus is taken from Q (see Lk 9:57–62). The third of the three sayings found in the source is absent from Matthew.

m. **8:18 The other side**: i.e., of the Sea of Galilee.

n. **8:19 Teacher:** for Matthew, this designation of Jesus is true, for he has Jesus using it of himself (Mt 10:24, 25; 23:8; 26:18), yet when it is used of him by others they are either his opponents (Mt 9:11; 12:38; 17:24; 22:16, 24, 36) or, as here and in Mt 19:16, well-disposed persons who cannot see more deeply. Thus it reveals an inadequate recognition of who Jesus is.

o. **8:20 Son of Man:** see note on Mk 8:31. This is the first occurrence in Matthew of a term that appears in the New Testament only in sayings of Jesus, except for Acts 7:56 and possibly Mt 9:6 (// Mk 2:10; Lk 5:24). In Matthew it refers to Jesus in his ministry (seven times, as here), in his passion and resurrection (nine times, e.g., Mt 17:22), and in his glorious coming at the end of the age (thirteen times, e.g., Mt 24:30).

p. **8:22 Let the dead bury their dead:** the demand of Jesus overrides what both the Jewish and the Hellenistic world regarded as a filial obligation of the highest importance. See note on Lk 9:60.

q. **8:23 His disciples followed him:** the first miracle in the second group (Mt 8:23–9:8) is introduced by a verse that links it with the preceding sayings by the catchword "follow." In Mark the initiative in entering the boat is taken by the disciples (Mk 4:35–41); here, Jesus enters first and the disciples follow.

r. **8:24 Storm:** literally, "earthquake," a word commonly used in apocalyptic literature for the shaking of the old world when God brings in his kingdom. All the synoptics use it in depicting the events preceding the parousia of the Son of Man (Mt 24:7; Mk 13:8; Lk 21:11). Matthew has introduced it here and in his account of the death and resurrection of Jesus (Mt 27:51–54; 28:2).

s. **8:25** The reverent plea of the disciples contrasts sharply with their reproach of Jesus in Mk 4:38.

t. **8:26 You of little faith:** see note on Mt 6:30. **Great calm:** Jesus' calming the sea may be meant to recall the Old Testament theme of God's control over the chaotic waters (Ps 65:8; 89:10; 93:3–4; 107:29).

u. **8:28 Gadarenes:** this is the reading of Codex Vaticanus, supported by other important textual witnesses. The original reading of Codex Sinaiticus was Gazarenes, later changed to Gergesenes, and a few versions have Gerasenes. Each of these readings points to a different territory connected, respectively, with the cities Gadara, Gergesa, and Gerasa (modern Jerash). There is the same confusion of readings in the parallel texts, Mk 5:1 and Lk 8:26; there the best reading seems to be "Gerasenes," whereas "Gadarenes" is probably the original reading in Matthew. The town of Gadara was about five miles southeast of the Sea of Galilee, and Josephus (*Life* 9:42) refers to it as possessing territory that lay on that sea. **Two demoniacs:** Mark (5:1–20) has one.

v. **8:29 What have you to do with us?:** see note on Jn 2:4. **Before the appointed time:** the notion that evil spirits were allowed by God to afflict human beings until the time of the final judgment is found in Enoch 16:1 and Jubilees 10:7–10.

w. **8:30** The tending of pigs, animals considered unclean by Mosaic law (Lv 11:6–7), indicates that the population was Gentile.

Chapter 9

The Healing of a Paralytic. 1 [a]He entered a boat, made the crossing, and came into his own town. **2** And there people brought to him a paralytic lying on a stretcher. When Jesus saw their faith, he said to the paralytic, "Courage, child, your sins are forgiven." **3** At that, some of the scribes[b] said to themselves, "This man is blaspheming." **4** Jesus knew what they were thinking, and said, "Why do you harbor evil thoughts? **5** Which is easier, to say, 'Your sins are forgiven,' or to say, 'Rise and walk'? **6** [c]But that you may know that the Son of Man has authority on earth to forgive sins"—he then said to the paralytic, "Rise, pick up your stretcher, and go home." **7** He rose and went home. **8** [d]When the crowds saw this they were struck with awe and glorified God who had given such authority to human beings.

The Call of Matthew.[e] **9** As Jesus passed on from there, he saw a man named Matthew[f] sitting at the customs post. He said to him, "Follow me." And he got up and followed him. **10** While he was at table in his house,[g] many tax collectors and sinners came and sat with Jesus and his disciples. **11** The Pharisees saw this and said to his disciples, "Why does your teacher[h] eat with tax collectors and sinners?" **12** He heard this and said, "Those who are well do not need a physician, but the sick do.[i] **13** Go and learn the meaning of the words, 'I desire mercy, not sacrifice.'[j] I did not come to call the righteous but sinners."

The Question About Fasting. 14 Then the disciples of John approached him and said, "Why do we and the Pharisees fast [much], but your disciples do not fast?" **15** Jesus answered them, "Can the wedding guests mourn as long as the bridegroom is with them? The days will come when the bridegroom is taken away from them, and then they will fast.[k] **16** No one patches an old cloak with a piece of unshrunken cloth,[l] for its fullness pulls away from the cloak and the tear gets worse. **17** People do not put new wine into old wineskins. Otherwise the skins burst, the wine spills out, and the skins are ruined. Rather, they pour new wine into fresh wineskins, and both are preserved."

The Official's Daughter and the Woman with a Hemorrhage. 18 [m]While he was saying these things to them, an official[n] came forward, knelt down before him, and said, "My daughter has just died. But come, lay your hand on her, and she will live." **19** Jesus rose and followed him, and so did his disciples. **20** A woman suffering hemorrhages for twelve years came up behind him and touched the tassel[o] on his cloak. **21** She said to herself, "If only I can touch his cloak, I shall be cured." **22** Jesus turned around and saw her, and said, "Courage, daughter! Your faith has saved you." And from that hour the woman was cured.

23 When Jesus arrived at the official's house and saw the flute players and the crowd who were making a commotion, **24** he said, "Go away!

The girl is not dead but sleeping."[p] And they ridiculed him. **25** When the crowd was put out, he came and took her by the hand, and the little girl arose. **26** And news of this spread throughout all that land.

The Healing of Two Blind Men.[q] **27** And as Jesus passed on from there, two blind men followed [him], crying out, "Son of David,[r] have pity on us!" **28** When he entered the house, the blind men approached him and Jesus said to them, "Do you believe that I can do this?" "Yes, Lord," they said to him. **29** Then he touched their eyes and said, "Let it be done for you according to your faith." **30** And their eyes were opened. Jesus warned them sternly, "See that no one knows about this." **31** But they went out and spread word of him through all that land.

The Healing of a Mute Person. **32** As they were going out,[s] a demoniac who could not speak was brought to him, **33** and when the demon was driven out the mute person spoke. The crowds were amazed and said, "Nothing like this has ever been seen in Israel." **34** [t]But the Pharisees said, "He drives out demons by the prince of demons."

The Compassion of Jesus. **35** [u]Jesus went around to all the towns and villages, teaching in their synagogues, proclaiming the gospel of the kingdom, and curing every disease and illness. **36** At the sight of the crowds, his heart was moved with pity for them because they were troubled and abandoned,[v] like sheep without a shepherd. **37** [w]Then he said to his disciples, "The harvest is abundant but the laborers are few; **38** so ask the master of the harvest to send out laborers for his harvest."

Notes

a. **9:1 His own town:** Capernaum; see Mt 4:13.

b. **9:3 Scribes:** see note on Mk 2:6. Matthew omits the reason given in the Marcan story for the charge of blasphemy: "Who but God alone can forgive sins?" (Mk 2:7).

c. **9:6** It is not clear whether **But that you may know . . . to forgive sins** is intended to be a continuation of the words of Jesus or a parenthetical comment of the evangelist to those who would hear or read this gospel. In any case, Matthew here follows the Marcan text.

d. **9:8 Who had given such authority to human beings:** a significant difference from Mk 2:12 ("They . . . glorified God, saying, 'We have never seen anything like this'"). Matthew's extension to **human beings** of the authority to forgive sins points to the belief that such authority was being claimed by Matthew's church.

e. **9:9–17** In this section the order is the same as that of Mk 2:13–22.

f. **9:9 A man named Matthew:** Mark names this tax collector Levi (Mk 2:14). No such name appears in the four lists of the twelve who were the closest companions of Jesus (Mt 10:2–4; Mk 3:16–19; Lk 6:14–16; Acts 1:13 [eleven, because of the defection of Judas Iscariot]), whereas all four list a **Matthew**, designated in Mt 10:3 as "the tax collector." The evangelist may have changed the "Levi" of his source to Matthew so that this man, whose call is given special notice, like that of the first four disciples (Mt 4:18–22), might be included among the twelve. Another reason for the change may be that the disciple Matthew was the source of traditions peculiar to the church for which the evangelist was writing.

g. **9:10 His house:** it is not clear whether his refers to Jesus or Matthew. **Tax collectors:** see note on Mt 5:46. Table association with such persons would cause ritual impurity.

h. **9:11 Teacher:** see note on Mt 8:19.

i. **9:12** See note on Mk 2:17.

j. **9:13 Go and learn . . . not sacrifice:** Matthew adds the prophetic statement of Hos 6:6 to the Marcan account (see also Mt 12:7). If mercy is superior to the temple sacrifices, how much more to the laws of ritual impurity.

k. **9:15** Fasting is a sign of mourning and would be as inappropriate at this time of joy, when Jesus is proclaiming the kingdom, as it would be at a marriage feast. Yet the saying looks forward to the time when Jesus will no longer be with the disciples visibly, the time of Matthew's church. **Then they will fast:** see *Didache* 8:1.

l. **9:16–17** Each of these parables speaks of the unsuitability of attempting to combine the old and the new. Jesus' teaching is not a patching up of Judaism, nor can the gospel be contained within the limits of Mosaic law.

m. **9:18–34** In this third group of miracles, the first (Mt 9:18–26) is clearly dependent on Mark (Mk 5:21–43). Though it tells of two miracles, the cure of the woman had already been included within the story of the raising of the official's daughter, so that the two were probably regarded as a single unit. The other miracles seem to have been derived from Mark and Q, respectively, though there Matthew's own editing is much more evident.

n. **9:18 Official:** literally, "ruler." Mark calls him "one of the synagogue officials" (Mk 5:22). **My daughter has just died:** Matthew heightens the Marcan "my daughter is at the point of death" (Mk 5:23).

o. **9:20 Tassel:** possibly "fringe." The Mosaic law prescribed that tassels be worn on the corners of one's garment as a reminder to keep the commandments (see Nm 15:37–39; Dt 22:12).

p. **9:24 Sleeping:** sleep is a biblical metaphor for death (see Ps 87:6 LXX; Dn 12:2; 1 Thes 5:10). Jesus' statement is not a denial of the child's real death, but an assurance that she will be roused from her sleep of death.

q. **9:27–31** This story was probably composed by Matthew out of Mark's story of the healing of a blind man named Bartimaeus (Mk 10:46–52). Mark places the event late in Jesus' ministry, just before his entrance into Jerusalem, and

Matthew has followed his Marcan source at that point in his gospel also (see Mt 20:29–34). In each of the Matthean stories the single blind man of Mark becomes two. The reason why Matthew would have given a double version of the Marcan story and placed the earlier one here may be that he wished to add a story of Jesus' curing the blind at this point in order to prepare for Jesus' answer to the emissaries of the Baptist (Mt 11:4–6) in which Jesus, recounting his works, begins with his giving sight to the blind.

r. **9:27 Son of David:** this messianic title is connected once with the healing power of Jesus in Mark (Mk 10:47–48) and Luke (Lk 18:38–39) but more frequently in Matthew (see also Mt 12:23; 15:22; 20:30–31).

s. **9:32–34** The source of this story seems to be Q (see Lk 11:14–15). As in the preceding healing of the blind, Matthew has two versions of this healing, the later in Mt 12:22–24 and the earlier here.

t. **9:34** This spiteful accusation foreshadows the growing opposition to Jesus in Mt 11 and 12.

u. **9:35** See notes on Mt 4:23–25; Mt 8:1–9:38.

v. **9:36** See Mk 6:34; Nm 27:17; 1 Kgs 22:17.

w. **9:37–38** This Q saying (see Lk 10:2) is only imperfectly related to this context. It presupposes that only God (**the master of the harvest**) can take the initiative in sending out preachers of the gospel, whereas in Matthew's setting it leads into Mt 10 where Jesus does so.

Chapter 10

The Mission of the Twelve. 1 [a]Then he summoned his twelve disciples[b] and gave them authority over unclean spirits to drive them out and to cure every disease and every illness. **2** The names of the twelve apostles[c] are these: first, Simon called Peter, and his brother Andrew; James, the son of Zebedee, and his brother John; **3** Philip and Bartholomew, Thomas and Matthew the tax collector; James, the son of Alphaeus, and Thaddeus; **4** Simon the Cananean, and Judas Iscariot who betrayed him.

The Commissioning of the Twelve. 5 Jesus sent out these twelve[d] after instructing them thus, "Do not go into pagan territory or enter a Samaritan town. **6** Go rather to the lost sheep of the house of Israel. **7** As you go, make this proclamation: 'The kingdom of heaven is at hand.' **8** [e]Cure the sick, raise the dead, cleanse lepers, drive out demons. Without cost you have received; without cost you are to give. **9** Do not take gold or silver or copper for your belts; **10** no sack for the journey, or a second tunic, or sandals, or walking stick. The laborer deserves his keep. **11** Whatever town or village you enter, look for a worthy person in it, and stay there until you leave. **12** As you enter a house, wish it peace. **13** If the house is worthy, let your peace come upon it; if not, let your peace return to you.[f] **14** [g]Whoever will not receive you or listen to your words—go outside that house or town and shake the dust from your feet. **15** Amen, I say to you, it will be more tolerable for the land of Sodom and Gomorrah on the day of judgment than for that town.

Coming Persecutions. 16 "Behold, I am sending you like sheep in the midst of wolves; so be shrewd as serpents and simple as doves. **17** [h]But beware of people, for they will hand you over to courts and scourge you in their synagogues, **18** and you will be led before governors and kings for my sake as a witness before them and the pagans. **19** When they hand you over, do not worry about how you are to speak or what you are to say. You will be given at that moment what you are to say. **20** For it will not be you who speak but the Spirit of your Father speaking through you. **21** [i]Brother will hand over brother to death, and the father his child; children will rise up against parents and have them to death. **22** You will be hated by all because of my name, but whoever endures to the end[j] will be saved. **23** When they persecute you in one town, flee to another. Amen, I say to you, you will not finish the towns of Israel before the Son of Man comes.[k] **24** No disciple is above his teacher, no slave above his master. **25** It is enough for the disciple that he become like his teacher, for the slave that he become like his master. If they have called the master of the house Beelzebul,[l] how much more those of his household!

Courage Under Persecution. 26 "Therefore do not be afraid of them. Nothing is concealed that will not be revealed, nor secret that will not be known.^m **27** What I say to you in the darkness, speak in the light; what you hear whispered, proclaim on the housetops. **28** And do not be afraid of those who kill the body but cannot kill the soul; rather, be afraid of the one who can destroy both soul and body in Gehenna. **29** Are not two sparrows sold for a small coin? Yet not one of them falls to the ground without your Father's knowledge. **30** Even all the hairs of your head are counted. **31** So do not be afraid; you are worth more than many sparrows. **32** ⁿEveryone who acknowledges me before others I will acknowledge before my heavenly Father. **33** But whoever denies me before others, I will deny before my heavenly Father.

Jesus: A Cause of Division. 34 "Do not think that I have come to bring peace upon the earth. I have come to bring not peace but the sword. **35** For I have come to set

> a man 'against his father,
>> a daughter against her mother,
> and a daughter-in-law against her mother-in-law;
>
> **36**   and one's enemies will be those of his household.'

The Conditions of Discipleship. 37 "Whoever loves father or mother more than me is not worthy of me, and whoever loves son or daughter more than me is not worthy of me; **38** and whoever does not take up his cross[o] and follow after me is not worthy of me. **39** ^pWhoever finds his life will lose it, and whoever loses his life for my sake will find it.

Rewards. 40 "Whoever receives you receives me,^q and whoever receives me receives the one who sent me. **41** ^rWhoever receives a prophet because he is a prophet will receive a prophet's reward, and whoever receives a righteous man because he is righteous will receive a righteous man's reward. **42** And whoever gives only a cup of cold water to one of these little ones to drink because he is a disciple—amen, I say to you, he will surely not lose his reward."

Notes

a. **10:1–11:1** After an introductory narrative (Mt 10:1–4), the second of the discourses of the gospel. It deals with the mission now to be undertaken by the disciples (Mt 10:5–15), but the perspective broadens and includes the missionary activity of the church between the time of the resurrection and the parousia.

b. **10:1 His twelve disciples:** although, unlike Mark (Mk 3:13–14) and Luke (Lk 6:12–16), Matthew has no story of Jesus' choosing the Twelve, he assumes that the group is known to the reader. The earliest New Testament text to speak of it is 1 Cor 15:5. The number probably is meant to recall the twelve tribes of Israel and implies Jesus' authority to call all Israel into the kingdom. While Luke (Lk 6:13) and probably Mark (Mk 4:10, 34) distinguish between the Twelve and a larger group also termed disciples, Matthew tends to identify the disciples and the Twelve. **Authority . . . every illness:** activities the same as those of Jesus;

see Mt 4:23; Mt 9:35; 10:8. The Twelve also share in his proclamation of the kingdom (Mt 10:7). But although he teaches (Mt 4:23; 7:28; 9:35), they do not. Their commission to teach comes only after Jesus' resurrection, after they have been fully instructed by him (Mt 28:20).

c. **10:2–4** Here, for the only time in Matthew, the Twelve are designated **apostles**. The word "apostle" means "one who is sent," and therefore fits the situation here described. In the Pauline letters, the place where the term occurs most frequently in the New Testament, it means primarily one who has seen the risen Lord and has been commissioned to proclaim the resurrection. With slight variants in Luke and Acts, the names of those who belong to this group are the same in the four lists given in the New Testament (see note on Mt 9:9). **Cananean:** this represents an Aramaic word meaning "zealot." The meaning of that designation is unclear (see note on Lk 6:15).

d. **10:5–6** Like Jesus (Mt 15:24), the Twelve are sent only to Israel. This saying may reflect an original Jewish Christian refusal of the mission to the Gentiles, but for Matthew it expresses rather the limitation that Jesus himself observed during his ministry.

e. **10:8–11** The Twelve have received their own call and mission through God's gift, and the benefits they confer are likewise to be given freely. They are not to take with them money, provisions, or unnecessary clothing; their lodging and food will be provided by those who receive them.

f. **10:13** The greeting of peace is conceived of not merely as a salutation but as an effective word. If it finds no worthy recipient, it will return to the speaker.

g. **10:14 Shake the dust from your feet:** this gesture indicates a complete disassociation from such unbelievers.

h. **10:17** The persecutions attendant upon the post-resurrection mission now begin to be spoken of. Here Matthew brings into the discourse sayings found in Mk 13 which deals with events preceding the parousia.

i. **10:21** See Mi 7:6 which is cited in Mt 10:35, 36.

j. **10:22 To the end:** the original meaning was probably "until the parousia." But it is not likely that Matthew expected no missionary disciples to suffer death before then, since he envisages the martyrdom of other Christians (Mt 10:21). For him, **the end** is probably that of the individual's life (see Mt 10:28).

k. **10:23 Before the Son of Man comes:** since the coming of the Son of Man at the end of the age had not taken place when this gospel was written, much less during the mission of the Twelve during Jesus' ministry, Matthew cannot have meant the coming to refer to the parousia. It is difficult to know what he understood it to be: perhaps the "proleptic parousia" of Mt 28:16–20, or the destruction of the temple in A.D. 70, viewed as a coming of Jesus in judgment on unbelieving Israel.

l. **10:25 Beelzebul:** see Mt 9:34 for the charge linking Jesus with "the prince of demons," who is named **Beelzebul** in Mt 12:24. The meaning of the name is uncertain; possibly, "lord of the house."

m. **10:26** The **concealed** and **secret** coming of the kingdom is to be proclaimed by them, and no fear must be allowed to deter them from that proclamation.

n. **10:32–33** In the Q parallel (Lk 12:8–9), the Son of Man will acknowledge those who have acknowledged Jesus, and those who deny him will be denied (by the Son of Man) before the angels of God at the judgment. Here Jesus and the Son of Man are identified, and the acknowledgment or denial will be before his heavenly Father.

o. **10:38** The first mention of the cross in Matthew, explicitly that of the disciple, but implicitly that of Jesus (**and follow after me**). Crucifixion was a form of capital punishment used by the Romans for offenders who were not Roman citizens.

p. **10:39** One who denies Jesus in order to save one's earthly life will be condemned to everlasting destruction; loss of earthly life for Jesus' sake will be rewarded by everlasting life in the kingdom.

q. **10:40–42** All who receive the disciples of Jesus receive him, and God who sent him, and will be rewarded accordingly.

r. **10:41 A prophet:** one who speaks in the name of God; here, the Christian prophets who proclaim the gospel. **Righteous man:** since righteousness is demanded of all the disciples, it is difficult to take the **righteous man** of this verse and **one of these little ones** (Mt 10:42) as indicating different groups within the followers of Jesus. Probably all three designations are used here of Christian missionaries as such.

Chapter 11

1 When Jesus finished giving these commands to his twelve disciples,[a] he went away from that place to teach and to preach in their towns.

IV. Opposition from Israel

The Messengers from John the Baptist. 2 [b]When John heard in prison[c] of the works of the Messiah, he sent his disciples to him **3** [d]with this question, "Are you the one who is to come, or should we look for another?" **4** Jesus said to them in reply, "Go and tell John what you hear and see: **5** [e]the blind regain their sight, the lame walk, lepers are cleansed, the deaf hear, the dead are raised, and the poor have the good news proclaimed to them. **6** And blessed is the one who takes no offense at me."

Jesus' Testimony to John.[f] **7** As they were going off, Jesus began to speak to the crowds about John, "What did you go out to the desert to see? A reed swayed by the wind? **8** Then what did you go out to see? Someone dressed in fine clothing? Those who wear fine clothing are in royal palaces. **9** Then why did you go out? To see a prophet?[g] Yes, I tell you, and more than a prophet. **10** This is the one about whom it is written:

'Behold, I am sending my messenger ahead of you;
he will prepare your way before you.'

11 Amen, I say to you, among those born of women there has been none greater than John the Baptist; yet the least in the kingdom of heaven is greater than he.[h] **12** From the days of John the Baptist until now, the kingdom of heaven suffers violence,[i] and the violent are taking it by force. **13** All the prophets and the law[j] prophesied up to the time of John. **14** And if you are willing to accept it, he is Elijah, the one who is to come. **15** Whoever has ears ought to hear.

16 "To what shall I compare this generation?[k] It is like children who sit in marketplaces and call to one another, **17** 'We played the flute for you, but you did not dance, we sang a dirge but you did not mourn.' **18** For John came neither eating nor drinking, and they said, 'He is possessed by a demon.' **19** The Son of Man came eating and drinking and they said, 'Look, he is a glutton and a drunkard, a friend of tax collectors and sinners.' But wisdom is vindicated by her works."

Reproaches to Unrepentant Towns. 20 Then he began to reproach the towns where most of his mighty deeds had been done, since they had not repented. **21** "Woe to you, Chorazin! Woe to you, Bethsaida! For if the mighty deeds done in your midst had been done in Tyre and Sidon,[l] they would long ago have repented in sackcloth and ashes. **22** But I tell you, it will be more tolerable for Tyre and Sidon on the day of judgment than for you. **23** [m]And as for you, Capernaum:

'Will you be exalted to heaven?
You will go down to the netherworld.'

For if the mighty deeds done in your midst had been done in Sodom, it would have remained until this day. **24** But I tell you, it will be more tolerable for the land of Sodom on the day of judgment than for you."

The Praise of the Father. 25 At that time Jesus said in reply,[n] "I give praise to you, Father, Lord of heaven and earth, for although you have hidden these things from the wise and the learned you have revealed them to the childlike. **26** Yes, Father, such has been your gracious will. **27** All things have been handed over to me by my Father. No one knows the Son except the Father, and no one knows the Father except the Son and anyone to whom the Son wishes to reveal him.

The Gentle Mastery of Christ. 28 [o]"Come to me, all you who labor and are burdened,[p] and I will give you rest. **29** [q]Take my yoke upon you and learn from me, for I am meek and humble of heart; and you will find rest for yourselves. **30** For my yoke is easy, and my burden light."

Notes

a. **11:1** The closing formula of the discourse refers back to the original addressees, the Twelve.

b. **11:2–12:50** The narrative section of the third book deals with the growing opposition to Jesus. It is largely devoted to disputes and attacks relating to faith and discipleship and thus contains much sayings-material, drawn in large part from Q.

c. **11:2 In prison:** see Mt 4:12; 14:1–12. **The works of the Messiah:** the deeds of Mt 8–9.

d. **11:3** The question probably expresses a doubt of the Baptist that Jesus is **the one who is to come** (cf. Mal 3:1) because his mission has not been one of fiery judgment as John had expected (Mt 3:2).

e. **11:5–6** Jesus' response is taken from passages of Isaiah (Is 26:19; 29:18–19; 35:5–6; 61:1) that picture the time of salvation as marked by deeds such as those that Jesus is doing. The beatitude is a warning to the Baptist not to disbelieve because his expectations have not been met.

f. **11:7–19** Jesus' rebuke of John is counterbalanced by a reminder of the greatness of the Baptist's function (Mt 11:7–15) that is followed by a complaint about those who have heeded neither John nor Jesus (Mt 11:16–19).

g. **11:9–10** In common Jewish belief there had been no prophecy in Israel since the last of the Old Testament prophets, Malachi. The coming of a new prophet was eagerly awaited, and Jesus agrees that John was such. Yet he was **more than a prophet**, for he was the precursor of the one who would bring in the new and final age. The Old Testament quotation is a combination of Mal 3:1; Ex 23:20 with the significant change that the **before me** of Malachi becomes **before you**. The messenger now precedes not God, as in the original, but Jesus.

h. **11:11** John's preeminent greatness lies in his function of announcing the imminence of the kingdom (Mt 3:1). But to be in the kingdom is so great a privilege that the least who has it is greater than the Baptist.

i. **11:12** The meaning of this difficult saying is probably that the opponents of Jesus are trying to prevent people from accepting the kingdom and to snatch it away from those who have received it.

j. **11:13 All the prophets and the law:** Matthew inverts the usual order, "law and prophets," and says that both have **prophesied**. This emphasis on the prophetic character of the law points to its fulfillment in the teaching of Jesus and to the transitory nature of some of its commandments (see note on Mt 5:17–20).

k. **11:16–19** See Lk 7:31–35. The meaning of the parable (Mt 11:16–17) and its explanation (Mt 11:18–19b) is much disputed. A plausible view is that the **children** of the parable are two groups, one of which proposes different entertainments to the other that will not agree with either proposal. The first represents John, Jesus, and their disciples; the second those who reject John for his asceticism and Jesus for his table association with those despised by the religiously observant. Mt 11:19c (**her works**) forms an inclusion with Mt 11:2 ("the works of the Messiah"). The original form of the saying is better preserved in Lk 7:35 " . . . wisdom is vindicated by all her children." There John and Jesus are the children of Wisdom; here the works of Jesus the Messiah are those of divine Wisdom, of which he is the embodiment. Some important textual witnesses, however, have essentially the same reading as in Luke.

l. **11:21** Tyre and Sidon were pagan cities denounced for their wickedness in the Old Testament; cf. Jl 4:4–7.

m. **11:23** Capernaum's pride and punishment are described in language taken from the taunt song against the king of Babylon (Is 14:13–15).

n. **11:25–27** This Q saying, identical with Lk 10:21–22 except for minor variations, introduces a joyous note into this section, so dominated by the theme of unbelief. **While the wise and the learned**, the scribes and Pharisees, have rejected Jesus' preaching and the significance of his mighty deeds, **the childlike** have accepted them. Acceptance depends upon the Father's revelation, but this is granted to those who are open to receive it and refused to the arrogant. Jesus can speak of all mysteries because he is **the Son** and there is perfect reciprocity of knowledge between him and the Father; what has been **handed over** to him is revealed only to those whom he wishes.

o. **11:28–29** These verses are peculiar to Matthew and are similar to Ben Sirach's invitation to learn wisdom and submit to her yoke (Sir 51:23, 26).

p. **11:28 Who labor and are burdened:** burdened by the law as expounded by the scribes and Pharisees (Mt 23:4).

q. **11:29** In place of the yoke of the law, complicated by scribal interpretation, Jesus invites the burdened to take the yoke of obedience to his word, under which they **will find rest**; cf. Jer 6:16.

Chapter 12

Picking Grain on the Sabbath. 1 [a]At that time Jesus was going through a field of grain on the sabbath. His disciples were hungry and began to pick the heads[b] of grain and eat them. **2** When the Pharisees saw this, they said to him, "See, your disciples are doing what is unlawful to do on the sabbath." **3** He said to them,[c] "Have you not read what David did when he and his companions were hungry, **4** how he went into the house of God and ate the bread of offering, which neither he nor his companions but only the priests could lawfully eat? **5** [d]Or have you not read in the law that on the sabbath the priests serving in the temple violate the sabbath and are innocent? **6** I say to you, something greater than the temple is here. **7** [e]If you knew what this meant, 'I desire mercy, not sacrifice,' you would not have condemned these innocent men. **8** [f]For the Son of Man is Lord of the sabbath."

The Man with a Withered Hand. 9 Moving on from there, he went into their synagogue. **10** And behold, there was a man there who had a withered hand. They questioned him, "Is it lawful to cure on the sabbath?"[g] so that they might accuse him. **11** [h]He said to them, "Which one of you who has a sheep that falls into a pit on the sabbath will not take hold of it and lift it out? **12** How much more valuable a person is than a sheep. So it is lawful to do good on the sabbath." **13** Then he said to the man, "Stretch out your hand." He stretched it out, and it was restored as sound as the other. **14** But the Pharisees[i] went out and took counsel against him to put him to death.

The Chosen Servant.[j] **15** When Jesus realized this, he withdrew from that place. Many [people] followed him, and he cured them all,[k] **16** but he warned them not to make him known. **17** This was to fulfill what had been spoken through Isaiah the prophet:

18 "Behold, my servant whom I have chosen,
      my beloved in whom I delight;
   I shall place my spirit upon him,
      and he will proclaim justice to the Gentiles.
19 He will not contend[l] or cry out,
      nor will anyone hear his voice in the streets.
20 A bruised reed he will not break,
      a smoldering wick he will not quench,
   until he brings justice to victory.
21   And in his name the Gentiles will hope."[m]

Jesus and Beelzebul.[n] **22** Then they brought to him a demoniac who was blind and mute. He cured the mute person so that he could speak and see. **23** [o]All the crowd was astounded, and said, "Could this perhaps be the Son of David?" **24** [p]But when the Pharisees heard this, they said, "This man drives out demons only by the power of Beelzebul, the prince of demons." **25** But he knew what they were thinking and said to them,[q] "Every kingdom divided against itself will be laid waste, and no town or house divided against itself will stand. **26** And if Satan drives out Satan, he is divided against himself; how, then, will his kingdom stand? **27** And if I drive out demons by Beelzebul, by whom do your own people[r] drive them out? Therefore they will be your judges. **28** [s]But if it is by the Spirit of God that I drive out demons, then the kingdom of God has come upon you. **29** [t]How can anyone enter a strong man's house and steal his property, unless he first ties up the strong man? Then he can plunder his house. **30** [u]Whoever is not with me is against me, and whoever does not gather with me scatters. **31** Therefore, I say to you, every sin and blasphemy will be forgiven people, but blasphemy against the Spirit[v] will not be forgiven. **32** And whoever speaks a word against the Son of Man will be forgiven; but whoever speaks against the holy Spirit will not be forgiven, either in this age or in the age to come.

A Tree and Its Fruits. 33 "Either declare[w] the tree good and its fruit is good, or declare the tree rotten and its fruit is rotten, for a tree is known by its fruit. **34** [x]You brood of vipers, how can you say good things when you are evil? For from the fullness of the heart the mouth speaks. **35** A good person brings forth good out of a store of goodness, but an evil person brings forth evil out of a store of evil. **36** [y]I tell you, on the day of judgment people will render an account for every careless word they speak. **37** By your words you will be acquitted, and by your words you will be condemned."

The Demand for a Sign.[z] **38** Then some of the scribes and Pharisees said to him, "Teacher,[aa] we wish to see a sign from you." **39** He said to them in reply, "An evil and unfaithful[ab] generation seeks a sign, but no sign will be given it except the sign of Jonah the prophet. **40** Just as Jonah was in the belly of the whale three days and three nights,[ac] so will the Son of Man be in the heart of the earth three days and three nights. **41** [ad]At the judgment, the men of Nineveh will arise with this generation and condemn it, because they repented at the preaching of Jonah; and there is something greater than Jonah here. **42** At the judgment the queen of the south will arise with this generation and condemn it, because she came from the ends of the earth to hear the wisdom of Solomon; and there is something greater than Solomon here.

The Return of the Unclean Spirit.[ae] **43** "When an unclean spirit goes out of a person it roams through arid regions searching for rest but finds none. **44** Then it says, 'I will return to my home from which I came.' But upon returning, it finds it empty, swept clean, and put in order. **45** Then it goes and brings back with itself seven other spirits more evil than itself, and they move in and dwell there; and the last condition of that person is worse than the first. Thus it will be with this evil generation."

The True Family of Jesus.[af] **46** While he was still speaking to the crowds, his mother and his brothers appeared outside, wishing to speak with him. **47** [Someone told him, "Your mother and your brothers are standing outside, asking to speak with you."][ag] **48** But he said in reply to the one who told him, "Who is my mother? Who are my brothers?" **49** And stretching out his hand toward his disciples, he said, "Here are my mother and my brothers. **50** For whoever does the will of my heavenly Father is my brother, and sister, and mother."

Notes

a. **12:1–14** Matthew here returns to the Marcan order that he left in Mt 9:18. The two stories depend on Mk 2:23–28; 3:1–6, respectively, and are the only places in either gospel that deal explicitly with Jesus' attitude toward sabbath observance.

b. **12:1–2** The picking of the heads of grain is here equated with reaping, which was forbidden on the sabbath (Ex 34:21).

c. **12:3–4** See 1 Sm 21:2–7. In the Marcan parallel (Mk 2:25–26) the high priest is called Abiathar, although in 1 Samuel this action is attributed to Ahimelech. The Old Testament story is not about a violation of the sabbath rest; its pertinence to this dispute is that a violation of the law was permissible because of David's men being without food.

d. **12:5–6** This and the following argument (Mt 12:7) are peculiar to Matthew. The temple service seems to be the changing of the showbread on the sabbath (Lv 24:8) and the doubling on the sabbath of the usual daily holocausts (Nm 28:9–10). The argument is that the law itself requires work that breaks the sabbath rest, because of the higher duty of temple service. If temple duties outweigh the sabbath law, how much more does the presence of Jesus, with his proclamation of the kingdom (**something greater than the temple**), justify the conduct of his disciples.

e. **12:7** See note on Mt 9:13.

f. **12:8** The ultimate justification for the disciples' violation of the sabbath rest is that Jesus, the Son of Man, has supreme authority over the law.

g. **12:10** Rabbinic tradition later than the gospels allowed relief to be given to a sufferer on the sabbath if life was in danger. This may also have been the view of Jesus' Pharisaic contemporaries. But the case here is not about one in danger of death.

h. **12:11** Matthew omits the question posed by Jesus in Mk 3:4 and substitutes one about rescuing a sheep on the sabbath, similar to that in Lk 14:5.

i. **12:14** See Mk 3:6. Here the plan to bring about Jesus' death is attributed to the Pharisees only. This is probably due to the situation of Matthew's church, when the sole opponents were the Pharisees.

j. **12:15–21** Matthew follows Mk 3:7–12 but summarizes his source in two verses (Mt 12:15, 16) that pick up the withdrawal, the healings, and the command for silence. To this he adds a fulfillment citation from the first Servant Song (Is 42:1–4) that does not correspond exactly to either the Hebrew or the LXX of that passage. It is the longest Old Testament citation in this gospel, emphasizing the meekness of Jesus, the Servant of the LORD, and foretelling the extension of his mission to the Gentiles.

k. **12:15** Jesus' knowledge of the Pharisees' plot and his healing all are peculiar to Matthew.

l. **12:19** The servant's not contending is seen as fulfilled in Jesus' withdrawal from the disputes narrated in Mt 12:1–14.

m. **12:21** Except for a minor detail, Matthew here follows the LXX, although the meaning of the Hebrew ("the coastlands will wait for his teaching") is similar.

n. **12:22–32** For the exorcism, see note on Mt 9:32–34. The long discussion combines Marcan and Q material (Mk 3:22–30; Lk 11:19–20, 23; 12:10). Mk 3:20–21 is omitted, with a consequent lessening of the sharpness of Mt 12:48.

o. **12:23** See note on Mt 9:27.

p. **12:24** See note on Mt 10:25.

q. **12:25–26** Jesus' first response to the Pharisees' charge is that if it were true, Satan would be destroying his own kingdom.

r. **12:27** Besides pointing out the absurdity of the charge, Jesus asks how the work of Jewish exorcists (**your own people**) is to be interpreted. Are they, too, to be charged with collusion with Beelzebul? For an example of Jewish exorcism see Josephus, *Antiquities* 8:42–49.

s. **12:28** The Q parallel (Lk 11:20) speaks of the "finger" rather than of the "spirit" of God. While the difference is probably due to Matthew's editing, he retains **the kingdom of God** rather than changing it to his usual "kingdom of heaven." **Has come upon you**: see Mt 4:17.

t. **12:29** A short parable illustrates what Jesus is doing. The **strong man** is Satan, whom Jesus has tied up and whose house he is **plundering**. Jewish expectation was that Satan would be chained up in the last days (Rev 20:2); Jesus' exorcisms indicate that those days have begun.

u. **12:30** This saying, already attached to the preceding verses in Q (see Lk 11:23), warns that there can be no neutrality where Jesus is concerned. Its pertinence in a context where Jesus is addressing not the neutral but the bitterly opposed is not clear. The accusation of scattering, however, does fit the situation. Jesus is the shepherd of God's people (Mt 2:6), his mission is to the lost sheep of Israel (Mt 15:24); the Pharisees, who oppose him, are guilty of scattering the sheep.

v. **12:31 Blasphemy against the Spirit:** the sin of attributing to Satan (Mt 12:24) what is the work of the Spirit of God (Mt 12:28).

w. **12:33 Declare:** literally, "make." The meaning of this verse is obscure. Possibly it is a challenge to the Pharisees either to declare Jesus and his exorcisms good or both of them bad. A tree is known by its fruit; if the fruit is good, so must the tree be. If the driving out of demons is good, so must its source be.

x. **12:34** The admission of Jesus' goodness cannot be made by the Pharisees, for they are evil, and the words that proceed from their evil hearts cannot be good.

y. **12:36–37** If on the day of judgment people will be held accountable for even their **careless** words, the vicious accusations of the Pharisees will surely lead to their condemnation.

z. **12:38–42** This section is mainly from Q (see Lk 11:29–32). Mk 8:11–12, which Matthew has followed in Mt 16:1–4, has a similar demand for a sign. The scribes and Pharisees refuse to accept the exorcisms of Jesus as authentication of his claims and demand a sign that will end all possibility of doubt. Jesus' response is that no such sign will be given. Because his opponents are evil and see him as an agent of Satan, nothing will convince them.

aa. **12:38 Teacher:** see note on Mt 8:19. In Mt 16:1 the request is for a sign "from heaven" (Mk 8:11).

ab. **12:39 Unfaithful:** literally, "adulterous." The covenant between God and Israel was portrayed as a marriage bond, and unfaithfulness to the covenant as adultery; cf. Hos 2:4–14; Jer 3:6–10.

ac. **12:40** See Jon 2:1. While in Q the sign was simply Jonah's preaching to the Ninevites (Lk 11:30, 32), Matthew here adds Jonah's sojourn **in the belly of the whale** for **three days and three nights**, a prefigurement of Jesus' sojourn in the abode of the dead and, implicitly, of his resurrection.

ad. **12:41–42** The Ninevites who **repented** (see Jon 3:1–10) and **the queen of the south** (i.e., of Sheba; see 1 Kgs 10:1–13) were pagans who responded to lesser opportunities than have been offered to Israel in the ministry of Jesus, **something greater than Jonah** or **Solomon.** At the final judgment they will condemn the faithless **generation** that has rejected him.

ae. **12:43–45** Another Q passage; cf. Mt 11:24–26. Jesus' ministry has broken Satan's hold over Israel, but the refusal of **this evil generation** to accept him will lead to a worse situation than what preceded his coming.

af. **12:46–50** See Mk 3:31–35. Matthew has omitted Mk 3:20–21 which is taken up in Mk 3:31 (see note on Mt 12:22–32), yet the point of the story is the same in both gospels: natural kinship with Jesus counts for nothing; only one who **does the will** of his **heavenly Father** belongs to his true family.

ag. **12:47** This verse is omitted in some important textual witnesses, including Codex Sinaiticus (original reading) and Codex Vaticanus.

Chapter 13

The Parable of the Sower. 1 ᵃOn that day, Jesus went out of the house and sat down by the sea. 2 Such large crowds gathered around him that he got into a boat and sat down, and the whole crowd stood along the shore. 3 ᵇAnd he spoke to them at length in parables,ᶜ saying: "A sower went out to sow. 4 And as he sowed, some seed fell on the path, and birds came and ate it up. 5 Some fell on rocky ground, where it had little soil. It sprang up at once because the soil was not deep, 6 and when the sun rose it was scorched, and it withered for lack of roots. 7 Some seed fell among thorns, and the thorns grew up and choked it. 8 But some seed fell on rich soil, and produced fruit, a hundred or sixty or thirtyfold. 9 Whoever has ears ought to hear."

The Purpose of Parables. 10 The disciples approached him and said, "Why do you speak to them in parables?" 11 ᵈHe said to them in reply, "Because knowledge of the mysteries of the kingdom of heaven has been granted to you, but to them it has not been granted. 12 To anyone who has, more will be givenᵉ and he will grow rich; from anyone who has not, even what he has will be taken away. 13 ᶠThis is why I speak to them in parables, because 'they look but do not see and hear but do not listen or understand.' 14 Isaiah's prophecy is fulfilled in them, which says:

> 'You shall indeed hear but not understand,
> you shall indeed look but never see.
15   Gross is the heart of this people,
> they will hardly hear with their ears,
> they have closed their eyes,
> lest they see with their eyes
> and hear with their ears
> and understand with their heart and be converted,
> and I heal them.'

The Privilege of Discipleship.ᵍ 16 "But blessed are your eyes, because they see, and your ears, because they hear. 17 Amen, I say to you, many prophets and righteous people longed to see what you see but did not see it, and to hear what you hear but did not hear it.

The Explanation of the Parable of the Sower.ʰ 18 "Hear then the parable of the sower. 19 The seed sown on the path is the one who hears the word of the kingdom without understanding it, and the evil one comes and steals away what was sown in his heart. 20 The seed sown on rocky ground is the one who hears the word and receives it at once with joy. 21 But he has no root and lasts only for a time. When some tribulation or persecution comes because of the word, he immediately falls away. 22 The seed sown among thorns is the one who hears the word, but then worldly anxiety and the lure of riches choke the word and it bears no fruit. 23 But the seed sown on rich soil is the one who hears the word and understands it, who indeed bears fruit and yields a hundred or sixty or thirtyfold."

The Parable of the Weeds Among the Wheat. **24** He proposed another parable to them.[i] "The kingdom of heaven may be likened to a man who sowed good seed in his field. **25** While everyone was asleep his enemy came and sowed weeds[j] all through the wheat, and then went off. **26** When the crop grew and bore fruit, the weeds appeared as well. **27** The slaves of the householder came to him and said, 'Master, did you not sow good seed in your field? Where have the weeds come from?' **28** He answered, 'An enemy has done this.' His slaves said to him, 'Do you want us to go and pull them up?' **29** He replied, 'No, if you pull up the weeds you might uproot the wheat along with them. **30** Let them grow together until harvest;[k] then at harvest time I will say to the harvesters, "First collect the weeds and tie them in bundles for burning; but gather the wheat into my barn."'"

The Parable of the Mustard Seed.[l] **31** He proposed another parable to them. "The kingdom of heaven is like a mustard seed that a person took and sowed in a field. **32** [m]It is the smallest of all the seeds, yet when full-grown it is the largest of plants. It becomes a large bush, and the 'birds of the sky come and dwell in its branches.'"

The Parable of the Yeast. **33** He spoke to them another parable. "The kingdom of heaven is like yeast[n] that a woman took and mixed with three measures of wheat flour until the whole batch was leavened."

The Use of Parables. **34** [o]All these things Jesus spoke to the crowds in parables. He spoke to them only in parables, **35** to fulfill what had been said through the prophet:[p]

> "I will open my mouth in parables,
> I will announce what has lain hidden
> from the foundation [of the world]."

The Explanation of the Parable of the Weeds. **36** Then, dismissing the crowds,[q] he went into the house. His disciples approached him and said, "Explain to us the parable of the weeds in the field." **37** [r]He said in reply, "He who sows good seed is the Son of Man, **38** the field is the world,[s] the good seed the children of the kingdom. The weeds are the children of the evil one, **39** and the enemy who sows them is the devil. The harvest is the end of the age,[t] and the harvesters are angels. **40** Just as weeds are collected and burned [up] with fire, so will it be at the end of the age. **41** The Son of Man will send his angels, and they will collect out of his kingdom[u] all who cause others to sin and all evildoers. **42** They will throw them into the fiery furnace, where there will be wailing and grinding of teeth. **43** [v]Then the righteous will shine like the sun in the kingdom of their Father. Whoever has ears ought to hear.

More Parables.ᵂ **44** "The kingdom of heaven is like a treasure buried in a field,ˣ which a person finds and hides again, and out of joy goes and sells all that he has and buys that field. **45** Again, the kingdom of heaven is like a merchant searching for fine pearls. **46** When he finds a pearl of great price, he goes and sells all that he has and buys it. **47** Again, the kingdom of heaven is like a net thrown into the sea, which collects fish of every kind. **48** When it is full they haul it ashore and sit down to put what is good into buckets. What is bad they throw away. **49** Thus it will be at the end of the age. The angels will go out and separate the wicked from the righteous **50** and throw them into the fiery furnace, where there will be wailing and grinding of teeth.

Treasures New and Old. 51 "Do you understandʸ all these things?" They answered, "Yes." **52** ᶻAnd he replied, "Then every scribe who has been instructed in the kingdom of heaven is like the head of a household who brings from his storeroom both the new and the old." **53** When Jesus finished these parables, he went away from there.

V. Jesus, the Kingdom, and the Church

The Rejection at Nazareth. 54 ᵃᵃHe came to his native place and taught the people in their synagogue. They were astonishedᵃᵇ and said, "Where did this man get such wisdom and mighty deeds? **55** Is he not the carpenter's son? Is not his mother named Mary and his brothers James, Joseph, Simon, and Judas? **56** Are not his sisters all with us? Where did this man get all this?" **57** And they took offense at him. But Jesus said to them, "A prophet is not without honor except in his native place and in his own house." **58** And he did not work many mighty deeds there because of their lack of faith.

Notes

a. **13:1–53** The discourse in parables is the third great discourse of Jesus in Matthew and constitutes the second part of the third book of the gospel. Matthew follows the Marcan outline (Mk 4:1–35) but has only two of Mark's parables, the five others being from Q and M. In addition to the seven parables, the discourse gives the reason why Jesus uses this type of speech (Mt 13:10–15), declares the blessedness of those who understand his teaching (Mt 13:16–17), explains the parable of the sower (Mt 13:18–23) and of the weeds (Mt 13:36–43), and ends with a concluding statement to the disciples (Mt 13:51–52).

b. **13:3 In parables:** the word "parable" (Greek *parabolē*) is used in the LXX to translate the Hebrew *māshāl*, a designation covering a wide variety of literary forms such as axioms, proverbs, similitudes, and allegories. In the New Testament the same breadth of meaning of the word is found, but there it primarily designates stories that are illustrative comparisons between Christian truths and events of everyday life. Sometimes the event has a strange element that is quite different from usual experience (e.g., in Mt 13:33 the enormous amount of dough in the parable of the yeast); this is meant to sharpen the curiosity of the hearer. If each detail of such a story is given a figurative meaning, the story is an allegory. Those who maintain a sharp distinction between parable and allegory insist that a parable has only one point of comparison, and that while parables were characteristic of Jesus' teaching, to see allegorical details in them is to introduce meanings that go beyond their original intention and even falsify it. However, to exclude any allegorical elements from a parable is an excessively rigid mode of interpretation, now abandoned by many scholars.

c. **13:3–8** Since in Palestine sowing often preceded plowing, much of the seed is scattered on ground that is unsuitable. Yet while much is wasted, the seed that falls on good ground bears fruit in extraordinarily large measure. The point of the parable is that, in spite of some failure because of opposition and indifference, the message of Jesus about the coming of the kingdom will have enormous success.

d. **13:11** Since a parable is figurative speech that demands reflection for understanding, only those who are prepared to explore its meaning can come to know it. To understand is a gift of God, granted to the disciples but not to the crowds. In Semitic fashion, both the disciples' understanding and the crowd's obtuseness are attributed to God. The question of human responsibility for the obtuseness is not dealt with, although it is asserted in Mt 13:13. **The mysteries:** as in Lk 8:10; Mk 4:11 has "the mystery." The word is used in Dn 2:18, 19, 27 and in the Qumran literature (1QpHab 7:8; 1QS 3:23; 1QM 3:9) to designate a divine plan or decree affecting the course of history that can be known only when revealed. **Knowledge of the mysteries of the kingdom of heaven** means recognition that the kingdom has become present in the ministry of Jesus.

e. **13:12** In the New Testament use of this axiom of practical "wisdom" (see Mt 25:29; Mk 4:25; Lk 8:18; 19:26), the reference transcends the original level. God gives further understanding to one who accepts the revealed mystery; from the one who does not, he will take it away (note the "theological passive," **more will be given, what he has will be taken away**).

f. **13:13 Because 'they look . . . or understand':** Matthew softens his Marcan source, which states that Jesus speaks in parables so that the crowds may not understand (Mk 4:12), and makes such speaking a punishment given **because** they have not accepted his previous clear teaching. However, his citation of Is 6:9–10 in Mt 13:14 supports the harsher Marcan view.

g. **13:16–17** Unlike the unbelieving crowds, the disciples have seen that which the **prophets** and the **righteous** of the Old Testament **longed to see** without having their longing fulfilled.

h. **13:18–23** See Mk 4:14–20; Lk 8:11–15. In this explanation of the parable the emphasis is on the various types of soil on which the seed falls, i.e., on the dispositions with which the preaching of Jesus is received. The second and third types particularly are explained in such a way as to support the view held by many scholars that the explanation derives not from Jesus but from early Christian reflection upon apostasy from the faith that was the consequence of persecution and worldliness, respectively. Others, however, hold that the explanation may come basically from Jesus even though it was developed in the light of later Christian experience. The four types of persons envisaged are (1) those who never accept **the word of the kingdom** (Mt 13:19); (2) those who believe for a while but fall away because of **persecution** (Mt 13:20–21); (3) those who believe, but in whom **the word** is choked by **worldly anxiety** and the seduction of **riches** (Mt 13:22); (4) those who respond to **the word** and produce **fruit** abundantly (Mt 13:23).

i. **13:24–30** This parable is peculiar to Matthew. The comparison in Mt 13:24 does not mean that **the kingdom of heaven may be likened** simply to the person in question but to the situation narrated in the whole story. The refusal of the **householder** to allow his **slaves** to separate **the wheat** from **the weeds** while they are still growing is a warning to the disciples not to attempt to anticipate the final judgment of God by a definitive exclusion of sinners from the kingdom. In its present stage it is composed of the good and the bad. The judgment of God alone will eliminate the sinful. Until then there must be patience and the preaching of repentance.

j. **13:25 Weeds:** darnel, a poisonous weed that in its first stage of growth resembles wheat.

k. **13:30 Harvest:** a common biblical metaphor for the time of God's judgment; cf. Jer 51:33; Jl 4:13; Hos 6:11.

l. **13:31–33** See Mk 4:30–32; Lk 13:18–21. The parables of the mustard seed and the yeast illustrate the same point: the amazing contrast between the small beginnings of the kingdom and its marvelous expansion.

m. **13:32** See Dn 4:7–9, 17–19 where the birds nesting in the tree represent the people of Nebuchadnezzar's kingdom. See also Ez 17:23; 31:6.

n. **13:33** Except in this Q parable and in Mt 16:12, **yeast** (or "leaven") is, in New Testament usage, a symbol of corruption (see Mt 16:6, 11–12; Mk 8:15; Lk 12:1; 1 Cor 5:6–8; Gal 5:9). **Three measures:** an enormous amount, enough to feed a hundred people. The exaggeration of this element of the parable points to the greatness of the kingdom's effect.

o. **13:34 Only in parables:** see Mt 13:10–15.

p. **13:35 The prophet:** some textual witnesses read "Isaiah the prophet." The quotation is actually from Ps 78:2; the first line corresponds to the LXX text of the psalm. The psalm's title ascribes it to Asaph, the founder of one of the guilds of temple musicians. He is called "the prophet" (NAB "the seer") in 2 Chr 29:30, but it is doubtful that Matthew averted to that; for him, any Old Testament text that could be seen as fulfilled in Jesus was prophetic.

q. **13:36 Dismissing the crowds:** the return of Jesus to the house marks a break with the crowds, who represent unbelieving Israel. From now on his attention is directed more and more to his disciples and to their instruction. The rest of the discourse is addressed to them alone.

r. **13:37–43** In the explanation of the parable of the weeds emphasis lies on the fearful end of the wicked, whereas the parable itself concentrates on patience with them until judgment time.

s. **13:38 The field is the world:** this presupposes the resurrection of Jesus and the granting to him of "all power in heaven and on earth" (Mt 28:18).

t. **13:39 The end of the age:** this phrase is found only in Matthew (13:40, 49; 24:3; 28:20).

u. **13:41 His kingdom:** the kingdom of the **Son of Man** is distinguished from that of the Father (Mt 13:43); see 1 Cor 15:24–25. The church is the place where Jesus' kingdom is manifested, but his royal authority embraces the entire world; see note on Mt 13:38.

v. **13:43** See Dn 12:3.

w. **13:44–50** The first two of the last three parables of the discourse have the same point. The **person** who **finds** a buried **treasure** and the **merchant** who finds a **pearl of great price** sell **all** that they have to acquire these finds; similarly, the one who understands the supreme value of the kingdom gives up whatever he must to obtain it. The **joy** with which this is done is made explicit in the first parable, but it may be presumed in the second also. The concluding parable of the fishnet resembles the explanation of the parable of the weeds with its stress upon the final exclusion of evil persons from the kingdom.

x. **13:44** In the unsettled conditions of Palestine in Jesus' time, it was not unusual to guard valuables by burying them in the ground.

y. **13:51** Matthew typically speaks of the understanding of the disciples.

z. **13:52** Since Matthew tends to identify the disciples and the Twelve (see note on Mt 10:1), this saying about the Christian **scribe** cannot be taken as applicable to all who accept the message of Jesus. While the Twelve are in many ways representative of all who believe in him, they are also distinguished from them in certain respects. The church of Matthew has leaders among whom are a group designated as "scribes" (Mt 23:34). Like the scribes of Israel, they are teachers. It is the Twelve and these their later counterparts to whom this verse applies. **The scribe . . . instructed in the kingdom of heaven** knows both the teaching of Jesus (**the new**) and the law and prophets (**the old**) and provides in his own teaching **both the new and the old** as interpreted and fulfilled by **the new**. On the translation **head of a household** (for the same Greek word translated **householder** in Mt 13:27), see note on Mt 24:45–51.

aa. **13:54–17:27** This section is the narrative part of the fourth book of the gospel.

ab. **13:54–58** After the Sermon on the Mount the crowds are in admiring astonishment at Jesus' teaching (Mt 7:28); here the astonishment is of those who take **offense at him.** Familiarity with his background and family leads them to regard him as pretentious. Matthew modifies his Marcan source (Mt 6:1–6). Jesus is not the carpenter but **the carpenter's son** (Mt 13:55), "and among his own kin" is omitted (Mt 13:57), **he did not work many mighty deeds** in face of such unbelief (Mt 13:58) rather than the Marcan " . . . he was not able to perform any mighty deed there" (Mt 6:5), and there is no mention of his amazement at his townspeople's lack of faith.

Chapter 14

Herod's Opinion of Jesus. 1 [a]At that time Herod the tetrarch[b] heard of the reputation of Jesus **2** and said to his servants, "This man is John the Baptist. He has been raised from the dead; that is why mighty powers are at work in him."

The Death of John the Baptist. 3 Now Herod had arrested John, bound [him], and put him in prison on account of Herodias,[c] the wife of his brother Philip, **4** for John had said to him, "It is not lawful for you to have her." **5** Although he wanted to kill him, he feared the people, for they regarded him as a prophet. **6** But at a birthday celebration for Herod, the daughter of Herodias performed a dance before the guests and delighted Herod **7** so much that he swore to give her whatever she might ask for. **8** Prompted by her mother, she said, "Give me here on a platter the head of John the Baptist." **9** The king was distressed, but because of his oaths and the guests who were present, he ordered that it be given, **10** and he had John beheaded in the prison. **11** His head was brought in on a platter and given to the girl, who took it to her mother. **12** His disciples came and took away the corpse and buried him; and they went and told Jesus.

The Return of the Twelve and the Feeding of the Five Thousand.[d] **13** When Jesus heard of it, he withdrew in a boat to a deserted place by himself. The crowds heard of this and followed him on foot from their towns. **14** When he disembarked and saw the vast crowd, his heart was moved with pity for them, and he cured their sick. **15** When it was evening, the disciples approached him and said, "This is a deserted place and it is already late; dismiss the crowds so that they can go to the villages and buy food for themselves." **16** [Jesus] said to them, "There is no need for them to go away; give them some food yourselves." **17** But they said to him, "Five loaves and two fish are all we have here." **18** Then he said, "Bring them here to me," **19** and he ordered the crowds to sit down on the grass. Taking[e] the five loaves and the two fish, and looking up to heaven, he said the blessing, broke the loaves, and gave them to the disciples, who in turn gave them to the crowds. **20** They all ate and were satisfied, and they picked up the fragments left over[f]—twelve wicker baskets full. **21** Those who ate were about five thousand men, not counting women and children.

The Walking on the Water.[g] **22** Then he made the disciples get into the boat and precede him to the other side, while he dismissed the crowds. **23** After doing so, he went up on the mountain by himself to pray. When it was evening he was there alone. **24** Meanwhile the boat, already a few miles offshore, was being tossed about by the waves, for the wind was against it. **25** During the fourth watch of the night,[h] he came toward them, walking on the sea. **26** When the disciples saw him walking on the sea they were terrified. "It is a ghost," they said, and they cried out in fear. **27** At once [Jesus] spoke to them, "Take courage, it is I;[i] do not be afraid." **28** Peter said to him in reply, "Lord, if it is you, command me to come to you on the water." **29** He said, "Come." Peter got out of the boat and began to walk on the water toward Jesus. **30** But when he saw how [strong] the wind was he became frightened; and, beginning to sink, he cried out, "LORD, save me!" **31** Immediately Jesus stretched out his hand and caught him, and said to him, "O you of little faith,[j] why did you doubt?" **32** After they got into the boat, the wind died down. **33** [k]Those who were in the boat did him homage, saying, "Truly, you are the Son of God."

   The Healings at Gennesaret. 34 After making the crossing, they came to land at Gennesaret. **35** When the men of that place recognized him, they sent word to all the surrounding country. People brought to him all those who were sick **36** and begged him that they might touch only the tassel on his cloak, and as many as touched it were healed.

Notes

a. **14:1–12** The murder of the Baptist by Herod Antipas prefigures the death of Jesus (see Mt 17:12). The Marcan source (Mk 6:14–29) is much reduced and in some points changed. In Mark Herod reveres John as a holy man and the desire to kill him is attributed to Herodias (Mk 6:19, 20), whereas here that desire is Herod's from the beginning (Mt 14:5).

b. **14:1 Herod the tetrarch:** Herod Antipas, son of Herod the Great. When the latter died, his territory was divided among three of his surviving sons, Archelaus who received half of it (Mt 2:23), Herod Antipas who became ruler of Galilee and Perea, and Philip who became ruler of northern Transjordan. Since he received a quarter of his father's domain, Antipas is accurately designated **tetrarch** ("ruler of a fourth [part]"), although in Mt 14:9 Matthew repeats the "king" of his Marcan source (Mk 6:26).

c. **14:3** Herodias was not the wife of Herod's half-brother Philip but of another half-brother, Herod Boethus. The union was prohibited by Lv 18:16; 20:21. According to Josephus (*Antiquities* 18:116–19), Herod imprisoned and then executed John because he feared that the Baptist's influence over the people might enable him to lead a rebellion.

d. **14:13–21** The feeding of the five thousand is the only miracle of Jesus that is recounted in all four gospels. The principal reason for that may be that it was seen as anticipating the Eucharist and the final banquet in the kingdom (Mt 8:11; 26:29), but it looks not only forward but backward, to the feeding of Israel with manna in the desert at the time of the Exodus (Ex 16), a miracle that in some contemporary Jewish expectation would be repeated in the messianic age (2 Bar 29:8). It may also be meant to recall Elisha's feeding a hundred men with small provisions (2 Kgs 4:42–44).

e. **14:19** The **taking,** saying the blessing, breaking, and giving to the disciples correspond to the actions of Jesus over the bread at the Last Supper (Mt 26:26). Since they were usual at any Jewish meal, that correspondence does not necessarily indicate a eucharistic reference here. Matthew's silence about Jesus' dividing the fish among the people (Mk 6:41) is perhaps more significant in that regard.

f. **14:20 The fragments left over:** as in Elisha's miracle, food was **left over** after all had been fed. The word **fragments** (Greek *klasmata*) is used, in the singular, of the broken bread of the Eucharist in *Didache* 9:3–4.

g. **14:22–33** The disciples, laboring against the turbulent sea, are saved by Jesus. For his power over the waters, see note on Mt 8:26. Here that power is expressed also by his **walking on the sea** (Mt 14:25; cf. Ps 77:20; Jb 9:8). Matthew has inserted into the Marcan story (Mk 6:45–52) material that belongs to his special traditions on Peter (Mt 14:28–31).

h. **14:25 The fourth watch of the night:** between 3 A.M. and 6 A.M. The Romans divided the twelve hours between 6 P.M. and 6 A.M. into four equal parts called "watches."

i. **14:27 It is I:** see note on Mk 6:50.

j. **14:31 You of little faith:** see note on Mt 6:30. **Why did you doubt?:** the verb is peculiar to Matthew and occurs elsewhere only in Mt 28:17.

k. **14:33** This confession is in striking contrast to the Marcan parallel (Mk 6:51) where the disciples are "completely astounded."

Chapter 15

The Tradition of the Elders.ᵃ **1** Then Pharisees and scribes came to Jesus from Jerusalem and said, **2** "Why do your disciples break the tradition of the elders?ᵇ They do not wash [their] hands when they eat a meal." **3** He said to them in reply, "And why do you break the commandment of Godᶜ for the sake of your tradition? **4** For God said, 'Honor your father and your mother,' and 'Whoever curses father or mother shall die.' **5** ᵈBut you say, 'Whoever says to father or mother, "Any support you might have had from me is dedicated to God," **6** need not honor his father.' You have nullified the word of God for the sake of your tradition. **7** Hypocrites, well did Isaiah prophesy about you when he said:

8   'This people honors me with their lips,ᵉ
       but their hearts are far from me;
9   in vain do they worship me,
       teaching as doctrines human precepts.'"

10 He summoned the crowd and said to them, "Hear and understand. **11** It is not what enters one's mouth that defiles that person; but what comes out of the mouth is what defiles one." **12** Then his disciples approached and said to him, "Do you know that the Pharisees took offense when they heard what you said?" **13** He said in reply,ᶠ "Every plant that my heavenly Father has not planted will be uprooted. **14** Let them alone; they are blind guides (of the blind). If a blind person leads a blind person, both will fall into a pit." **15** Then Peterᵍ said to him in reply, "Explain [this] parable to us." **16** He said to them, "Are even you still without understanding? **17** Do you not realize that everything that enters the mouth passes into the stomach and is expelled into the latrine? **18** But the things that come out of the mouth come from the heart, and they defile. **19** ʰFor from the heart come evil thoughts, murder, adultery, unchastity, theft, false witness, blasphemy. **20** These are what defile a person, but to eat with unwashed hands does not defile."

The Canaanite Woman's Faith.ⁱ **21** Then Jesus went from that place and withdrew to the region of Tyre and Sidon. **22** And behold, a Canaanite woman of that district came and called out, "Have pity on me, Lord, Son of David! My daughter is tormented by a demon." **23** But he did not say a word in answer to her. His disciples came and asked him, "Send her away, for she keeps calling out after us." **24** ʲHe said in reply, "I was sent only to the lost sheep of the house of Israel." **25** But the woman came and did him homage, saying, "Lord, help me." **26** He said in reply, "It is not right to take the food of the childrenᵏ and throw it to the dogs." **27** She said, "Please, Lord, for even the dogs eat the scraps that fall from the table of their masters." **28** Then Jesus said to her in reply, "O woman, great is your faith!ˡ Let it be done for you as you wish." And her daughter was healed from that hour.

The Healing of Many People. 29 Moving on from there Jesus walked by the Sea of Galilee, went up on the mountain, and sat down there. **30** Great crowds came to him, having with them the lame, the blind, the deformed, the mute, and many others. They placed them at his feet, and he cured them. **31** The crowds were amazed when they saw the mute speaking, the deformed made whole, the lame walking, and the blind able to see, and they glorified the God of Israel.

The Feeding of the Four Thousand.[m] **32** Jesus summoned his disciples and said, "My heart is moved with pity for the crowd, for they have been with me now for three days and have nothing to eat. I do not want to send them away hungry, for fear they may collapse on the way." **33** The disciples said to him, "Where could we ever get enough bread in this deserted place to satisfy such a crowd?" **34** Jesus said to them, "How many loaves do you have?" "Seven," they replied, "and a few fish." **35** He ordered the crowd to sit down on the ground. **36** Then he took the seven loaves and the fish, gave thanks,[n] broke the loaves, and gave them to the disciples, who in turn gave them to the crowds. **37** They all ate and were satisfied. They picked up the fragments left over—seven baskets full. **38** Those who ate were four thousand men, not counting women and children. **39** And when he had dismissed the crowds, he got into the boat and came to the district of Magadan.

Notes

a. **15:1–20** This dispute begins with the question of the Pharisees and scribes why Jesus' disciples are breaking **the tradition of the elders** about washing one's hands before eating (Mt 15:2). Jesus' counterquestion accuses his opponents of breaking **the commandment of God for the sake of** their **tradition** (Mt 15:3) and illustrates this by their interpretation of the commandment of the Decalogue concerning parents (Mt 15:4–6). Denouncing them as hypocrites, he applies to them a derogatory prophecy of Isaiah (Mt 15:7–8). Then with a wider audience (**the crowd**, Mt 15:10) he goes beyond the violation of tradition with which the dispute has started. The parable (Mt 15:11) is an attack on the Mosaic law concerning clean and unclean foods, similar to those antitheses that abrogate the law (Mt 5:31–32, 33–34, 38–39). After a warning to his disciples not to follow the moral guidance of the Pharisees (Mt 15:13–14), he explains the **parable** (Mt 15:15) to them, saying that defilement comes not from what **enters the mouth** (Mt 15:17) but from the evil thoughts and deeds that rise from within, **from the heart** (Mt 15:18–20). The last verse returns to the starting point of the dispute (eating **with unwashed hands**). Because of Matthew's omission of Mk 7:19b, some scholars think that Matthew has weakened the Marcan repudiation of the Mosaic food laws. But that half verse is ambiguous in the Greek, which may be the reason for its omission here.

b. **15:2 The tradition of the elders:** see note on Mk 7:5. The purpose of the handwashing was to remove defilement caused by contact with what was ritually unclean.

c. **15:3–4** For the commandment see Ex 20:12 (Dt 5:16); 21:17. The honoring of one's parents had to do with supporting them in their needs.

d. **15:5** See note on Mk 7:11.

e. **15:8** The text of Is 29:13 is quoted approximately according to the Septuagint.

f. **15:13–14** Jesus leads his disciples away from the teaching authority of the Pharisees.

g. **15:15** Matthew specifies **Peter** as the questioner, unlike Mk 7:17. Given his tendency to present the disciples as more understanding than in his Marcan source, it is noteworthy that here he retains the Marcan rebuke, although in a slightly milder form. This may be due to his wish to correct the Jewish Christians within his church who still held to the food laws and thus separated themselves from Gentile Christians who did not observe them.

h. **15:19** The Marcan list of thirteen things that defile (Mk 7:21–22) is here reduced to seven that partially cover the content of the Decalogue.

i. **15:21–28** See note on Mt 8:5–13.

j. **15:24** See note on Mt 10:5–6.

k. **15:26 The children:** the people of Israel. **Dogs:** see note on Mt 7:6.

l. **15:28** As in the case of the cure of the centurion's servant (Mt 8:10), Matthew ascribes Jesus' granting the request to the woman's **great faith**, a point not made equally explicit in the Marcan parallel (Mk 7:24–30).

m. **15:32–39** Most probably this story is a doublet of that of the feeding of the five thousand (Mt 14:13–21). It differs from it notably only in that Jesus takes the initiative, not the disciples (Mt 15:32), and in the numbers: the crowd has been with Jesus **three days** (Mt 15:32), **seven loaves** are multiplied (Mt 15:36), **seven baskets of fragments** remain after the feeding (Mt 15:37), and **four thousand** men are fed (Mt 15:38).

n. **15:36 Gave thanks:** see Mt 14:19, "said the blessing." There is no difference in meaning. The thanksgiving was a blessing of God for his benefits.

Chapter 16

The Demand for a Sign. 1 ªThe Pharisees and Sadducees came and, to test him, asked him to show them a sign from heaven. 2 ᵇHe said to them in reply, "[In the evening you say, 'Tomorrow will be fair, for the sky is red'; 3 and, in the morning, 'Today will be stormy, for the sky is red and threatening.' You know how to judge the appearance of the sky, but you cannot judge the signs of the times.] 4 An evil and unfaithful generation seeks a sign, but no sign will be given it except the sign of Jonah."ᶜ Then he left them and went away.

The Leaven of the Pharisees and Sadducees. 5 In coming to the other side of the sea,ᵈ the disciples had forgotten to bring bread. 6 Jesus said to them, "Look out, and beware of the leavenᵉ of the Pharisees and Sadducees." 7 ᶠThey concluded among themselves, saying, "It is because we have brought no bread." 8 When Jesus became aware of this he said, "You of little faith, why do you conclude among yourselves that it is because you have no bread? 9 Do you not yet understand, and do you not remember the five loaves for the five thousand, and how many wicker baskets you took up? 10 Or the seven loaves for the four thousand, and how many baskets you took up? 11 How do you not comprehend that I was not speaking to you about bread? Beware of the leaven of the Pharisees and Sadducees." 12 Then they understoodᵍ that he was not telling them to beware of the leaven of bread, but of the teaching of the Pharisees and Sadducees.

Peter's Confession About Jesus.ʰ 13 When Jesus went into the region of Caesarea Philippiⁱ he asked his disciples, "Who do people say that the Son of Man is?" 14 They replied, "Some say John the Baptist,ʲ others Elijah, still others Jeremiah or one of the prophets." 15 He said to them, "But who do you say that I am?" 16 ᵏSimon Peter said in reply, "You are the Messiah, the Son of the living God." 17 Jesus said to him in reply, "Blessed are you, Simon son of Jonah. For flesh and bloodˡ has not revealed this to you, but my heavenly Father. 18 And so I say to you, you are Peter, and upon this rock I will build my church,ᵐ and the gates of the netherworld shall not prevail against it. 19 I will give you the keys to the kingdom of heaven.ⁿ Whatever you bind on earth shall be bound in heaven; and whatever you loose on earth shall be loosed in heaven." 20 ᵒThen he strictly ordered his disciples to tell no one that he was the Messiah.

The First Prediction of the Passion.ᵖ 21 From that time on, Jesus began to show his disciples that he[q] must go to Jerusalem and suffer greatly from the elders, the chief priests, and the scribes, and be killed and on the third day be raised. 22 ʳThen Peter took him aside and began to rebuke him, "God forbid, Lord! No such thing shall ever happen to you." 23 He turned and said to Peter, "Get behind me, Satan! You are an obstacle to me. You are thinking not as God does, but as human beings do."

The Conditions of Discipleship.[s] **24** Then Jesus said to his disciples, "Whoever wishes to come after me must deny himself,[t] take up his cross, and follow me. **25** For whoever wishes to save his life will lose it, but whoever loses his life for my sake will find it.[u] **26** What profit would there be for one to gain the whole world and forfeit his life? Or what can one give in exchange for his life? **27** [v]For the Son of Man will come with his angels in his Father's glory, and then he will repay everyone according to his conduct. **28** [w]Amen, I say to you, there are some standing here who will not taste death until they see the Son of Man coming in his kingdom."

Notes

a. **16:1 A sign from heaven:** see note on Mt 12:38–42.

b. **16:2–3** The answer of Jesus in these verses is omitted in many important textual witnesses, and it is very uncertain that it is an original part of this gospel. It resembles Lk 12:54–56 and may have been inserted from there. It rebukes the Pharisees and Sadducees who are able to read indications of coming weather but not the indications of the coming kingdom in the signs that Jesus does offer, his mighty deeds and teaching.

c. **16:4** See notes on Mt 12:39, 40.

d. **16:5–12** Jesus' warning his disciples against **the teaching of the Pharisees and Sadducees** comes immediately before his promise to confer on Peter the authority to bind and to loose on earth (Mt 16:19), an authority that will be confirmed in heaven. Such authority most probably has to do, at least in part, with teaching. The rejection of the teaching authority of the Pharisees (see also Mt 12:12–14) prepares for a new one derived from Jesus.

e. **16:6 Leaven:** see note on Mt 13:33. **Sadducees:** Matthew's Marcan source speaks rather of "the leaven of Herod" (Mk 8:15).

f. **16:7–11** The disciples, men **of little faith**, misunderstand Jesus' metaphorical use of **leaven**, forgetting that, as the feeding of the crowds shows, he is not at a loss to provide them with bread.

g. **16:12** After his rebuke, the disciples understand that by **leaven** he meant the corrupting influence of the **teaching of the Pharisees and Sadducees.** The evangelist probably understands this **teaching** as common to both groups. Since at the time of Jesus' ministry the two differed widely on points of teaching, e.g., the resurrection of the dead, and at the time of the evangelist the Sadducee party was no longer a force in Judaism, the supposed common teaching fits neither period. The disciples' eventual understanding of Jesus' warning contrasts with their continuing obtuseness in the Marcan parallel (Mk 8:14–21).

h. **16:13–20** The Marcan confession of Jesus as Messiah, made by Peter as spokesman for the other disciples (Mk 8:27–29; cf. also Lk 9:18–20), is modified significantly here. The confession is of Jesus both as **Messiah** and as **Son of the living God** (Mt 16:16). Jesus' response, drawn principally from material peculiar to Matthew, attributes the confession to a divine revelation granted to

Peter alone (Mt 16:17) and makes him the **rock** on which Jesus **will build** his **church** (Mt 16:18) and the disciple whose authority in the church **on earth** will be confirmed in **heaven**, i.e., by God (Mt 16:19).

i. **16:13 Caesarea Philippi:** situated about twenty miles north of the Sea of Galilee in the territory ruled by Philip, a son of Herod the Great, tetrarch from 4 B.C. until his death in A.D. 34 (see note on Mt 14:1). He rebuilt the town of Paneas, naming it **Caesarea** in honor of the emperor, and **Philippi** ("of Philip") to distinguish it from the seaport in Samaria that was also called Caesarea. **Who do people say that the Son of Man is?:** although the question differs from the Marcan parallel (Mk 8:27: "Who . . . that I am?"), the meaning is the same, for Jesus here refers to himself as the **Son of Man** (cf. Mt 16:15).

j. **16:14 John the Baptist:** see Mt 14:2. **Elijah:** cf. Mal 3:32–34; Sir 48:10; and see note on Mt 3:4. **Jeremiah:** an addition of Matthew to the Marcan source.

k. **16:16 The Son of the living God:** see Mt 2:15; 3:17. The addition of this exalted title to the Marcan confession eliminates whatever ambiguity was attached to the title Messiah. This, among other things, supports the view proposed by many scholars that Matthew has here combined his source's confession with a post-resurrectional confession of faith in Jesus as **Son of the living God** that belonged to the appearance of the risen Jesus to Peter; cf. 1 Cor 15:5; Lk 24:34.

l. **16:17 Flesh and blood:** a Semitic expression for human beings, especially in their weakness. **Has not revealed this . . . but my heavenly Father:** that Peter's faith is spoken of as coming not through human means but through a revelation from God is similar to Paul's description of his recognition of who Jesus was; see Gal 1:15–16, " . . . when he [God] . . . was pleased to reveal his Son to me . . . ."

m. **16:18 You are Peter, and upon this rock I will build my church:** the Aramaic word *kēpā'* meaning rock and transliterated into Greek as *Kēphas* is the name by which Peter is called in the Pauline letters (1 Cor 1:12; 3:22; 9:5; 15:4; Gal 1:18; 2:9, 11, 14) except in Gal 2:7–8 ("Peter"). It is translated as *Petros* ("Peter") in Jn 1:42. The presumed original Aramaic of Jesus' statement would have been, in English, "You are the Rock (*Kēpā'*) and upon this rock (*kēpā'*) I will build my church." The Greek text probably means the same, for the difference in gender between the masculine noun *petros*, the disciple's new name, and the feminine noun *petra* (rock) may be due simply to the unsuitability of using a feminine noun as the proper name of a male. Although the two words were generally used with slightly different nuances, they were also used interchangeably with the same meaning, "rock." **Church:** this word (Greek *ekklēsia*) occurs in the gospels only here and in Mt 18:17 (twice). There are several possibilities for an Aramaic original. Jesus' **church** means the community that he will gather and that, like a building, will have Peter as its solid foundation. That function of Peter consists in his being witness to Jesus as **the Messiah, the Son of the living God. The gates of the netherworld shall not prevail against it:** the netherworld (Greek *Hadēs*, the abode of the dead) is conceived of as a walled city whose **gates** will not close in upon the church of Jesus, i.e., it will not be overcome by the power of death.

n. **16:19 The keys to the kingdom of heaven:** the image of the keys is probably drawn from Is 22:15–25 where Eliakim, who succeeds Shebna as master of the palace, is given "the key of the House of David," which he authoritatively "opens" and "shuts" (Is 22:22). **Whatever you bind . . . loosed in heaven:** there are many instances in rabbinic literature of the binding-loosing imagery. Of the several meanings given there to the metaphor, two are of special importance here: the giving of authoritative teaching, and the lifting or imposing of the ban of excommunication. It is disputed whether the image of **the keys** and that of binding and loosing are different metaphors meaning the same thing. In any case, the promise of the keys is given to Peter alone. In Mt 18:18 all the disciples are given the power of binding and loosing, but the context of that verse suggests that there the power of excommunication alone is intended. That **the keys** are those to the **kingdom of heaven** and that Peter's exercise of authority in the church **on earth** will be confirmed **in heaven** show an intimate connection between, but not an identification of, the church and the **kingdom of heaven.**

o. **16:20** Cf. Mk 8:30. Matthew makes explicit that the prohibition has to do with speaking of Jesus as **the Messiah**; see note on Mk 8:27–30.

p. **16:21–23** This first prediction of the passion follows Mk 8:31–33 in the main and serves as a corrective to an understanding of Jesus' messiahship as solely one of glory and triumph. By his addition of **from that time on** (Mt 16:21) Matthew has emphasized that Jesus' revelation of his coming suffering and death marks a new phase of the gospel. Neither this nor the two later passion predictions (Mt 17:22–23; 20:17–19) can be taken as sayings that, as they stand, go back to Jesus himself. However, it is probable that he foresaw that his mission would entail suffering and perhaps death, but was confident that he would ultimately be vindicated by God (see Mt 26:29).

q. **16:21 He:** the Marcan parallel (Mk 8:31) has "the Son of Man." Since Matthew has already designated Jesus by that title (Mt 15:13), its omission here is not significant. The Matthean prediction is equally about the sufferings of the Son of Man. **Must:** this necessity is part of the tradition of all the synoptics; cf. Mk 8:31; Lk 9:21. **The elders, the chief priests, and the scribes:** see note on Mk 8:31. **On the third day:** so also Lk 9:22, against the Marcan "after three days" (Mk 8:31). Matthew's formulation is, in the Greek, almost identical with the pre-Pauline fragment of the kerygma in 1 Cor 15:4 and also with Hos 6:2, which many take to be the Old Testament background to the confession that Jesus was raised **on the third day.** Josephus uses "after three days" and "on the third day" interchangeably (*Antiquities* 7:280–81; 8:214, 218) and there is probably no difference in meaning between the two phrases.

r. **16:22–23** Peter's refusal to accept Jesus' predicted suffering and death is seen as a satanic attempt to deflect Jesus from his God-appointed course, and the disciple is addressed in terms that recall Jesus' dismissal of the devil in the temptation account (Mt 4:10: "Get away, Satan!"). Peter's satanic purpose is emphasized by Matthew's addition to the Marcan source of the words **You are an obstacle to me.**

s. **16:24–28** A readiness to follow Jesus even to giving up one's life for him is the condition for true discipleship; this will be repaid by him at the final judgment.

t. **16:24 Deny himself:** to deny someone is to disown him (see Mt 10:33; 26:34–35) and to deny oneself is to disown oneself as the center of one's existence.

u. **16:25** See notes on Mt 10:38, 39.

v. **16:27** The parousia and final judgment are described in Mt 25:31 in terms almost identical with these.

w. **16:28 Coming in his kingdom:** since the **kingdom of the Son of Man** has been described as "the world" and Jesus' sovereignty precedes his final coming in glory (Mt 13:38, 41), the coming in this verse is not the parousia as in the preceding but the manifestation of Jesus' rule after his resurrection; see notes on Mt 13:38, 41.

Chapter 17

The Transfiguration of Jesus.[a] **1** After six days Jesus took Peter, James, and John his brother, and led them up a high mountain by themselves.[b] **2** [c]And he was transfigured before them; his face shone like the sun and his clothes became white as light. **3** [d]And behold, Moses and Elijah appeared to them, conversing with him. **4** Then Peter said to Jesus in reply, "Lord, it is good that we are here. If you wish, I will make three tents[e] here, one for you, one for Moses, and one for Elijah." **5** While he was still speaking, behold, a bright cloud cast a shadow over them,[f] then from the cloud came a voice that said, "This is my beloved Son, with whom I am well pleased; listen to him." **6** [g]When the disciples heard this, they fell prostrate and were very much afraid. **7** But Jesus came and touched them, saying, "Rise, and do not be afraid." **8** And when the disciples raised their eyes, they saw no one else but Jesus alone.

The Coming of Elijah.[h] **9** As they were coming down from the mountain, Jesus charged them, "Do not tell the vision[i] to anyone until the Son of Man has been raised from the dead." **10** [j]Then the disciples asked him, "Why do the scribes say that Elijah must come first?" **11** He said in reply,[k] "Elijah will indeed come and restore all things; **12** but I tell you that Elijah has already come, and they did not recognize him but did to him whatever they pleased. So also will the Son of Man suffer at their hands." **13** [l]Then the disciples understood that he was speaking to them of John the Baptist.

The Healing of a Boy with a Demon.[m] **14** When they came to the crowd a man approached, knelt down before him, **15** and said, "Lord, have pity on my son, for he is a lunatic[n] and suffers severely; often he falls into fire, and often into water. **16** I brought him to your disciples, but they could not cure him." **17** Jesus said in reply, "O faithless and perverse[o] generation, how long will I be with you? How long will I endure you? Bring him here to me." **18** Jesus rebuked him and the demon came out of him,[p] and from that hour the boy was cured. **19** Then the disciples approached Jesus in private and said, "Why could we not drive it out?" **20** [q]He said to them, "Because of your little faith. Amen, I say to you, if you have faith the size of a mustard seed, you will say to this mountain, 'Move from here to there,' and it will move. Nothing will be impossible for you." [21][r]

The Second Prediction of the Passion.[s] **22** As they were gathering in Galilee, Jesus said to them, "The Son of Man is to be handed over to men, **23** and they will kill him, and he will be raised on the third day." And they were overwhelmed with grief.

Payment of the Temple Tax.[t] **24** When they came to Capernaum, the collectors of the temple tax[u] approached Peter and said, "Doesn't your teacher pay the temple tax?" **25** "Yes," he said.[v] When he came into the house, before he had time to speak, Jesus asked him, "What is your opinion, Simon? From whom do the kings of the earth take tolls or census tax?

From their subjects or from foreigners?" **26** ᵂWhen he said, "From foreigners," Jesus said to him, "Then the subjects are exempt. **27** But that we may not offend them,ˣ go to the sea, drop in a hook, and take the first fish that comes up. Open its mouth and you will find a coin worth twice the temple tax. Give that to them for me and for you."

Notes

a. **17:1–8** The account of the transfiguration confirms that Jesus is the **Son** of God (Mt 17:5) and points to fulfillment of the prediction that he will come **in his Father's glory** at the end of the age (Mt 16:27). It has been explained by some as a resurrection appearance retrojected into the time of Jesus' ministry, but that is not probable since the account lacks many of the usual elements of the resurrection-appearance narratives. It draws upon motifs from the Old Testament and noncanonical Jewish apocalyptic literature that express the presence of the heavenly and the divine, e.g., brilliant light, white garments, and the overshadowing cloud.

b. **17:1** These three disciples are also taken apart from the others by Jesus in Gethsemane (Mt 26:37). **A high mountain:** this has been identified with Tabor or Hermon, but probably no specific mountain was intended by the evangelist or by his Marcan source (Mk 9:2). Its meaning is theological rather than geographical, possibly recalling the revelation to Moses on Mount Sinai (Ex 24:12–18) and to Elijah at the same place (1 Kgs 19:8–18; Horeb = Sinai).

c. **17:2 His face shone like the sun:** this is a Matthean addition; cf. Dn 10:6. **His clothes became white as light:** cf. Dn 7:9, where the clothing of God appears "snow bright." For the white garments of other heavenly beings, see Rev 4:4; 7:9; 19:14.

d. **17:3** See note on Mk 9:5.

e. **17:4 Three tents:** the booths in which the Israelites lived during the feast of Tabernacles (cf. Jn 7:2) were meant to recall their ancestors' dwelling in booths during the journey from Egypt to the promised land (Lv 23:39–42). The same Greek word, *skēnē*, here translated **tents**, is used in the LXX for the booths of that feast, and some scholars have suggested that there is an allusion here to that liturgical custom.

f. **17:5 Cloud cast a shadow over them:** see note on Mk 9:7. **This is my beloved Son . . . listen to him:** cf. Mt 3:17. The voice repeats the baptismal proclamation about Jesus, with the addition of the command **listen to him**. The latter is a reference to Dt 18:15 in which the Israelites are commanded to **listen to** the prophet like Moses whom God will raise up for them. The command to listen to Jesus is general, but in this context it probably applies particularly to the preceding predictions of his passion and resurrection (Mt 16:21) and of his coming (Mt 16:27, 28).

g. **17:6–7** A Matthean addition; cf. Dn 10:9–10, 18–19.

h. **17:9–13** In response to the disciples' question about the expected return of Elijah, Jesus interprets the mission of the Baptist as the fulfillment of that expectation. But that was not suspected by those who opposed and finally killed him, and Jesus predicts a similar fate for himself.

i. **17:9 The vision:** Matthew alone uses this word to describe the transfiguration. **Until the Son of Man has been raised from the dead:** only in the light of Jesus' resurrection can the meaning of his life and mission be truly understood; until then no testimony to **the vision** will lead people to faith.

j. **17:10** See notes on Mt 3:4; 16:14.

k. **17:11–12** The preceding question and this answer may reflect later controversy with Jews who objected to the Christian claims for Jesus that Elijah had not yet come.

l. **17:13** See Mt 11:14.

m. **17:14–20** Matthew has greatly shortened the Marcan story (Mk 9:14–29). Leaving aside several details of the boy's illness, he concentrates on the need for faith, not so much on the part of the boy's father (as does Mark, for Matthew omits Mk 9:22b–24) but on that of his own disciples whose inability to drive out the demon is ascribed to their **little faith** (Mt 17:20).

n. **17:15 A lunatic:** this description of the boy is peculiar to Matthew. The word occurs in the New Testament only here and in Mt 4:24 and means one affected or struck by the moon. The symptoms of the boy's illness point to epilepsy, and attacks of this were thought to be caused by phases of the moon.

o. **17:17 Faithless and perverse:** so Matthew and Luke (Lk 9:41) against Mark's **faithless** (Mk 9:19). The Greek word here translated perverse is the same as that in Dt 32:5 LXX, where Moses speaks to his people. There is a problem in knowing to whom the reproach is addressed. Since the Matthean Jesus normally chides his disciples for their **little faith** (as in Mt 17:20), it would appear that the charge of lack of faith could not be made against them and that the reproach is addressed to unbelievers among the Jews. However in Mt 17:20b **(if you have faith the size of a mustard seed)**, which is certainly addressed to the disciples, they appear to have not even the smallest faith; if they had, they would have been able to cure the boy. In the light of Mt 17:20b the reproach of Mt 17:17 could have applied to the disciples. There seems to be an inconsistency between the charge of **little faith** in Mt 17:20a and that of not even a little in Mt 17:20b.

p. **17:18 The demon came out of him:** not until this verse does Matthew indicate that the boy's illness is a case of demoniacal possession.

q. **17:20** The entire verse is an addition of Matthew who (according to the better attested text) omits the reason given for the disciples' inability in Mk 9:29. **Little faith:** see note on Mt 6:30. **Faith the size of a mustard seed ... and it will move:** a combination of a Q saying (cf. Lk 17:6) with a Marcan saying (cf. Mk 11:23).

r. **17:21** Some manuscripts add, "But this kind does not come out except by prayer and fasting"; this is a variant of the better reading of Mk 9:29.

s. **17:22–23** The second passion prediction (cf. Mt 16:21–23) is the least detailed of the three and may be the earliest. In the Marcan parallel the disciples do not understand (Mk 9:32); here they understand and are **overwhelmed with grief** at the prospect of Jesus' death (Mt 17:23).

t. **17:24–27** Like Mt 14:28–31 and Mt 16:16b–19, this episode comes from Matthew's special material on Peter. Although the question of **the collectors** concerns Jesus' payment of the **temple tax**, it is put to Peter. It is he who receives instruction from Jesus about freedom from the obligation of payment and yet why it should be made. The means of doing so is provided miraculously. The pericope deals with a problem of Matthew's church, whether its members should pay the temple tax, and the answer is given through a word of Jesus conveyed to Peter. Some scholars see here an example of the teaching authority of Peter exercised in the name of Jesus (see Mt 16:19). The specific problem was a Jewish Christian one and may have arisen when the Matthean church was composed largely of that group.

u. **17:24 The temple tax:** before the destruction of the Jerusalem temple in A.D. 70 every male Jew above nineteen years of age was obliged to make an annual contribution to its upkeep (cf. Ex 30:11–16; Neh 10:33). After the destruction the Romans imposed upon Jews the obligation of paying that tax for the temple of Jupiter Capitolinus. There is disagreement about which period the story deals with.

v. **17:25 From their subjects or from foreigners?:** the Greek word here translated **subjects** literally means "sons."

w. **17:26 Then the subjects are exempt:** just as **subjects** are not bound by laws applying to **foreigners**, neither are Jesus and his disciples, who belong to the kingdom of heaven, bound by the duty of paying the temple tax imposed on those who are not of the kingdom. If the Greek is translated "sons," the freedom of Jesus, the Son of God, and of his disciples, children ("sons") of the kingdom (cf. Mt 13:38), is even more clear.

x. **17:27 That we may not offend them:** though they are exempt (Mt 17:26), Jesus and his disciples are to avoid giving offense; therefore the tax is to be paid. **A coin worth twice the temple tax:** literally, "a stater," a Greek coin worth two double drachmas. Two double drachmas were equal to the Jewish shekel and the tax was a half-shekel. **For me and for you:** not only Jesus but Peter pays the tax, and this example serves as a standard for the conduct of all the disciples.

Chapter 18[a]

The Greatest in the Kingdom. 1 At that time the disciples[b] approached Jesus and said, "Who is the greatest in the kingdom of heaven?" **2** He called a child over, placed it in their midst, **3** and said, "Amen, I say to you, unless you turn and become like children,[c] you will not enter the kingdom of heaven. **4** Whoever humbles himself like this child is the greatest in the kingdom of heaven. **5** [d]And whoever receives one child such as this in my name receives me.

Temptations to Sin. 6 "Whoever causes one of these little ones[e] who believe in me to sin, it would be better for him to have a great millstone hung around his neck and to be drowned in the depths of the sea. **7** [f]Woe to the world because of things that cause sin! Such things must come, but woe to the one through whom they come! **8** If your hand or foot causes you to sin,[g] cut it off and throw it away. It is better for you to enter into life maimed or crippled than with two hands or two feet to be thrown into eternal fire. **9** And if your eye causes you to sin, tear it out and throw it away. It is better for you to enter into life with one eye than with two eyes to be thrown into fiery Gehenna.

The Parable of the Lost Sheep.[h] **10** "See that you do not despise one of these little ones,[i] for I say to you that their angels in heaven always look upon the face of my heavenly Father. [11][j] **12** What is your opinion? If a man has a hundred sheep and one of them goes astray, will he not leave the ninety-nine in the hills and go in search of the stray? **13** And if he finds it, amen, I say to you, he rejoices more over it than over the ninety-nine that did not stray. **14** In just the same way, it is not the will of your heavenly Father that one of these little ones be lost.

A Brother Who Sins.[k] **15** "If your brother[l] sins [against you], go and tell him his fault between you and him alone. If he listens to you, you have won over your brother. **16** [m]If he does not listen, take one or two others along with you, so that 'every fact may be established on the testimony of two or three witnesses.' **17** If he refuses to listen to them, tell the church.[n] If he refuses to listen even to the church, then treat him as you would a Gentile or a tax collector. **18** [o]Amen, I say to you, whatever you bind on earth shall be bound in heaven, and whatever you loose on earth shall be loosed in heaven. **19** [p]Again, [amen,] I say to you, if two of you agree on earth about anything for which they are to pray, it shall be granted to them by my heavenly Father. **20** [q]For where two or three are gathered together in my name, there am I in the midst of them."

The Parable of the Unforgiving Servant.[r] **21** Then Peter approaching asked him, "Lord, if my brother sins against me, how often must I forgive him? As many as seven times?" **22** [s]Jesus answered, "I say to you, not seven times but seventy-seven times. **23** That is why the kingdom of heaven may be likened to a king who decided to settle accounts with his servants. 24 ᵗWhen he began the accounting, a debtor was brought before him who owed him a huge amount. **25** Since he had no way of paying it back, his master ordered him to be sold, along with his wife, his children, and all his property, in payment of the debt. **26** ᵘAt that, the servant fell down, did him homage, and said, 'Be patient with me, and I will pay you back in full.' **27** Moved with compassion the master of that servant let him go and forgave him the loan. **28** When that servant had left, he found one of his fellow servants who owed him a much smaller amount.ᵛ He seized him and started to choke him, demanding, 'Pay back what you owe.' **29** Falling to his knees, his fellow servant begged him, 'Be patient with me, and I will pay you back.' **30** But he refused. Instead, he had him put in prison until he paid back the debt. **31** Now when his fellow servants saw what had happened, they were deeply disturbed, and went to their master and reported the whole affair. **32** His master summoned him and said to him, 'You wicked servant! I forgave you your entire debt because you begged me to. **33** Should you not have had pity on your fellow servant, as I had pity on you?' **34** Then in anger his master handed him over to the torturers until he should pay back the whole debt.ʷ **35** ˣSo will my heavenly Father do to you, unless each of you forgives his brother from his heart."

Notes

a. **18:1–35** This discourse of the fourth book of the gospel is often called the "church order" discourse, but it lacks most of the considerations usually connected with church order, such as various offices in the church and the duties of each, and deals principally with the relations that must obtain among the members of the church. Beginning with the warning that greatness in the **kingdom of heaven** is measured not by rank or power but by childlikeness (Mt 18:1–5), it deals with the care that the disciples must take not to cause the **little ones to sin** or to neglect them if they stray from the community (Mt 18:6–14), the correction of members who sin (Mt 18:15–18), the efficacy of the prayer of the disciples because of the presence of Jesus (Mt 18:19–20), and the forgiveness that must be repeatedly extended to sinful members who repent (Mt 18:21–35).

b. **18:1** The initiative is taken not by Jesus as in the Marcan parallel (Mk 9:33–34) but by the disciples. **Kingdom of heaven:** this may mean **the kingdom** in its fullness, i.e., after the parousia and the final judgment. But what follows about causes of sin, church discipline, and forgiveness, all dealing with the present age, suggests that the question has to do with rank also in the church, where the kingdom is manifested here and now, although only partially and by anticipation; see notes on Mt 3:2; 4:17.

c. **18:3 Become like children:** the child is held up as a model for the disciples not because of any supposed innocence of children but because of their complete dependence on, and trust in, their parents. So must the disciples be, in respect to God.

d. **18:5** Cf. Mt 10:40.

e. **18:6 One of these little ones:** the thought passes from the child of Mt 18:2–4 to the disciples, **little ones** because of their becoming **like children**. It is difficult to know whether this is a designation of all who are disciples or of those who are insignificant in contrast to others, e.g., the leaders of the community. Since apart from this chapter the designation **little ones** occurs in Matthew only in Mt 10:42 where it means disciples as such, that is its more likely meaning here. **Who believe in me:** since discipleship is impossible without at least some degree of faith, this further specification seems superfluous. However, it serves to indicate that the warning against causing a **little one** to sin is principally directed against whatever would lead such a one to a weakening or loss of faith. The Greek verb *skandalizein*, here translated **causes . . . to sin**, means literally "causes to stumble"; what the stumbling is depends on the context. It is used of falling away from faith in Mt 13:21. According to the better reading of Mk 9:42, **in me** is a Matthean addition to the Marcan source. **It would be better . . . depths of the sea:** cf. Mk 9:42.

f. **18:7** This is a Q saying; cf. Lk 17:1. The inevitability of **things that cause sin** (literally, "scandals") does not take away the responsibility of **the one through whom they come.**

g. **18:8–9** These verses are a doublet of Mt 5:29–30. In that context they have to do with causes of sexual sin. As in the Marcan source from which they have been drawn (Mk 9:42–48), they differ from the first warning about scandal, which deals with causing another person to sin, for they concern what **causes** oneself **to sin** and they do not seem to be related to another's loss of faith, as the first warning is. It is difficult to know how Matthew understood the logical connection between these verses and Mt 18:6–7.

h. **18:10–14** The first and last verses are peculiar to Matthew. The parable itself comes from Q; see Lk 15:3–7. In Luke it serves as justification for Jesus' table-companionship with sinners; here, it is an exhortation for the disciples to seek out fellow disciples who have gone **astray.** Not only must no one cause a fellow disciple to sin, but those who have strayed must be sought out and, if possible, brought back to the community. The joy of the shepherd on finding the sheep, though not absent in Mt 18:13 is more emphasized in Luke. By his addition of Mt 18:10, 14 Matthew has drawn out explicitly the application of the parable to the care of the **little ones.**

i. **18:10 Their angels in heaven . . . my heavenly Father:** for the Jewish belief in angels as guardians of nations and individuals, see Dn 10:13, 20–21; Tb 5:4–7; 1QH 5:20–22; as intercessors who present the prayers of human beings to God, see Tb 13:12, 15. The high worth of the **little ones** is indicated by their being represented before God by these heavenly beings.

j. **18:11** Some manuscripts add, "For the Son of Man has come to save what was lost"; cf. Mt 9:13. This is practically identical with Lk 19:10 and is probably a copyist's addition from that source.

k. **18:15–20** Passing from the duty of Christian disciples toward those who have strayed from their number, the discourse now turns to how they are to deal with one who sins and yet remains within the community. First there is to be private correction (Mt 18:15); if this is unsuccessful, further correction before **two or three witnesses** (Mt 18:16); if this fails, the matter is to be brought before the assembled community (the church), and if the sinner refuses to attend to the correction **of the church**, he is to be expelled (Mt 18:17). The church's judgment will be ratified **in heaven**, i.e., by God (Mt 18:18). This three-step process of correction corresponds, though not exactly, to the procedure of the Qumran community; see 1QS 5:25–6:1; 6:24–7:25; CD 9:2–8. The section ends with a saying about the favorable response of God to prayer, even to that of a very small number, for Jesus is in the midst of any gathering of his disciples, however small (Mt 18:19–20). Whether this prayer has anything to do with the preceding judgment is uncertain.

l. **18:15 Your brother:** a fellow disciple; see Mt 23:8. The bracketed words, **against you**, are widely attested but they are not in the important codices Sinaiticus and Vaticanus or in some other textual witnesses. Their omission broadens the type of sin in question. **Won over:** literally, "gained."

m. **18:16** Cf. Dt 19:15.

n. **18:17 The church:** the second of the only two instances of this word in the gospels; see note on Mt 16:18. Here it refers not to the entire **church** of Jesus, as in Mt 16:18, but to the local congregation. **Treat him . . . a Gentile or a tax collector:** just as the observant Jew avoided the company of Gentiles and tax collectors, so must the congregation of Christian disciples separate itself from the arrogantly sinful member who refuses to repent even when convicted of his sin by the whole **church**. Such a one is to be set outside the fellowship of the community. The harsh language about **Gentile** and **tax collector** probably reflects a stage of the Matthean **church** when it was principally composed of Jewish Christians. That time had long since passed, but the principle of exclusion for such a sinner remained. Paul makes a similar demand for excommunication in 1 Cor 5:1–13.

o. **18:18** Except for the plural of the verbs **bind** and **loose**, this verse is practically identical with Mt 16:19b and many scholars understand it as granting to all the disciples what was previously given to Peter alone. For a different view, based on the different contexts of the two verses, see note on Mt 16:19.

p. **18:19–20** Some take these verses as applying to prayer on the occasion of the church's gathering to deal with the sinner of Mt 18:17. Unless an a *fortiori* argument is supposed, this seems unlikely. God's answer to the prayer of **two or three** envisages a different situation from one that involves the entire congregation. In addition, the object of this prayer is expressed in most general terms as **anything for which they are to pray**.

q. **18:20 For where two or three . . . midst of them:** the presence of Jesus guarantees the efficacy of the prayer. This saying is similar to one attributed to a rabbi executed in A.D. 135 at the time of the second Jewish revolt: " . . . When two sit and there are between them the words of the Torah, the divine presence (*Shekinah*) rests upon them" (*Pirqê 'Abôt* 3, 3).

r. **18:21–35** The final section of the discourse deals with the forgiveness that the disciples are to give to their fellow disciples who sin against them. To the question of Peter how often forgiveness is to be granted (Mt 18:21), Jesus answers that it is to be given without limit (Mt 18:22) and illustrates this with the parable of the unmerciful servant (Mt 18:23–34), warning that his **heavenly Father** will give those who do not forgive the same treatment as that given to the unmerciful servant (Mt 18:35). Mt 18:21–22 correspond to Lk 17:4; the parable and the final warning are peculiar to Matthew. That the parable did not originally belong to this context is suggested by the fact that it really does not deal with repeated forgiveness, which is the point of Peter's question and Jesus' reply.

s. **18:22 Seventy-seven times:** the Greek corresponds exactly to the LXX of Gn 4:24. There is probably an allusion, by contrast, to the limitless vengeance of Lamech in the Genesis text. In any case, what is demanded of the disciples is limitless forgiveness.

t. **18:24 A huge amount:** literally, "ten thousand talents." The talent was a unit of coinage of high but varying value depending on its metal (gold, silver, copper) and its place of origin. It is mentioned in the New Testament only here and in Mt 25:14–30.

u. **18:26 Pay you back in full:** an empty promise, given the size of the debt.

v. **18:28 A much smaller amount:** literally, "a hundred denarii." A denarius was the normal daily wage of a laborer. The difference between the two debts is enormous and brings out the absurdity of the conduct of the Christian who has received the great forgiveness of God and yet refuses to forgive the relatively minor offenses done to him.

w. **18:34** Since the debt is so great as to be unpayable, the punishment will be endless.

x. **18:35** The Father's forgiveness, already given, will be withdrawn at the final judgment for those who have not imitated his forgiveness by their own.

VI. Ministry in Judea and Jerusalem

Chapter 19

Marriage and Divorce. 1 ᵃWhen Jesusᵇ finished these words,ᶜ he left Galilee and went to the district of Judea across the Jordan. **2** Great crowds followed him, and he cured them there. **3** Some Pharisees approached him, and tested him,ᵈ saying, "Is it lawful for a man to divorce his wife for any cause whatever?" **4** ᵉHe said in reply, "Have you not read that from the beginning the Creator 'made them male and female' **5** and said, 'For this reason a man shall leave his father and mother and be joined to his wife, and the two shall become one flesh'? **6** So they are no longer two, but one flesh. Therefore, what God has joined together, no human being must separate." **7** ᶠThey said to him, "Then why did Moses command that the man give the woman a bill of divorce and dismiss [her]?" **8** He said to them, "Because of the hardness of your hearts Moses allowed you to divorce your wives, but from the beginning it was not so. **9** I say to you,ᵍ whoever divorces his wife (unless the marriage is unlawful) and marries another commits adultery." **10** [His] disciples said to him, "If that is the case of a man with his wife, it is better not to marry." **11** He answered, "Not all can accept [this] word,ʰ but only those to whom that is granted. **12** Some are incapable of marriage because they were born so; some, because they were made so by others; some, because they have renounced marriageⁱ for the sake of the kingdom of heaven. Whoever can accept this ought to accept it."

Blessing of the Children.ʲ **13** Then children were brought to him that he might lay his hands on them and pray. The disciples rebuked them, **14** but Jesus said, "Let the children come to me, and do not prevent them; for the kingdom of heaven belongs to such as these." **15** After he placed his hands on them, he went away.

The Rich Young Man.ᵏ **16** Now someone approached him and said, "Teacher, what good must I do to gain eternal life?"ˡ **17** He answered him, "Why do you ask me about the good? There is only One who is good.ᵐ If you wish to enter into life, keep the commandments." **18** ⁿHe asked him, "Which ones?" And Jesus replied, " 'You shall not kill; you shall not commit adultery; you shall not steal; you shall not bear false witness; **19** honor your father and your mother'; and 'you shall love your neighbor as yourself.'" **20** ᵒThe young man said to him, "All of these I have observed. What do I still lack?" **21** Jesus said to him, "If you wish to be perfect,ᵖ go, sell what you have and give to [the] poor, and you will have treasure in heaven. Then come, follow me." **22** When the young man heard this statement, he went away sad, for he had many possessions. **23** ᑫThen Jesus said to his disciples, "Amen, I say to you, it will be hard for one who is rich to enter the kingdom of heaven. **24** Again I say to you, it is easier for a camel to pass through the eye of a needle than for one who is rich to enter the kingdom of God." **25** ᵣWhen the disciples heard this, they were greatly astonished and said, "Who then can be saved?" **26** Jesus looked at them and said, "For human beings this is impossible, but for God all things are possible." **27** Then Peter said to him in reply, "We have given up everything and followed you. What will there be for us?" **28** ˢJesus said to them, "Amen, I say to you that you who have followed me, in the new age, when the Son of Man is seated on his throne of glory, will yourselves sit on twelve thrones, judging the twelve tribes of Israel. **29** And everyone who has given up houses or brothers or sisters or father or mother or children or lands for the sake of my name will receive a hundred times more, and will inherit eternal life. **30** ᵗBut many who are first will be last, and the last will be first.

Notes

a. **19:1–23:39** The narrative section of the fifth book of the gospel. The first part (Mt 19:1–20:34) has for its setting the journey of Jesus from Galilee to Jerusalem; the second (Mt 21:1–23:39) deals with Jesus' ministry in Jerusalem up to the final great discourse of the gospel (Mt 24–25). Matthew follows the Marcan sequence of events, though adding material both special to this gospel and drawn from Q. The second part ends with the denunciation of the scribes and Pharisees (Mt 23:1–36) followed by Jesus' lament over Jerusalem (Mt 23:37–39). This long and important speech raises a problem for the view that Matthew is structured around five other discourses of Jesus (see Introduction) and that this one has no such function in the gospel. However, it is to be noted that this speech lacks the customary concluding formula that follows the five discourses (see note on Mt 7:28), and that those discourses are all addressed either exclusively (Mt 10; 18; 24; 25) or primarily (Mt 5–7; 13) to the disciples, whereas this is addressed primarily to the scribes and Pharisees (Mt 23:13–36). Consequently, it seems plausible to maintain that the evangelist did not intend to give it the structural importance of the five other discourses, and that, in spite of its being composed of sayings-material, it belongs to the narrative section of this book. In that regard, it is similar to the sayings-material of Mt 11:7–30. Some have proposed that Matthew wished to regard it as part of the final discourse of Mt 24–25, but the intervening material (Mt 24:1–4) and the change in matter and style of those chapters do not support that view.

b. **19:1** In giving Jesus' teaching on divorce (Mt 19:3–9), Matthew here follows his Marcan source (Mk 10:2–12) as he does Q in Mt 5:31–32 (cf. Lk 16:18). Mt 19:10–12 are peculiar to Matthew.

c. **19:1 When Jesus finished these words:** see note on Mt 7:28–29. **The district of Judea across the Jordan:** an inexact designation of the territory. Judea did not extend **across the Jordan;** the territory east of the river was Perea. The route to Jerusalem by way of Perea avoided passage through Samaria.

d. **19:3 Tested him:** the verb is used of attempts of Jesus' opponents to embarrass him by challenging him to do something they think impossible (Mt 16:1; Mk

8:11; Lk 11:16) or by having him say something that they can use against him (Mt 22:18, 35; Mk 10:2; 12:15). **For any cause whatever:** this is peculiar to Matthew and has been interpreted by some as meaning that Jesus was being asked to take sides in the dispute between the schools of Hillel and Shammai on the reasons for divorce, the latter holding a stricter position than the former. It is unlikely, however, that to ask Jesus' opinion about the differing views of two Jewish schools, both highly respected, could be described as "testing" him, for the reason indicated above.

e. **19:4–6** Matthew recasts his Marcan source, omitting Jesus' question about Moses' command (Mk 10:3) and having him recall at once two Genesis texts that show the will and purpose of **the Creator** in making human beings **male and female** (Gn 1:27), namely, that a **man** may **be joined to his wife** in marriage in the intimacy of **one flesh** (Gn 2:24). **What God has** thus **joined** must not be separated by any human being. (The NAB translation of the Hebrew *bāśār* of Gn 2:24 as "body" rather than "flesh" obscures the reference of Matthew to that text.)

f. **19:7** See Dt 24:1–4.

g. **19:9** Moses' concession to human sinfulness (**the hardness of your hearts**, Mt 19:8) is repudiated by Jesus, and the original will of the Creator is reaffirmed against that concession. **(Unless the marriage is unlawful):** see note on Mt 5:31–32. There is some evidence suggesting that Jesus' absolute prohibition of divorce was paralleled in the Qumran community (see 11QTemple 57:17–19; CD 4:12b–5:14). Matthew removes Mark's setting of this verse as spoken to the disciples alone "in the house" (Mk 10:10) and also his extension of the divorce prohibition to the case of a woman's divorcing her husband (Mk 10:12), probably because in Palestine, unlike the places where Roman and Greek law prevailed, the woman was not allowed to initiate the divorce.

h. **19:11 [This] word:** probably the disciples' **"it is better not to marry"** (Mt 19:10). Jesus agrees but says that celibacy is not for all but only for those **to whom that is granted** by God.

i. **19:12 Incapable of marriage:** literally, "eunuchs." Three classes are mentioned, eunuchs from birth, eunuchs by castration, and those who have voluntarily **renounced marriage** (literally, "have made themselves eunuchs") **for the sake of the kingdom**, i.e., to devote themselves entirely to its service. Some scholars take the last class to be those who have been divorced by their spouses and have refused to enter another marriage. But it is more likely that it is rather those who have chosen never to marry, since that suits better the optional nature of the decision: **whoever can . . . ought to accept it.**

j. **19:13–15** This account is understood by some as intended to justify the practice of infant baptism. That interpretation is based principally on the command not to **prevent** the children from coming, since that word sometimes has a baptismal connotation in the New Testament; see Acts 8:36.

k. **19:16–30** Cf. Mk 10:17–31. This story does not set up a "two-tier" morality, that of those who seek (only) **eternal life** (Mt 19:16) and that of those who **wish to be perfect** (Mt 19:21). It speaks rather of the obstacle that riches constitute for the following of Jesus and of the impossibility, humanly speaking, for one who has **many possessions** (Mt 19:22) **to enter the kingdom** (Mt 19:24). Actual renunciation of riches is not demanded of all; Matthew counts the rich Joseph of Arimathea as a disciple of Jesus (Mt 27:57). But only the poor in spirit (Mt 5:3) can **enter the kingdom** and, as here, such poverty may entail the sacrifice of one's **possessions**. The Twelve, who **have given up everything** (Mt 19:27) to follow Jesus, will have as their reward a share in Jesus' (the Son of Man's) **judging the twelve tribes of Israel** (Mt 19:28), and all who have similarly sacrificed family or property for his sake **will inherit eternal life** (Mt 19:29).

l. **19:16 Gain eternal life:** this is equivalent to "entering into life" (Mt 19:17) and "being saved" (Mt 19:25); the **life** is that of the new age after the final judgment (see Mt 25:46). It probably is also equivalent here to "entering the kingdom of heaven" (Mt 19:23) or "the kingdom of God" (Mt 19:24), but see notes on Mt 3:2; 4:17; 18:1 for the wider reference of **the kingdom** in Matthew.

m. **19:17** By Matthew's reformulation of the Marcan question and reply (Mk 10:17–18) Jesus' repudiation of the term "good" for himself has been softened. Yet the Marcan assertion that "no one is good but God alone" stands, with only unimportant verbal modification.

n. **19:18–19** The first five commandments cited are from the Decalogue (see Ex 20:12–16; Dt 5:16–20). Matthew omits Mark's "you shall not defraud" (Mk 10:19; see Dt 24:14) and adds Lv 19:18. This combination of commandments of the Decalogue with Lv 19:18 is partially the same as Paul's enumeration of the demands of Christian morality in Rom 13:9.

o. **19:20 Young man:** in Matthew alone of the synoptics the questioner is said to be a **young man**; thus the Marcan "from my youth" (Mk 10:20) is omitted.

p. **19:21 If you wish to be perfect: to be perfect** is demanded of all Christians; see Mt 5:48. In the case of this man, it involves selling his possessions and giving to the poor; only so can he **follow** Jesus.

q. **19:23–24** Riches are an obstacle to entering **the kingdom** that cannot be overcome by human power. The comparison with the impossibility of a camel's passing **through the eye of a needle** should not be mitigated by such suppositions as that **the eye of a needle** means a low or narrow gate. **The kingdom of God:** as in Mt 12:28; 21:31, 43 instead of Matthew's usual **kingdom of heaven.**

r. **19:25–26** See note on Mk 10:23–27.

s. **19:28** This saying, directed to the Twelve, is from Q; see Lk 22:29–30. **The new age:** the Greek word here translated "new age" occurs in the New Testament only here and in Ti 3:5. Literally, it means "rebirth" or "regeneration," and is used in Titus of spiritual rebirth through baptism. Here it means the "rebirth" effected by the coming of the kingdom. Since that coming has various stages (see notes on Mt 3:2; 4:17), the **new age** could be taken as referring to the time after the resurrection when the Twelve will govern the true Israel, i.e., the church of Jesus. (For "judge" in the sense of "govern," cf. Jgs 12:8, 9, 11; 15:20; 16:31; Ps 2:10). But since it is connected here with the time when the **Son of Man** will be **seated on his throne of glory,** language that Matthew uses in Mt

25:31 for the time of final judgment, it is more likely that what the Twelve are promised is that they will be joined with Jesus then in judging the people of Israel.

t. **19:30** Different interpretations have been given to this saying, which comes from Mk 10:31. In view of Matthew's associating it with the following parable (Mt 20:1–15) and substantially repeating it (in reverse order) at the end of that parable (Mt 20:16), it may be that his meaning is that all who respond to the call of Jesus, at whatever time (**first** or **last**), will be the same in respect to inheriting the benefits of the kingdom, which is the gift of God.

Chapter 20

The Workers in the Vineyard.[a] **1** "The kingdom of heaven is like a landowner who went out at dawn to hire laborers for his vineyard. **2** After agreeing with them for the usual daily wage, he sent them into his vineyard. **3** Going out about nine o'clock, he saw others standing idle in the marketplace, **4** [b]and he said to them, 'You too go into my vineyard, and I will give you what is just.' **5** So they went off. [And] he went out again around noon, and around three o'clock, and did likewise. **6** Going out about five o'clock, he found others standing around, and said to them, 'Why do you stand here idle all day?' **7** They answered, 'Because no one has hired us.' He said to them, 'You too go into my vineyard.' **8** [c]When it was evening the owner of the vineyard said to his foreman, 'Summon the laborers and give them their pay, beginning with the last and ending with the first.' **9** When those who had started about five o'clock came, each received the usual daily wage. **10** So when the first came, they thought that they would receive more, but each of them also got the usual wage. **11** And on receiving it they grumbled against the landowner, **12** saying, 'These last ones worked only one hour, and you have made them equal to us, who bore the day's burden and the heat.' **13** He said to one of them in reply, 'My friend, I am not cheating you.[d] Did you not agree with me for the usual daily wage? **14** [e]Take what is yours and go. What if I wish to give this last one the same as you? **15** [Or] am I not free to do as I wish with my own money? Are you envious because I am generous?' **16** [f]Thus, the last will be first, and the first will be last."

The Third Prediction of the Passion.[g] **17** As Jesus was going up to Jerusalem, he took the twelve [disciples] aside by themselves, and said to them on the way, **18** "Behold, we are going up to Jerusalem, and the Son of Man will be handed over to the chief priests and the scribes, and they will condemn him to death, **19** and hand him over to the Gentiles to be mocked and scourged and crucified, and he will be raised on the third day."

The Request of James and John.[h] **20** Then the mother[i] of the sons of Zebedee approached him with her sons and did him homage, wishing to ask him for something. **21** He said to her, "What do you wish?" She answered him, "Command that these two sons of mine sit, one at your right and the other at your left, in your kingdom." **22** Jesus said in reply, "You do not know what you are asking.[j] Can you drink the cup that I am going to drink?" They said to him, "We can." **23** He replied, "My cup you will indeed drink, but to sit at my right and at my left [, this] is not mine to give but is for those for whom it has been prepared by my Father." **24** When the ten heard this, they became indignant at the two brothers. **25** But Jesus summoned them and said, "You know that the rulers of the Gentiles Lord it over them, and the great ones make their authority over them felt. **26** But it shall not be so among you. Rather, whoever wishes to be great among you shall be your servant; **27** whoever wishes to be first among you shall be your slave. **28** Just so, the Son of Man did not come to be served but to serve and to give his life as a ransom[k] for many."

The Healing of Two Blind Men.[l] **29** As they left Jericho, a great crowd followed him. **30** Two blind men were sitting by the roadside, and when they heard that Jesus was passing by, they cried out, "[Lord,][m] Son of David, have pity on us!" **31** The crowd warned them to be silent, but they called out all the more, "Lord, Son of David, have pity on us!" **32** Jesus stopped and called them and said, "What do you want me to do for you?" **33** They answered him, "Lord, let our eyes be opened." **34** Moved with pity, Jesus touched their eyes. Immediately they received their sight, and followed him.

Notes

a. **20:1–16** This parable is peculiar to Matthew. It is difficult to know whether the evangelist composed it or received it as part of his traditional material and, if the latter is the case, what its original reference was. In its present context its close association with Mt 19:30 suggests that its teaching is the equality of all the disciples in the reward of inheriting eternal life.

b. **20:4 What is just:** although the wage is not stipulated as in the case of those first hired, it will be fair.

c. **20:8 Beginning with the last . . . the first:** this element of the parable has no other purpose than to show how **the first** knew what **the last** were given (Mt 20:12).

d. **20:13 I am not cheating you:** literally, "I am not treating you unjustly."

e. **20:14–15** The owner's conduct involves no violation of justice (Mt 20:4, 13), and that all the workers receive the same wage is due only to his generosity to the latest arrivals; the resentment of the first comes from envy.

f. **20:16** See note on Mt 19:30.

g. **20:17–19** Cf. Mk 10:32–34. This is the third and the most detailed of the passion predictions (Mt 16:21–23; 17:22–23). It speaks of Jesus' being **handed over to the Gentiles** (Mt 27:2), his being **mocked** (Mt 27:27–30), **scourged** (Mt 27:26), and **crucified** (Mt 27:31, 35). In all but the last of these points Matthew agrees with his Marcan source, but whereas Mark speaks of Jesus' being killed (Mk 10:34), Matthew has the specific **to be . . . crucified**.

h. **20:20–28** Cf. Mk 10:35–45. The request of the sons of Zebedee, made through their mother, for the highest places of honor in the **kingdom**, and the indignation of **the** other **ten** disciples at this request, show that neither **the two brothers** nor the others have understood that what makes for greatness in the kingdom is not Lordly power but humble service. Jesus gives the example, and his ministry of service will reach its highest point when he gives his life for the deliverance of the human race from sin.

i. **20:20–21** The reason for Matthew's making **the mother** the petitioner (cf. Mk 10:35) is not clear. Possibly he intends an allusion to Bathsheba's seeking the kingdom for Solomon; see 1 Kgs 1:11–21. **Your kingdom:** see note on Mt 16:28.

j. **20:22 You do not know what you are asking:** the Greek verbs are plural and, with the rest of the verse, indicate that the answer is addressed not to the woman but to her sons. **Drink the cup:** see note on Mk 10:38–40. Matthew omits the Marcan "or be baptized with the baptism with which I am baptized" (Mk 10:38).

k. **20:28 Ransom:** this noun, which occurs in the New Testament only here and in the Marcan parallel (Mk 10:45), does not necessarily express the idea of liberation by payment of some price. The cognate verb is used frequently in the LXX of God's liberating Israel from Egypt or from Babylonia after the Exile; see Ex 6:6; 15:13; Ps 77:16 (76 LXX); Is 43:1; 44:22. The liberation brought by Jesus' death will be **for many**; cf. Is 53:12. **Many** does not mean that some are excluded, but is a Semitism designating the collectivity who benefit from the service of the one, and is equivalent to "all." While there are few verbal contacts between this saying and the fourth Servant Song (Is 52:13–53:12), the ideas of that passage are reflected here.

l. **20:29–34** The cure of the blind men is probably symbolic of what will happen to the disciples, now blind to the meaning of Jesus' passion and to the necessity of their sharing his suffering. As the men are given sight, so, after the resurrection, will the disciples come to see that to which they are now blind. Matthew has abbreviated his Marcan source (Mk 10:46–52) and has made Mark's one man two. Such doubling is characteristic of this gospel; see Mt 8:28–34 (// Mk 5:1–20) and the note on Mt 9:27–31.

m. **20:30 [Lord,]:** some important textual witnesses omit this, but that may be because copyists assimilated this verse to Mt 9:27. **Son of David:** see note on Mt 9:27.

Chapter 21

The Entry into Jerusalem.[a] **1** When they drew near Jerusalem and came to Bethphage[b] on the Mount of Olives, Jesus sent two disciples, **2** saying to them, "Go into the village opposite you, and immediately you will find an ass tethered, and a colt with her.[c] Untie them and bring them here to me. **3** And if anyone should say anything to you, reply, 'The master has need of them.' Then he will send them at once." **4** [d]This happened so that what had been spoken through the prophet might be fulfilled:

5 "Say to daughter Zion,
 'Behold, your king comes to you,
  meek and riding on an ass,
   and on a colt, the foal of a beast of burden.'"

6 The disciples went and did as Jesus had ordered them. **7** [e]They brought the ass and the colt and laid their cloaks over them, and he sat upon them. **8** [f]The very large crowd spread their cloaks on the road, while others cut branches from the trees and strewed them on the road. **9** The crowds preceding him and those following kept crying out and saying:

"Hosanna[g] to the Son of David;
 blessed is he who comes in the name of the Lord;
 hosanna in the highest."

10 And when he entered Jerusalem the whole city was shaken[h] and asked, "Who is this?" **11** And the crowds replied, "This is Jesus the prophet,[i] from Nazareth in Galilee."

The Cleansing of the Temple.[j] **12** Jesus entered the temple area and drove out all those engaged in selling and buying there. He overturned the tables of the money changers and the seats of those who were selling doves.[k] **13** And he said to them, "It is written:

'My house shall be a house of prayer,'[l]
 but you are making it a den of thieves."

14 The blind and the lame[m] approached him in the temple area, and he cured them. **15** When the chief priests and the scribes saw the wondrous things[n] he was doing, and the children crying out in the temple area, "Hosanna to the Son of David," they were indignant **16** [o]and said to him, "Do you hear what they are saying?" Jesus said to them, "Yes; and have you never read the text, 'Out of the mouths of infants and nurslings you have brought forth praise'?" **17** And leaving them, he went out of the city to Bethany, and there he spent the night.

The Cursing of the Fig Tree.[p] **18** When he was going back to the city in the morning, he was hungry. **19** Seeing a fig tree by the road, he went over to it, but found nothing on it except leaves. And he said to it, "May no fruit ever come from you again." And immediately the fig tree withered.

20 When the disciples saw this, they were amazed and said, "How was it that the fig tree withered immediately?" **21** [q]Jesus said to them in reply, "Amen, I say to you, if you have faith and do not waver, not only will you do what has been done to the fig tree, but even if you say to this mountain, 'Be lifted up and thrown into the sea,' it will be done. **22** Whatever you ask for in prayer with faith, you will receive."

The Authority of Jesus Questioned.[r] **23** When he had come into the temple area, the chief priests and the elders of the people approached him as he was teaching and said, "By what authority are you doing these things?[s] And who gave you this authority?" **24** Jesus said to them in reply, "I shall ask you one question,[t] and if you answer it for me, then I shall tell you by what authority I do these things. **25** Where was John's baptism from? Was it of heavenly or of human origin?" They discussed this among themselves and said, "If we say 'Of heavenly origin,' he will say to us, 'Then why did you not believe him?' **26** [u]But if we say, 'Of human origin,' we fear the crowd, for they all regard John as a prophet." **27** So they said to Jesus in reply, "We do not know." He himself said to them, "Neither shall I tell you by what authority I do these things.[v]

The Parable of the Two Sons.[w] **28** "What is your opinion? A man had two sons. He came to the first and said, 'Son, go out and work in the vineyard today.' **29** He said in reply, 'I will not,' but afterwards he changed his mind and went. **30** The man came to the other son and gave the same order. He said in reply, 'Yes, sir,' but did not go. **31** [x]Which of the two did his father's will?" They answered, "The first." Jesus said to them, "Amen, I say to you, tax collectors and prostitutes are entering the kingdom of God before you. **32** [y]When John came to you in the way of righteousness, you did not believe him; but tax collectors and prostitutes did. Yet even when you saw that, you did not later change your minds and believe him.

The Parable of the Tenants.[z] **33** "Hear another parable. There was a landowner who planted a vineyard,[aa] put a hedge around it, dug a wine press in it, and built a tower. Then he leased it to tenants and went on a journey. **34** When vintage time drew near, he sent his servants[ab] to the tenants to obtain his produce. **35** But the tenants seized the servants and one they beat, another they killed, and a third they stoned. **36** Again he sent other servants, more numerous than the first ones, but they treated them in the same way. **37** Finally, he sent his son to them, thinking, 'They will respect my son.' **38** [ac]But when the tenants saw the son, they said to one another, 'This is the heir. Come, let us kill him and acquire his inheritance.' **39** [ad]They seized him, threw him out of the vineyard, and killed him. **40** What will the owner of the vineyard do to those tenants when he comes?" **41** They answered[ae] him, "He will put those wretched men to a wretched death and lease his vineyard to other tenants who will give him the produce at the proper times." **42** [af]Jesus said to them, "Did you never read in the scriptures:

'The stone that the builders rejected
   has become the cornerstone;
by the Lord has this been done,
   and it is wonderful in our eyes'?

43 [ag]Therefore, I say to you, the kingdom of God will be taken away from you and given to a people that will produce its fruit. **44** [[ah] The one who falls on this stone will be dashed to pieces; and it will crush anyone on whom it falls.]" **45** When the chief priests and the Pharisees[ai] heard his parables, they knew that he was speaking about them. **46** And although they were attempting to arrest him, they feared the crowds, for they regarded him as a prophet.

Notes

a. **21:1–11** Jesus' coming to Jerusalem is in accordance with the divine will that he must go there (cf. Mt 16:21) to suffer, die, and be raised. He prepares for his entry into the city in such a way as to make it a fulfillment of the prophecy of Zec 9:9 (Mt 21:2) that emphasizes the humility of the **king** who **comes** (Mt 21:5). That prophecy, absent from the Marcan parallel account (Mk 11:1–11) although found also in the Johannine account of the entry (Jn 12:15), is the center of the Matthean story. During the procession from Bethphage to Jerusalem, Jesus is acclaimed as the Davidic messianic king by the crowds who accompany him (Mt 21:9). On his arrival the **whole city was shaken**, and to the inquiry of the amazed populace about Jesus' identity the crowds with him reply that he is **the prophet, from Nazareth in Galilee** (Mt 21:10, 11).

b. **21:1 Bethphage:** a village that can no longer be certainly identified. Mark mentions it before Bethany (Mk 11:1), which suggests that it lay to the east of the latter. **The Mount of Olives:** the hill east of Jerusalem that is spoken of in Zec 14:4 as the place where the Lord will come to rescue Jerusalem from the enemy nations.

c. **21:2 An ass tethered, and a colt with her:** instead of the one animal of Mk 11:2, Matthew has two, as demanded by his understanding of Zec 9:9.

d. **21:4–5 The prophet:** this fulfillment citation is actually composed of two distinct Old Testament texts, Is 62:11 (**Say to daughter Zion**) and Zec 9:9. The **ass** and the **colt** are the same animal in the prophecy, mentioned twice in different ways, the common Hebrew literary device of poetic parallelism. That Matthew takes them as two is one of the reasons why some scholars think that he was a Gentile rather than a Jewish Christian who would presumably not make that mistake (see Introduction).

e. **21:7 Upon them:** upon the two animals; an awkward picture resulting from Matthew's misunderstanding of the prophecy.

f. **21:8 Spread . . . on the road:** cf. 2 Kgs 9:13. There is a similarity between the cutting and strewing of the branches and the festivities of Tabernacles (Lv 23:39–40); see also 2 Mc 10:5–8 where the celebration of the rededication of the temple is compared to that of Tabernacles.

g. **21:9 Hosanna:** the Hebrew means "(O Lord) grant salvation"; see Ps 118:25, but that invocation had become an acclamation of jubilation and welcome. **Blessed is he . . . in the name of the Lord:** see Ps 118:26 and the note on Jn 12:13. **In the highest:** probably only an intensification of the acclamation, although **Hosanna in the highest** could be taken as a prayer, "May God save (him)."

h. **21:10 Was shaken:** in the gospels this verb is peculiar to Matthew where it is used also of the earthquake at the time of the crucifixion (Mt 27:51) and of the terror of the guards of Jesus' tomb at the appearance of the angel (Mt 28:4). For Matthew's use of the cognate noun, see note on Mt 8:24.

i. **21:11 The prophet:** see Mt 16:14 ("one of the prophets") and 21:46.

j. **21:12–17** Matthew changes the order of (Mk 11:11, 12, 15) and places the cleansing of the temple on the same day as the entry into Jerusalem, immediately after it. The activities going on in **the temple area** were not secular but connected with the temple worship. Thus Jesus' attack on those so engaged and his charge that they were **making** God's **house of prayer a den of thieves** (Mt 21:12–13) constituted a claim to authority over the religious practices of Israel and were a challenge to the priestly authorities. Mt 21:14–17 are peculiar to Matthew. Jesus' healings and his countenancing the children's cries of praise rouse the indignation of **the chief priests and the scribes** (Mt 21:15). These two groups appear in the infancy narrative (Mt 2:4) and have been mentioned in the first and third passion predictions (Mt 16:21; 20:18). Now, as the passion approaches, they come on the scene again, exhibiting their hostility to Jesus.

k. **21:12** These activities were carried on in the court of the Gentiles, the outermost court of **the temple area**. Animals for sacrifice were sold; the **doves** were for those who could not afford a more expensive offering; see Lv 5:7. **Tables of the money changers:** only the coinage of Tyre could be used for the purchases; other money had to be exchanged for that.

l. **21:13 'My house . . . prayer':** cf. Is 56:7. Matthew omits the final words of the quotation, "for all peoples" ("all nations"), possibly because for him the worship of the God of Israel by all nations belongs to the time after the resurrection; see Mt 28:19. **A den of thieves:** the phrase is taken from Jer 7:11.

m. **21:14 The blind and the lame:** according to 2 Sm 5:8 LXX **the blind and the lame** were forbidden to enter "the house of the Lord," the temple. These are the last of Jesus' healings in Matthew.

n. **21:15 The wondrous things:** the healings.

o. **21:16 'Out of the mouths . . . praise':** cf. Ps 8:3 LXX.

p. **21:18–22** In Mark the effect of Jesus' cursing the fig tree is not immediate; see Mk 11:14, 20. By making it so, Matthew has heightened the miracle. Jesus' act seems arbitrary and ill-tempered, but it is a prophetic action similar to those of Old Testament prophets that vividly symbolize some part of their preaching; see, e.g., Ez 12:1–20. It is a sign of the judgment that is to come upon the Israel that with all its apparent piety lacks the fruit of good deeds (Mt 3:10) and will soon bear the punishment of its fruitlessness (Mt 21:43). Some scholars propose that this story is the development in tradition of a parable of Jesus about the destiny of a fruitless tree, such as Lk 13:6–9. Jesus' answer to the question of the amazed disciples (Mt 21:20) makes the miracle an example of the power of prayer made with unwavering **faith** (Mt 21:21–22).

q. **21:21** See Mt 17:20.

r. **21:23–27** Cf. Mk 11:27–33. This is the first of five controversies between Jesus and the religious authorities of Judaism in Mt 21:23–22:46, presented in the form of questions and answers.

s. **21:23 These things:** probably his entry into the city, his cleansing of the temple, and his healings there.

t. **21:24** To reply by counterquestion was common in rabbinical debate.

u. **21:26 We fear . . . as a prophet:** cf. Mt 14:5.

v. **21:27** Since through embarrassment on the one hand and fear on the other the religious authorities claim ignorance of the origin of John's baptism, they show themselves incapable of speaking with authority; hence Jesus refuses to discuss with them the grounds of his authority.

w. **21:28–32** The series of controversies is interrupted by three parables on the judgment of Israel (Mt 21:28–22:14) of which this, peculiar to Matthew, is the first. The second (Mt 21:33–46) comes from Mark (12:1–12), and the third (Mt 22:1–14) from Q; see Lk 14:15–24. This interruption of the controversies is similar to that in Mark, although Mark has only one parable between the first and second controversy. As regards Matthew's first parable, Mt 21:28–30 if taken by themselves could point simply to the difference between saying and doing, a theme of much importance in this gospel (cf. Mt 7:21; 12:50); that may have been the parable's original reference. However, it is given a more specific application by the addition of Mt 21:31–32. The two sons represent, respectively, the religious leaders and the religious outcasts who followed John's call to repentance. By the answer they give to Jesus' question (Mt 21:31) the leaders condemn themselves. There is much confusion in the textual tradition of the parable. Of the three different forms of the text given by important textual witnesses, one has the leaders answer that the son who agreed to go but did not was the one who did the father's will. Although some scholars accept that as the original reading, their arguments in favor of it seem unconvincing. The choice probably lies only between a reading that puts the son who agrees and then disobeys before the son who at first refuses and then obeys, and the reading followed in the present translation. The witnesses to the latter reading are slightly better than those that support the other.

x. **21:31 Entering . . . before you:** this probably means "they enter; you do not."

y. **21:32** Cf. Lk 7:29–30. Although the thought is similar to that of the Lucan text, the formulation is so different that it is improbable that the saying comes from Q. **Came to you . . . way of righteousness:** several meanings are possible: that John himself was righteous, that he taught righteousness to others, or that he had an important place in God's plan of salvation. For the last, see note on Mt 3:14–15.

z. **21:33–46** Cf. Mk 12:1–12. In this parable there is a close correspondence between most of the details of the story and the situation that it illustrates, the dealings of God with his people. Because of that heavy allegorizing, some scholars think that it does not in any way go back to Jesus, but represents the theology of the later church. That judgment applies to the Marcan parallel as well, although the allegorizing has gone farther in Matthew. There are others who believe that while many of the allegorical elements are due to church sources, they have been added to a basic parable spoken by Jesus. This view is now supported by the Gospel of Thomas, 65, where a less allegorized and probably more primitive form of the parable is found.

aa. **21:33 Planted a vineyard . . . a tower:** cf. Is 5:1–2. The **vineyard** is defined in Is 5:7 as "the house of Israel."

ab. **21:34–35 His servants:** Matthew has two sendings of **servants** as against Mark's three sendings of a single servant (Mk 12:2–5a) followed by a statement about the sending of "many others" (Mk 12:2, 5b). That these servants stand for the prophets sent by God to Israel is clearly implied but not made explicit here, but see Mt 23:37. **His produce:** cf. Mk 12:2 "some of the produce." The **produce** is the good works demanded by God, and his claim to them is total.

ac. **21:38 Acquire his inheritance:** if a Jewish proselyte died without heir, the tenants of his land would have final claim on it.

ad. **21:39 Threw him out . . . and killed him:** the change in the Marcan order where the son is killed and his corpse then thrown out (Mk 12:8) was probably made because of the tradition that Jesus died outside the city of Jerusalem; see Jn 19:17; Hb 13:12.

ae. **21:41 They answered:** in Mk 12:9 the question is answered by Jesus himself; here the leaders answer and so condemn themselves; cf. Mt 21:31. Matthew adds that the new **tenants** to whom the vineyard will be transferred **will give** the owner the **produce at the proper times.**

af. **21:42** Cf. Ps 118:22–23. The psalm was used in the early church as a prophecy of Jesus' resurrection; see Acts 4:11; 1 Pt 2:7. If, as some think, the original parable ended at Mt 21:39 it was thought necessary to complete it by a reference to Jesus' vindication by God.

ag. **21:43** Peculiar to Matthew. **Kingdom of God:** see note on Mt 19:23–24. Its presence here instead of Matthew's usual "kingdom of heaven" may indicate that the saying came from Matthew's own traditional material. **A people that will produce its fruit:** believing Israelites and Gentiles, the church of Jesus.

ah. **21:44** The majority of textual witnesses omit this verse. It is probably an early addition to Matthew from Lk 20:18 with which it is practically identical.

ai. **21:45 The Pharisees:** Matthew inserts into the group of Jewish leaders (Mt 21:23) those who represented the Judaism of his own time.

Chapter 22

The Parable of the Wedding Feast.[a] **1** Jesus again in reply spoke to them in parables, saying, **2** "The kingdom of heaven may be likened to a king who gave a wedding feast[b] for his son. **3** [c]He dispatched his servants to summon the invited guests to the feast, but they refused to come. **4** A second time he sent other servants, saying, 'Tell those invited: "Behold, I have prepared my banquet, my calves and fattened cattle are killed, and everything is ready; come to the feast."' **5** Some ignored the invitation and went away, one to his farm, another to his business. **6** The rest laid hold of his servants, mistreated them, and killed them. **7** [d]The king was enraged and sent his troops, destroyed those murderers, and burned their city. **8** Then he said to his servants, 'The feast is ready, but those who were invited were not worthy to come. **9** Go out, therefore, into the main roads and invite to the feast whomever you find.' **10** The servants went out into the streets and gathered all they found, bad and good alike,[e] and the hall was filled with guests. **11** [f]But when the king came in to meet the guests he saw a man there not dressed in a wedding garment. **12** He said to him, 'My friend, how is it that you came in here without a wedding garment?' But he was reduced to silence. **13** [g]Then the king said to his attendants, 'Bind his hands and feet, and cast him into the darkness outside, where there will be wailing and grinding of teeth.' **14** Many are invited, but few are chosen."

Paying Taxes to the Emperor.[h] **15** Then the Pharisees[i] went off and plotted how they might entrap him in speech. **16** They sent their disciples to him, with the Herodians,[j] saying, "Teacher, we know that you are a truthful man and that you teach the way of God in accordance with the truth. And you are not concerned with anyone's opinion, for you do not regard a person's status. **17** [k]Tell us, then, what is your opinion: Is it lawful to pay the census tax to Caesar or not?" **18** Knowing their malice, Jesus said, "Why are you testing me, you hypocrites? **19** [l]Show me the coin that pays the census tax." Then they handed him the Roman coin. **20** He said to them, "Whose image is this and whose inscription?" **21** They replied, "Caesar's."[m] At that he said to them, "Then repay to Caesar what belongs to Caesar and to God what belongs to God." **22** When they heard this they were amazed, and leaving him they went away.

The Question About the Resurrection.[n] **23** On that day Sadducees approached him, saying that there is no resurrection.[o] They put this question to him, **24** saying, "Teacher, Moses said, 'If a man dies[p] without children, his brother shall marry his wife and raise up descendants for his brother.' **25** Now there were seven brothers among us. The first married and died and, having no descendants, left his wife to his brother. **26** The same happened with the second and the third, through all seven. **27** Finally the woman died. **28** Now at the resurrection, of the seven, whose wife will she be? For they all had been married to her." **29** ᵠJesus said to them in reply, "You are misled because you do not know the scriptures or the power of God. **30** At the resurrection they neither marry nor are given in marriage but are like the angels in heaven. **31** And concerning the resurrection of the dead, have you not read what was said to youʳ by God, **32** 'I am the God of Abraham, the God of Isaac, and the God of Jacob'? He is not the God of the dead but of the living." **33** When the crowds heard this, they were astonished at his teaching.

The Greatest Commandment.ˢ **34** When the Pharisees heard that he had silenced the Sadducees, they gathered together, **35** and one of them [a scholar of the law]ᵗ tested him by asking, **36** "Teacher,ᵘ which commandment in the law is the greatest?" **37** He said to him,ᵛ "You shall love the Lord, your God, with all your heart, with all your soul, and with all your mind. **38** This is the greatest and the first commandment. **39** The second is like it:ʷ You shall love your neighbor as yourself. **40** ˣThe whole law and the prophets depend on these two commandments."

The Question About David's Son.ʸ **41** While the Pharisees were gathered together, Jesus questioned them,ᶻ **42** ᵃᵃsaying, "What is your opinion about the Messiah? Whose son is he?" They replied, "David's." **43** He said to them, "How, then, does David, inspired by the Spirit, call him 'Lord,' saying:

44   'The Lord said to my Lord,
          "Sit at my right hand
          until I place your enemies under your feet"'?

45 ᵃᵇIf David calls him 'Lord,' how can he be his son?" **46** No one was able to answer him a word, nor from that day on did anyone dare to ask him any more questions.

Notes

a. **22:1–14** This parable is from Q; see Lk 14:15–24. It has been given many allegorical traits by Matthew, e.g., the burning of the **city** of the guests who refused the invitation (Mt 22:7), which corresponds to the destruction of Jerusalem by the Romans in A.D. 70. It has similarities with the preceding parable of the tenants: the sending of two groups of **servants** (Mt 22:3, 4), the murder of the **servants** (Mt 22:6), the punishment of the **murderers** (Mt 22:7), and the entrance of a new group into a privileged situation of which the others had proved themselves unworthy (Mt 22:8–10). The parable ends with a section that is peculiar to Matthew (Mt 22:11–14), which some take as a distinct parable. Matthew presents the **kingdom** in its double aspect, already present and something that can be entered here and now (Mt 22:1–10), and something that will be possessed only by those present members who can stand the scrutiny of the final judgment (Mt 22:11–14). The parable is not only a statement of God's judgment on Israel but a warning to Matthew's church.

b. **22:2 Wedding feast:** the Old Testament's portrayal of final salvation under the image of a banquet (Is 25:6) is taken up also in Mt 8:11; cf. Lk 13:15.

c. **22:3–4 Servants . . . other servants:** probably Christian missionaries in both instances; cf. Mt 23:34.

d. **22:7** See note on Mt 22:1–14.

e. **22:10 Bad and good alike:** cf. Mt 13:47.

f. **22:11 A wedding garment:** the repentance, change of heart and mind, that is the condition for entrance into the kingdom (Mt 3:2; 4:17) must be continued in a life of good deeds (Mt 7:21–23).

g. **22:13 Wailing and grinding of teeth:** the Christian who lacks the wedding garment of good deeds will suffer the same fate as those Jews who have rejected Jesus; see note on Mt 8:11–12.

h. **22:15–22** The series of controversies between Jesus and the representatives of Judaism (see note on Mt 21:23–27) is resumed. As in the first (Mt 21:23–27), here and in the following disputes Matthew follows his Marcan source with few modifications.

i. **22:15 The Pharisees:** while Matthew retains the Marcan union of Pharisees and Herodians in this account, he clearly emphasizes the Pharisees' part. They alone are mentioned here, and the Herodians are joined with them only in a prepositional phrase of Mt 22:16. **Entrap him in speech:** the question that they will pose is intended to force Jesus to take either a position contrary to that held by the majority of the people or one that will bring him into conflict with the Roman authorities.

j. **22:16 Herodians:** see note on Mk 3:6. They would favor payment of the tax; the Pharisees did not.

k. **22:17 Is it lawful:** the law to which they refer is the law of God.

l. 22:19 **They handed him the Roman coin:** their readiness in producing the money implies their use of it and their acceptance of the financial advantages of the Roman administration in Palestine.

m. **22:21 Caesar's:** the emperor Tiberius (A.D. 14–37). **Repay to Caesar what belongs to Caesar:** those who willingly use the coin that is Caesar's should **repay** him in kind. The answer avoids taking sides in the question of the lawfulness of the tax. **To God what belongs to God:** Jesus raises the debate to a new level. Those who have hypocritically asked about tax in respect to its relation to the law of **God** should be concerned rather with repaying God with the good deeds that are his due; cf. Mt 21:41, 43.

n. **22:23–33** Here Jesus' opponents are the **Sadducees**, members of the powerful priestly party of his time; see note on Mt 3:7. Denying the resurrection of the dead, a teaching of relatively late origin in Judaism (cf. Dn 12:2), they appeal to a law of the Pentateuch (Dt 25:5–10) and present a case based on it that would make resurrection from the dead ridiculous (Mt 22:24–28). Jesus chides them for knowing neither the **scriptures** nor **the power of God** (Mt 22:29). His argument in respect to God's power contradicts the notion, held even by many proponents as well as by opponents of the teaching, that the life of those raised from the dead would be essentially a continuation of the type of life they had had before death (Mt 22:30). His argument based on the scriptures (Mt 22:31–32) is of a sort that was accepted as valid among Jews of the time.

o. **22:23 Saying that there is no resurrection:** in the Marcan parallel (Mk 22:12, 18) the Sadducees are correctly defined as those "who say there is no resurrection"; see also Lk 20:27. Matthew's rewording of Mark can mean that these particular Sadducees deny the resurrection, which would imply that he was not aware that the denial was characteristic of the party. For some scholars this is an indication of his being a Gentile Christian; see note on Mt 21:4–5.

p. **22:24 'If a man dies . . . his brother':** this is known as the "law of the levirate," from the Latin *levir*, "brother-in-law." Its purpose was to continue the family line of the deceased brother (Dt 25:6).

q. **22:29** The sexual relationships of this world will be transcended; the risen body will be the work of the creative **power of God.**

r. **22:31–32** Cf. Ex 3:6. In the Pentateuch, which the Sadducees accepted as normative for Jewish belief and practice, God speaks even now (**to you**) of himself as the God of the patriarchs who died centuries ago. He identifies himself in relation to them, and because of their relation to him, the living God, they too are alive. This might appear no argument for the resurrection, but simply for life after death as conceived in Wis 3:1–3. But the general thought of early first-century Judaism was not influenced by that conception; for it human immortality was connected with the existence of the body.

s. **22:34–40** The Marcan parallel (Mk 12:28–34) is an exchange between Jesus and a scribe who is impressed by the way in which Jesus has conducted himself in the previous controversy (Mk 12:28), who compliments him for the answer he gives him (Mk 12:32), and who is said by Jesus to be "not far from the kingdom of God" (Mk 12:34). Matthew has sharpened that scene. The questioner, as the representative of other Pharisees, tests Jesus by his question (Mt 22:34–35), and both his reaction to Jesus' reply and Jesus' commendation of him are lacking.

t. **22:35 [A scholar of the law]:** meaning "scribe." Although this reading is supported by the vast majority of textual witnesses, it is the only time that the Greek word so translated occurs in Matthew. It is relatively frequent in Luke, and there is reason to think that it may have been added here by a copyist since it occurs in the Lucan parallel (Lk 10:25–28). **Tested:** see note on Mt 19:3.

u. **22:36** For the devout Jew all the commandments were to be kept with equal care, but there is evidence of preoccupation in Jewish sources with the question put to Jesus.

v. **22:37–38** Cf. Dt 6:5. Matthew omits the first part of Mark's fuller quotation (Mk 12:29; Dt 6:4–5), probably because he considered its monotheistic emphasis needless for his church. The love of God must engage the total person (**heart, soul, mind**).

w. **22:39** Jesus goes beyond the extent of the question put to him and joins **to the greatest and the first commandment a second**, that of **love** of **neighbor**, Lv

19:18; see note on Mt 19:18–19. This combination of the two commandments may already have been made in Judaism.

x. **22:40** The double commandment is the source from which **the whole law and the prophets** are derived.

y. **22:41–46** Having answered the questions of his opponents in the preceding three controversies, Jesus now puts a question to them about the sonship of the Messiah. Their easy response (Mt 22:43a) is countered by his quoting a verse of Ps 110 that raises a problem for their response (43b–45). They are unable to solve it and **from that day on** their questioning of him is ended.

z. **22:41 The Pharisees . . . questioned them:** Mark is not specific about who are questioned (Mk 12:35).

aa. **22:42–44 David's:** this view of the Pharisees was based on such Old Testament texts as Is 11:1–9; Jer 23:5; and Ez 34:23; see also the extrabiblical Psalms of Solomon 17:21. **How, then . . . saying:** Jesus cites Ps 110:1 accepting the Davidic authorship of the psalm, a common view of his time. The psalm was probably composed for the enthronement of a Davidic king of Judah. Matthew assumes that the Pharisees interpret it as referring to the Messiah, although there is no clear evidence that it was so interpreted in the Judaism of Jesus' time. It was widely used in the early church as referring to the exaltation of the risen Jesus. **My Lord:** understood as the Messiah.

ab. **22:45** Since Matthew presents Jesus both as Messiah (Mt 16:16) and as Son of David (Mt 1:1; see also note on Mt 9:27), the question is not meant to imply Jesus' denial of Davidic sonship. It probably means that although he is the Son of David, he is someone greater, Son of Man and Son of God, and recognized as greater by David who calls him my '**Lord.**'

Chapter 23[a]

Denunciation of the Scribes and Pharisees. 1 Then Jesus spoke to the crowds and to his disciples, **2** [b]saying, "The scribes and the Pharisees have taken their seat on the chair of Moses. **3** Therefore, do and observe all things whatsoever they tell you, but do not follow their example. For they preach but they do not practice. **4** They tie up heavy burdens[c] [hard to carry] and lay them on people's shoulders, but they will not lift a finger to move them. **5** [d]All their works are performed to be seen. They widen their phylacteries and lengthen their tassels. **6** [e]They love places of honor at banquets, seats of honor in synagogues, **7** greetings in marketplaces, and the salutation 'Rabbi.' **8** [f]As for you, do not be called 'Rabbi.' You have but one teacher, and you are all brothers. **9** Call no one on earth your father; you have but one Father in heaven. **10** Do not be called 'Master'; you have but one master, the Messiah. **11** The greatest among you must be your servant. **12** Whoever exalts himself will be humbled; but whoever humbles himself will be exalted.

13 [g]"Woe to you, scribes and Pharisees, you hypocrites. You lock the kingdom of heaven[h] before human beings. You do not enter yourselves, nor do you allow entrance to those trying to enter. [**14**][i]

15 [j]"Woe to you, scribes and Pharisees, you hypocrites. You traverse sea and land to make one convert, and when that happens you make him a child of Gehenna twice as much as yourselves.

16 [k]"Woe to you, blind guides, who say, 'If one swears by the temple, it means nothing, but if one swears by the gold of the temple, one is obligated.' **17** Blind fools, which is greater, the gold, or the temple that made the gold sacred? **18** And you say, 'If one swears by the altar, it means nothing, but if one swears by the gift on the altar, one is obligated.' **19** You blind ones, which is greater, the gift, or the altar that makes the gift sacred? **20** One who swears by the altar swears by it and all that is upon it; **21** one who swears by the temple swears by it and by him who dwells in it; **22** one who swears by heaven swears by the throne of God and by him who is seated on it.

23 "Woe to you, scribes and Pharisees, you hypocrites. You pay tithes[l] of mint and dill and cummin, and have neglected the weightier things of the law: judgment and mercy and fidelity. [But] these you should have done, without neglecting the others. **24** [m]Blind guides, who strain out the gnat and swallow the camel!

25 [n]"Woe to you, scribes and Pharisees, you hypocrites. You cleanse the outside of cup and dish, but inside they are full of plunder and self-indulgence. **26** Blind Pharisee, cleanse first the inside of the cup, so that the outside also may be clean.

27 [o]"Woe to you, scribes and Pharisees, you hypocrites. You are like whitewashed tombs, which appear beautiful on the outside, but inside are full of dead men's bones and every kind of filth. **28** Even so, on the outside you appear righteous, but inside you are filled with hypocrisy and evildoing.

29 [p]"Woe to you, scribes and Pharisees,[q] you hypocrites. You build the tombs of the prophets and adorn the memorials of the righteous, **30** and you say, 'If we had lived in the days of our ancestors, we would not have joined them in shedding the prophets' blood.' **31** Thus you bear witness against yourselves that you are the children of those who murdered the prophets; **32** now fill up what your ancestors measured out! **33** You serpents, you brood of vipers, how can you flee from the judgment of Gehenna? **34** [r]Therefore, behold, I send to you prophets and wise men and scribes; some of them you will kill and crucify, some of them you will scourge in your synagogues and pursue from town to town, **35** so that there may come upon you all the righteous blood shed upon earth, from the righteous blood of Abel to the blood of Zechariah, the son of Barachiah, whom you murdered between the sanctuary and the altar. **36** Amen, I say to you, all these things will come upon this generation.

The Lament over Jerusalem.[s] **37** "Jerusalem, Jerusalem, you who kill the prophets and stone those sent to you, how many times I yearned to gather your children together, as a hen gathers her young under her wings, but you were unwilling! **38** Behold, your house will be abandoned, desolate. **39** I tell you, you will not see me again until you say, 'Blessed is he who comes in the name of the Lord.'"

Notes

a. **23:1–39** The final section of the narrative part of the fifth book of the gospel is a denunciation by Jesus of the scribes and the Pharisees (see note on Mt 3:7). It depends in part on Mark and Q (cf. Mk 12:38–39; Lk 11:37–52; 13:34–35), but in the main it is peculiar to Matthew. (For the reasons against considering this extensive body of sayings-material either as one of the structural discourses of this gospel or as part of the one that follows in Mt 24–25, see note on Mt 19:1–23:39.) While the tradition of a deep opposition between Jesus and the Pharisees is well founded, this speech reflects an opposition that goes beyond that of Jesus' ministry and must be seen as expressing the bitter conflict between Pharisaic Judaism and the church of Matthew at the time when the gospel was composed. The complaint often made that the speech ignores the positive qualities of Pharisaism and of its better representatives is true, but the complaint overlooks the circumstances that gave rise to the invective. Nor is the speech purely anti-Pharisaic. The evangelist discerns in his church many of the same faults that he finds in its opponents and warns his fellow Christians to look to their own conduct and attitudes.

b. **23:2–3 Have taken their seat . . . Moses:** it is uncertain whether this is simply a metaphor for Mosaic teaching authority or refers to an actual **chair** on which the teacher sat. It has been proved that there was a seat so designated in synagogues of a later period than that of this gospel. **Do and observe . . . they tell**

you: since the Matthean Jesus abrogates Mosaic law (Mt 5:31–42), warns his disciples against the teaching of the Pharisees (Mt 14:1–12), and, in this speech, denounces the Pharisees as blind guides in respect to their teaching on oaths (Mt 23:16–22), this commandment **to observe all things whatsoever they** (the scribes and Pharisees) **tell you** cannot be taken as the evangelist's understanding of the proper standard of conduct for his church. The saying may reflect a period when the Matthean community was largely Jewish Christian and was still seeking to avoid a complete break with the synagogue. Matthew has incorporated this traditional material into the speech in accordance with his view of the course of salvation history, in which he portrays the time of Jesus' ministry as marked by the fidelity to the law, although with significant pointers to the new situation that would exist after his death and resurrection (see note on Mt 5:17–20). The crowds and the disciples (Mt 23:1) are exhorted not to **follow** the **example** of the Jewish leaders, whose deeds do not conform to their teaching (Mt 23:3).

c. **23:4 Tie up heavy burdens:** see note on Mt 11:28.

d. **23:5** To the charge of preaching but not practicing (Mt 23:3), Jesus adds that of acting in order to earn praise. The disciples have already been warned against this same fault (see note on Mt 6:1–18). **Phylacteries:** the Mosaic law required that during prayer small boxes containing parchments on which verses of scripture were written be worn on the left forearm and the forehead (see Ex 13:9, 16; Dt 6:8; 11:18). **Tassels:** see note on Mt 9:20. The widening of **phylacteries** and the lengthening of **tassels** were for the purpose of making these evidences of piety more noticeable.

e. **23:6–7** Cf. Mk 12:38–39. '**Rabbi**': literally, "my great one," a title of respect for teachers and leaders.

f. **23:8–12** These verses, warning against the use of various titles, are addressed to the disciples alone. While only the title '**Rabbi**' has been said to be used in addressing the scribes and Pharisees (Mt 23:7), the implication is that **Father** and '**Master**' also were. The prohibition of these titles to the disciples suggests that their use was present in Matthew's church. The Matthean Jesus forbids not only the titles but the spirit of superiority and pride that is shown by their acceptance. **Whoever exalts . . . will be exalted:** cf. Lk 14:11.

g. **23:13–36** This series of seven "woes," directed against the **scribes and Pharisees** and addressed to them, is the heart of the speech. The phrase woe to occurs often in the prophetic and apocalyptic literature, expressing horror of a sin and punishment for those who commit it. **Hypocrites:** see note on Mt 6:2. The hypocrisy of the **scribes and Pharisees** consists in the difference between their speech and action (Mt 23:3) and in demonstrations of piety that have no other purpose than to enhance their reputation as religious persons (Mt 23:5).

h. **23:13 You lock the kingdom of heaven:** cf. Mt 16:19 where Jesus tells Peter that he will give him the keys to **the kingdom of heaven**. The purpose of the authority expressed by that metaphor is to give entrance into the kingdom (the kingdom is closed only to those who reject the authority); here the charge is made that the authority of the **scribes and Pharisees** is exercised in such a way as to be an obstacle to entrance. Cf. Lk 11:52 where the accusation against the "scholars of the law" (Matthew's **scribes**) is that they "have taken away the key of knowledge."

i. **23:14** Some manuscripts add a verse here or after Mt 23:12, "Woe to you, scribes and Pharisees, you hypocrites. You devour the houses of widows and, as a pretext, recite lengthy prayers. Because of this, you will receive a very severe condemnation." Cf. Mk 12:40; Lk 20:47. This "woe" is almost identical with Mk 12:40 and seems to be an interpolation derived from that text.

j. **23:15** In the first century A.D. until the First Jewish Revolt against Rome (A.D. 66–70), many Pharisees conducted a vigorous missionary campaign among Gentiles. **Convert:** literally, "proselyte," a Gentile who accepted Judaism fully by submitting to circumcision and all other requirements of Mosaic law. **Child of Gehenna:** worthy of everlasting punishment; for **Gehenna**, see note on Mt 5:22. **Twice as much as yourselves:** possibly this refers simply to the zeal of the **convert**, surpassing that of the one who converted him.

k. **23:16–22** An attack on the casuistry that declared some oaths binding (**one is obligated**) and others not (**it means nothing**) and held the binding oath to be the one made by something of lesser value (**the gold; the gift on the altar**). Such teaching, which inverts the order of values, reveals the teachers to be **blind guides**; cf. Mt 15:14. Since the Matthean Jesus forbids all oaths to his disciples (Mt 5:33–37), this woe does not set up a standard for Christian moral conduct, but ridicules the Pharisees on their own terms.

l. **23:23** The Mosaic law ordered tithing of the produce of the land (Lv 27:30; Dt 14:22–23), and the scribal tradition is said here to have extended this law to even the smallest herbs. The practice is criticized not in itself but because it shows the Pharisees' preoccupation with matters of less importance while they neglect **the weightier things of the law**.

m. **23:24** Cf. Lv 11:41–45 that forbids the eating of any "swarming creature." The Pharisees' scrupulosity about minor matters and neglect of greater ones (Mt 23:23) is further brought out by this contrast between straining liquids that might contain a tiny "swarming creature" and yet swallowing **the camel**. The latter was one of the unclean animals forbidden by the law (Lv 11:4), but it is hardly possible that the scribes and Pharisees are being denounced as guilty of so gross a violation of the food laws. To **swallow the camel** is only a hyperbolic way of speaking of their neglect of what is important.

n. **23:25–26** The ritual washing of utensils for dining (cf. Mk 7:4) is turned into a metaphor illustrating a concern for appearances while inner purity is ignored. The **scribes and Pharisees** are compared to cups carefully washed on the outside but filthy within. **Self-indulgence:** the Greek word here translated means lack of self-control, whether in drinking or in sexual conduct.

o. **23:27–28** The sixth **woe**, like the preceding one, deals with concern for externals and neglect of what is **inside**. Since contact with dead bodies, even when one was unaware of it, caused ritual impurity (Nm 19:11–22), tombs were whitewashed so that no one would contract such impurity inadvertently.

p. **23:29–36** The final **woe** is the most serious indictment of all. It portrays the **scribes and Pharisees** as standing in the same line as their **ancestors** who murdered **the prophets** and **the righteous**.

q. **23:29–32** In spite of honoring the slain dead by building their **tombs** and adorning their **memorials**, and claiming that they would not have joined in their ancestors' crimes if they **had lived in** their **days**, the **scribes and Pharisees** are true children of their ancestors and are defiantly ordered by Jesus to **fill up** what those **ancestors measured out**. This order reflects the Jewish notion that there was an allotted measure of suffering that had to be completed before God's final judgment would take place.

r. **23:34–36** There are important differences between the Matthean and the Lucan form of this Q material; cf. Lk 11:49–51. In Luke the one who sends the emissaries is the "wisdom of God." If, as many scholars think, that is the original wording of Q, Matthew, by making Jesus the sender, has presented him as the personified divine wisdom. In Luke, wisdom's emissaries are the Old Testament "prophets" and the Christian "apostles." Matthew's **prophets and wise men and scribes** are probably Christian disciples alone; cf. Mt 10:41 and see note on Mt 13:52. **You will kill:** see Mt 24:9. **Scourge in your synagogues . . . town to town:** see Mt 10:17, 23 and the note on Mt 10:17. **All the righteous blood shed upon the earth:** the slaying of the disciples is in continuity with all the shedding of **righteous blood** beginning with that of **Abel**. The persecution of Jesus' disciples by **this generation** involves the persecutors in the guilt of their murderous ancestors. **The blood of Zechariah:** see note on Lk 11:51. By identifying him as **the son of Barachiah** Matthew understands him to be Zechariah the Old Testament minor prophet; see Zec 1:1.

s. **23:37–39** Cf. Lk 13:34–35. The denunciation of Pharisaic Judaism ends with this lament over **Jerusalem**, which has repeatedly rejected and murdered those whom God has **sent** to her. **How many times:** this may refer to various visits of Jesus to the city, an aspect of his ministry found in John but otherwise not in the synoptics. **As a hen . . . under her wings:** for imagery similar to this, see Ps 17:8; 91:4. **Your house . . . desolate:** probably an allusion to the destruction of the temple in A.D. 70. **You will not see me . . . in the name of the Lord:** Israel will not see Jesus again until he comes in glory for the final judgment. The acclamation has been interpreted in contrasting ways, as an indication that Israel will at last accept Jesus at that time, and as its troubled recognition of him as its dreaded judge who will pronounce its condemnation; in support of the latter view see Mt 24:30.

Chapter 24

The Destruction of the Temple Foretold. 1 ªJesus left the temple area and was going away, when his disciples approached him to point out the temple buildings. **2** ᵇHe said to them in reply, "You see all these things, do you not? Amen, I say to you, there will not be left here a stone upon another stone that will not be thrown down."

The Beginning of Calamities. 3 As he was sitting on the Mount of Olives,ᶜ the disciples approached him privately and said, "Tell us, when will this happen, and what sign will there be of your coming, and of the end of the age?" **4** ᵈJesus said to them in reply, "See that no one deceives you. **5** For many will come in my name, saying, 'I am the Messiah,' and they will deceive many. **6** You will hear of warsᵉ and reports of wars; see that you are not alarmed, for these things must happen, but it will not yet be the end. **7** Nation will rise against nation, and kingdom against kingdom; there will be famines and earthquakes from place to place. **8** ᶠAll these are the beginning of the labor pains. **9** ᵍThen they will hand you over to persecution, and they will kill you. You will be hated by all nations because of my name. **10** And then many will be led into sin; they will betray and hate one another. **11** Many false prophets will arise and deceive many; **12** and because of the increase of evildoing, the love of many will grow cold. **13** But the one who perseveres to the end will be saved. **14** And this gospel of the kingdom will be preached throughout the world as a witness to all nations,[h] and then the end will come.

The Great Tribulation.ⁱ 15 "When you see the desolating abominationʲ spoken of through Daniel the prophet standing in the holy place (let the reader understand), **16** then those in Judea must fleeᵏ to the mountains, **17** ˡa person on the housetop must not go down to get things out of his house, **18** a person in the field must not return to get his cloak. **19** Woe to pregnant women and nursing mothers in those days. **20** ᵐPray that your flight not be in winter or on the sabbath, **21** ⁿfor at that time there will be great tribulation, such as has not been since the beginning of the world until now, nor ever will be. **22** And if those days had not been shortened, no one would be saved; but for the sake of the elect they will be shortened. **23** If anyone says to you then, 'Look, here is the Messiah!' or, 'There he is!' do not believe it. **24** False messiahs and false prophets will arise, and they will perform signs and wonders so great as to deceive, if that were possible, even the elect. **25** Behold, I have told it to you beforehand. **26** So if they say to you, 'He is in the desert,' do not go out there; if they say, 'He is in the inner rooms,' do not believe it.º **27** For just as lightning comes from the east and is seen as far as the west, so will the coming of the Son of Man be. **28** Wherever the corpse is, there the vultures will gather.

The Coming of the Son of Man. **29** [p]"Immediately after the tribulation of those days,

the sun will be darkened,
  and the moon will not give its light,
and the stars will fall from the sky,
  and the powers of the heavens will be shaken.

30 And then the sign of the Son of Man[q] will appear in heaven, and all the
tribes of the earth will mourn, and they will see the Son of Man coming
upon the clouds of heaven with power and great glory. **31** And he will
send out his angels[r] with a trumpet blast, and they will gather his elect
from the four winds, from one end of the heavens to the other.

The Lesson of the Fig Tree.[s] **32** "Learn a lesson from the fig tree. When
its branch becomes tender and sprouts leaves, you know that summer is
near. **33** In the same way, when you see all these things, know that he is
near, at the gates. **34** Amen, I say to you, this generation[t] will not pass
away until all these things have taken place. **35** Heaven and earth will
pass away, but my words will not pass away.

The Unknown Day and Hour.[u] **36** "But of that day and hour no one
knows, neither the angels of heaven, nor the Son,[v] but the Father alone. **37**
[w]For as it was in the days of Noah, so it will be at the coming of the Son of
Man. **38** In [those] days before the flood, they were eating and drinking,
marrying and giving in marriage, up to the day that Noah entered the ark.
39 They did not know until the flood came and carried them all away. So
will it be [also] at the coming of the Son of Man. **40** [x]Two men will be out
in the field; one will be taken, and one will be left. **41** Two women will be
grinding at the mill; one will be taken, and one will be left. **42** [y]Therefore,
stay awake! For you do not know on which day your Lord will come. **43**
Be sure of this: if the master of the house had known the hour of night
when the thief was coming, he would have stayed awake and not let his
house be broken into. **44** So too, you also must be prepared, for at an hour
you do not expect, the Son of Man will come.

The Faithful or the Unfaithful Servant.[z] **45** "Who, then, is the faithful
and prudent servant, whom the master has put in charge of his household
to distribute to them their food at the proper time?[aa] **46** Blessed is that
servant whom his master on his arrival finds doing so. **47** Amen, I say to
you, he will put him in charge of all his property. **48** [ab]But if that wicked
servant says to himself, 'My master is long delayed,' **49** and begins to beat
his fellow servants, and eat and drink with drunkards, **50** the servant's
master will come on an unexpected day and at an unknown hour **51** and
will punish him severely[ac] and assign him a place with the hypocrites,
where there will be wailing and grinding of teeth.

Notes

a. **24:1–25:46** The discourse of the fifth book, the last of the five around which the gospel is structured. It is called the "eschatological" discourse since it deals with the coming of the new age (the *eschaton*) in its fullness, with events that will precede it, and with how the disciples are to conduct themselves while awaiting an event that is as certain as its exact time is unknown to all but the Father (Mt 24:36). The discourse may be divided into two parts, Mt 24:1–44 and Mt 24:45–25:46. In the first, Matthew follows his Marcan source (Mk 13:1–37) closely. The second is drawn from Q and from the evangelist's own traditional material. Both parts show Matthew's editing of his sources by deletions, additions, and modifications. The vigilant waiting that is emphasized in the second part does not mean a cessation of ordinary activity and concentration only on what is to come, but a faithful accomplishment of duties at hand, with awareness that the end, for which the disciples must always be ready, will entail the great judgment by which the everlasting destiny of all will be determined.

b. **24:2** As in Mark, Jesus predicts the destruction of the temple. By omitting the Marcan story of the widow's contribution (Mk 12:41–44) that immediately precedes the prediction in that gospel, Matthew has established a close connection between it and Mt 23:38, " . . . your house will be abandoned desolate."

c. **24:3 The Mount of Olives:** see note on Mt 21:1. **The disciples:** cf. Mk 13:3–4 where only Peter, James, John, and Andrew put the question that is answered by the discourse. In both gospels, however, the question is put **privately**: the ensuing discourse is only for those who are **disciples** of Jesus. **When will this happen . . . end of the age?:** Matthew distinguishes carefully between the destruction of the temple (**this**) and the **coming** of Jesus that will bring **the end of the age.** In Mark the two events are more closely connected, a fact that may be explained by Mark's believing that the one would immediately succeed the other. **Coming:** this translates the Greek word *parousia*, which is used in the gospels only here and in Mt 24:27, 37, 39. It designated the official visit of a ruler to a city or the manifestation of a saving deity, and it was used by Christians to refer to the final coming of Jesus in glory, a term first found in the New Testament with that meaning in 1 Thes 2:19. **The end of the age:** see note on Mt 13:39.

d. **24:4–14** This section of the discourse deals with calamities in the world (Mt 24:6–7) and in the church (Mt 24:9–12). The former **must happen** before **the end** comes (Mt 24:6), but they are only the **beginning of the labor pains** (Mt 24:8). (It may be noted that the Greek word translated **the end** in Mt 24:6 and in Mt 24:13–14 is not the same as the phrase "the end of the age" in Mt 24:3, although the meaning is the same.) The latter are sufferings of the church, both from within and without, that will last **until the gospel is preached . . . to all nations. Then the end will come** and those who have endured the sufferings with fidelity **will be saved** (Mt 24:13–14).

e. **24:6–7** The disturbances mentioned here are a commonplace of apocalyptic language, as is the assurance that they **must happen** (see Dn 2:28 LXX), for that is the plan of God. **Kingdom against kingdom:** see Is 19:2.

f. **24:8 The labor pains:** the tribulations leading up to the end of the age are compared to the pains of a woman about to give birth. There is much attestation for rabbinic use of the phrase "the woes (or birth pains) of the Messiah" after the New Testament period, but in at least one instance it is attributed to a rabbi who lived in the late first century A.D. In this Jewish usage it meant the distress of the time preceding the coming of the Messiah; here, the **labor pains** precede the coming of the Son of Man in glory.

g. **24:9–12** Matthew has used Mk 13:9–12 in his missionary discourse (Mt 10:17–21) and omits it here. Besides the sufferings, including death, and the hatred of **all nations** that the disciples will have to endure, there will be worse affliction within the church itself. This is described in Mt 24:10–12, which are peculiar to Matthew. **Will be led into sin:** literally, "will be scandalized," probably meaning that they will become apostates; see Mt 13:21 where "fall away" translates the same Greek word as here. **Betray:** in the Greek this is the same word as the **hand over** of Mt 24:9. The handing over to persecution and hatred from outside will have their counterpart within the church. **False prophets:** these are Christians; see note on Mt 7:15–20. **Evildoing:** see Mt 7:23. Because of the apocalyptic nature of much of this discourse, the literal meaning of this description of the church should not be pressed too hard. However, there is reason to think that Matthew's addition of these verses reflects in some measure the condition of his community.

h. **24:14** Except for the last part (**and then the end will come**), this verse substantially repeats Mk 13:10. The Matthean addition raises a problem since what follows in Mt 24:15–23 refers to the horrors of the First Jewish Revolt including the destruction of the temple, and Matthew, writing after that time, knew that the parousia of Jesus was still in the future. A solution may be that the evangelist saw the events of those verses as foreshadowing the cosmic disturbances that he associates with the parousia (Mt 24:29) so that the period in which the former took place could be understood as belonging to **the end**.

i. **24:15–28** Cf. Mk 13:14–23; Lk 17:23–24, 37. A further stage in the tribulations that will precede the coming of the Son of Man, and an answer to the question of Mt 24:3a, "when will this (the destruction of the temple) happen?"

j. **24:15 The desolating abomination:** in 167 B.C. the Syrian king Antiochus IV Epiphanes desecrated the temple by setting up in it a statue of Zeus Olympios (see 1 Mc 1:54). That event is referred to in Dn 12:11 LXX as the "desolating abomination" (NAB "horrible abomination") and the same Greek term is used here; cf. also Dn 9:27; 11:31. Although the desecration had taken place before Daniel was written, it is presented there as a future event, and Matthew sees that "prophecy" fulfilled in the desecration of the temple by the Romans. **In the holy place:** the temple; more precise than Mark's **where he should not** (Mk 13:14). **Let the reader understand:** this parenthetical remark, taken from Mk 13:14 invites **the reader** to realize the meaning of Daniel's "prophecy."

k. **24:16** The tradition that the Christians of Jerusalem fled from that city to Pella, a city of Transjordan, at the time of the First Jewish Revolt is found in Eusebius (*Ecclesiastical History*, 3:5:3), who attributes the flight to "a certain oracle given by revelation before the war." The tradition is not improbable but the

Matthean command, derived from its Marcan source, is vague in respect to the place of flight (**to the mountains**), although some scholars see it as applicable to the flight to Pella.

l. **24:17–19** Haste is essential, and the journey will be particularly difficult for women who are burdened with unborn or infant children.

m. **24:20 On the sabbath:** this addition to **in winter** (cf. Mk 13:18) has been understood as an indication that Matthew was addressed to a church still observing the Mosaic law of sabbath rest and the scribal limitations upon the length of journeys that might lawfully be made on that day. That interpretation conflicts with Matthew's view on sabbath observance (cf. Mt 12:1–14). The meaning of the addition may be that those undertaking on the sabbath a journey such as the one here ordered would be offending the sensibilities of law-observant Jews and would incur their hostility.

n. **24:21** For the unparalleled distress of that time, see Dn 12:1.

o. **24:26–28** Claims that the Messiah is to be found in some distant or secret place must be ignored. **The coming of the Son of Man** will be as clear as **lightning** is to all and as **the corpse** of an animal is to **vultures**; cf. Lk 17:24, 37. Here there is clear identification of the **Son of Man** and the Messiah; cf. Mt 24:23.

p. **24:29** The answer to the question of Mt 24:3b, "What will be the sign of your coming?" **Immediately after . . . those days:** the shortening of time between the preceding **tribulation** and the parousia has been explained as Matthew's use of a supposed device of Old Testament prophecy whereby certainty that a predicted event will occur is expressed by depicting it as imminent. While it is questionable that that is an acceptable understanding of the Old Testament predictions, it may be applicable here, for Matthew knew that the parousia had not come **immediately after** the fall of Jerusalem, and it is unlikely that he is attributing a mistaken calculation of time to Jesus. **The sun . . . be shaken:** cf. Is 13:10, 13.

q. **24:30 The sign of the Son of Man:** perhaps this means **the sign** that is the glorious appearance **of the Son of Man**; cf. Mt 12:39–40 where "the sign of Jonah" is Jonah's being in the "belly of the whale." **Tribes of the earth will mourn:** peculiar to Matthew; cf. Zec 12:12–14. **Coming upon the clouds . . . glory:** cf. Dn 7:13, although there the "one like a son of man" comes to God to receive kingship; here the **Son of Man** comes from heaven for judgment.

r. **24:31 Send out his angels:** cf. Mt 13:41 where they are sent out to collect the wicked for punishment. **Trumpet blast:** cf. Is 27:13; 1 Thes 4:16.

s. **24:32–35** Cf. Mk 13:28–31.

t. **24:34** The difficulty raised by this verse cannot be satisfactorily removed by the supposition that **this generation** means the Jewish people throughout the course of their history, much less the entire human race. Perhaps for Matthew it means the **generation** to which he and his community belonged.

u. **24:36–44** The statement of Mt 24:34 is now counterbalanced by one that declares that the exact time of the parousia is known only **to the Father** (Mt 24:36), and the disciples are warned to be always ready for it. This section is drawn from Mark and Q (cf. Lk 17:26–27, 34–35; 12:39–40).

v. **24:36** Many textual witnesses omit **nor the Son**, which follows Mk 13:32. Since its omission can be explained by reluctance to attribute this ignorance to **the Son**, the reading that includes it is probably original.

w. **24:37–39** Cf. Lk 17:26–27. **In the days of Noah:** the Old Testament account of the flood lays no emphasis upon what is central for Matthew, i.e., the unexpected coming of the flood upon those who were unprepared for it.

x. **24:40–41** Cf. Lk 17:34–35. **Taken . . . left:** the former probably means **taken** into the kingdom; the latter, **left** for destruction. People in the same situation will be dealt with in opposite ways. In this context, the discrimination between them will be based on their readiness for the coming of the Son of Man.

y. **24:42–44** Cf. Lk 12:39–40. The theme of vigilance and readiness is continued with the bold comparison of the Son of Man to a thief who comes to break into a house.

z. **24:45–51** The second part of the discourse (see note on Mt 24:1–25:46) begins with this parable of **the faithful** or unfaithful **servant**; cf. Lk 12:41–46. It is addressed to the leaders of Matthew's church; **the servant has** been **put in charge** of his master's **household** (Mt 24:45) even though that household is composed of those who are his **fellow servants** (Mt 24:49).

aa. **24:45 To distribute . . . proper time:** readiness for the master's return means a vigilance that is accompanied by faithful performance of the duty assigned.

ab. **24:48 My master . . . delayed:** the note of delay is found also in the other parables of this section; cf. Mt 25:5, 19.

ac. **24:51 Punish him severely:** the Greek verb, found in the New Testament only here and in the Lucan parallel (Lk 12:46), means, literally, "cut in two." **With the hypocrites:** see note on Mt 6:2. Matthew classes the unfaithful Christian leader with the unbelieving leaders of Judaism. **Wailing and grinding of teeth:** see note on Mt 8:11–12.

Chapter 25

The Parable of the Ten Virgins.[a] **1** "Then[b] the kingdom of heaven will be like ten virgins who took their lamps and went out to meet the bridegroom. **2** [c]Five of them were foolish and five were wise. **3** The foolish ones, when taking their lamps, brought no oil with them, **4** but the wise brought flasks of oil with their lamps. **5** Since the bridegroom was long delayed, they all became drowsy and fell asleep. **6** At midnight, there was a cry, 'Behold, the bridegroom! Come out to meet him!' **7** Then all those virgins got up and trimmed their lamps. **8** The foolish ones said to the wise, 'Give us some of your oil, for our lamps are going out.' **9** But the wise ones replied, 'No, for there may not be enough for us and you. Go instead to the merchants and buy some for yourselves.' **10** While they went off to buy it, the bridegroom came and those who were ready went into the wedding feast with him. Then the door was locked. **11** [d]Afterwards the other virgins came and said, 'Lord, Lord, open the door for us!' **12** But he said in reply, 'Amen, I say to you, I do not know you.' **13** Therefore, stay awake,[e] for you know neither the day nor the hour.

The Parable of the Talents.[f] **14** "It will be as when a man who was going on a journey[g] called in his servants and entrusted his possessions to them. **15** To one he gave five talents;[h] to another, two; to a third, one—to each according to his ability. Then he went away. Immediately **16** the one who received five talents went and traded with them, and made another five. **17** Likewise, the one who received two made another two. **18** [i]But the man who received one went off and dug a hole in the ground and buried his master's money. **19** After a long time the master of those servants came back and settled accounts with them. **20** The one who had received five talents came forward bringing the additional five.[j] He said, 'Master, you gave me five talents. See, I have made five more.' **21** His master said to him, 'Well done, my good and faithful servant. Since you were faithful in small matters, I will give you great responsibilities. Come, share your master's joy.' **22** [Then] the one who had received two talents also came forward and said, 'Master, you gave me two talents. See, I have made two more.' **23** His master said to him, 'Well done, my good and faithful servant. Since you were faithful in small matters, I will give you great responsibilities. Come, share your master's joy.' **24** Then the one who had received the one talent came forward and said, 'Master, I knew you were a demanding person, harvesting where you did not plant and gathering where you did not scatter; **25** so out of fear I went off and buried your talent in the ground. Here it is back.' **26** His master said to him in reply, 'You wicked, lazy servant![k] So you knew that I harvest where I did not plant and gather where I did not scatter? **27** Should you not then have put my money in the bank so that I could have got it back with interest on my return? **28** Now then! Take the talent from him and give it to the one with ten. **29** ^lFor to everyone who has, more will be given and he will grow rich; but from the one who has not, even what he has will be taken away. **30** ^mAnd throw this useless servant into the darkness outside, where there will be wailing and grinding of teeth.'

The Judgment of the Nations.[n] **31** "When the Son of Man comes in his glory, and all the angels with him, he will sit upon his glorious throne, **32** and all the nations[o] will be assembled before him. And he will separate them one from another, as a shepherd separates the sheep from the goats. **33** He will place the sheep on his right and the goats on his left. **34** Then the king will say to those on his right, 'Come, you who are blessed by my Father. Inherit the kingdom prepared for you from the foundation of the world. **35** For I was hungry and you gave me food, I was thirsty and you gave me drink, a stranger and you welcomed me, **36** naked and you clothed me, ill and you cared for me, in prison and you visited me.' **37** Then the righteous[p] will answer him and say, 'Lord, when did we see you hungry and feed you, or thirsty and give you drink? **38** When did we see you a stranger and welcome you, or naked and clothe you? **39** When did we see you ill or in prison, and visit you?' **40** And the king will say to them in reply, 'Amen, I say to you, whatever you did for one of these least brothers of mine, you did for me.' **41** ^qThen he will say to those on his left, 'Depart from me, you accursed, into the eternal fire prepared for the devil and his angels. **42** For I was hungry and you gave me no food, I was thirsty and you gave me no drink, **43** a stranger and you gave me no welcome, naked and you gave me no clothing, ill and in prison, and you did not care for me.' **44** ^rThen they will answer and say, 'Lord, when did we see you hungry or thirsty or a stranger or naked or ill or in prison, and not minister to your needs?' **45** He will answer them, 'Amen, I say to you, what you did not do for one of these least ones, you did not do for me.' **46** And these will go off to eternal punishment, but the righteous to eternal life."

Notes

a. **25:1–13** Peculiar to Matthew.

b. **25:1 Then:** at the time of the parousia. **Kingdom . . . will be like:** see note on Mt 13:24–30.

c. **25:2–4 Foolish . . . wise:** cf. the contrasted "wise man" and "fool" of Mt 7:24, 26 where the two are distinguished by good deeds and lack of them, and such deeds may be signified by the oil of this parable.

d. **25:11–12 Lord, Lord:** cf. Mt 7:21. **I do not know you:** cf. Mt 7:23 where the Greek verb is different but synonymous.

e. **25:13 Stay awake:** some scholars see this command as an addition to the original parable of Matthew's traditional material, since in Mt 25:5 all the virgins, wise and foolish, fall asleep. But the wise virgins are adequately equipped for their task, and stay awake may mean no more than to be prepared; cf. Mt 24:42, 44.

f. **25:14–30** Cf. Lk 19:12–27.

g. **25:14 It will be as when . . . journey:** literally, "For just as a man who was going on a journey." Although the comparison is not completed, the sense is clear; the kingdom of heaven is like the situation here described. Faithful use of one's gifts will lead to participation in the fullness of the kingdom, lazy inactivity to exclusion from it.

h. **25:15 Talents:** see note on Mt 18:24.

i. **25:18 Buried his master's money:** see note on Mt 13:44.

j. **25:20–23** Although the first two servants have received and doubled large sums, their faithful trading is regarded by the master as fidelity **in small matters** only, compared with **the great responsibilities** now to be given to them. The latter are unspecified. **Share your master's joy:** probably the joy of the banquet of the kingdom; cf. Mt 8:11.

k. **25:26–28 Wicked, lazy servant:** this man's inactivity is not negligible but seriously culpable. As punishment, he loses the gift he had received, that is now given to the first servant, whose possessions are already great.

l. **25:29** See note on Mt 13:12 where there is a similar application of this maxim.

m. **25:30** See note on Mt 8:11–12.

n. **25:31–46** The conclusion of the discourse, which is peculiar to Matthew, portrays the final judgment that will accompany the parousia. Although often called a "parable," it is not really such, for the only parabolic elements are the depiction of **the Son of Man** as a **shepherd** and of **the righteous** and the wicked as **sheep** and **goats**, respectively (Mt 25:32–33). The criterion of judgment will be the deeds of mercy that have been done for the **least** of Jesus' **brothers** (Mt 25:40). A difficult and important question is the identification of these **least brothers**. Are they all people who have suffered hunger, thirst, etc. (Mt 25:35, 36) or a particular group of such sufferers? Scholars are divided in their response and arguments can be made for either side. But leaving aside the problem of what the traditional material that Matthew edited may have meant, it seems that a stronger case can be made for the view that in the evangelist's sense the sufferers are Christians, probably Christian missionaries whose sufferings were brought upon them by their preaching of the gospel. The criterion of judgment for **all the nations** is their treatment of those who have borne to the world the message of Jesus, and this means ultimately their acceptance or rejection of Jesus himself; cf. Mt 10:40, "Whoever receives you, receives me." See note on Mt 16:27.

o. **25:32 All the nations:** before the end the gospel will have been preached throughout the world (Mt 24:14); thus the Gentiles will be judged on their response to it. But the phrase **all the nations** includes the Jews also, for at the judgment "the Son of Man . . . will repay everyone according to his conduct" (Mt 16:27).

p. 25:37–40 The **righteous** will be astonished that in caring for the needs of the sufferers they were ministering to the **Lord** himself. **One of these least brothers of mine:** cf. Mt 10:42.

q. **25:41 Fire prepared . . . his angels:** cf. 1 Enoch 10:13 where it is said of the evil angels and Semyaza, their leader, "In those days they will lead them into the bottom of the fire—and in torment—in the prison (where) they will be locked up forever."

r. **25:44–45 The accursed** (Mt 25:41) will be likewise astonished that their neglect of the sufferers was neglect of the **Lord** and will receive from him a similar answer.

VII. The Passion and Resurrection

Chapter 26

The Conspiracy Against Jesus. 1 [a]When Jesus finished all these words,[b] he said to his disciples, **2** "You know that in two days' time it will be Passover, and the Son of Man will be handed over to be crucified." **3** [c]Then the chief priests and the elders of the people assembled in the palace of the high priest, who was called Caiaphas, **4** and they consulted together to arrest Jesus by treachery and put him to death. **5** But they said, "Not during the festival,[d] that there may not be a riot among the people."

The Anointing at Bethany.[e] **6** Now when Jesus was in Bethany in the house of Simon the leper, **7** a woman came up to him with an alabaster jar of costly perfumed oil, and poured it on his head while he was reclining at table. **8** When the disciples saw this, they were indignant and said, "Why this waste? **9** It could have been sold for much, and the money given to the poor." **10** Since Jesus knew this, he said to them, "Why do you make trouble for the woman? She has done a good thing for me. **11** The poor you will always have with you; but you will not always have me. **12** [f]In pouring this perfumed oil upon my body, she did it to prepare me for burial. **13** Amen, I say to you, wherever this gospel is proclaimed in the whole world, what she has done will be spoken of, in memory of her."

The Betrayal by Judas. 14 Then one of the Twelve, who was called Judas Iscariot,[g] went to the chief priests **15** [h]and said, "What are you willing to give me if I hand him over to you?" They paid him thirty pieces of silver, **16** and from that time on he looked for an opportunity to hand him over.

Preparations for the Passover. 17 On the first day of the Feast of Unleavened Bread,[i] the disciples approached Jesus and said, "Where do you want us to prepare for you to eat the Passover?" **18** [j]He said, "Go into the city to a certain man and tell him, 'The teacher says, "My appointed time draws near; in your house I shall celebrate the Passover with my disciples."'" **19** The disciples then did as Jesus had ordered, and prepared the Passover.

The Betrayer. 20 When it was evening, he reclined at table with the Twelve. **21** And while they were eating, he said, "Amen, I say to you, one of you will betray me."[k] **22** Deeply distressed at this, they began to say to him one after another, "Surely it is not I, Lord?" **23** He said in reply, "He who has dipped his hand into the dish with me is the one who will betray me. **24** [l]The Son of Man indeed goes, as it is written of him, but woe to that man by whom the Son of Man is betrayed. It would be better for that man if he had never been born." **25** [m]Then Judas, his betrayer, said in reply, "Surely it is not I, Rabbi?" He answered, "You have said so."

The Lord's Supper. 26 [n]While they were eating, Jesus took bread, said the blessing, broke it, and giving it to his disciples said, "Take and eat; this is my body."[o] **27** Then he took a cup, gave thanks,[p] and gave it to them, saying, "Drink from it, all of you, **28** for this is my blood of the covenant, which will be shed on behalf of many for the forgiveness of sins. **29** [q]I tell you, from now on I shall not drink this fruit of the vine until the day when I drink it with you new in the kingdom of my Father." **30** [r]Then, after singing a hymn, they went out to the Mount of Olives.

Peter's Denial Foretold. 31 Then Jesus said to them, "This night all of you will have your faith in me shaken,[s] for it is written:

'I will strike the shepherd,
and the sheep of the flock will be dispersed';

32 but after I have been raised up, I shall go before you to Galilee." **33** Peter said to him in reply, "Though all may have their faith in you shaken, mine will never be." **34** [t]Jesus said to him, "Amen, I say to you, this very night before the cock crows, you will deny me three times." **35** Peter said to him, "Even though I should have to die with you, I will not deny you." And all the disciples spoke likewise.

The Agony in the Garden. 36 [u]Then Jesus came with them to a place called Gethsemane,[v] and he said to his disciples, "Sit here while I go over there and pray." **37** He took along Peter and the two sons of Zebedee,[w] and began to feel sorrow and distress. **38** Then he said to them, "My soul is sorrowful even to death.[x] Remain here and keep watch with me." **39** He advanced a little and fell prostrate in prayer, saying, "My Father,[y] if it is possible, let this cup pass from me; yet, not as I will, but as you will." **40** When he returned to his disciples he found them asleep. He said to Peter, "So you could not keep watch with me for one hour? **41** Watch and pray that you may not undergo the test.[z] The spirit is willing, but the flesh is weak." **42** [aa]Withdrawing a second time, he prayed again, "My Father, if it is not possible that this cup pass without my drinking it, your will be done!" **43** Then he returned once more and found them asleep, for they could not keep their eyes open. **44** He left them and withdrew again and prayed a third time, saying the same thing again. **45** Then he returned to his disciples and said to them, "Are you still sleeping and taking your rest? Behold, the hour is at hand when the Son of Man is to be handed over to sinners. **46** Get up, let us go. Look, my betrayer is at hand."

The Betrayal and Arrest of Jesus. 47 While he was still speaking, Judas, one of the Twelve, arrived, accompanied by a large crowd, with swords and clubs, who had come from the chief priests and the elders of the people. **48** His betrayer had arranged a sign with them, saying, "The man I shall kiss is the one; arrest him." **49** Immediately he went over to Jesus and said, "Hail, Rabbi!"[ab] and he kissed him. **50** Jesus answered him, "Friend, do what you have come for." Then stepping forward they laid hands on Jesus and arrested him. **51** And behold, one of those who accompanied Jesus put his hand to his sword, drew it, and struck the high priest's servant, cutting off his ear. **52** Then Jesus said to him, "Put your sword back into its sheath, for all who take the sword will perish by the sword. **53** Do you think that I cannot call upon my Father and he will not provide me at this moment with more than twelve legions of angels? **54** But then how would the scriptures be fulfilled which say that it must come to pass in this way?" **55** [ac]At that hour Jesus said to the crowds, "Have you come out as against a robber, with swords and clubs to seize me? Day after day I sat teaching in the temple area, yet you did not arrest me. **56** But all this has come to pass that the writings of the prophets may be fulfilled." Then all the disciples left him and fled.

Jesus Before the Sanhedrin.[ad] **57** Those who had arrested Jesus led him away to Caiaphas[ae] the high priest, where the scribes and the elders were assembled. **58** Peter was following him at a distance as far as the high priest's courtyard, and going inside he sat down with the servants to see the outcome. **59** The chief priests and the entire Sanhedrin[af] kept trying to obtain false testimony against Jesus in order to put him to death, **60** but they found none, though many false witnesses came forward. Finally two[ag] came forward **61** who stated, "This man said, 'I can destroy the temple of God and within three days rebuild it.'" **62** The high priest rose and addressed him, "Have you no answer? What are these men testifying against you?" **63** But Jesus was silent.[ah] Then the high priest said to him, "I order you to tell us under oath before the living God whether you are the Messiah, the Son of God." **64** Jesus said to him in reply, "You have said so.[ai] But I tell you:

> From now on you will see 'the Son of Man
>> seated at the right hand of the Power'
>> and 'coming on the clouds of heaven.'"

65 Then the high priest tore his robes and said, "He has blasphemed![aj] What further need have we of witnesses? You have now heard the blasphemy; **66** what is your opinion?" They said in reply, "He deserves to die!" **67** [ak]Then they spat in his face and struck him, while some slapped him, **68** saying, "Prophesy for us, Messiah: who is it that struck you?"

Peter's Denial of Jesus. 69 Now Peter was sitting outside in the courtyard. One of the maids came over to him and said, "You too were with Jesus the Galilean." **70** [al]But he denied it in front of everyone, saying, "I do not know what you are talking about!" **71** As he went out to the gate, another girl saw him and said to those who were there, "This man was with Jesus the Nazorean." **72** Again he denied it with an oath, "I do not know the man!" **73** [am]A little later the bystanders came over and said to Peter, "Surely you too are one of them; even your speech gives you away." **74** At that he began to curse and to swear, "I do not know the man." And immediately a cock crowed. **75** Then Peter remembered the word that

Jesus had spoken: "Before the cock crows you will deny me three times."
He went out and began to weep bitterly.

Notes

a. **26:1–28:20** The five books with alternating narrative and discourse (Mt 3:1–25:46) that give this gospel its distinctive structure lead up to the climactic events that are the center of Christian belief and the origin of the Christian church, the passion and resurrection of Jesus. In his passion narrative (Mt 26 and 27) Matthew follows his Marcan source closely but with omissions (e.g., Mk 14:51–52) and additions (e.g., Mt 27:3–10, 19). Some of the additions indicate that he utilized traditions that he had received from elsewhere; others are due to his own theological insight (e.g., Mt 26:28 " . . . for the forgiveness of sins"; Mt 27:52). In his editing Matthew also altered Mark in some minor details. But there is no need to suppose that he knew any passion narrative other than Mark's.

b. **26:1–2 When Jesus finished all these words:** see note on Mt 7:28–29. **"You know . . . crucified":** Matthew turns Mark's statement of the time (Mk 14:1) into Jesus' final prediction of his passion. **Passover:** see note on Mk 14:1.

c. **26:3** Caiaphas was high priest from A.D. 18 to 36.

d. **26:5 Not during the festival:** the plan to delay Jesus' arrest and execution until after **the festival** was not carried out, for according to the synoptics he was arrested on the night of Nisan 14 and put to death the following day. No reason is given why the plan was changed.

e. **26:6–13** See notes on Mk 14:3–9 and Jn 12:1–8.

f. **26:12 To prepare me for burial:** cf. Mk 14:8. In accordance with the interpretation of this act as Jesus' **burial** anointing, Matthew, more consistent than Mark, changes the purpose of the visit of the women to Jesus' tomb; they do not go to anoint him (Mk 16:1) but "to see the tomb" (Mt 28:1).

g. **26:14 Iscariot:** see note on Lk 6:16.

h. **26:15** The motive of avarice is introduced by Judas's question about the price for betrayal, which is absent in the Marcan source (Mk 14:10–11). **Hand him over:** the same Greek verb is used to express the saving purpose of God by which Jesus is handed over to death (cf. Mt 17:22; 20:18; 26:2) and the human malice that hands him over. **Thirty pieces of silver:** the price of the betrayal is found only in Matthew. It is derived from Zec 11:12 where it is the wages paid to the rejected shepherd, a cheap price (Zec 11:13). That amount is also the compensation paid to one whose slave has been gored by an ox (Ex 21:32).

i. **26:17 The first day of the Feast of Unleavened Bread:** see note on Mk 14:1. Matthew omits Mark's "when they sacrificed the Passover lamb."

j. **26:18** By omitting much of Mk 14:13–15, adding **My appointed time draws near**, and turning the question into a statement, **in your house I shall celebrate the Passover**, Matthew has given this passage a solemnity and majesty greater than that of his source.

k. **26:21** Given Matthew's interest in the fulfillment of the Old Testament, it is curious that he omits the Marcan designation of Jesus' betrayer as "one who is eating with me" (Mk 14:18), since that is probably an allusion to Ps 41:10. However, the shocking fact that the betrayer is one who shares table fellowship with Jesus is emphasized in Mt 26:23.

l. **26:24 It would be better . . . born:** the enormity of the deed is such that it would be better not to exist than to do it.

m. 26:25 Peculiar to Matthew. **You have said so:** cf. Mt 26:64; 27:11. This is a half-affirmative. Emphasis is laid on the pronoun and the answer implies that the statement would not have been made if the question had not been asked.

n. **26:26–29** See note on Mk 14:22–24. The Marcan-Matthean is one of the two major New Testament traditions of the words of Jesus when instituting the Eucharist. The other (and earlier) is the Pauline-Lucan (1 Cor 11:23–25; Lk 22:19–20). Each shows the influence of Christian liturgical usage, but the Marcan-Matthean is more developed in that regard than the Pauline-Lucan. The words over the bread and cup succeed each other without the intervening meal mentioned in 1 Cor 11:25; Lk 22:20; and there is parallelism between the consecratory words (**this is my body . . . this is my blood**). Matthew follows Mark closely but with some changes.

o. **26:26** See note on Mt 14:19. **Said the blessing:** a prayer blessing God. **Take and eat:** literally, **Take, eat. Eat** is an addition to Mark's "take it" (literally, "take"; Mk 14:22). **This is my body:** the bread is identified with Jesus himself.

p. **26:27–28 Gave thanks:** see note on Mt 15:36. **Gave it to them . . . all of you:** cf. Mk 14:23–24. In the Marcan sequence the disciples drink and then Jesus says the interpretative words. Matthew has changed this into a command to **drink** followed by those words. **My blood:** see Lv 17:11 for the concept that the **blood** is "the seat of life" and that when placed on the altar it "makes atonement." **Which will be shed:** the present participle, "being shed" or "going to be shed," is future in relation to the Last Supper. **On behalf of:** Greek *peri*; see note on Mk 14:24. **Many:** see note on Mt 20:28. **For the forgiveness of sins:** a Matthean addition. The same phrase occurs in Mk 1:4 in connection with John's baptism but Matthew avoids it there (Mt 3:11). He places it here probably because he wishes to emphasize that it is the sacrificial death of Jesus that brings **forgiveness of sins.**

q. **26:29** Although his death will interrupt the table fellowship he has had with the disciples, Jesus confidently predicts his vindication by God and a new table fellowship with them at the banquet of the kingdom.

r. **26:30** See note on Mk 14:26.

s. **26:31 Will have . . . shaken:** literally, "will be scandalized in me"; see note on Mt 24:9–12. **I will strike . . . dispersed:** cf. Zec 13:7.

t. **26:34 Before the cock crows:** see note on Mt 14:25. The third watch of the night was called "cockcrow." **Deny me:** see note on Mt 16:24.

u. **26:36–56** Cf. Mk 14:32–52. The account of Jesus in Gethsemane is divided between that of his agony (Mt 26:36–46) and that of his betrayal and arrest (Mt

26:47–56). Jesus' **sorrow and distress** (Mt 26:37) in face of death is unrelieved by the presence of his three disciples who, though urged to **watch with** him (Mt 26:38, 41), fall asleep (Mt 26:40, 43). He prays that **if . . . possible** his death may be avoided (Mt 26:39) but that his Father's will be done (Mt 26:39, 42, 44). Knowing then that his death must take place, he announces to his companions that **the hour** for his being **handed over** has come (Mt 26:45). Judas arrives with an armed band provided by the Sanhedrin and greets Jesus with a kiss, the prearranged sign for his identification (Mt 26:47–49). After his arrest, he rebukes a disciple who has attacked the **high priest's servant** with a **sword** (Mt 26:51–54), and chides those who have come out to seize him with **swords and clubs** as if he were a **robber** (Mt 26:55–56). In both rebukes Jesus declares that the treatment he is now receiving is the fulfillment of the scriptures (Mt 26:55, 56). The subsequent flight of **all the disciples** is itself the fulfillment of his own prediction (cf. 31). In this episode, Matthew follows Mark with a few alterations.

v. **26:36 Gethsemane:** the Hebrew name means "oil press" and designates an olive orchard on the western slope of the Mount of Olives; see note on Mt 21:1. The name appears only in Matthew and Mark. The place is called a "garden" in Jn 18:1.

w. **26:37 Peter and the two sons of Zebedee:** cf. Mt 17:1.

x. **26:38** Cf. Ps 42:6, 12. In the Septuagint (Ps 41:5, 12) the same Greek word for **sorrowful** is used as here. **To death:** i.e., "enough to die"; cf. Jon 4:9.

y. **26:39 My Father:** see note on Mk 14:36. Matthew omits the Aramaic *'abbā'* and adds the qualifier **my**. **This cup:** see note on Mk 10:38–40.

z. **26:41 Undergo the test:** see note on Mt 6:13. In that verse "the final test" translates the same Greek word as is here translated **the test**, and these are the only instances of the use of that word in Matthew. It is possible that the passion of Jesus is seen here as an anticipation of the great tribulation that will precede the parousia (see notes on Mt 24:8; 24:21) to which Mt 6:13 refers, and that just as Jesus prays to be delivered from death (Mt 26:39), so he exhorts the disciples to pray that they will not have to **undergo** the great **test** that his passion would be for them. Some scholars, however, understand **not undergo** (literally, "not enter") **the test** as meaning not that the disciples may be spared **the test** but that they may not yield to the temptation of falling away from Jesus because of his passion even though they will have to endure it.

aa. **26:42 Your will be done:** cf. Mt 6:10.

ab. **26:49 Rabbi:** see note on Mt 23:6–7. Jesus is so addressed twice in Matthew (Mt 26:25), both times by Judas. For the significance of the closely related address "teacher" in Matthew, see note on Mt 8:19.

ac. **26:55 Day after day . . . arrest me:** cf. Mk 14:49. This suggests that Jesus had taught for a relatively long period in Jerusalem, whereas Mt 21:1–11 puts his coming to the city for the first time only a few days before.

ad. **26:57–68** Following Mk 14:53–65 Matthew presents the nighttime appearance of Jesus before the **Sanhedrin** as a real trial. After **many false witnesses** bring charges against him that do not suffice for the death sentence (Mt 26:60), **two came forward** who charge him with claiming to be able to **destroy the temple . . . and within three days** to rebuild it (Mt 26:60–61). Jesus makes no answer even when challenged to do so by **the high priest,** who then orders him to declare **under oath . . . whether** he is the **Messiah, the Son of God** (Mt 26:62–63). Matthew changes Mark's clear affirmative response (Mk 14:62) to the same one as that given to Judas (Mt 26:25), but follows Mark almost verbatim in Jesus' predicting that his judges will see him **(the Son of Man) seated at the right hand of God and coming on the clouds of heaven** (Mt 26:64). **The high priest** then charges him with blasphemy (Mt 26:65), a charge with which the other members of **the Sanhedrin** agree by declaring that **he deserves to die** (Mt 26:66). They then attack him (Mt 26:67) and mockingly demand that he **prophesy** (Mt 26:68). This account contains elements that are contrary to the judicial procedures prescribed in the Mishnah, the Jewish code of law that dates in written form from ca. A.D. 200, e.g., trial on a feast day, a night session of the court, pronouncement of a verdict of condemnation at the same session at which testimony was received. Consequently, some scholars regard the account entirely as a creation of the early Christians without historical value. However, it is disputable whether the norms found in the Mishnah were in force at the time of Jesus. More to the point is the question whether the Matthean-Marcan night trial derives from a combination of two separate incidents, a nighttime preliminary investigation (cf. Jn 18:13, 19–24) and a formal trial on the following morning (cf. Lk 22:66–71).

ae. **26:57 Caiaphas:** see note on Mt 26:3.

af. **26:59 Sanhedrin:** see note on Lk 22:66.

ag. **26:60–61 Two:** cf. Dt 19:15. **I can destroy . . . rebuild it:** there are significant differences from the Marcan parallel (Mk 14:58). Matthew omits "made with hands" and "not made with hands" and changes Mark's "will destroy" and "will build another" to **can destroy** and (can) **rebuild.** The charge is probably based on Jesus' prediction of the temple's destruction; see notes on Mt 23:37–39; 24:2; and Jn 2:19. A similar prediction by Jeremiah was considered as deserving death; cf. Jer 7:1–15; 26:1–8.

ah. **26:63 Silent:** possibly an allusion to Is 53:7. **I order you . . . living God:** peculiar to Matthew; cf. Mk 14:61.

ai. **26:64 You have said so:** see note on Mt 26:25. **From now on . . . heaven:** the Son of Man who is to be crucified (cf. Mt 20:19) will be seen in glorious majesty (cf. Ps 110:1) and **coming on the clouds of heaven** (cf. Dn 7:13). **The Power:** see note on Mk 14:61–62.

aj. **26:65 Blasphemed:** the punishment for **blasphemy** was death by stoning (see Lv 24:10–16). According to the Mishnah, to be guilty of blasphemy one had to pronounce "the Name itself," i.e., Yahweh; cf. **Sanhedrin** 7:4, 5. Those who judge the gospel accounts of Jesus' trial by the later Mishnah standards point out that Jesus uses the surrogate "the Power," and hence no Jewish court would have regarded him as guilty of blasphemy; others hold that the Mishnah's narrow understanding of blasphemy was a later development.

ak. **26:67–68** The physical abuse, apparently done to Jesus by the members of the Sanhedrin themselves, recalls the sufferings of the Isaian Servant of the Lord; cf. Is 50:6. The mocking challenge to **prophesy** is probably motivated by Jesus' prediction of his future glory (Mt 26:64).

al. **26:70 Denied it in front of everyone:** see Mt 10:33. Peter's repentance (Mt 26:75) saves him from the fearful destiny of which Jesus speaks there.

am. **26:73 Your speech . . . away:** Matthew explicates Mark's "you too are a Galilean" (Mk 14:70).

Chapter 27

Jesus Before Pilate. 1 [a]When it was morning, all the chief priests and the elders of the people took counsel[b] against Jesus to put him to death. **2** They bound him, led him away, and handed him over to Pilate, the governor.

The Death of Judas. 3 Then Judas, his betrayer, seeing that Jesus had been condemned, deeply regretted what he had done. He returned the thirty pieces of silver[c] to the chief priests and elders, **4** saying, "I have sinned in betraying innocent blood." They said, "What is that to us? Look to it yourself." **5** [d]Flinging the money into the temple, he departed and went off and hanged himself. **6** The chief priests gathered up the money, but said, "It is not lawful to deposit this in the temple treasury, for it is the price of blood." **7** After consultation, they used it to buy the potter's field as a burial place for foreigners. **8** That is why that field even today is called the Field of Blood. **9** Then was fulfilled what had been said through Jeremiah the prophet,[e] "And they took the thirty pieces of silver, the value of a man with a price on his head, a price set by some of the Israelites, **10** and they paid it out for the potter's field just as the Lord had commanded me."

Jesus Questioned by Pilate. 11 Now Jesus stood before the governor, and he questioned him, "Are you the king of the Jews?"[f] Jesus said, "You say so." **12** And when he was accused by the chief priests and elders,[g] he made no answer. **13** Then Pilate said to him, "Do you not hear how many things they are testifying against you?" **14** But he did not answer him one word, so that the governor was greatly amazed.

The Sentence of Death. 15 [h]Now on the occasion of the feast the governor was accustomed to release to the crowd one prisoner whom they wished. **16** [i]And at that time they had a notorious prisoner called [Jesus] Barabbas. **17** So when they had assembled, Pilate said to them, "Which one do you want me to release to you, [Jesus] Barabbas, or Jesus called Messiah?" **18** [j]For he knew that it was out of envy that they had handed him over. **19** [k]While he was still seated on the bench, his wife sent him a message, "Have nothing to do with that righteous man. I suffered much in a dream today because of him." **20** The chief priests and the elders persuaded the crowds to ask for Barabbas but to destroy Jesus. **21** The governor said to them in reply, "Which of the two do you want me to release to you?" They answered, "Barabbas!" **22** [l]Pilate said to them, "Then what shall I do with Jesus called Messiah?" They all said, "Let him be crucified!" **23** But he said, "Why? What evil has he done?" They only shouted the louder, "Let him be crucified!" **24** [m]When Pilate saw that he was not succeeding at all, but that a riot was breaking out instead, he took water and washed his hands in the sight of the crowd, saying, "I am innocent of this man's blood. Look to it yourselves." **25** And the whole people said in reply, "His blood be upon us and upon our children." **26** Then he released

Barabbas to them, but after he had Jesus scourged,[n] he handed him over to be crucified.

Mockery by the Soldiers. 27 Then the soldiers of the governor took Jesus inside the praetorium[o] and gathered the whole cohort around him. **28** They stripped off his clothes and threw a scarlet military cloak[p] about him. **29** Weaving a crown out of thorns,[q] they placed it on his head, and a reed in his right hand. And kneeling before him, they mocked him, saying, "Hail, King of the Jews!" **30** They spat upon him[r] and took the reed and kept striking him on the head. **31** And when they had mocked him, they stripped him of the cloak, dressed him in his own clothes, and led him off to crucify him.

The Way of the Cross.[s] **32** As they were going out, they met a Cyrenian named Simon; this man they pressed into service to carry his cross.

The Crucifixion. 33 And when they came to a place called Golgotha (which means Place of the Skull), **34** they gave Jesus wine to drink mixed with gall.[t] But when he had tasted it, he refused to drink. **35** After they had crucified him, they divided his garments[u] by casting lots; **36** then they sat down and kept watch over him there. **37** And they placed over his head the written charge[v] against him: This is Jesus, the King of the Jews. **38** Two revolutionaries[w] were crucified with him, one on his right and the other on his left. **39** [x]Those passing by reviled him, shaking their heads **40** and saying, "You who would destroy the temple and rebuild it in three days, save yourself, if you are the Son of God, [and] come down from the cross!" **41** Likewise the chief priests with the scribes and elders mocked him and said, **42** "He saved others; he cannot save himself. So he is the king of Israel![y] Let him come down from the cross now, and we will believe in him. **43** [z]He trusted in God; let him deliver him now if he wants him. For he said, 'I am the Son of God.'" **44** The revolutionaries who were crucified with him also kept abusing him in the same way.

The Death of Jesus. 45 [aa]From noon onward, darkness came over the whole land until three in the afternoon. **46** And about three o'clock Jesus cried out in a loud voice, "Eli, Eli, lema sabachthani?"[ab] which means, "My God, my God, why have you forsaken me?" **47** [ac]Some of the bystanders who heard it said, "This one is calling for Elijah." **48** Immediately one of them ran to get a sponge; he soaked it in wine, and putting it on a reed, gave it to him to drink. **49** But the rest said, "Wait, let us see if Elijah comes to save him." **50** [ad]But Jesus cried out again in a loud voice, and gave up his spirit. **51** And behold, the veil of the sanctuary was torn in two from top to bottom.[ae] The earth quaked, rocks were split, **52** tombs were opened, and the bodies of many saints who had fallen asleep were raised. **53** And coming forth from their tombs after his resurrection, they entered the holy city and appeared to many. **54** [af]The centurion and the men with him who were keeping watch over Jesus feared greatly when they saw the earthquake and all that was happening, and they said, "Truly, this was the Son of God!" **55** There were many women there, looking on from a distance,[ag] who had followed Jesus from Galilee, ministering to him. **56** Among them were Mary Magdalene and Mary the mother of James and Joseph, and the mother of the sons of Zebedee.

The Burial of Jesus.[ah] **57** When it was evening, there came a rich man from Arimathea named Joseph, who was himself a disciple of Jesus. **58** He went to Pilate and asked for the body of Jesus; then Pilate ordered it to be handed over. **59** Taking the body, Joseph wrapped it [in] clean linen **60** and laid it in his new tomb that he had hewn in the rock. Then he rolled a huge stone across the entrance to the tomb and departed. **61** But Mary Magdalene and the other Mary remained sitting there, facing the tomb.

The Guard at the Tomb.[ai] **62** The next day, the one following the day of preparation,[aj] the chief priests and the Pharisees gathered before Pilate **63** and said, "Sir, we remember that this impostor while still alive said, 'After three days I will be raised up.' **64** Give orders, then, that the grave be secured until the third day, lest his disciples come and steal him and say to the people, 'He has been raised from the dead.' This last imposture would be worse than the first."[ak] **65** Pilate said to them, "The guard is yours;[al] go secure it as best you can." **66** So they went and secured the tomb by fixing a seal to the stone and setting the guard.

Notes

a. **27:1–31** Cf. Mk 15:1–20. Matthew's account of the Roman trial before **Pilate** is introduced by a consultation of the Sanhedrin after which Jesus is **handed over to . . . the governor** (Mt 27:1–2). Matthew follows his Marcan source closely but adds some material that is peculiar to him, the death of **Judas** (Mt 27:3–10), possibly the name **Jesus** as the name of **Barabbas** also (Mt 27:16–17), the intervention of Pilate's **wife** (Mt 27:19), Pilate's washing **his hands** in token of his disclaiming responsibility for Jesus' death (Mt 27:24), and the assuming of that responsibility by **the whole people** (Mt 27:25).

b. **27:1** There is scholarly disagreement about the meaning of the Sanhedrin's taking **counsel** (*symboulion elabon*; cf. Mt 12:14; 22:15; 27:7; 28:12); see note on Mk 15:1. Some understand it as a discussion about the strategy for putting their death sentence against **Jesus** into effect since they lacked the right to do so themselves. Others see it as the occasion for their passing that sentence, holding that Matthew, unlike Mark (Mk 14:64), does not consider that it had been passed in the night session (Mt 26:66). Even in the latter interpretation, their handing **him over to Pilate** is best explained on the hypothesis that they did not have competence to put their sentence into effect, as is stated in Jn 18:31.

c. **27:3 The thirty pieces of silver:** see Mt 26:15.

d. **27:5–8** For another tradition about the death of Judas, cf. Acts 1:18–19. The two traditions agree only in the purchase of a field with **the money** paid to Judas for his betrayal of Jesus and the name given to the field, **the Field of Blood.**

In Acts Judas himself buys the field and its name comes from his own blood shed in his fatal accident on it. **The potter's field:** this designation of the field is based on the fulfillment citation in Mt 27:10.

e. **27:9–10** Cf. Mt 26:15. Matthew's attributing this text to Jeremiah is puzzling, for there is no such text in that book, and **the thirty pieces of silver** thrown by Judas "into the temple" (Mt 27:5) recall rather Zec 11:12–13. It is usually said that the attribution of the text to Jeremiah is due to Matthew's combining the Zechariah text with texts from Jeremiah that speak of a **potter** (Jer 18:2–3), the buying of a **field** (Jer 32:6–9), or the breaking of a potter's flask at Topheth in the valley of Ben-Hinnom with the prediction that it will become a burial place (Jer 19:1–13).

f. **27:11 King of the Jews:** this title is used of Jesus only by pagans. The Matthean instances are, besides this verse, Mt 2:2; 27:29, 37. Matthew equates it with "Messiah"; cf. Mt 2:2, 4 and Mt 27:17, 22 where he has changed "the king of the Jews" of his Marcan source (Mk 15:9, 12) to "(Jesus) called Messiah." The normal political connotation of both titles would be of concern to the Roman **governor. You say so:** see note on Mt 26:25. An unqualified affirmative response is not made because Jesus' kingship is not what Pilate would understand it to be.

g. **27:12–14** Cf. Mt 26:62–63. As in the trial before the Sanhedrin, Jesus' silence may be meant to recall Is 53:7. **Greatly amazed:** possibly an allusion to Is 52:14–15.

h. **27:15–26** The choice that Pilate offers **the crowd** between **Barabbas** and **Jesus** is said to be in accordance with a custom of releasing at the Passover feast **one prisoner** chosen by **the crowd** (Mt 27:15). This custom is mentioned also in Mk 15:6 and Jn 18:39 but not in Luke; see note on Lk 23:17. Outside of the gospels there is no direct attestation of it, and scholars are divided in their judgment of the historical reliability of the claim that there was such a practice.

i. **27:16–17 [Jesus] Barabbas:** it is possible that the double name is the original reading; **Jesus** was a common Jewish name; see note on Mt 1:21. This reading is found in only a few textual witnesses, although its absence in the majority can be explained as an omission of **Jesus** made for reverential reasons. That name is bracketed because of its uncertain textual attestation. The Aramaic name **Barabbas** means "son of the father"; the irony of the choice offered between him and Jesus, the true son of the Father, would be evident to those addressees of Matthew who knew that.

j. **27:18** Cf. Mk 14:10. This is an example of the tendency, found in varying degree in all the gospels, to present Pilate in a relatively favorable light and emphasize the hostility of the Jewish authorities and eventually of the people.

k. **27:19** Jesus' innocence is declared by a Gentile woman. **In a dream:** in Matthew's infancy narrative, dreams are the means of divine communication; cf. Mt 1:20; 2:12, 13, 19, 22.

l. **27:22 Let him be crucified:** incited by the chief priests and elders (Mt 27:20), the crowds demand that Jesus be executed by crucifixion, a peculiarly horrible form of Roman capital punishment. The Marcan parallel, "Crucify him" (Mk

15:3), addressed to Pilate, is changed by Matthew to the passive, probably to emphasize the responsibility of the crowds.

m. **27:24–25** Peculiar to Matthew. **Took water . . . blood:** cf. Dt 21:1–8, the hand-washing prescribed in the case of a murder when the killer is unknown. The elders of the city nearest to where the corpse is found must wash their hands, declaring, "Our hands did not shed this blood." **Look to it yourselves:** cf. Mt 27:4. **The whole people:** Matthew sees in those who speak these words **the** entire **people** (Greek *laos*) of Israel. **His blood . . . and upon our children:** cf. Jer 26:15. The responsibility for Jesus' death is accepted by the nation that was God's special possession (Ex 19:5), his own **people** (Hos 2:25), and they thereby lose that high privilege; see Mt 21:43 and the note on that verse. The controversy between Matthew's church and Pharisaic Judaism about which was the true people of God is reflected here. As the Second Vatican Council has pointed out, guilt for Jesus' death is not attributable to all the Jews of his time or to any Jews of later times.

n. **27:26 He had Jesus scourged:** the usual preliminary to crucifixion.

o. **27:27 The praetorium:** the residence of the Roman governor. His usual place of residence was at Caesarea Maritima on the Mediterranean coast, but he went to Jerusalem during the great feasts, when the influx of pilgrims posed the danger of a nationalistic riot. It is disputed whether **the praetorium** in Jerusalem was the old palace of Herod in the west of the city or the fortress of Antonia northwest of the temple area. **The whole cohort:** normally six hundred soldiers.

p. **27:28 Scarlet military cloak:** so Matthew as against the royal purple of Mk 15:17 and Jn 19:2.

q. **27:29 Crown out of thorns:** probably of long **thorns** that stood upright so that it resembled the "radiant" **crown**, a diadem with spikes worn by Hellenistic kings. The soldiers' purpose was mockery, not torture. **A reed:** peculiar to Matthew; a mock scepter.

r. **27:30 Spat upon him:** cf. Mt 26:67 where there also is a possible allusion to Is 50:6.

s. **27:32** See note on Mk 15:21. **Cyrenian named Simon:** Cyrenaica was a Roman province on the north coast of Africa and Cyrene was its capital city. The city had a large population of Greek-speaking Jews. **Simon** may have been living in Palestine or have come there for the Passover as a pilgrim. **Pressed into service:** see note on Mt 5:41.

t. **27:34 Wine . . . mixed with gall:** cf. Mk 15:23 where the drink is "wine drugged with myrrh," a narcotic. Matthew's text is probably an inexact allusion to Ps 69:22. That psalm belongs to the class called the individual lament, in which a persecuted just man prays for deliverance in the midst of great suffering and also expresses confidence that his prayer will be heard. That theme of the suffering Just One is frequently applied to the sufferings of Jesus in the passion narratives.

u. **27:35** The clothing of an executed criminal went to his executioner(s), but the description of that procedure in the case of Jesus, found in all the gospels, is plainly inspired by Ps 22:19. However, that psalm verse is quoted only in Jn 19:24.

v. **27:37** The offense of a person condemned to death by crucifixion was written on a tablet that was displayed on his cross. The charge against **Jesus** was that he had claimed to be the **King of the Jews** (cf. Mt 27:11), i.e., the Messiah (cf. Mt 27:17, 22).

w. **27:38 Revolutionaries:** see note on Jn 18:40 where the same Greek word as that found here is used for Barabbas.

x. **27:39–40 Reviled him . . . heads:** cf. Ps 22:8. **You who would destroy . . . three days;** cf. Mt 26:61. **If you are the Son of God:** the same words as those of the devil in the temptation of Jesus; cf. Mt 4:3, 6.

y. **27:42 King of Israel:** in their mocking of Jesus the members of the Sanhedrin call themselves and their people not "the Jews" but **Israel**.

z. **27:43** Peculiar to Matthew. **He trusted in God . . . wants him:** cf. Ps 22:9. **He said . . . of God:** probably an allusion to Wis 2:12–20 where the theme of the suffering Just One appears.

aa. **27:45** Cf. Am 8:9 where on the day of the Lord "the sun will set at midday."

ab. **27:46** *Eli, Eli, lema sabachthani?:* Jesus cries out in the words of Ps 22:2a, a psalm of lament that is the Old Testament passage most frequently drawn upon in this narrative. In Mark the verse is cited entirely in Aramaic, which Matthew partially retains but changes the invocation of God to the Hebrew *Eli*, possibly because that is more easily related to the statement of the following verse about Jesus' calling for Elijah.

ac. **27:47 Elijah:** see note on Mt 3:4. This prophet, taken up into heaven (2 Kgs 2:11), was believed to come to the help of those in distress, but the evidences of that belief are all later than the gospels.

ad. **27:50 Gave up his spirit:** cf. the Marcan parallel (Mk 15:37), "breathed his last." Matthew's alteration expresses both Jesus' control over his destiny and his obedient giving up of his life to God.

ae. **27:51–53 Veil of the sanctuary . . . bottom:** cf. Mk 15:38; Lk 23:45. Luke puts this event immediately before the death of Jesus. There were two veils in the Mosaic tabernacle on the model of which the temple was constructed, the outer one before the entrance of the Holy Place and the inner one before the Holy of Holies (see Ex 26:31–36). Only the high priest could pass through the latter and that only on the Day of Atonement (see Lv 16:1–18). Probably the torn veil of the gospels is the inner one. The meaning of the scene may be that now, because of Jesus' death, all people have access to the presence of God, or that the temple, its holiest part standing exposed, is now profaned and will soon be destroyed. **The earth quaked . . . appeared to many:** peculiar to Matthew. The earthquake, the splitting of the **rocks**, and especially the resurrection of the dead **saints** indicate the coming of the final age. In the Old Testament the coming of God is frequently portrayed with the imagery of an earthquake (see

Ps 68:9; 77:19), and Jesus speaks of the earthquakes that will accompany the "labor pains" that signify the beginning of the dissolution of the old world (Mt 24:7–8). For the expectation of the resurrection of the dead at the coming of the new and final age, see Dn 12:1–3. Matthew knows that the end of the old age has not yet come (Mt 28:20), but the new age has broken in with the death (and resurrection; cf. the earthquake in Mt 28:2) of Jesus; see note on Mt 16:28. **After his resurrection:** this qualification seems to be due to Matthew's wish to assert the primacy of Jesus' **resurrection** even though he has placed the resurrection of the dead **saints** immediately after Jesus' death.

af. **27:54** Cf. Mk 15:39. The Christian confession of faith is made by Gentiles, not only **the centurion,** as in Mark, but the other soldiers **who were keeping watch over Jesus** (cf. Mt 27:36).

ag. **27:55–56 Looking on from a distance:** cf. Ps 38:12. **Mary Magdalene . . . Joseph:** these two women are mentioned again in Mt 27:61 and Mt 28:1 and are important as witnesses of the reality of the empty tomb. A **James** and **Joseph** are referred to in Mt 13:55 as brothers of Jesus.

ah. **27:57–61** Cf. Mk 15:42–47. Matthew drops Mark's designation of **Joseph of Arimathea** as "a distinguished member of the council" (the Sanhedrin), and makes him **a rich man** and a **disciple of Jesus.** The former may be an allusion to Is 53:9 (the Hebrew reading of that text is disputed and the one followed in the NAB OT has nothing about the rich, but they are mentioned in the LXX version). That the tomb was the **new tomb** of **a rich man** and that it was seen by the women are indications of an apologetic intent of Matthew; there could be no question about the identity of Jesus' burial place. **The other Mary:** the mother of James and Joseph (Mt 27:56).

ai. **27:62–66** Peculiar to Matthew. The story prepares for Mt 28:11–15 and the Jewish charge that the tomb was empty because the disciples had stolen the body of Jesus (Mt 28:13, 15).

aj. **27:62 The next day . . . preparation:** the sabbath. According to the synoptic chronology, in that year **the day of preparation** (for the sabbath) was the Passover; cf. Mk 15:42. **The Pharisees:** the principal opponents of Jesus during his ministry and, in Matthew's time, of the Christian church, join with the **chief priests** to guarantee against a possible attempt of Jesus' **disciples** to steal his body.

ak. **27:64 This last imposture . . . the first:** the claim that Jesus **has been raised from the dead** is clearly the **last imposture; the first** may be either his claim that he would **be raised up** (Mt 27:63) or his claim that he was the one with whose ministry the kingdom of God had come (see Mt 12:28).

al. **27:65 The guard is yours:** literally, "have a guard" or "you have a guard." Either the imperative or the indicative could mean that Pilate granted the petitioners some Roman soldiers as guards, which is the sense of the present translation. However, if the verb is taken as an indicative it could also mean that Pilate told them to use their own Jewish guards.

Chapter 28[a]

The Resurrection of Jesus. 1 After the sabbath, as the first day of the week was dawning,[b] Mary Magdalene and the other Mary came to see the tomb. **2** [c]And behold, there was a great earthquake; for an angel of the Lord descended from heaven, approached, rolled back the stone, and sat upon it. **3** His appearance was like lightning and his clothing was white as snow. **4** The guards were shaken with fear of him and became like dead men. **5** Then the angel said to the women in reply, "Do not be afraid! I know that you are seeking Jesus the crucified. **6** [d]He is not here, for he has been raised just as he said. Come and see the place where he lay. **7** Then go quickly and tell his disciples, 'He has been raised from the dead, and he is going before you to Galilee; there you will see him.' Behold, I have told you." **8** Then they went away quickly from the tomb, fearful yet overjoyed, and ran to announce[e] this to his disciples. **9** [f]And behold, Jesus met them on their way and greeted them. They approached, embraced his feet, and did him homage. **10** Then Jesus said to them, "Do not be afraid. Go tell my brothers to go to Galilee, and there they will see me."

The Report of the Guard.[g] **11** While they were going, some of the guard went into the city and told the chief priests all that had happened. **12** They assembled with the elders and took counsel; then they gave a large sum of money to the soldiers, **13** telling them, "You are to say, 'His disciples came by night and stole him while we were asleep.' **14** And if this gets to the ears of the governor, we will satisfy [him] and keep you out of trouble." **15** The soldiers took the money and did as they were instructed. And this story has circulated among the Jews to the present [day].

The Commissioning of the Disciples.[h] **16** The eleven[i] disciples went to Galilee, to the mountain to which Jesus had ordered them. **17** [j]When they saw him, they worshiped, but they doubted. **18** [k]Then Jesus approached and said to them, "All power in heaven and on earth has been given to me. **19** Go, therefore,[l] and make disciples of all nations, baptizing them in the name of the Father, and of the Son, and of the holy Spirit, **20** teaching them to observe all that I have commanded you.[m] And behold, I am with you always, until the end of the age."

Notes

a. **28:1–20** Except for Mt 28:1–8 based on Mk 16:1–8, the material of this final chapter is peculiar to Matthew. Even where he follows Mark, Matthew has altered his source so greatly that a very different impression is given from that of the Marcan account. The two points that are common to the resurrection testimony of all the gospels are that the tomb of Jesus had been found empty and that the risen Jesus had appeared to certain persons, or, in the original form of Mark, that such an appearance was promised as soon to take place (see Mk 16:7). On this central and all-important basis, Matthew has constructed an account that interprets the resurrection as the turning of the ages (Mt 28:2–4), shows the Jewish opposition to Jesus as continuing **to the present** in the claim that the resurrection is a deception perpetrated by the **disciples** who stole his body from the tomb (Mt 28:11–15), and marks a new stage in the mission of **the disciples** once limited to Israel (Mt 10:5–6); now they are to **make disciples of all nations.** In this work they will be strengthened by the presence of the exalted Son of Man, who will be with them **until** the kingdom comes in fullness at **the end of the age** (Mt 28:16–20).

b. **28:1 After the Sabbath . . . dawning:** since the sabbath ended at sunset, this could mean in the early evening, for **dawning** can refer to the appearance of the evening star; cf. Lk 23:54. However, it is probable that Matthew means the morning dawn of the day after the sabbath, as in the similar though slightly different text of Mark, "when the sun had risen" (Mk 16:2). **Mary Magdalene and the other Mary:** see notes on Mt 27:55–56; 57–61. **To see the tomb:** cf. Mk 16:1–2 where the purpose of the women's visit is to anoint Jesus' body.

c. **28:2–4** Peculiar to Matthew. **A great earthquake:** see note on Mt 27:51–53. **Descended from heaven:** this trait is peculiar to Matthew, although his interpretation of the "young man" of his Marcan source (Mk 16:5) as an **angel** is probably true to Mark's intention; cf. Lk 24:23 where the "two men" of Mt 24:4 are said to be "angels." **Rolled back the stone . . . upon it:** not to allow the risen Jesus to leave the tomb but to make evident that the tomb is empty (see Mt 24:6). Unlike the apocryphal Gospel of Peter (9:35—11:44), the New Testament does not describe the resurrection of Jesus, nor is there anyone who sees it. **His appearance was like lightning . . . snow:** see note on Mt 17:2.

d. **28:6–7** Cf. Mk 16:6–7. **Just as he said:** a Matthean addition referring to Jesus' predictions of his resurrection, e.g., Mt 16:21; 17:23; 20:19. **Tell his disciples:** like the angel of the Lord of the infancy narrative, the angel interprets a fact and gives a commandment about what is to be done; cf. Mt 1:20–21. Matthew omits Mark's "and Peter" (Mk 16:7); considering his interest in Peter, this omission is curious. Perhaps the reason is that the Marcan text may allude to a first appearance of Jesus to Peter alone (cf. 1 Cor 15:5; Lk 24:34) which Matthew has already incorporated into his account of Peter's confession at Caesarea Philippi; see note on Mt 16:16. **He is going . . . Galilee:** like Mk 16:7, a reference to Jesus' prediction at the Last Supper (Mt 26:32; Mk 14:28). Matthew changes Mark's "as he told you" to a declaration of the angel.

e. **28:8** Contrast Mk 16:8 where the women in their fear "said nothing to anyone."

f. **28:9–10** Although these verses are peculiar to Matthew, there are similarities between them and John's account of the appearance of Jesus to Mary Magdalene (Jn 20:17). In both there is a touching of Jesus' body, and a command of Jesus to bear a message to his disciples, designated as his **brothers.** Matthew may have drawn upon a tradition that appears in a different form in John. Jesus' words to the women are mainly a repetition of those of the angel (Mt 28:5a, 7b).

g. **28:11–15** This account indicates that the dispute between Christians and Jews about the empty tomb was not whether the tomb was empty but why.

h. **28:16–20** This climactic scene has been called a "proleptic parousia," for it gives a foretaste of the final glorious coming of the Son of Man (Mt 26:64). Then his triumph will be manifest to all; now it is revealed only to **the disciples**, who are commissioned to announce it to **all nations** and bring them to belief in Jesus and obedience to his commandments.

i. **28:16 The eleven:** the number recalls the tragic defection of Judas Iscariot. **To the mountain . . . ordered them:** since the message to the **disciples** was simply that they were to go to Galilee (Mt 28:10), some think that **the mountain** comes from a tradition of the message known to Matthew and alluded to here. For the significance of the mountain, see note on Mt 17:1.

j. **28:17 But they doubted:** the Greek can also be translated, "but some doubted." The verb occurs elsewhere in the New Testament only in Mt 14:31 where it is associated with Peter's being of "little faith." For the meaning of that designation, see note on Mt 6:30.

k. **28:18 All power . . . me:** the Greek word here translated **power** is the same as that found in the LXX translation of Dn 7:13–14 where one "like a son of man" is given **power** and an everlasting kingdom by God. The risen Jesus here claims universal power, i.e., **in heaven and on earth.**

l. **28:19 Therefore:** since universal power belongs to the risen Jesus (Mt 28:18), he gives the eleven a mission that is universal. They are to **make disciples of all nations.** While **all nations** is understood by some scholars as referring only to all Gentiles, it is probable that it included the Jews as well. **Baptizing them:** baptism is the means of entrance into the community of the risen one, the Church. **In the name of the Father . . . holy Spirit:** this is perhaps the clearest expression in the New Testament of trinitarian belief. It may have been the baptismal formula of Matthew's church, but primarily it designates the effect of baptism, the union of the one baptized with the Father, Son, and holy Spirit.

m. **28:20 All that I have commanded you:** the moral teaching found in this gospel, preeminently that of the Sermon on the Mount (Mt 5–7). The commandments of Jesus are the standard of Christian conduct, not the Mosaic law as such, even though some of the Mosaic commandments have now been invested with the authority of Jesus. **Behold, I am with you always:** the promise of Jesus' real though invisible presence echoes the name Emmanuel given to him in the infancy narrative; see note on Mt 1:23. **End of the age:** see notes on Mt 13:39 and Mt 24:3.

from The Confessions

Saint Augustine

Book 6

I

(1) O GOD, my hope from my youth,[1] where were You all this time, where had You gone?[2] For was it not You who created me and distinguished me from the beasts of the field and made me wiser than the birds of the air?[3] Yet I walked through dark and slippery places,[4] and I went out of myself in the search for You[5] and did not find the God of my heart.[6] I had come into the depths of the sea[7] and I had lost faith and all hope of discovering the truth.

By this time my mother had come to me, following me over sea and land[8] with the courage of piety and relying upon You in all perils. For they were in danger from a storm, and she reassured even the sailors—by whom travellers newly ventured upon the deep are ordinarily reassured—promising them safe arrival because thus You had promised her in a vision. She found me in a perilous state through my deep despair of ever discovering the truth. But even when I told her that if I was not yet a Catholic Christian, I was no longer a Manichean, she was not greatly exultant as at some unlooked-for good news, because she had already received assurance upon that part of my misery; she bewailed me as one dead certainly, but certainly to be raised again by You, offering me in her mind as one stretched out dead, that You might say to the widow's son: *Young man, I say to thee arise:*[9] and he should sit up and begin to speak and You should give him to his mother. So her heart was not shaken with any tumult of exultation at hearing that what daily she had begged of You with tears had in so large part happened: for I was at least rescued from heresy, even if I had not yet attained the truth. In fact, because she was certain that You would give her what remained since You had promised her all, she answered me serenely and with a heart full of confidence that in Christ she believed that she would see me a faithful Catholic before she died. So much she said to me. But to You, O Fount of mercy, she multiplied her prayers and her tears that You should hasten Your help[10] and enlighten my darkness:[11] and she hastened to church more zealously than ever and drank in the words of Ambrose as a fountain of water springing up into life everlasting.[12] She loved that man as an angel of God[13] because she had

learned that it was by him that I had been brought so far as to the wavering state I was now in; through which she took it for granted that I had
to pass on my way from sickness to health, with some graver peril yet to
come, analogous to what doctors call the crisis.[14]

II

(2) My mother had brought meal and bread and wine to certain oratories built to the memory of saints, as was her custom in Africa. But the
sacristan prevented her. When she learned that the bishop himself had
forbidden the practice, she received the prohibition so devoutly and obe-
diently that I wondered at the ease with which she turned into a critic of
her own former custom rather than of the present prohibition. For her
soul was not a slave to wine—drinking, nor had she any love of wine to
provoke her to hatred of the truth, like so many of both sexes who are
as much sickened by a hymn of sobriety as drunkards would be if one
poured water into their wine. But when my mother brought her basket
with those accustomed dainties—of which she meant to eat a little and
give away the rest—she never allowed herself more than one small cup
diluted to her sober palate, and from this she would sip no more than was
fitting. And if there were many oratories of departed saints to be honoured
in that way, she took round with her the same cup to be used in each place:
and this, not only diluted with water but by now lukewarm, she would
share with others present in small sips, for her concern was with piety and
not with the pleasure of the wine.

But when she found that the custom was forbidden by so famous a
preacher and so pious a bishop even to those who used it soberly, lest it
might be an occasion of gluttony to the heavier drinkers; and because in
any event these funeral feasts in honour of our parents in the faith were
too much like the superstitions of the heathens, she abandoned the practice quite willingly.[15] In place of her basket filled with the fruits of the earth,
she learned to offer at the shrines of the martyrs a breast full of prayers
purer than any such gifts. Thus she was able to give what she could to the
needy; and the communion of the Lord's Body was celebrated where the
martyrs had been immolated and crowned in the likeness of His Passion.[16]

But yet, O Lord my God, it does seem to me—and upon this matter
my heart is in Your sight—that my mother might not so easily have borne
the breaking of her custom if it had been forbidden by some other whom
she did not love as she loved Ambrose. For on account of my salvation she
loved him dearly; and he loved her on account of her most religious way of
life, for she was fervent in spirit[17] and ever doing good,[18] and she haunted
the church. So that when he saw me he often broke out in her praises, con-
gratulating me that I had such a mother, and not realising what sort of a
son she had: for I doubted all these things and did not believe that the way
of life[19] could be discovered.

III

(3) Nor did I then groan in prayer for Your help. My mind was intent upon inquiry and unquiet for argumentation. I regarded Ambrose as a lucky man by worldly standards to be held in honour by such important people: only his celibacy seemed to me a heavy burden. I had no means of guessing, and no experience of my own to learn from, what hope he bore within him, what struggles he might have against the temptations that went with his high place, what was his consolation in adversity, and on what joys of Your bread the hidden mouth of his heart fed. Nor did he know how I was inflamed nor the depth[20] of my peril. I could not ask of him what I wished as I wished, for I was kept from any face to face conversation with him by the throng of men with their own troubles, whose infirmities he served.[21] The very little time he was not with these he was refreshing either his body with necessary food or his mind with reading. When he read, his eyes travelled across the page and his heart sought into the sense, but voice and tongue were silent.[22] No one was forbidden to approach him nor was it his custom to require that visitors should be announced: but when we came into him we often saw him reading and always to himself; and after we had sat long in silence, unwilling to interrupt a work on which he was so intent, we would depart again. We guessed that in the small time he could find for the refreshment of his mind, he would wish to be free from the distraction of other men's affairs and not called away from what he was doing. Perhaps he was on his guard lest [if he read aloud] someone listening should be troubled and want an explanation if the author he was reading expressed some idea over obscurely, and it might be necessary to expound or discuss some of the more difficult questions. And if he had to spend time on this, he would get through less reading than he wished. Or it may be that his real reason for reading to himself was to preserve his voice, which did in fact readily grow tired. But whatever his reason for doing it, that man certainly had a good reason.

(4) Anyhow I was given no opportunity of putting such questions as I desired to that holy oracle of Yours, his breast, unless they were of a sort to be heard briefly. But the agitation working in me required that he should be fully at leisure if I were to pour it out before him; and I never found him so. Still I heard him every Sunday[23] preaching the word of truth[24] to his congregation; and I became more and more certain that all those knots of cunning and calumny, which those who deceived me had tangled up against the holy books, could be untangled. I learned that the phrase, "man created by You in Your own image,"[25] was not taken by Your spiritual children, whom of our Catholic mother You have made to be born anew by grace, to mean that You are bounded within the shape of a human body. And although I had not the vaguest or most shadowy notion[26] how

a spiritual substance could be, yet I was filled with shame—but joyful too—that I had been barking all these years not against the Catholic faith but against mere figments of carnal imaginations. I had been rash and impious in that I had spoken in condemnation of things which I should have learned more truly of by inquiry. For You, O highest and nearest, most hidden and most present, have not parts greater and smaller; You are wholly everywhere, yet nowhere limited within space, nor are You of any bodily form. And yet You have made man in Your own image, and man is in space from head to foot.

IV

(5) Thus I was ignorant how this image of Yours could be; but I should have knocked at the door[27] and proposed the question how it was to be believed, and not jeeringly opposed it as if it were believed in this or that particular way. The anxiety as to what I should hold as sure gnawed at my heart all the more keenly, as my shame increased at having been so long tricked and deceived by the promise of certainty, and at having with a rashness of error worthy of a child gone on spouting forth so many uncertainties as confidently as if I had known them for sure. That they were false, I saw clearly only later. Yet already I was certain that they were at least uncertain, and that I had taken them for certain, when in the blindness of my opposition I attacked Your Catholic church. I did not yet know that she was teaching the truth, but I had found that she did not teach the things of which I had so strongly accused her. So I was first confounded and then enlightened. And I rejoiced, O my God, that Your only church, the Body of Your only Son,[28] in which the name of Christ had been put upon me while I was still an infant,[29] had no taste for such puerile nonsense; nor in her sound doctrine had she the notion of somehow packing You, the Creator of all things, into any space—however mighty and ample yet bounded upon all sides—in the shape of a human body.

(6) I was glad also that the old Scriptures of the law and the prophets were set before me now, no longer in that light in which they had formerly seemed absurd, when I criticised Your holy ones for thinking this or that which in plain fact they did not think. And it was a joy to hear Ambrose who often repeated to his congregation, as if it were a rule he was most strongly urging upon them, the text: *the letter killeth, but the spirit giveth life.*[30] And he would go on to draw aside the veil of mystery[31] and lay open the spiritual meaning of things which taken literally would have seemed to teach falsehood.[32] Nothing of what he said struck me as false, although I did not as yet know whether what he said was true. I held back my heart from accepting anything, fearing that I might fall once more, whereas in fact the hanging in suspense was more deadly. I wanted to be as certain of things unseen as that seven and three make ten. For I had not reached the point of madness which denies that even this can be known; but I wanted

to know other things as clearly as this, either such material things as were not present to my senses, or spiritual things which I did not know how to conceive save corporeally. By believing I might have been cured; for then the eye of my mind would have been clearer and so might in some way have been directed towards Your truth which abides for ever[33] and knows no defect. But as usually happens, the man who has tried a bad doctor is afraid to trust even a good one: so it was with the health of my soul, which could not be healed save by believing, and refused to be healed that way for fear of believing falsehood. Thus I was resisting Your hands,[34] for You first prepared for us the medicine of faith and then applied it to the diseases of the world and gave it such great power.[35]

V

(7) From this time on I found myself preferring the Catholic doctrine, realising that it acted more modestly and honestly in requiring things to be believed which could not be proved—whether they were in themselves provable though not by this or that person, or were not provable at all—than the Manichees who derided credulity and made impossible promises of certain knowledge, and then called upon men to believe so many utterly fabulous and absurd things because they could not be demonstrated. Next, Lord, with gentle and most merciful hand You worked upon my heart and rectified it. I began to consider the countless things I believed which I had not seen, or which had happened with me not there—so many things in the history of nations, so many facts about places and cities which I had never seen, so many things told me by friends, by doctors, by this man, by that man: and unless we accepted these things, we should do nothing at all in this life. Most strongly of all it struck me how firmly and unshakeably I believed that I was born of a particular father and mother, which I could not possibly know unless I believed it upon the word of others. Thus You brought me to see that those who believed Your Bible, which You have established among almost all peoples with such authority, were not to be censured, but rather those who did not believe it, and that I must give no heed to any who might say to me: "How do you know that those Scriptures were given to mankind by the Spirit of the One true and most true God?" For this point above all was to be believed; because no assault of fallacious questions which I had read in such multitude in the philosophers—who in any event contradicted each other—could constrain me not to believe both that You are, though what might be Your nature I did not know, and that the government of human affairs belongs to You.

(8) But though I held these truths sometimes more strongly, sometimes less, yet I always believed both that You are and that You have a care of us: even if I did not know what I must hold as to Your substance, or what way leads to You—or leads back to You. Thus, since men had not the strength[36]

to discover the truth by pure reason and therefore we needed the authority of Holy Writ, I was coming to believe that You would certainly not
have bestowed such eminent authority upon those Scriptures throughout
the world, unless it had been Your will that by them men should believe
in You and in them seek You.

Now that I heard them expounded so convincingly, I saw that many
passages in these books, which had at one time struck me as absurdities,
must be referred to the profundity of mystery. Indeed the authority of
Scripture seemed to be more to be revered and more worthy of devoted
faith in that it was at once a book that all could read and read easily, and
yet preserved the majesty of its mystery in the deepest part of its meaning:
for it offers itself to all in the plainest words and the simplest expressions,
yet demands the closest attention of the most serious minds.[37] Thus it
receives all within its welcoming arms, and at the same time brings a few
direct to You by narrow ways:[38] yet these few would be fewer still but for
this twofold quality by which it stands so lofty in authority yet draws the
multitude to its bosom by its holy lowliness. So I dwelt upon these things
and You were near me, I sighed and You heard me, I was wavering uncer-
tainly and You guided me, I was going the broad way of the world and
You did not forsake me.

VI

(9) I was all hot for honours, money, marriage: and You made mock
of my hotness.[39] In my pursuit of these, I suffered most bitter disappointments, but in this You were good to me since I was thus prevented from
taking delight in anything not Yourself Look now into my heart. Lord, by
whose will I remember all this and confess it to You. Let my soul cleave
toYou[40] now that You have freed it from the tenacious hold of death.
At that time my soul was in misery, and You pricked the soreness of its
wound, that leaving all things it might turn to You, who are over all[41] and
without whom all would return to nothing, that it might turn to You and
be healed.[42]

I was in utter misery and there was one day especially on which You
acted to bring home to me the realisation of my misery. I was preparing an
oration in praise of the Emperor in which I was to utter any number of lies
to win the applause of people who knew they were lies.[43] My heart was
much wrought upon by the shame of this and inflamed with the fever of
the thoughts that consumed it. I was passing along a certain street in Milan
when I noticed a beggar. He was jesting and laughing and I imagine more
than a little drunk. I fell into gloom and spoke to the friends who were
with me about the endless sorrows that our own insanity brings us: for
here was I striving away, dragging the load of my unhappiness under the
spurring of my desires, and making it worse by dragging it: and with all
our striving, our one aim was to arrive at some sort of happiness without

care: the beggar had reached the same goal before us, and we might quite well never reach it at all. The very thing that he had attained by means of a few pennies begged from passers-by—namely the pleasure of a temporary happiness—I was plotting for with so many a weary twist and turn.

Certainly his joy was no true joy; but the joy I sought in my ambition was emptier still. In any event he was cheerful and I worried, he had no cares and I nothing but cares. Now if anyone had asked me whether I would rather be cheerful or fearful, I would answer, "Cheerful": but if he had gone on to ask whether I would rather be like that beggar or as I actually was, I would certainly have chosen my own state though so troubled and anxious. Now this was surely absurd. It could not be for any true reason. I ought not to have preferred my own state rather than his merely because I was the more learned, since I got no joy from my learning, but sought only to please men by it—not even to teach them, only to please them. Therefore did You break my bones[44] with the rod of Your discipline.[45]

(10) Let my soul pay no heed to those who would say: "It makes a difference what one is happy about. The beggar found joy in his drunkenness, you sought joy in glory." But what glory, Lord? A glory not in You.[46] For my glory was no truer than his joy, and it turned my head even more. That very night he would sleep off his drunkenness: but how often and often I had gone to bed with mine and woken up with it, and would in the future go to bed with it and wake up with it. It does indeed make a difference what one is happy about: I know it, and I know that the happiness of a sure hope is incomparably beyond all such vanity. And there was indeed a difference between him and me—for he was much the happier man: not only because he was soaked in his merriment while I was eaten up with cares, but also because he by wishing luck to all comers had at least got wine, while I by lying was aiming only to get empty praise.

I spoke much to this effect to the friends that were with me: and I often observed that it was with them as it was with me, and I found it very ill with me. So I worried and by worrying doubled the ill. And when by chance prosperity smiled in my direction, I lacked the spirit to seize it, for it fled away almost before I could get my hand upon it.

VII

(11) We were gloomy together with such thoughts, I and those who were closest to me. I discussed the problem especially with Alypius[47] and Nebridius.[48] Alypius was born in the same town as I. His parents were of high rank there. He was younger than I, indeed he had studied under me both when I began my teaching in our native town and afterwards at Carthage. He was much attached to me because he thought me kindly and learned, and I to him because of the great bent towards virtue that

was so marked in him so young. But at Carthage the maelstrom of ill morals—and especially the passion for idle spectacles—had sucked him in, his special madness being for the Circus[49]. When he first came into the grip of this wretched craving, I had set up a school for the public and was teaching rhetoric. He had not come to me as a pupil because of some difference that had arisen between his father and me. I discovered that he was quite fatally devoted to the Games, and I was much worried because it seemed to me that so much promise was to be thrown away, or had already been thrown away. But I had no way of advising him or forcibly restraining him, neither the good will of a friend nor the right of a master. For I took for granted that he would feel about me as his father did. In fact he did not. He took his own line in the matter rather than his father's, and fell into the way of greeting me when we met and of coming sometimes into my school to listen awhile and be off again.

(12) But it had passed from my mind that I could do anything to prevent the waste of so good a mind in the blind and ruinous pursuit of the empty pastimes he was in. But You, Lord, who hold the helm of all that You have created, had not forgotten him—and indeed he was one day to be numbered amongst Your children as a high priest of Your sacrament.[50] That his amendment might be obviously due to You, You brought it about through me, and without my being aware of it. For one day when I was sitting in my usual place with my students in front of me, he came in, greeted me, sat down and gave his attention to what was being discussed. I had in hand a passage that I was expounding: and it suddenly struck me that it could be very well illustrated by a comparison taken from the Games—a comparison which would make the point I was establishing clearer and more amusing, and which involved biting mockery of those who were slaves to that particular insanity. You know, O my God and his,[51] that I was not thinking of Alypius or his need to be cured of that disease. But he applied it instantly to himself and thought I had said it solely on his account. Another might have taken it as a reason for being angry with me, but the youth was honest enough to take it as a reason for being angry with himself and for warmer attachment to me. You said long ago and caused it to be written in Your Book: *Rebuke a wise man and he will love you.*[52]

As a matter of fact I had not been rebuking him, but You use all men with or without their knowledge for a purpose known to Yourself—and that purpose is just. Thus of my heart and tongue You made burning coals[53] to cauterise and heal a mind of such promise, though it lay sick. Let him who does not realise Your mercies, which my soul's depths confess to You,[54] pass over Your praises in silence. As a result of what he had heard me say, he wrenched himself up out of the deep pit in which he had chosen to be plunged and in the darkness of whose pleasures he had been so woefully blinded. He braced his mind and shook it till all the filth of the Games fell away from it and he went no more.

Then he prevailed upon his unwilling father to let him be one of my students. His father did at last yield. Alypius began to take lessons from me again and so came to be involved with me in the same superstitions. He loved especially the pretence the Manichees made of continence, which he took to be quite genuine. But in fact it was a senseless and misleading continence, which seduced precious souls[55] not yet able to reach the profound depth of virtue and easily deceived with the surface appearance of what was only an unreal counterfeit of virtue.[56]

VIII

(13) In pursuit of the worldly career whose necessity his parents were always dinning into his ears, he had gone before me to Rome to study Law: and there incredibly he had been carried away by an incredible passion for gladiatorial shows. He had turned from such things and utterly detested them. But it happened one day that he met some friends and fellow-students coming from dinner: and though he flatly refused and vigorously resisted, they used friendly violence and forced him along with them to the amphitheatre on a day of these cruel and murderous Games. He protested "Even if you drag my body to the place, can you force me to turn my mind and my eyes on the show? Though there, I shall not be there, and so I shall defeat both you and it."

Hearing this his companions led him on all the faster, wishing to discover whether he could do as he had said. When they had reached the arena and had got such seats as they could, the whole place was in a frenzy of hideous delight. He closed up the door of his eyes and forbade his mind to pay attention to things so evil. If only he could have stopped his ears too! For at a certain critical point in the fight, the vast roar of the whole audience beat upon him. His curiosity got the better of him, and thinking that he would be able to treat the sight with scorn—whatever the sight might be—he opened his eyes and was stricken with a deeper wound in the soul than the man whom he had opened his eyes to see got in the body. He fell more miserably than the gladiator whose fall had set the crowd to that roar—a roar which had entered his ears and unlocked his eyes, so that his soul was stricken and beaten down. But in truth the reason was that its courage had so far been only audaciousness, and it was weak because it had relied upon itself when it should have trusted only in You.[57] Seeing the blood he drank deep of the savagery. He did not turn away but fixed his gaze upon the sight. He drank in all the frenzy, with no thought of what had happened to him, revelled in the wickedness of the contest and was drunk with lust for blood. He was no longer the man who had come there but one of the crowd to which he had come, a fit companion for those who had brought him.

What more need I say? He continued to gaze, shouted, grew hot, and when he departed took with him a madness by which he was to be goaded to come back again, not only with those who at first took him there, but even more than they and leading on others. Yet out of all this You drew him with strong and merciful hand, teaching him to have confidence in You, not in himself.[58] But this was long after.

IX

(14) For the time, the matter was only laid up in his memory for his future healing. So also was an incident which had happened earlier while he was still a student in my school at Carthage. He was in the market-place at noon one day going over in his mind something that he had to say by heart (as students usually have to do) when You allowed him to be arrested as a thief by the officers in charge of the market. I imagine that You allowed this, O our God, for no other cause than that one who was to be so great should learn thus early that in judging cases man must not too easily be condemned by man through rash credulity. As he was walking by himself before the judgment-seat with his tablets and his pen, the real thief, a young man who was also a student, came along with an axe concealed under his clothes and quite unseen by Alypius went up to the leaden gratings which are over the silversmiths' shops and began to cut away the lead. When they heard the sound of the axe the silversmiths underneath began to call out and sent men to seize whomever they might find. The thief heard their voices and ran away leaving his axe behind for fear that he might be caught with it.

Now Alypius who had not seen the man arrive saw him depart, observed the speed of his departure, and wondering what it was all about went up to the place. He found the axe and stood looking at it with surprise. At this moment those who had been sent found him alone and carrying the weapon whose noise had startled them and brought them there. They seized him, dragged him off, and gathering the neighbouring shopkeepers made a great boast of having caught the thief in the act. They took him off to hand him over to the officers of the law.

(15) But his lesson stopped there. For at that point, Lord, You came to the aid of his innocence, of which indeed You were the only witness.[59] For as he was being led off to imprisonment or torture, they were met by a certain architect, who had the principal charge of public buildings. They were particularly pleased to meet him just then, because they were themselves under suspicion of stealing the goods that were lost out of the marketplace, and they felt that at last he would know who had done the stealing. But this man had often seen Alypius at the house of a certain senator whom he himself frequently visited. He knew him at once and taking him by the hand drew him away from the crowd and enquired the cause

of all the trouble. He heard what had happened and commanded the rabble who thronged about raging and threatening Alypius to come with him. They came to the house of the young man who had done the deed. There was a boy outside the door who was quite ready to tell the whole thing, being too young to fear that any harm would come to his master from what he said: for he had gone with him to the market place. Alypius remembered seeing the boy and told the architect, who showed the hatchet to the boy and asked him whose it was. "Ours," replied the boy immediately. He was questioned further and disclosed everything. Thus the guilt was transferred to the man who lived in that house, to the great confusion of the crowd which had been hurling its taunts at Alypius. Alypius indeed, who was later to be a dispenser of Your word and to investigate many cases in Your Church, went off very much wiser for the experience.[60]

X

(16) I found him at Rome when I came there and he became my close friend. He went with me to Milan, so that he might be still with me, and might at the same time practise the law he had studied, but this rather to please his parents than of his own wish. He had already sat three times as an assessor,[61] displaying an integrity that caused others to marvel—whereas he marvelled that any should prefer money to honesty. His character was tested further, not only by the temptation of bribery but also by the threat of danger to himself. At Rome he had been Assessor to the Chancellor of the Italian Treasury.[62] There was at the time a very powerful senator, to whom many were bound by favours received, while many stood in fear of him. He wanted to have permission granted him for something forbidden by the law. Ordinarily so powerful a man would have got it as a matter of course. But Alypius refused. A bribe was offered: he treated it with complete contempt. He was threatened and treated the threats likewise. Everyone was amazed at so rare a spirit, in that he neither courted the friendship nor feared the enmity of a man so important and so well known for the innumerable means at his disposal for advancing or damaging others. The judge himself, to whom Alypius acted as assessor, did not want to grant the permit, but would not openly refuse it: he put the blame upon Alypius, claiming that Alypius would not let him do it: and in truth if he had tried, Alypius would have left the court.

The only thing that did tempt him was his love of study: he thought of having books copied for him at the reduced rates allowed to praetors.[63] But considering the equity of the matter he came to a better decision, holding justice which forbade it more valuable than the power to do it. All that I have so far said is small: yet *he that is faithful in that which is least, is faithful also in that which is greater;*[64] nor is that word void which proceeded from the mouth of Your Truth:[65] *If then you have not been faithful in the unjust mammon, who will trust you with that which is the true? and if you have not been faithful in that which is another's, who will give you that which is your own?*[66] Such then was the man who was so close a friend, and shared my wavering as to the course of life we should adopt.

(17) I have mentioned Nebridius. He had left his native place near Carthage: he had left Carthage itself where he had mainly lived, had left his rich family estate and his house and his mother, for she would not come with him. All these things he had left and had come to Milan for no other reason than to be with me: for with a real passion for truth and wisdom, he was in the same anguish as I and the same uncertain wavering; and he continued his ardent search for the way of happiness and his close investigation of the most difficult questions. Thus there were together the mouths of three needy souls, bitterly confessing to one another their spiritual poverty and waiting upon You that You *might give them their food in due season.*[67] And amidst the bitter disappointments which through Your mercy followed all our worldly affairs, darkness clouded our souls as we tried to see why we suffered these things. And we turned away in deepest gloom saying, "How long shall these things be?"[68] This question was ever on our lips, but for all that we did not give up our worldly ways, because we still saw no certitude which it was worth changing our way of life to grasp.

XI

(18) I was much exercised in mind as I remembered how long it was since that nineteenth year of my age in which I first felt the passion for true knowledge and resolved that when I found it I would give up all the empty hopes and lying follies of vain desires.[69] And here I was going on for thirty, still sticking in the same mire,[70] greedy for the enjoyment of things present though they ever eluded me and wasted my soul, and at every moment saying: "Tomorrow I shall find it: it will be all quite clear and I shall grasp it. Faustus will come and explain everything. And those mighty Academics—is it true that nothing can be grasped with certainty for the directing of life? No: we must search the more closely and not despair. For now the things in the Scriptures which used to seem absurd are no longer absurd, but can be quite properly understood in another sense. I shall set my foot upon that step on which my parents placed me as a child, until I clearly find the truth. But where shall I search? When shall I search? Ambrose is busy. I am myself too busy to read. And in any event where can I find the books? Who has them, or when can I procure them? Can I borrow them from anyone? I must appoint set times, set apart certain hours for the health of my soul. A great hope has dawned: the Catholic faith does not teach the things I thought and vainly accused it of Catholic scholars hold it blasphemy to believe God limited within the shape of a human body. Do I hesitate to knock, that other truths may be opened?[71] My pupils occupy

the morning hours, but what do I do with the rest? Why not do this? But if I do, when shall I have time to visit the powerful friends of whose influence I stand in need,[72] or when prepare the lessons I sell to my pupils, or when refresh myself by relaxing my mind from too close preoccupation with my heavy concerns?

(19) "But perish all this. Let me dismiss this vanity and emptiness and give myself wholly to the search for truth. Life is a poor thing, death may come at any time: if it were to come upon me suddenly, in what state should I depart this life? And where am I to learn the things I have neglected? Or must I not rather suffer the punishment of my negligence? Or does death perhaps cut off and end all care along with our bodily sense? This too must be settled. But God forbid that it should be so. It is not for nothing or any mere emptiness that the magnificence of the authority of the Christian faith is spread over all the world. Such great and wonderful things would never have been wrought for us by God, if the life of the soul were ended by the death of the body. Why then do I delay to drop my hopes of this world and give myself wholly to the search for God and true happiness?

"Yet stay a moment. After all, these worldly things are pleasant, they have their own charm and it is no small charm. The mind is not easily cut off from them merely because it would be base to go back to them. Again, it would not be too difficult to win some post of honour: and what more should I have to wish for? I have a body of powerful friends: even if I press on to nothing more ambitious, I could at least get a governorship. And then I could marry a wife, with some little money of her own, so that she would not increase my expenditure.[73] And so I should have reached the limit of ambition. Many great men, well worthy of our imitation, have given themselves to the pursuit of wisdom even though they had wives."

(20) These things went through my mind, and the wind blew one way and then another, and tossed my heart this way and that. Time was passing and I delayed to turn to the Lord.[74] From day to day I postponed life in You, but I did not postpone the death that daily I was dying in myself. I was in love with the idea of happiness, yet I feared it where it was, and fled away from it in my search for it. The plain truth is that I thought I should be impossibly miserable if I had to forego the embraces of a woman: and I did not think of Your mercy as a healing medicine for that weakness,[75] because I had never tried it. I thought that continency was a matter of our own strength, and I knew that I had not the strength: for in my utter foolishness I did not know the word of Your Scripture that none can be continent unless You give it.[76] And truly You would have given it if with groaning of spirit I had assailed Your ears[77] and with settled faith had cast my care upon You.[78]

XII

(21) It was Alypius indeed who kept me from marrying, with his unvarying argument that if I did we could not possibly live together with untroubled leisure in the pursuit of wisdom,[79] as we had so long desired. For on that side of things he was quite extraordinarily chaste. Early in adolescence he had had the experience of sexual intercourse, but it took no hold upon him. Indeed he regretted having done it and despised it and from then on lived in complete continence. I brought up the example of those who had pursued wisdom in the married state and served God faithfully,[80] and faithfully kept and cherished their friends. But indeed I was far enough from their greatness of spirit. I was bound by this need of the flesh, and dragged with me the chain of its poisonous delight, fearing to be set free: and I rejected his words of wise counsel, pushing away the hand that would set me free as though it were hurting a sore place. Moreover, through me the serpent began to speak to Alypius himself. By my tongue the devil wove fascinating snares[81] and scattered them in his path for the entangling of his hitherto untrammelled feet.

(22) For he marvelled to see me, of whom he thought so much, stuck so fast in the grip of that particular lust as to affirm whenever we talked of it that I could not possibly lead a single life. I urged on my side, when I saw how puzzled he was, that there was a great difference between the snatched and furtive experience of sex which he had had as a boy—and now scarcely remembered and could therefore brush aside with no particular trouble—and the enjoyment of my permanent state. It only needed the honourable name of marriage, and he would have had no cause to wonder why I could not give up that way of life. The result was that he began to desire marriage himself, not through any lust for the pleasure of it but solely through curiosity: for as he explained, he wanted to discover what the thing was without which my life—which to him seemed so pleasing— would have seemed to me no life at all but torment. For his mind, itself free from the chain, marvelled at my enslavement; and from marvelling he came to a desire to try it. Thus he might well have entered upon the same experience and so fallen into the enslavement which at present he found so incomprehensible: for he was willing to make a covenant with death,[82] and *he that loves danger shall fall into it.*[83] Such honour as there is in marriage from the duty of well-ordered life together and the having of children, had very small influence with either of us. What held me so fiercely bound was principally the sheer habit of sating a lust that could never be satisfied, and what drew him who was not yet bound was curiosity about me. Thus we stood until You, O most High, not forsaking our dust[84] but pitying our pitifulness, helped us by secret and wonderful ways.

XIII

(23) Great effort was made to get me married. I proposed, the girl was promised me. My mother played a great part in the matter for she wanted to have me married and then cleansed with the saving waters of baptism, rejoicing to see me grow every day more fitted for baptism and feeling that her prayers and Your promises were to be fulfilled in my faith. By my request and her own desire she begged You daily with the uttermost intensity of her heart to show her in a vision something of my future marriage, but You would never do it. She did indeed see certain vain fantasies, under the pressure of her mind's preoccupation with the matter; and she told them to me, not, however, with the confidence she always had when You had shown things to her, but as if she set small store by them; for she said that there was a certain unanalysable savour, not to be expressed in words, by which she could distinguish between what You revealed and the dreams of her own spirit. Still she pushed on with the matter of my marriage, and the girl was asked for. She was still two years short of the age for marriage,[85] but I liked her and agreed to wait.

XIV

(24) There was a group of us friends who had much serious discussion together, concerning the cares and troubles of human life which we found so hard to endure. We had almost decided to seek a life of peace,[86] away from the throng of men. This peace we hoped to attain by putting together whatever we could manage to get, and making one common household for all of us: so that in the clear trust of friendship, things should not belong to this or that individual, but one thing should be made of all our possessions, and belong wholly to each one of us, and everybody own everything. It seemed that there might be perhaps ten men in this fellowship. Among us there were some very rich men, especially Romanianus, our fellow townsman, who had been a close friend of mine from childhood and had been brought to the court in Milan by the press of some very urgent business.[87] He was strongest of all for the idea and he had considerable influence in persuasion because his wealth was much greater than anyone else's. We agreed that two officers should be chosen every year to handle the details of our life together, leaving the rest undisturbed. But then we began to wonder whether our wives would agree, for some of us already had wives and I meant to have one. So the whole plan, which we had built up so neatly, fell to pieces in our hands and was simply dropped. We returned to our old sighing and groaning and treading of this world's broad and beaten ways:[88] for many thoughts were in our hearts, but *Thy counsel standeth forever.*[89] And out of Thy counsel didst Thou deride ours and didst prepare Thine own things for us, meaning to *give us meat in due season and to open Thy hands and fill our souls with Thy blessing.*[90]

XV

(25) Meanwhile my sins were multiplied.[91] She with whom I had lived so long was torn from my side as a hindrance to my forthcoming marriage. My heart which had held her very dear was broken and wounded and shed blood. She went back to Africa, swearing that she would never know another man, and left with me the natural son I had had of her. But I in my unhappiness could not, for all my manhood, imitate her resolve. I was unable to bear the delay of two years which must pass before I was to get the girl I had asked for in marriage. In fact it was not really marriage that I wanted. I was simply a slave to lust. So I took another woman, not of course as a wife; and thus my soul's disease was nourished and kept alive as vigorously as ever, indeed worse than ever, that it might reach the realm of matrimony in the company of its ancient habit. Nor was the wound healed that had been made by the cutting off of my former mistress. For there was first burning and bitter grief; and after that it festered, and as the pain grew duller it only grew more hopeless.[92]

XVI

(26) Praise be to Thee, glory to Thee,[93] O Fountain of mercies. I became more wretched and Thou more close to me. Thy right hand was ready to pluck me from the mire and wash me clean, though I knew it not. So far nothing called me back from the depth of the gulf of carnal pleasure save fear of death and of the judgment to come, which, through all the fluctuations of my opinions, never left my mind. I discussed with my friends Alypius and Nebridius concerning the nature of good and evil, and Epicurus would certainly have won the palm in my judgment if I had not believed that after death there remained life for the soul and treatment according to its deserts, which Epicurus did not hold. And I put the question, supposing we were immortals and could live in perpetual enjoyment of the body without any fear of loss, why we should not then be happy, or what else should we seek.[94] I did not realise that it belonged to the very heart of my wretchedness to be so drowned and blinded in it that I could not conceive that light of honour, and of beauty loved for its own sake, which the eye of the flesh does not see but only the innermost soul. I was so blind that I never came to ask myself what was the source of the pleasure I found in discussing these ideas (worthless as they were) with friends, and of my inability to be happy without friends, even in the sense of happiness which I then held, no matter how great the abundance of carnal pleasure. For truly I loved my friends, for their own sake, and I knew that I was in turn so loved by them. O, tortuous ways! Woe to my soul with its rash hope of finding something better if it forsook Thee! My soul turned and turned again, on back and sides and belly, and the bed was always hard. For Thou alone art her rest. And behold Thou art close

at hand[95] to deliver us from the wretchedness of error and establish us in Thy way,[96] and console us with Thy word: "Run,[97] I shall bear you up and bring you and carry you to the end."[98]

Notes

1. See Ps. 70(71):5.

2. Literally, "to where did you withdraw"? See Ps. 9:22(10:1).

3. See Job 35:11 Old Latin.

4. See Ps. 34:6.

5. See X.27.38.

6. See Ps. 72(73):26.

7. See Ps. 67:23(68:22).

8. In one of the most poignant scenes of the *Aeneid,* the mother of Euryalus sees the mangled corpse of her son and asks, "Is it for this that I followed after you by land and by sea?" (Virgil, *Aeneid* 9.492).

9. Luke 7:14.

10. See Ps. 69:2(70:1).

11. See Ps. 17:29(18:28).

12. See John 4:14.

13. See Gal. 4:14.

14. The *accessio critica* is the heightening of the fever before it finally breaks. See *Explanations of the Psalms* 72.

15. As bishop of Hippo Augustine would also forbid the practice, though his efforts were not always met with success.

16. Literally, "in imitation of the Passion." Because of their willingness to die for their faith, the martyrs are particularly conspicuous imitators of Christ, and hence the cult of the martyrs was closely linked to the Mass and the Eucharist, the sacramental re-presencing of the crucifixion and resurrection of Christ.

17. See Rom. 12:11.

18. See 1 Tim. 5:10.

19. See Ps. 15(16): 11; Prov. 6:23, 10:17, 15:10.

20. Literally, "the pit," a common biblical image. See Ps. 7:16(15), 56:7(57:6); Prov. 26:27; Matt. 15:14.

21. One of the duties of a bishop in late antiquity was to act as judge of what was essentially a small claims court (see p. xvi).

22. Although reading silently was not unheard of in the ancient world, it was far more common until the late Middle Ages to read aloud even when one was alone.

23. Literally, "every Lord's Day." Augustine eschewed the use of the word *Sunday* (named after the sun or the sun god) for the day sanctified by Christ's resurrection from the dead.

24. See 2 Tim. 2:1 5.

25. Cen. 1:26. Cf. III.7.12, V.10.20.

26. See 1 Cor. 13:12.

27. See Matt. 7:7.

28. See Col. 1:18,24.

29. See 1.11.17.

30. 2 Cor. 3:6.

31. See 2 Cor. 3:14ff.

32. See "Typological Exegesis," pp. 333–34.

33. See Ps. 116(117):2.

34. See Ps. 16:8(17:7); Dan. 4:32(35).

35. As Augustine writes in *On True Religion*, God uses two principal ways of healing the wounds of sin: reason and the authority of faith (24.45).

36. Literally, "when we were weak." See Rom. 5:6.

37. Literally, "of those who are not light of heart." See Ecclus.(Sir.) 19:4.

38. See Matt. 7:13–14.

39. See Ps. 2:4, 36(37):13.

40. See Ps. 62:9(63:8), 72(73):28.

41. See Rom. 9:5.

42. See Isa. 6:10; Matt. 13:15.

43. Panegyrics of this kind were a common part of the orator's life. According to Henry Chadwick, Augustine most likely delivered this speech to Emperor Valentinian II on November 22, 384.

44. See Ps. 41:11(42:10).

45. See Ps. 22(23):4.

46. See Jer. 9:24; 1 Cor. 1:31; 2 Cor. 10:17.

47. Alypius was a native of Thagaste, bom after 354 into a family nobler than Augustine's; he died sometime around 427 or 428. Most of what we know about him comes from Augustine's writings.

48. See note on IV.3.6.

49. Although the "Circus Games," or simply "The Games," specifically designated chariot races, they could also signify other forms of spectacle.

50. The word for "high priest" (*antistes*) was also used to designate a Catholic bishop. Alypius became the bishop of Thagaste some time prior to March 395.

51. See Ps. 68:6(68:5).

52. Prov. 9:8 Old Latin.

53. See Ezek. 1:13.

54. See. Ps. 106(107):8. Literally, "your mercies which confess to you from my marrow," that is, from my innermost being (cf. Heb. 4:12).

55. See Prov. 6:26.

56. The celibacy that the Manichean Elders claimed to practice was, according to Augustine, inauthentic and often feigned. Some Elders may have taken celibacy seriously, but they tried to remain continent by dint of their own efforts. As Augustine comes to learn, true continence is a gift from God (see VIII.11.27, IX.1.1, X.29.40).

57. See Jth. 6:15.

58. See Isa. 57:13.

59. See Wis. 1:6; Jer. 29:23.

60. Since one of the duties of a bishop in the fourth and fifth centuries was arbitrating legal disputes (see notes at VI.3.3 and XI.2.2), Alypius' brush with a wrongful conviction was a providential lesson in the difficulties of determining innocence and guilt from appearances.

61. An expert who advised magistrates on the administration of law.

62. Literally, the "Count of Italian Largesse" (*largitionum*). The holder of this office supervised monetary taxes and the minting of currency for all of Italy.

63. Praetors in the fourth century were minor administrators. Copying books at a discount was no small temptation in an age when the cost of a single transcribed manuscript could be considerable.

64. Luke 16:10–11.

65. See Isa. 55:11.

66. Luke 16:11–12.

67. Ps. 144(145): 1 5.

68. See Ps. 12:2(13:1).

69. See Ps. 39:5(40:4).

70. See Terence, *Phormio* 780.

71. See Matt. 7:7–8.

72. As Alypius' encounter with the powerful senator illustrates, patronage was essential to worldly success In Roman life. In a custom called the *salutatio matutina*, or morning greeting, clients would visit their patrons at the start of the day to pay their respects.

73. Augustine would have probably had to bribe key officials—or at least entertain them lavishly—in order to solidify his hold on a provincial governorship.

74. See Ecclus.(Sir.) 5:8.

75. See Matt. 4:23.

76. See Wis. 8:21.

77. Literally, "knocked upon your ears." See Matt. 7:7.

78. See Ps. 54:23(55:22).

79. Literally, "in the love of wisdom," that is, in philosophy. See III.4.8.

80. Literally, "found favor with God." See Heb. 13:16.

81. See III.6.10; V.3.3; X.36.59.

82. See Wis. 1:16; Isa. 28:18.

83. Ecclus.(Sir.) 3:27.

84. See Gen. 2:7.

85. The Code of Justinian set the legal age at twelve years old for girls and fourteen for boys (*Inst.* 1.22). The short life spans of the era made early marriage desirable, while the strong social support available to young and inexperienced spouses made it possible.

86. Literally, "to live leisurely." When used in a philosophical context, leisure (*otium*) implies not idleness but the life of contemplation.

87. Romanianus, a native of Thagaste, was a wealthy benefactor whose generosity made Augustine's studies at Carthage possible (*Against the Academics* 2.23). He was related to Augustine (*Letter* 26), though precisely how is not clear. After persuading Romanianus to join the Manichean sect, Augustine dedicated *Against the Academics* to him in order to win him over to philosophy and *On True Religion* in order to encourage his conversion to Christianity. What "urgent business" drew him to Milan is not known, though it is mentioned in *Against the Academics* as calamitous (1.1.2).

88. See Matt. 7:13.

89. Prov. 19:21.

90. Ps. 144(145):15–16.

91. See Ecclus.(Sir.) 23:3.

92. See "Concubinage in Antiquity," pp. 327–29

93. See 1 Par. (Chron.) 29:11–12.

94. See Cicero's summary of this Epicurean tenet in *De finibus* 1.12.40.

95. See Ps. 138(139):8.

96. See Ps. 31(32):8.

97. See 1 Cor. 9:24.

98. See Isa. 46:4.

Book 7

I

(1) NOW my evil sinful youth was over and I had come on into young manhood;[1] but the older in years, the baser was my vanity, in that I could not conceive any other kind of substance than what these eyes are accustomed to see. I did not indeed, O God, think of You under the figure of a human body From the moment I began to know anything of philosophy, I had rejected that idea; and I rejoiced to find the same rejection in the faith of our spiritual mother. Your Catholic Church. But what else to think You I did not know.

As a man, though so poor a man, I set myself to think of You as the supreme and sole and true God;[2] and with all my heart I believed You incorruptible and inviolable and immutable, for though I did not see whence or how, yet I saw with utter certainty that what can be corrupted is lower than what cannot be corrupted, that the inviolable is beyond question better than the violable, and that what can suffer no change is better than what can be changed. My heart cried out passionately against all my imaginings; and I tried with this one truth to beat away all that circling host of uncleannesses[3] from the eyes of my mind. But they were scarce gone for the space of a single glance.[4] They came again close packed upon me, pressed upon my gaze and so clouded it that though I did not even then think of You under the shape of a human body, yet I could not but think of You as some corporeal substance, occupying all space, whether infused in the world, or else diffused through infinite space beyond the world.[5] Yet even at this I thought of You as incorruptible and inviolable and immutable, and I still saw those as better than corruptible and violable and mutable. But whatever I tried to see as not in space seemed to me to be nothing, absolutely nothing, not even a void: for if a body were taken out of its place and the place remained without any body, whether of earth or water or air or sky, it would still be an empty place, a space-occupying nothingness.

(2) Thus I was so gross of mind[6]—not seeing even myself clearly—that whatever was not extended in space, either diffused or massed together or swollen out or having some such qualities or at least capable of having them, I thought must be nothing whatsoever. My mind was in search of such images as the forms my eye was accustomed to see; and I did not realise that the mental act by which I formed these images was not itself a bodily image: yet it could not have formed them unless it were something and something great. I conceived of You, Life of my life, as mighty everywhere and throughout infinite space, piercing through the whole mass of the world, and spread measureless and limitless every way beyond the world, so that the earth should have You and the sky should have You and

all things should have You, and that they should be bounded in You but You nowhere bounded. For as the body of the air, which is above the earth, does not hinder the sun's light from passing through it, and that light penetrates it, yet does not break it or cut it but fills it wholly: so I thought that the body not only of the sky and air and sea but of the earth also was penetrable by You and easily to be pierced in all its parts, great and small, for the receiving of Your presence, while Your secret inspiration governed inwardly and outwardly all the things You had created.

This I held because I could think of nothing else. But it was false. For if it were so, a greater part of the earth would have contained a greater part of You, and a lesser a lesser; and all things should be filled with You in such a way that the body of an elephant should contain more of You than the body of a sparrow simply because it is larger and takes up so much more room; and so You would make Your parts present in the parts of the world piece by piece, little pieces in the little pieces, great masses in the great masses. That of course is not the truth of it. But You had not as yet enlightened my darkness.[7]

II

(3) But against [the Manichees] who deceived others because they were deceived themselves, and whose speech was dumbness because Your word did not sound from them, that argument was sufficient which long before, as far back as our Carthage days, had been proposed by Nebridius. I remember that when we heard it we were all powerfully struck by it. What would that imaginary brood of Darkness, which the Manichees were wont to set up as an opposing substance, have done against You if You had refused to fight with it?[8] For if the answer was that it would have done You some damage, that would have been to make You violable and subject to corruption. But if the answer was that it could in no way have harmed You, then they would show no reason for Your fighting with it. But it was precisely the result of Your fighting that some part or member of You, some offspring of Your substance, was mingled with those contrary powers, those natures not created by You; and was so far corrupted by them and changed for the worse as to be turned from beatitude into misery and to need assistance to deliver it and make it clean. This was the human soul. It was enslaved, contaminated and corrupted; and to its aid came Your Word in its freedom and purity and integrity. But that Word was itself corruptible, because it was from one and the same substance [as the soul]. Thus if they affirmed You, whatever You are—that is Your substance by which You are—to be incorruptible, all these ideas of theirs must be false and execrable; but if they affirm You corruptible, that would on the face of it be false and to be abominated. Therefore this argument of Nebridius was sufficient against these men, and I should utterly have

vomited them up from my overcharged breast, because they had no way of escape, without horrible sacrilege of heart and tongue, from what they held and said of You.

III

(4) But though I said and firmly held that the Lord God was incorrupt-ible and unalterable and in no way changeable, the true God who made not only our souls but our bodies also, and not only our souls and bodies but all things whatsoever, as yet I did not see, clear and unravelled, what was the cause of evil. Whatever that cause might be, I saw that no expla-nation would do which would force me to believe the immutable God mutable; for if I did that I should have been the very thing I was trying to find [namely a cause of evil]. From now it was with no anxiety that I sought it, for I was sure that what the Manichees said was not true. With all my heart I rejected them, because I saw that while they inquired as to the source of evil, they were full of evil themselves,[9] in that they preferred rather to hold that Your substance suffered evil than that their own sub-stance committed it.

(5) So I set myself to examine an idea I had heard—namely that our free will is the cause of our doing evil, and Your just judgment[10] the cause of our suffering evil. I could not clearly discern this. I endeavoured to draw the eye of my mind from the pit, but I was again plunged into it; and as often as I tried, so often was I plunged back. But it raised me a little towards Your light that I now was as much aware that I had a will as that I had a life. And when I willed to do or not do anything, I was quite cer-tain that it was myself and no other who willed, and I came to see that the cause of my sin lay there.

But what I did unwillingly, it still seemed to me that I rather suffered than did, and I judged it to be not my fault but my punishment: though as I held You most just, I was quite ready to admit that I was being justly punished.

But I asked further: "Who made me? Was it not my God, who is not only Good but Goodness itself? What root reason is there for my willing evil and failing to will good, which would make it just for me to be pun-ished? Who was it that set and ingrafted in me this root of bitterness,[11] since I was wholly made by my most loving God? If the devil is the author, where does the devil come from? And if by his own perverse will he was turned from a good angel into a devil, what was the origin in him of the perverse will by which he became a devil, since by the all-good Creator he was made wholly angel?" By such thoughts I was cast down again and almost stifled; yet I was not brought down so far as the hell of that error, where no man confesses unto You,[12] the error which holds rather that You suffer evil than that man does it.

IV

(6) I now tried to discover other truths, as I had already come to realise that incorruptible is better than corruptible, so that You must be incorruptible, whatever might be Your nature. For no soul ever has been able to conceive or ever will be able to conceive anything better than You, the supreme and perfect Good. Therefore since the incorruptible is unquestionably to be held greater than the corruptible—and I so held it—I could now draw the conclusion that unless You were incorruptible there was something better than my God. But seeing the superiority of the incorruptible, I should have looked for You in that truth and have learned from it where evil is—that is, learned the origin of the corruption by which Your substance cannot be violated. For there is no way in which corruption can affect our God, whether by His will or by necessity or by accident: for He is God, and what He wills is good, and Himself is Goodness; whereas to be corrupted is not good. Nor are You against Your will constrained to anything, for Your will is not greater than Your power. It would be greater only if You were greater than Yourself for God's will and God's power are alike God Himself.[13] And what unlooked-for accident can befall You, since You know all things? No nature exists save because You know it. Why indeed should I multiply reasons to show that the substance which is God is not corruptible, since if it were, it would not be God?

V

(7) I sought for the origin of evil, but I sought in an evil manner, and failed to see the evil that there was in my manner of enquiry. I ranged before the eyes of my mind the whole creation, both what we are able to see—earth and sea and air and stars and trees and mortal creatures; and what we cannot see—like the firmament of the heaven above, and all its angels and spiritual powers: though even these I imagined as if they were bodies disposed each in its own place. And I made one great mass of God's creation, distinguished according to the kinds of bodies in it, whether they really were bodies, or only such bodies as I imagined spirits to be. I made it huge, not as huge as it is, which I had no means of knowing, but as huge as might be necessary, though in every direction finite. And I saw You, Lord, in every part containing and penetrating it. Yourself altogether infinite: as if Your Being were a sea, infinite and immeasurable everywhere, though still only a sea: and within it there were some mighty but not infinite sponge, and that sponge filled in every part with the immeasurable sea.[14] Thus I conceived Your Creation as finite, and filled utterly by Yourself, and You were Infinite. And I said: "Here is God, and here is what God has created; and God is good, mightily and incomparably better than all these; but of His goodness He created them good: and see how He contains and fills them.

"Where then is evil, and what is its source, and how has it crept into the creation? What is its root, what is its seed? Can it be that it is wholly without being? But why should we fear and be on guard against what is not? Or if our fear of it is groundless, then our very fear is itself an evil thing. For by it the heart is driven and tormented for no cause; and that evil is all the worse, if there is nothing to fear yet we do fear. Thus either there is evil which we fear, or the fact that we fear is evil.

"Whence then is evil, since God who is good made all things good?[15] It was the greater and supreme Good who made these lesser goods, but Creator and Creation are alike good. Whence then comes evil? Was there perhaps some evil matter of which He made this creation, matter which He formed and ordered, while yet leaving in it some element which He did not convert into good? But why? Could He who was omnipotent be unable to change matter wholly so that no evil might remain in it? Indeed why did He choose to make anything of it and not rather by the same omnipotence cause it wholly not to be? Could it possibly have existed against His will? And if it had so existed from eternity, why did He allow it so long to continue through the infinite spaces of time past, and then after so long a while choose to make something of it? If He did suddenly decide to act, surely the Omnipotent should rather have caused it to cease to be, that He Himself, the true and supreme and infinite Good, alone should be. Or, since it was not good that He who was good should frame and create something not good, could He not have taken away and reduced to nothing that matter which was evil, and provided good matter of which to create all things? For He would not be omnipotent if He could not create something good without the aid of matter which He had not created."

Such thoughts I revolved in my unhappy heart, which was further burdened and gnawed at by the fear that I should die without having found the truth. But at least the faith of Your Christ, our Lord and Saviour,[16] taught by the Catholic Church, stood firm in my heart, though on many points I was still uncertain and swerving from the norm of doctrine. Yet my mind did not forsake it, but drank of it more deeply with every day that passed.

VI

(8) By now I had rejected the ridiculous prophesyings and blasphemous follies of the astrologers. Let Your own mercies, O my God, confess to You from the very depths of my soul.[17] For who else recalls us from the death that all error is, except the Life which cannot die, and the Wisdom which illumines the minds that need it and needs no illumination from any other, by which the world is governed even to the wind-blown leaves of the trees? It was You then who provided the cure for the obstinacy with which I argued with Vindicianus,[18] an old man of great mental acuteness,

and with Nebridius a young man of very fine soul. Vindicianus maintained with great vehemence, Nebridius not quite so vehemently but repeatedly, that there was no art for foreseeing the future, but that human guesses sometimes chanced to fall out right: those who said a great deal would often say things that did in fact come to pass, although those who said them did not really know, but merely happened to say them in the course of saying so many things. Then by Your provision came a man to help me in this matter, one who was a fairly frequent consulter of the astrologers. He was not himself skilled in the art, but as I have said he followed it up with some curiosity. One thing he did know, which he said that he had heard from his father: but he did not realise how utterly destructive it was to any belief in their art. This man, Firminus by name,[19] an educated man and trained in Rhetoric, consulted me as one very dear to him concerning certain affairs of his own in which he placed very considerable worldly hopes, wishing to know how I thought his constellations, as the astrologers call them, stood in the matter. I had now begun to turn towards Nebridius' opinion, yet for all my own uncertainty I did not absolutely refuse to read the stars and tell him what I saw; but I added that I was practically persuaded that the whole business was an empty folly. Thereupon he told me that his father had been deeply interested in the books of the astrologers and had had a friend as keen as himself in studying them. They studied and conferred together upon these follies each with the same burning zeal: they observed the moments at which the dumb animals about their houses brought forth their young, and noted the position of the sky at those moments, by way of getting experience in the art. And he said that he had heard from his father that when his mother was pregnant with him [Firminus], a female slave belonging to his father's friend happened to be pregnant at the same time. This her master could not be unaware of since he took such minute care to know about the whelping of his very dogs. The friends had numbered the days and hours and even the smallest parts of the hours, the one for his wife and the other for his servant, with the most careful observation. And it chanced that both women brought forth their child at the same instant. Thus they were compelled to cast the very same horoscope even to the exact minute for both children, the one for his son, the other for his slave. For when the women began to be in labour, each man let the other know what was happening in his own house, and they had messengers ready to send to each other as soon as either should know that the child had been born—and each of course would know instantly, since it was happening in his own household; and the messengers sent by each, so my friend said, met at a point equidistant from both houses, so that neither could observe any position of the stars or any moment of time different from the other. Yet Firminus, born to wealth in his parents' house, trod the pleasanter ways of life,[20] grew in riches and was raised to positions of honour; whereas the slave did not find the yoke of his condition relaxed, but served his masters. So Firminus who knew him told me.

(9) I heard all this, and I believed it, because of the man who told it. All my doubt was resolved and fell away. First I tried to win Firminus from his interest, by telling him that if I had had to consult his stars and truly foretell his future, I should surely have had to see in his horoscope that his parents had been people of standing in their neighbourhood, that his family was noble in his own city, that he was born free, that he was to have a sound education in the liberal arts. Whereas if the slave had consulted me upon the same constellations, for they were the very same, and asked me to foretell him the truth, then I ought to have seen in them that his family was lowborn, his condition servile, and all sorts of other particulars very different and very far removed from the first child's. Thus looking at the same constellations I must utter different things if I were to tell the truth, and if I said the same things I should be foretelling falsely. Thus I saw it as obvious that such things as happened to be said truly from the casting of horoscopes were true not by skill but by chance; and such things as were false were not due to want of skill in the art but merely that luck had fallen the other way.

(10) Having started upon this fine of reasoning I began to consider what I should answer if any one of those fools who got their living by astrology and whom I was already longing to assail and overwhelm with ridicule, should simply reply that either Firminus had told me, or his father had told him, falsely: so I set myself to considering the case of those who are born twins, who usually emerge from the womb so close to each other that the small interval of time involved—however much influence they claim that it has in nature—cannot be estimated by any human observation so as to be set down in the tables which the astrologer has to inspect in order to pronounce the truth. It will not be the truth. For instance, anyone inspecting those tables would have had to foretell the same future for Esau and Jacob, but the same things did not happen to them.[21] Therefore he would either have had to foretell falsely, or else if he foretold truly then he would have had to see different things in the same horoscope. So again we see that any truth he spoke would have been by chance not skill. For You, O Lord, the most just Ruler of the universe, can so act by Your secret influence upon both those who consult and those who are consulted—neither of them knowing what they do—that when a man consults he hears what it behooves him to hear, given the hidden merits of souls, from the abyss of Your just judgment.[22] Let no man say to You, "What is this or why is this?"[23] He must not say it, he must not say it. For he is a man.

VII

(11) Thus, O God my aid,[24] from those chains You had freed me. But I was still seeking what might be the source of evil and I could see no answer. Yet with all the ebb and flow of my thought You did not let me be carried away from the faith by which I believed that You were, and that Your substance was unchangeable, and that You cared for men and would judge them; and that in Christ Your Son our Lord, and in the Holy Scriptures which the authority of Your Catholic Church acknowledges, You had established the Way of man's salvation unto that Life which is to be after death.[25] But with these truths held safe and inviolably rooted in my mind, I was still on fire with the question whence comes evil. What were the agonies, what the anguish of my heart in labour, O my God!

But though I knew it not, You were listening. And when in silence I sought so vehemently, the voiceless contritions of my soul were strong cries to Your mercy. You knew what I was suffering and no man knew it. For how little it was that my tongue uttered of it in the ears even of my closest friends! Could they hear the tumult of my soul, for whose utterance no time or voice of mine would have been sufficient? Yet into Your hearing came all that I cried forth in the anguish of my heart, and my desire was in Your sight, and the sight of my eyes shone not for me.[26] For that sight was within, I looking outward.[27] Nor was that light in space: but I was intent upon things that are contained in space, and in them I found no place to rest. The things of space neither so received me that I could say, "It is enough, it is well," nor yet allowed me to return where I might find sufficiency and well-being. They were not good enough for me, I was not good enough for You: You are my true joy, and I am subject to You, and You have made subject to me the things below me that You have created. This was the right order and the middle way of salvation for me, that I should remain in Your image, and so in You should dominate my body. But when I rose against You in my pride and *ran upon my Lord with the thick neck of my shield*,[28] those lower things became greater than I and pressed me under so that I could neither loosen their grip nor so much as breathe. Wherever I looked they bore in upon me, massed thick; and when I tried to think, the images of corporeal things barred me from turning back towards the truth, as though they said: "Where are you going, base and unclean?" All these things had grown out of my wound, for You humble the proud like one wounded;[29] and I was separated from You by my own swollenness, as though my cheeks had swelled out and closed up my eyes.

VIII

(12) But You, O Lord, abide forever,[30] nor are You angry with us forever,[31] for You have pity upon our dust and ashes.[32] It was pleasing in Your sight[33] to reshape what was deformed in me.[34] And You kept stirring me

with Your secret goad[35] so that I should remain unquiet until You should become clear to the gaze of my soul. And from the secret hand of Your healing my swollenness abated, and the troubled and darkened sight of my mind was daily made better by the stinging ointment[36] of sorrow.

IX

(13) And first you willed to show me how You resist the proud and give grace to the humble,[37] and with how great mercy You have shown men the way of humility in that the Word was made flesh and dwelt among men.[38] Therefore You brought in my way by means of a certain man—an incredibly conceited man[39]—some books of the Platonists translated from Greek into Latin.[40] In them I found, though not in the very words, yet the thing itself and proved by all sorts of reasons: that *in the beginning was the Word and the Word was with God and the Word was God: the same was in the beginning with God; all things were made by Him and without Him was made nothing that was made; in Him was life and the life was the light of men, and the light shines in darkness and the darkness did not comprehend it.*[41] And I found in those same writings that the soul of man, though it *gives testimony of the light, yet is not itself the light;*[42] but the Word, God Himself, is *the true light which enlightens every man that comes into this world;*[43] and that *He was in the world and the world was made by Him, and the world knew Him not.*[44] But I did not read in those books that *He came unto His own, and His own received Him not, but to as many as received Him He gave power to be made the sons of God, to them that believed in His name.*[45]

(14) Again I found in them that the Word, God, was *born not of flesh nor of blood, nor of the will of man nor of the will of the flesh, but of God;*[46] but I did not find that *the Word became flesh.*[47]

I found it stated, differently and in a variety of ways, that the *Son being in the form of the Father thought it not robbery to be equal with God*[48] because by nature He was God. But these books did not tell me that *He emptied Himself, taking the form of a servant, being made in the likeness of men, and in habit found as a man;*[49] or that *He humbled Himself becoming obedient unto death, even to the death of the cross; for which cause God also hath exalted Him from the dead and given Him a name which is above all names, that in the name of Jesus every knee should bow of those that are in heaven, on earth, and under the earth; and that every tongue should confess that the Lord Jesus is in the glory of God the Father.*[50]

Further I read there that Your only—begotten Son was before all times and beyond all times and abides unchangeably, co-eternal with You, and that of *His fullness souls receive,*[51] that they may be blessed, and that by participation in that wisdom which abides in itself they are renewed[52] that they may be wise. But I did not read that *in due time He died for the ungodly,*[53] and that *Thou didst not spare Thy only-begotten Son but delivered*

Him up for us all.[54] For *Thou hast hid these things from the wise and hast revealed them to little ones,*[55] *that those who labour and are burdened should come to Him and He should refresh them, because He is meek and humble of heart;*[56] and *the meek He directs in judgment, and the gentle He teaches His ways,*[57] *beholding our lowness and our trouble and forgiving all our sins.*[58] But those who wear the high boots[59] of their sublimer doctrine do not hear Him saying, *Learn of me for I am meek and humble of heart and you shall find rest for your souls;*[60] and if *they know God, they have not glorified him as God or given thanks: but become vain in their thoughts; and their foolish heart is darkened. Professing themselves to be wise they become fools.*[61]

(15) Again I read in these books that they had *changed the glory of Thy incorruption* into idols and divers images, *into the likeness of the image of a corruptible man and of birds, and of four-footed beasts, and of creeping things*[62]— in fact into that Egyptian food for which Esau had lost his birthright,[63] since the people which was Your firstborn worshipped the head of a four-footed beast instead of You, turning in their heart back towards Egypt[64] and bowing down their soul, Your image, before the image of a calf that eats hay.[65] I found these things there and I did not feed upon them. For it pleased You, O Lord, to take away the reproach of inferiority from Jacob, so that the elder brother served the younger:[66] and You have called the Gentiles into Your inheritance.[67] From the Gentiles indeed I had come to You; and I fixed my mind upon the gold which You willed that Your people should bring with them from Egypt: for it was Yours, wherever it was.[68] And You had said to the Athenians by Your Apostle that in You we live and move and are, as certain of their own writers had said;[69] and obviously it was from [Athens] that these books came. But I did not fix my mind upon the idols of the Egyptians which they served with the gold that was Yours, *changing the truth of God into a lie and worshipping and serving a creature rather than the Creator.*[70]

X

(16) Being admonished by all this to return to myself,[71] I entered into my own depths, with You as guide; and I was able to do it because You were my helper.[72] I entered, and with the eye of my soul, such as it was, I saw Your unchangeable Light[73] shining over that same eye of my soul, over my mind. It was not the light of everyday that the eye of flesh can see, nor some greater light of the same order, such as might be if the brightness of our daily light should be seen shining with a more intense brightness and filling all things with its greatness. Your light was not that, but other, altogether other, than all such lights. Nor was it above my mind as oil above the water it floats on, nor as the sky is above the earth; it was above because it made me, and I was below because made by it. He who knows the truth knows that Light, and he that knows the Light knows eternity.[74]

Charity knows it. O eternal truth and true love and beloved eternity![75] Thou art my God, I sigh to Thee, by day and by night.[76] When first I knew Thee, Thou didst lift me up[77] so that I might see that there was something to see, but that I was not yet the man to see it. And Thou didst beat back the weakness of my gaze, blazing upon me too strongly, and I was shaken with love and with dread.[78] And I knew that I was far from Thee in the region of unlikeness,[79] as if I heard Thy voice from on high: "I am the food of grown men: grow and you shall eat Me. And you shall not change Me into yourself as bodily food, but into Me you shall be changed." And I learned that *Thou hast corrected man for iniquity and Thou didst make my soul shrivel up like a cobweb.*[80] And I said: "Is truth then nothing at all, since it is not extended either through finite spaces or infinite?" And thou didst cry to me from afar: *I am who am.*[81] And I heard Thee, as one hears in the heart; and there was from that moment no ground of doubt in me: I would more easily have doubted my own life than have doubted that truth is: which is *clearly seen, being understood by the things that are made.*[82]

XI

(17) Then I thought upon those other things that are less than You, and I saw that they neither absolutely are nor yet totally are not: they are, in as much as they are from You: they are not, in as much as they are not what You are. For that truly is, which abides unchangeably. But *it is good for me to adhere to my God,*[83] for if I abide not in Him, I cannot abide in myself. But He, in abiding in Himself, renews all things:[84] and *Thou art my God for Thou hast no need of my goods.*[85]

XII

(18) And it became clear to me that corruptible things are good:[86] if they were supremely good they could not be corrupted, but also if they were not good at all they could not be corrupted: if they were supremely good they would be incorruptible, if they were in no way good there would be nothing in them that might corrupt. For corruption damages; and unless it diminished goodness, it would not damage. Thus either corruption does no damage, which is impossible or—and this is the certain proof of it—all things that are corrupted are deprived of some goodness. But if they were deprived of all goodness, they would be totally without being. For if they might still be and yet could no longer be corrupted, they would be better than in their first state, because they would abide henceforth incorruptibly. What could be more monstrous than to say that things could be made better by losing all their goodness? If they were deprived of all goodness, they would be altogether nothing: therefore as long as they are, they are good. Thus whatsoever things are, are good; and that evil whose origin I sought is not a substance, because if it were a substance

it would be good. For either it would be an incorruptible substance, that is to say, the highest goodness; or it would be a corruptible substance, which would not be corruptible unless it were good. Thus I saw and clearly realised that You have made all things good, and that there are no substances not made by You. And because all the things You have made are not equal, they have a goodness [over and above] as a totality: because they are good individually, and they are very good all together, for our God has made all things very good.[87]

XIII

(19) To You, then evil utterly is not—and not only to You, but to Your whole creation likewise, evil is not: because there is nothing over and above Your creation that could break in or derange the order that You imposed upon it. But in certain of its parts there are some things which we call evil because they do not harmonise with other things; yet these same things do harmonise with still others and thus are good; and in themselves they are good. All these things which do not harmonise with one another, do suit well with that lower part of creation which we call the earth, which has its cloudy and windy sky in some way apt to it. God forbid that I should say: "I wish that these things were not"; because even if I saw only them, though I should want better things, yet even for them alone I should praise You: for that You are to be praised, things of earth show—*dragons, and all deeps, fire, hail, snow, ice, and stormy winds, which fulfill Thy word; mountains and all hills, fruitful trees and all cedars; beasts and all cattle, serpents and feathered fowl; kings of the earth and all people, princes and all judges of the earth; young men and maidens, old men and young, praise Thy name.*[88] And since from the heavens, O our God, *all Thy angels praise Thee in the high places, and all Thy hosts, sun and moon, all the stars and lights, the heavens of heavens, and the waters that are above the heavens, praise Thy name*[89]—I no longer desired better, because I had thought upon them all and with clearer judgment I realised that while certain higher things are better than lower things, yet all things together are better than the higher alone.

XIV

(20) There is no sanity[90] in those whom anything in creation displeases, any more than there was in me when I was displeased with many things that You had made. Because my soul did not dare to be displeased with my God, it would not allow that what displeased it was Yours. Thus it strayed off into the error of holding two substances, and it found no rest but talked wildly. Turning from that error it had made for itself a god occupying the infinite measures of all space, and had thought this god to be You, and had placed it in its heart,[91] and thus had once again become the temple of its own idol,[92] a temple abominable to You. But You caressed

my head, though I knew it not, and closed my eyes that they should not see vanity;[93] and I ceased from myself a little and found sleep from my madness. And from that sleep I awakened in You, and I saw You infinite in a different way; but that sight was not with the eyes of flesh.

XV

(21) And I looked upon other things, and I saw that they owed their being to You, and that all finite things are in You: but in a different manner, being in You not as in a place, but because You are and hold all things in the hand of Your truth, and all things are true inasmuch as they are: nor is falsehood anything, save that something is thought to be which is not. And I observed that all things harmonised not only with their places but also with their times; and that You, who alone are eternal, did not begin to work after innumerable spaces of time had gone by: since all the spaces of time, spaces past, spaces to come, could neither go nor come if You did not operate and abide.

XVI

(22) My own experience had shown me that there was nothing extraordinary in the same bread being loathsome to a sick palate and agreeable to a healthy, and in light being painful to sore eyes which is a joy to clear. Your justice displeases the wicked: but so do the viper and the smaller worms: yet these You have created good, and suited to the lower parts of Your creation—to which lower parts indeed the wicked themselves are well suited, insofar as they are unlike You, though they become suited to the higher parts as they grow more like You. So that when I now asked what is iniquity, I realised that it was not a substance but a swerving of the will which is turned towards lower things and away from You, O God, who are the supreme substance: so that it casts away what is most inward to it[94] and swells greedily for outward things.

XVII

(23) And I marvelled to find that at last I loved You and not some phantom instead of You; yet I did not stably enjoy my God, but was ravished to You by Your beauty, yet soon was torn away from You again by my own weight,[95] and fell again with torment to lower things. Carnal habit was that weight. Yet the memory of You remained with me and I knew without doubt that it was You to whom I should cleave, though I was not yet such as could cleave to You: *for the corruptible body is a load upon the soul, and the earthly habitation presses down the mind that muses upon many things.*[96] I was altogether certain that Your *invisible things are clearly seen from the creation of the world, being understood by the things that are made:*[97] so too are Your

everlasting power and Your Godhead. I was now studying the ground of my admiration for the beauty of bodies, whether celestial or of earth, and on what authority I might rightly judge of things mutable and say, "This ought to be so, that not so." Enquiring then what was the source of my judgment, when I did so judge I had discovered the immutable and true eternity of truth above my changing mind. Thus by stages I passed from bodies to the soul which uses the body for its perceiving, and from this to the soul's inner power, to which the body's senses present external things, as indeed the beasts are able; and from there I passed on to the reasoning power, to which is referred for judgment what is received from the body's senses. This too realised that it was mutable in me, and rose to its own understanding. It withdrew my thought from its habitual way,[98] abstracting from the confused crowds of phantasms that it might find what light suffused it, when with utter certainty it cried aloud that the immutable was to be preferred to the mutable, and how it had come to know the immutable itself: for if it had not come to some knowledge of the immutable, it could not have known it as certainly preferable to the mutable. Thus in the thrust of a trembling glance[99] my mind arrived at That Which Is.[100] Then indeed I saw clearly Your *invisible things which are understood by the things that are made;*[101] but I lacked the strength to hold my gaze fixed, and my weakness was beaten back again so that I returned to my old habits, bearing nothing with me but a memory of delight and a desire as for something of which I had caught the fragrance but which I had not yet the strength to eat.

XVIII

(24) So I set about finding a way to gain the strength that was necessary for enjoying You. And I could not find it until I embraced the *Mediator between God and man, the man Christ Jesus,*[102] *who is overall things, God blessed forever,*[103] who was calling unto me and saying, *I am the Way, the Truth, and the Life;*[104] and who brought into union with our nature that Food which I lacked the strength to take: for *the Word was made flesh*[105] that Your Wisdom, by which You created all things,[106] might give suck to our souls' infancy. For I was not yet lowly enough to hold the lowly Jesus as my God, nor did I know what lesson His embracing of our weakness was to teach. For Your Word, the eternal Truth, towering above the highest parts of Your creation, lifts up to Himself those that were cast down. He built for Himself here below a lowly house[107] of our clay,[108] that by it He might bring down from themselves and bring up to Himself those who were to be made subject, healing the swollenness of their pride and fostering their love: so that their self-confidence might grow no further but rather diminish, seeing the deity at their feet, humbled by the assumption of our coat of human nature:[109] to the end that weary at last they might cast themselves down upon His humanity and rise again in its rising.

XIX

(25) But I realised none of this at that time. I thought of Christ my Lord as of a man of marvellous wisdom, whom no other could possibly equal; and I saw His miraculous birth from a virgin—with the example it gave that temporal things are to be despised for the sake of immortality—as a mark of divine care for us, which surely merited for Him complete authority as our master. But the mystery contained in the truth that the Word was made flesh, I could not even faintly glimpse. From what had come down in writing about Him—that He ate and drank, slept, walked, was glad, was sad, preached—I had gathered that His body did not cleave to Your Word save through a human mind and soul. This anyone knows who grasps the immutability of Your Word, as I now grasped it in my own fashion and indeed held it unwaveringly. For at one moment to be moving the limbs by the will, at another keeping them still; now feeling some particular emotion, now not feeling it; now uttering wisdom in human speech, now silent—all these are properties of a mutable soul and a mutable mind. If Scripture told falsely of Christ on this matter, all of it would be involved in the peril of falsehood, and there would be no sure faith for mankind left in it. Taking then what was written there as truth, I saw Christ as complete man: not the body of a man only, or an animating soul without a rational mind, but altogether man; and I thought He was to be preferred to all others not as the very Person of Truth but because of the great excellence of His human nature and His more perfect participation in wisdom.

Alypius, on the other hand, imagined that Catholics believed that in Christ God was clothed in flesh—meaning that there was the godhead and a body in Him, but no soul. He thought they held that He had not a human mind. And since it seemed quite clear to him that what had been handed down to us concerning Christ could not have been done save by a creature both vital and rational, he was slower in his movement towards the Christian faith itself. But once he realised that this was the error of the Apollinarian heretics,[110] he liked the Catholic faith better and accepted it. But I admit that it was only some time later that I learned how, in the truth that the Word was made flesh, Catholic doctrine is distinguished from the error of Photinus.[111] In fact the refutation of heretics serves to bring into clearer light what Your Church holds and what sound doctrine is.[112] *For there must be also heresies: that they who are approved may be made manifest among the weak.*[113]

XX

(26) Now that I had read the books of the Platonists and had been set by them towards the search for a truth that is incorporeal, I came to see *Your invisible things which are understood by the things that are made.*[114] I was at

a standstill, yet I *felt* what through the darkness of my mind I was not able actually to see; I was certain that You are and that You are infinite, but not as being diffused through space whether finite or infinite: that You truly are and are ever the same,[115] not in any part or by any motion different or otherwise; and I knew that all other things are from You from the simple fact that they are at all. Of these things I was utterly certain, yet I had not the strength to enjoy You. I talked away as if I knew a great deal; but if I had not sought the way to You in Christ our Saviour,[116] I would have come not to instruction but to destruction. For I had begun to wish to appear wise, and this indeed was the fullness of my punishment; and I did not weep for my state, but was badly puffed up with my knowledge.[117] Where was that charity which builds[118] us up upon the foundation of humility, which is Christ Jesus?[119] Or when would those books have taught me that? Yet I think it was Your will that I should come upon these books before I had made study of the Scriptures, that it might be impressed on my memory how they had affected me: so that, when later I should have become responsive to You through Your Books with my wounds healed by the care of Your fingers, I might be able to discern the difference that there is between presumption and confession, between those who see what the goal is but do not see the way, and [those who see] the Way which leads to that country of blessedness, which we are meant not only to know but to dwell in. If I had been first formed by Your Holy Scriptures so that You had grown sweet to me through their familiar use, and had come later upon these books of the Platonists, they might have swept me away from the solid ground of piety; and even if I had remained firm in that disposition which for my health Scripture had taught me, I might perhaps have thought that the same disposition could have been acquired from those books if a man studied them alone.

XXI

(27) So now I seized greedily upon the adorable writing of Your Spirit, and especially upon the Apostle Paul. And I found that those difficulties, in which it had once seemed to me that he contradicted himself and that the text of his discourse did not agree with the testimonies of the law and the prophets,[120] vanished away. In that pure eloquence[121] I saw One Face, and I learned to rejoice with trembling.[122] I found that whatever truth I had read in the Platonists was said here with praise of Your grace: that he who sees should *not so glory as if he had not received*—and received, indeed, not only what he sees but even the power to see, *for what has he that he has not received?*[123] And further, that he [who sees] is not only taught to see You who are always the same, but is also strengthened to take hold of You; and that he who cannot see You from afar off, may yet walk on that way by which he may come and see and take hold. For though a man be *delighted*

with the law of God according to the inward man, what shall he do about that *other law in his members, fighting against the law of his mind and captivating him in the law of sin that is in his members?*[124] *For Thou art just, O Lord,*[125] but *we have sinned, we have committed iniquity, we have done wickedly*[126] and Thy hand has grown heavy upon us[127] and we are justly delivered over to that first sinner, the ruler of death,[128] because he has turned our will to the likeness of his will, whereby *he stood not in Thy truth.*[129] But what shall unhappy man do?[130] *Who shall deliver him from the body of this death, save the grace of God by Jesus Christ our Lord*[131] whom Thou hast begotten coeternally with Thee and *possessed in the beginning of Thy ways;*[132] *in whom the prince of this world*[133] found nothing worthy of death yet killed Him;[134] *and the handwriting was blotted out of the decree which was contrary to us.*[135]

The writings of the Platonists contain nothing of all this. Their pages show nothing of the face of that love, the tears of confession, Your sacrifice, an afflicted spirit, a contrite and humbled heart,[136] the salvation of Your people, the espoused city,[137] the promise of the Holy Spirit,[138] the chalice of our redemption.[139] In them no one sings: *Shall not my soul be submitted unto God? From Him is my salvation: for He is my God, my salvation, and my defence: I shall be no more moved.*[140] And we hear no voice calling: *Come unto me, all you that labour.*[141] They scorned to learn from Him, because He *is meek and humble of heart.*[142] *For thou hast hidden these things from the wise and prudent and hast revealed them to the little ones.*[143] It is one thing to see the land of peace from a wooded mountaintop, yet not find the way to it and struggle hopelessly far from the way, with hosts of those fugitive deserters from God, under their leader the Lion and the Dragon,[144] besetting us about and ever lying in wait; and quite another to hold to the way that leads there, a way guarded by the care of our heavenly General, where there are no deserters from the army of heaven to practise their robberies—for indeed they avoid that way as a torment. Marvellously these truths graved themselves in my heart when I read that least of Your Apostles[145] and looked upon Your works and trembled.[146]

Notes

1. That is, his youth (*adulescentia*), which lasted into his twenties, had ended, and he was entering into young manhood (*juventus*). See note on I.8.13.

2. See John 17:3.

3. The phrase is similar to Virgil's descriptions of the Harpies (*Aeneid* 3.233).

4. Literally, "in the twinkling of an eye" (1 Cor. 15:52).

5. See Plotinus, *Enneads* 6.5.2.

6. Literally, "fattened in heart." See Isa. 6:10 Old Latin; Matt. 13:15; Acts 28:27.

7. See Ps. 17:29(18:28).

8. See "Manichaeism," pp. 330–31.

9. See Rom. 1:29.

10. See Ps. 118(119):137.

11. See Heb. 12:15.

12. See Ps. 6:6(5).

13. Cf. Plotinus, *Enneads* 6.8.13.

14. Cf. Plotinus, *Enneads* 4.3.9.37–41, where the example of a net is used instead of a sponge.

15. See Gen. 1:31.

16. See 2 Pet. 2:20.

17. See Ps. 106(107):8.

18. See IV.3.5.

19. Little is known of Firminus outside of what Augustine tells us here.

20. Literally, he trod "the whitened roads of the world," a possible allusion to the lime mortar used in the construction of Roman roads.

21. See Gen. 25–27.

22. See Ps. 35:7(36:6).

23. See Ecclus.(Sir.) 39:26.

24. See Ps. 17:3(18:2).

25. See John 14:6.

26. See Ps. 37:9-11(38:8–10).

27. Cf. Plotinus, *Enneads* 6.5.12.

28. Job 15:26 Old Latin.

29. See Ps. 88:11(89:10).

30. See Ps. 101:13(102:12).

31. See Ps. 84:6(85:5).

32. See Job 42:6 Old Latin; 1.6.7 and X.5.7.

33. See Ps. 18:15(19:14).

34. Cf. X.27.38.

35. See Eccles. 12:11; Virgil, *Aeneid* 11.336–37.

36. Literally, "eye-salve." See Apoc.(Rev.) 3:18. Here and in other writings, Augustine uses the term for the incarnate Christ, whose sorrows were salutary for mankind.

37. 1 Pet. 5:5.

38. See John 1:14.

39. Possibly Manlius Theodorus, a Christian Neoplatonist to whom Augustine had enthusiastically dedicated *On the Happy Life*, a move which he later regretted (*Retractations* 1.2). In any event, the fact that Augustine names the heretic Faustus in V.3.3 but not his acquaintance here is noteworthy (see "Concubinage in Antiquity," pp. 327–29, final paragraph).

40. The exact identity of these books remains hotly contested. Though Augustine may have had some direct contact with Latin translations of Plato, it is far more likely that he is referring here to the writings of Plotinus and, to a lesser extent, Porphyry. Again it is noteworthy that he does not mention the texts by name, even though he does not hesitate to name Cicero's *Hortensius* in III.4.7.

41. John 1:1–5.

42. John 1:8.

43. John 1:9.

44. John 1:10.

45. John 1:11–12.

46. John 1:13.

47. John 1:14.

48. Phil. 2:6.

49. Phil. 2:7.

50. Phil. 2:8–11.

51. John 1:16.

52. See Wis. 7:27.

53. Rom. 5:6.

54. Rom. 8:32.

55. Matt. 11:25.

56. Matt. 11:28.

57. Ps. 24(25):9.

58. Ps. 24(2 5): 18.

59. *Cothurni* were buskins worn by tragic actors to increase their height.

60. Matt. 11:29.

61 Rom. 1:21–22.

62 Rom. 1:23.

63 See Gen. 25:33–34.

64 See Acts 7:39.

65 See Exod. 32:1–6; Ps. 105(106):20.

66 See Gen. 25:23; Rom. 9:12.

67. See Ps. 78(79):1.

68. See Exod. 3:22; 11:2. That is, just as God commanded the Hebrews to despoil the Egyptians of their gold, so too does He instruct Christians to take secular learning (in this case, Platonic philosophy) and put it to good use. See *On Christian Doctrine* 2.40.60.

69. See Acts 17:27–28.

70. Rom. 1:25. That is, Augustine was careful not to make the same mistake as the Hebrews in the wilderness: taking pagan goods (gold, wisdom, etc.) and using them for idolatrous rather than pious purposes.

71. Cf. Luke 15:17 (the Prodigal Son) and Plotinus, *Enneads* 1.6.9.

72. See Ps. 29:11(30:10).

73. See John 1:9.

74. See John 14:7.

75. An interlocking invocation of the Trinity.

76. See Ps. 1:2, 41:4(42:3); Jer. 9:1.

77. See Ps. 26(27):10.

78. See Plotinus, *Enneads* 1.6.7.12–19.

79. See Luke 15:13 (Prodigal Son); Plotinus, *Enneads* 1.8.13; Plato, *Statesman* 273d.

80. Ps. 38:12 (39:11). An *aranea* can mean either a spider or its web. Augustine takes the word to mean the latter, as when he writes: "What is more wasted away than a cobweb?. . . place your finger on it lightly, and it is ruined. . . . You have made my soul to be as such . . . by teaching me about my iniquity" (*Explanations of the Psalms* 38.18).

81. Exod. 3:14.

82. Rom. 1:20.

83. Ps. 72(73):28.

84. See Wis. 7:27.

85. Ps. 15(16):20.

86. See Plotinus, *Enneads* 3.2.5.25–32.

87. See Gen. 1:31.

88. Ps. 148:7–12.

89. Ps. 148:1–4.

90. *Sanitas* can also mean health or soundness. See Ps. 37:4, 8(38:3,7).

91. See Ezek. 14:7.

92. See 1 Cor. 6:16.

93. See Ps. 118(119):37.

94. See Ecclus.(Sir.) 10:10.

95. See Plotinus, *Enneads* 6.9.14.16–23.

96. Wis. 9:15.

97. Rom. 1:20.

98. See Cicero, *Disputationes Tusculanae* 1.6.38.

99. See 1 Cor. 15:52.

100. See Exod. 3:14. For the ways in which these stages of ascent recapitulate as well as depart from Plotinus', see *Enneads* 5.1.11.

101. Rom. 1:20.

102. 1 Tim. 2:5.

103. Rom. 9:5.

104. John 14:6.

105. John 1:14.

106. See Col. 1:16.

107. See Prov. 9:1.

108. See Gen. 2:7; 1.11.18; XIII.12.13, 17.20.

109. Literally, "our coat of skin," a reference to the animal skins Adam and Eve wore after their expulsion from Paradise (Gen. 1:21). According to Augustine and several other Church Fathers, the skins symbolize the mortality that mankind has taken on as a result of original sin (see XIII.15.16).

110. Apollinaris the Younger (*fl.* 4th c.) was a bishop of Laodicea who taught that Jesus Christ had a human body and a human sensitive soul but no rational faculty of the soul, the Divine Word having taken its place. His teachings were condemned by two Roman synods in 374 and 380 and at the Council of Constantinople in 381.

111. Photinus, Bishop of Sirmium in Rannonia (d. 376), held that Jesus Christ was a mere man since He did not exist as the Divine Word prior to the Incarnation.

112. See 1 Tim. 1:10; 2 Tim. 4:3-4; Tit. 1:9, 2:1.

113. Cor. 11:19.

114. Rom. 1:20.

115. See Ps. 101:28(102:27); Heb. 1:12.

116. See Tit. 1:4.

117. See 1 Cor. 8:1.

118. See 1 Cor. 8:1.

119. See 1 Cor. 3:11.

120. See Matt. 5:17, 7:12; Luke 16:16.

121. Literally, "chaste words." See Ps. 11:7(12:6).

122. See Ps. 2:11.

123. 1 Cor. 4:7.

124. Rom. 7:22–23.

125. Dan. 3:27; see Tob. 3:2; Est. 14:7; Ps. 118(119):137; Jer. 12:1; Apoc.(Rev.) 16:5.

126. Dan. 3:29.

127. See Ps. 31 (32):4.

128. See Heb. 2:14-15.

129. John 8:44.

130. See Rom. 7:24.

131. Rom. 7:24.

132. Prov. 8:22.

133. John 12:31, 14:30, 16:11.

134. See Luke 23:4, 14–15, 22; John 18:38; 19:4, 6.

135. Col. 2:14.

136. See Ps. 50:19(51:17).

137. See Apoc.(Rev.) 21:2.

138. Literally, "the earnest-money of the Holy Spirit" (see 2 Cor. 1:22, 5:5). As it follows mention of an espousal, this may be a reference to the money pledged by a groom for the financial security of his bride.

139. Most likely the Precious Blood of the Eucharist though, given the nuptial imagery in this passage, it may also be seen as a loving cup.

140. Ps. 61:2–3(62:1–2).

141. Matt. 11:28.

142. Matt. 11:29.

143. Matt. 11:25.

144. See Ps. 90(91):13. This passage compares the demons, or fallen angels, to deserters from the Roman imperial army who often went on to become high-way robbers.

145. St. Paul (see 1 Cor. 15:9).

146. See Hab. 3:2.

Book 8

I

(1) LET ME, O my God, remember with thanks to Thee[1] and confess Thy mercies upon me. Let my bones be pierced through with Thy love, and let them say, *Who is like unto Thee, O Lord?*[2] *Thou hast broken my bonds, I will sacrifice to Thee the sacrifice of praise.*[3] How Thou hast broken them I shall tell and all who adore Thee will say as they listen, "Blessed be the Lord in heaven and on earth,[4] great and wonderful is His name."[5]

Your words had rooted deep in my heart and I was fenced about on all sides by You.[6] Of Your eternal life I was now certain, though I saw it *in a dark manner and as through a glass.*[7] All my former doubt about an incorruptible substance from which every substance has its being was taken from me. My desire now was not to be more sure of You but more steadfast in You.

But in my temporal life all was uncertain; my heart had to be purged of the old leaven.[8] The way, our Saviour himself, delighted me; but I still shrank from actually walking a way so strait.[9] Then by You it came into my mind, and the idea appealed strongly to me,[10] to go to Simplicianus whom I knew to be Your good servant, for Your grace shone in him.[11] I had heard that from his youth he had lived in great love of You. He was now grown old; and it seemed to me that from a long lifetime spent in so firm a following of Your way he must have experienced much and learned much. And truly so it was. I hoped that if I conferred with him about my problems he might from that experience and learning show me the best way for one affected as I was to walk in Your path.

(2) For I saw the Church full; and one went this way, and one that.[12] But I was unhappy at the life I led in the world, and it was indeed a heavy burden, for the hope of honour and profit no longer inflamed my desire, as formerly, to help me bear so exacting a servitude. These things delighted me no longer in comparison with Your sweetness and the beauty of Your house which I loved.[13] But what still held me tight bound was my need of woman: nor indeed did the Apostle forbid me to marry, though he exhorted to a better state, wishing all men to be as he was himself.[14] But I in my weakness was for choosing the softer place, and this one thing kept me from taking a sure line upon others. I was weary and wasted with the cares that were eating into me, all because there were many things which I was unwilling to suffer but had to put up with for the sake of living with a wife, a way of life to which I was utterly bound. I had heard from the mouth of Truth itself that *there are eunuchs who have made themselves eunuchs for the kingdom of heaven;* but Christ had said. *He that can take it, let him take it.*[15] Certainly *all men are vain in whom there is not the knowledge of God and who cannot, by these good things that are seen, find Him that is.*[16] Now I was

no longer in that sort of vanity; I had gone beyond it and in the testimony of the whole creation I had found You, our Creator, and Your Word who is with You and one God with You, by whom You created all things.[17] But there is another sort of godlessness, that of the men who *knowing God have not glorified Him as God or given thanks.*[18] Into this also I had fallen, but Your right hand upheld me[19] and taking me out of it, placed me where I might find health. For You have said to man: *Behold, the fear of the Lord is wisdom;*[20] and again: *Be not desirous to seem wise,*[21] for *those who affirm themselves to be wise become fools.*[22] I had now found the pearl of great price,[23] and I ought to have sold all I had and bought it. But I hesitated still.

II

(3) So I went to Simplicianus, who had begotten Ambrose, now bishop, into Your grace, and whom indeed Ambrose loved as a father. I told him all the wanderings of my error. But when I told him that I had read certain books of the Platonists which had been translated into Latin by Victorinus, one—time professor of Rhetoric in Rome—who had, so I heard, died a Christian—he congratulated me for not having fallen upon the writings of other philosophers which are full of vain deceits, according to the elements of this world,[24] whereas in the Platonists God and his Word are everywhere implied. Then to draw me on to the humility of Christ, hidden from the wise and revealed to little ones,[25] he began to speak of Victorinus[26] himself whom he had known intimately when he was in Rome. Of Victorinus he told me what I shall now set down, for the story glorifies Your grace and it should be told to Your glory. For here was an old man deeply learned, trained in all the liberal sciences, a man who had read and weighed so many of the philosophers' writings, the teacher of so many distinguished senators, a man who on account of the brilliance of his teaching had earned and been granted a statue in the Roman forum—an honour the citizens of this world think so great.[27] He had grown old in the worship of idols, had taken part in their sacrilegious rites, for almost all the Roman nobility at that time was enthusiastic for them and was ever talking of "prodigies and the monster gods of every kind, and of the jackal-headed Anubis—who all had once fought against the Roman deities Neptune and Venus and Minerva"[28] and had been beaten: yet Rome was on its knees before these gods it had conquered. All this Victorinus with his thunder of eloquence had gone on championing for so many years even into old age:[29] yet he thought it no shame to be the child of Your Christ, an infant at Your font, bending his neck under the yoke of humility[30] and his forehead to the ignominy of the cross.[31]

(4) O Lord, Lord, who dost *bow down Thy heavens and descend, dost touch the mountains and they smoke;*[32] by what means didst Thou find Thy way into that breast? He read, so Simplicianus said, Holy Scripture; he

investigated all the Christian writings most carefully and minutely. And he said not publicly but to Simplicianus privately and as one friend to another: "I would have you know that I am now a Christian." Simplicianus answered: "I shall not believe it nor count you among Christians unless I see you in the Church of Christ." Victorinus asked with some faint mockery: "Then is it the walls that make Christians?" He went on saying that he was a Christian, and Simplicianus went on with the same denial, and Victorinus always repeated his retort about the walls. The fact was that he feared to offend his friends, important people and worshippers of these demons; he feared that their enmity might fall heavily upon him from the height of their Babylon dignity[33] as from the cedars of Lebanon which the Lord had not yet brought down.[34] But when by reading in all earnestness he had drawn strength, he grew afraid that Christ might deny him before His angels if he were ashamed to confess Christ before men.[35] He felt that he was guilty of a great crime in being ashamed of the sacraments of the lowliness of Your Word, when he had not been ashamed of the sacrilegious rites of those demons of pride whom in his pride he had worshipped. So he grew proud towards vanity and humble towards truth. Quite suddenly and without warning he said to Simplicianus, as Simplicianus told me: "Let us go to the church. I wish to be made a Christian." Simplicianus, unable to control his joy, went with him. He was instructed in the first mysteries of the faith,[36] and not long after gave in his name that he might be regenerated by baptism,[37] to the astonishment of Rome and the joy of the Church. The proud saw it and were enraged, ground their teeth and were livid with envy:[38] but the Lord God was the hope of His servant, so that he had no regard for vanities and lying follies.[39]

(5) Finally when the hour had come for his profession of faith—which at Rome was usually made by those who were about to enter into Your grace in a set form of words learned and memorised and spoken from a platform in the sight of the faithful[40]—Simplicianus told me that the priests offered Victorinus to let him make the profession in private, as the custom was with such as seemed likely to find the ordeal embarrassing. But he preferred to make profession of salvation in the sight of the congregation in church. For there had been no salvation in the Rhetoric he had taught, yet he had professed it publicly. Obviously therefore he should be in less fear of Your meek flock when he was uttering Your word, since he had had no fear of the throng of the deluded when uttering his own. When therefore he had gone up to make his profession all those who knew him began whispering his name to one another with congratulatory murmurs. And indeed who there did not know him? And from the lips of the rejoicing congregation sounded the whisper, "Victorinus, Victorinus." They were quick to utter their exultation at seeing him and as quickly fell silent to hear him. He uttered the true faith with glorious confidence, and

they would gladly have snatched him to their very heart. Indeed, they did take him to their heart in their love and their joy: with those hands they took him.

III

(6) O loving God, what is it in men that makes them rejoice more for the salvation of a soul that was despaired of or one delivered from a major peril, than if there had always been hope or the peril had been less? Even You, O Merciful Father, rejoice more *upon one sinner doing penance than upon ninety and nine just who need not penance.*[41] It is with special joy that we hear how the lost sheep is brought home upon the exultant shoulders of the shepherd[42] and how the coin is put back into Your treasury while the neighbours rejoice with the woman who found it.[43] And the joy we feel at Mass in Your church brings tears as we hear of that younger son who was dead and made alive again, who had been lost and was found.[44] You rejoice in us and in Your angels who stand fast in holy charity. For You are ever the same[45] because You ever know, and in the one way of knowing, all those things which are not always existent nor always the same.

(7) What is it in the soul, I ask again, that makes it delight more to have found or regained the things it loves than if it had always had them? Creatures other than man bear the same witness, and all things are filled with testimonies acclaiming that it is so. The victorious general has his triumph; but he would not have been victorious if he had not fought; and the greater danger there was in the battle, the greater rejoicing in the triumph. The storm tosses the sailors and threatens to wreck the ship; all are pale with the threat of death.[46] But the sky grows clear, the sea calm, and now they are as wild with exultation as before with fear. A friend is sick and his pulse threatens danger; all who want him well feel as if they shared his sickness. He begins to recover, though he cannot yet walk as strongly as of old: and there is more joy than there was before, when he was still well and could walk properly. Note too that men procure the actual pleasures of human life by way of pain—I mean not only the pain that comes upon us unlooked for and beyond our will, but unpleasantness planned and willingly accepted. There is no pleasure in eating or drinking, unless the discomfort of hunger and thirst come before. Drunkards eat salty things[47] to develop a thirst so great as to be painful, and pleasure arises when the liquor quenches the pain of the thirst. And it is the custom that promised brides do not give themselves at once lest the husband should hold the gift cheap unless delay had set him craving.

(8) We see this in base and dishonourable pleasure, but also in the pleasure that is licit and permitted, and again in the purest and most honourable friendship. We have seen it in the case of him who had been dead and was brought back to life, who had been lost and was found.[48]

Universally the greater joy is heralded by greater pain. What does this mean,[49] O Lord my God, when Thou art an eternal joy to Thyself, Thou Thyself art joy itself, and things about Thee ever rejoice in Thee? What does it mean that this part of creation thus alternates between need felt and need met, between discord and harmony? Is this their mode of being, this what Thou didst give them, when from the heights of heaven[50] to the lowest earth,[51] from the beginning of time to the end, from the angel to the worm, from the first movement to the last, Thou didst set all kinds of good things and all Thy just works each in its place, each in its season? Alas for me, how high art Thou in the highest,[52] how deep in the deepest! And Thou dost never depart from us, yet with difficulty do we return to Thee.

IV

(9) Come, Lord, work upon us, call us back, set us on fire and clasp us close, be fragrant to us, draw us to Thy loveliness: let us love, let us run to Thee. Do not many from a deeper pit of blindness than Victorinus come back to Thee, enlightened by that light[53] in which they receive from Thee the power to be made Thy sons?[54] But because they are not so well-known, there is less rejoicing over them even by those who do know them. For when many rejoice together, the joy of each one is richer: they warm themselves at each other's flame. Further, insofar as they are known widely, they guide many to salvation and are bound to be followed by many. So that even those who have gone before rejoice much on their account, because the rejoicing is not only on their account. It would be shameful if in Your tabernacle the persons of the rich should be welcome before the poor, or the nobly born before the rest: since *Thou hast rather chosen the weak things of the world to confound the strong, and hast chosen the base things of the world and the things that are contemptible, and things that are not, in order to bring to nought things that are.*[55] It was by Paul's tongue that You uttered these words. Yet when Paulus the proconsul[56] came under the light yoke of Christ[57] and became a simple subject of the great King, his pride brought low[58] by the Apostle's spiritual might, even that least of Your Apostles[59] now desired to be called Paul, in place of his former name of Saul, for the glory of so great a victory. Victory over the enemy is greater when we win from him a man whom he holds more strongly and through whom he holds more people. He has a firmer hold on the eminent by reason of their noble rank, and through them he holds very many people by reason of their authority. Therefore the heart of Victorinus was all the more welcome because the devil had held it as an impregnable fortress; and the tongue of Victorinus because it was a strong sharp weapon with which the devil had slain many. It was right for Your sons to rejoice with more abounding joy because our King had bound the strong man,[60] and

they saw his vessels taken from him and cleansed and made available unto Your honour and *profitable to the Lord unto every good work.*[61]

V

(10) Now when this man of Yours, Simplicianus, had told me the story of Victorinus, I was on fire to imitate him: which indeed was why he had told me. He added that in the time of the Emperor Julian, when a law was made prohibiting Christians from teaching Literature and Rhetoric,[62] Victorinus had obeyed the law, preferring to give up his own school of words rather than Your word, by which You make eloquent the tongues of babes.[63] In this he seemed to me not only courageous but actually fortunate, because it gave him the chance to devote himself wholly to You. I longed for the same chance, but I was bound not with the iron of another's chains, but by my own iron will. The enemy held my will; and of it he made a chain and bound me. Because my will was perverse it changed to lust, and lust yielded to become habit, and habit not resisted became necessity. These were like links hanging one on another—which is why I have called it a chain—and their hard bondage held me bound hand and foot. The new will which I now began to have, by which I willed to worship You freely[64] and to enjoy You, O God, the only certain Joy, was not yet strong enough to overcome that earlier will rooted deep through the years. My two wills, one old, one new,[65] one carnal, one spiritual,[66] were in conflict and in their conflict wasted my soul.

(11) Thus, with myself as object of the experiment, I came to understand what I had read, how the *flesh lusts against the spirit and the spirit against the flesh.*[67] I indeed was in both camps, but more in that which I approved in myself than in that which I disapproved. For in a sense it was now no longer I that was in this second camp, because in large part I rather suffered it unwillingly than did it with my will.[68] Yet habit had grown stronger against me by my own act, since I had come willingly where I did not now will to be. Who can justly complain when just punishment overtakes the sinner? I no longer had the excuse which I used to think I had for not yet forsaking the world and serving You, the excuse namely that I had no certain knowledge of the truth. By now I was quite certain; but I was still bound to earth and refused to take service in Your army;[69] I feared to be freed of all the things that impeded me, as strongly as I ought to have feared the being impeded by them.

(12) I was held down as agreeably by this world's baggage as one often is by sleep; and indeed the thoughts with which I meditated upon You[70] were like the efforts of a man who wants to get up but is so heavy with sleep that he simply sinks back into it again. There is no one who wants to be asleep always—for every sound judgment holds that it is best to be awake— yet a man often postpones the effort of shaking himself awake when he feels a sluggish heaviness in the limbs, and settles pleasurably

into another doze though he knows he should not, because it is time to get up. Similarly I regarded it as settled that it would be better to give myself to Your love rather than go on yielding to my own lust; but the first course delighted and convinced my mind, the second delighted my body and held it in bondage. For there was nothing I could reply when You called me: *Rise, thou that steepest and arise from the dead: and Christ shall enlighten thee;*[71] and whereas You showed me by every evidence that Your words were true, there was simply nothing I could answer save only laggard lazy words: "Soon," "Quite soon," "Give me just a little while." But "soon" and "quite soon" did not mean any particular time; and "just a little while" went on for a long while. It was in vain that *I delighted in Thy law according to the inner man, when that other law in my members rebelled against the law of my mind and led me captive in the law of sin that was in my members.*[72] For the law of sin is the fierce force of habit, by which the mind is drawn and held even against its will, and yet deservedly because it had fallen wilfully into the habit. Who *then should deliver me from the body of this death, but Thy grace only, through Jesus Christ our Lord?*[73]

VI

(13) Now, O Lord, my Helper and my Redeemer,[74] I shall tell and confess to Your name[75] how You delivered me from the chain of that desire of the flesh which held me so bound, and the servitude of worldly things. I went my usual way with a mind ever more anxious, and day after day I sighed for You. I would be off to Your church as often as my business, under the weight of which I groaned, left me free. Alypius was with me, at liberty from his legal office after a third term as Assessor[76] and waiting for private clients, to whom he might sell his legal advice—just as I sold skill in speaking, if indeed this can be bought. Nebridius had yielded to our friendship so far as to teach under Verecundus,[77] a great friend of all of us, a citizen and elementary school teacher of Milan, who had earnestly asked and indeed by right of friendship demanded from our company the help he badly needed. Nebridius was not influenced in the matter by any desire for profit, for he could have done better had he chosen, in a more advanced school; but he was a good and gracious friend and too kindly a man to refuse our requests. But he did it all very quietly, for he did not want to draw the attention of those persons whom the world[78] holds great; he thus avoided distraction of mind, for he wanted to have his mind free and at leisure for as many hours as possible to seek or read or hear truths concerning wisdom.

(14) On a certain day—Nebridius was away for some reason I cannot recall—there came to Alypius and me at our house one Ponticianus, a fellow countryman of ours, being from Africa, holder of an important post in the Emperor's court.[79] There was something or other he wanted of us

and we sat down to discuss the matter. As it happened he noticed a book on a gaming table by which we were sitting. He picked it up, opened it, and found that it was the Apostle Paul, which surprised him because he had expected that it would be one of the books I wore myself out teaching. Then he smiled a little and looked at me, and expressed pleasure but surprise too at having come suddenly upon that book, and only that book, lying before me. For he was a Christian and a devout Christian; he knelt before You in church, O our God, in daily prayer and many times daily. I told him that I had given much care to these writings. Whereupon he began to tell the story of the Egyptian monk Antony, whose name was held in high honour among Your servants, although Alypius and I had never heard it before that time.[80] When he learned this, he was the more intent upon telling the story, anxious to introduce so great a man to men ignorant of him, and very much marvelling at our ignorance. But Alypius and I stood amazed to hear of Your wonderful works, done in the true faith and in the Catholic Church so recently, practically in our own times, and with such numbers of witnesses. All three of us were filled with wonder, we because the deeds we were now hearing were so great, and he because we had never heard them before.

(15) From this story he went on to the great groups in the monasteries, and their ways all redolent of You, and the fertile deserts of the wilderness, of all of which we knew nothing. There was actually a monastery at Milan, outside the city walls. It was full of worthy brethren and under the care of Ambrose. And we had not heard of it. He continued with his discourse and we listened in absolute silence. It chanced that he told how on one occasion he and three of his companions—it was at Treves,[81] when the Emperor was at the chariot races in the Circus—had gone one afternoon to walk in the gardens close by the city walls. As it happened they fell into two groups, one of the others staying with him, and the other two likewise walking their own way. But as those other two strolled on they came into a certain house, the dwelling of some servants of Yours, poor in spirit, of whom is the kingdom of God.[82] There they found a small book in which was written the life of Antony.[83] One of them began to read it, marvelled at it, was inflamed by it. While he was actually reading he had begun to think how he might embrace such a life, and give up his worldly employment to serve You alone. For the two men were both state officials.[84] Suddenly the man who was doing the reading was filled with a love of holiness and angry at himself with righteous shame.[85] He looked at his friend and said to him: "Tell me, please, what is the goal of our ambition in all these labours of ours? What are we aiming at? What is our motive in being in the public service? Have we any higher hope at court than to be friends of the Emperor?[86] And at that level, is not everything uncertain and full of perils? And how many perils must we meet on the way to this greater peril? And how long before we are there? But if I should choose to be a

friend of God,[87] I can become one now." He said this, and all troubled with the pain of the new life coming to birth in him, he turned back his eyes to the book. He read on and was changed inwardly, where You alone could see; and the world dropped away from his mind, as soon appeared outwardly. For while he was reading and his heart thus tossing on its own flood, at length he broke out in heavy weeping, saw the better way and chose it for his own. Being now Your servant he said to his friend, "Now I have broken from that hope we had and have decided to serve God; and I enter upon that service from this hour, in this place. If you have no will to imitate me, at least do not try to dissuade me."

The other replied that he would remain his companion in so great a service for so great a prize. So the two of them, now Your servants, built a spiritual tower[88] at the only cost that is adequate, the cost of leaving all things and following You.[89] Then Ponticianus and the man who had gone walking with him in another part of the garden came looking for them in the same place, and when they found them suggested that they should return home as the day was now declining. But they told their decision and their purpose, and how that will had arisen in them and was now settled in them; and asked them not to try to argue them out of their decision, even if they would not also join them. Ponticianus and his friend, though not changed from their former state, yet wept for themselves, as he told us, and congratulated them in God and commended themselves to their prayers. Then with their own heart trailing in the dust they went off to the palace, while the other two, with their heart fixed upon heaven, remained in the hut. Both these men, as it happened, were betrothed, and when the two women heard of it they likewise dedicated their virginity to You.

VII

(16) This was the story Ponticianus told. But You, Lord, while he was speaking, turned me back towards myself, taking me from behind my own back[90] where I had put myself all the time that I preferred not to see myself. And You set me there before my own face[91] that I might see how vile I was, how twisted and unclean and spotted and ulcerous. I saw myself and was horrified; but there was no way to flee from myself. If I tried to turn my gaze from myself, there was Ponticianus telling what he was telling; and again You were setting me face to face with myself, forcing me upon my own sight, that I might see my iniquity and loathe it.[92] I had known it, but I had pretended not to see it, had deliberately looked the other way and let it go from my mind.

(17) But this time, the more ardently I approved those two as I heard of their determination to win health for their souls by giving themselves up wholly to Your healing, the more detestable did I find myself in comparison with them. For many years had flowed by—a dozen or more—from

the time when I was nineteen and was stirred by the reading of Cicero's
Hortensius to the study of wisdom;[93] and here was I still postponing the
giving up of this world's happiness to devote myself to the search for that
of which not the finding only but the mere seeking is better than to find
all the treasures and kingdoms of men, better than all the body's pleasures
though they were to be had merely for a nod.[94] But I in my great worthless-
ness—for it was greater thus early—had begged You for chastity, saying,
"Grant me chastity and continence, but not yet." For I was afraid that You
would hear my prayer too soon, and too soon would heal me from the
disease of lust which I wanted satisfied rather than extinguished. So I had
gone wandering in my sacrilegious superstition through the base ways
[of the Manicheans]:[95] not indeed that I was sure they were right but that
I preferred them to the Christians, whom I did not inquire about in the
spirit of religion but simply opposed through malice.

(18) I had thought that my reason for putting off from day to day[96]
the following of You alone to the contempt of earthly hopes was that I did
not see any certain goal towards which to direct my course. But now the
day was come when I stood naked in my own sight and my conscience
accused me: "Why is my voice not heard? Surely you are the man who
used to say that you could not cast off vanity's baggage for an uncertain
truth. Very well: now the truth is certain, yet you are still carrying the load.
Here are men who have been given wings to free their shoulders[97] from
the load, though they did not wear themselves out in searching nor spend
ten years or more thinking about it."

Thus was I inwardly gnawed at. And I was in the grip of the most horrible and confounding shame, while Ponticianus was telling his story. He
finished the tale and the business for which he had come; and he went his
way, and I to myself. What did I not say against myself, with what lashes
of condemnation did I not scourge my soul to make it follow me now that
I wanted to follow You! My soul hung back. It would not follow, yet found
no excuse for not following. All its arguments had already been used and
refuted. There remained only trembling silence: for it feared as very death
the cessation of that habit of which in truth it was dying.

VIII

(19) In the midst of that great tumult of my inner dwelling place, the
tumult I had stirred up against my own soul in the chamber of my heart,[98]
I turned upon Alypius, wild in look and troubled in mind, crying out:
"What is wrong with us? What is this that you heard? The unlearned arise
and take heaven by force,[99] and here are we with all our learning, stuck
fast in flesh and blood![100] Is there any shame in following because they
have gone before us, would it not be a worse shame not to follow at once?"

These words and more of the same sort I uttered, then the violence of my feeling tore me from him while he stood staring at me thunderstruck. For I did not sound like myself. My brow, cheeks, eyes, flush, the pitch of my voice, spoke my mind more powerfully than the words I uttered. There was a garden attached to our lodging, of which we had the use, as indeed we had of the whole house: for our host, the master of the house, did not live there. To this garden the storm in my breast somehow brought me, for there no one could intervene in the fierce suit I had brought against myself, until it should reach its issue: though what the issue was to be, You knew, not I: but there I was, going mad on my way to sanity, dying on my way to life, aware how evil I was, unaware that I was to grow better in a little while. So I went off to the garden, and Alypius close on my heels: for it was still privacy for me to have him near, and how could he leave me to myself in that state? We found a seat as far as possible from the house. I was frantic in mind,[101] in a frenzy of indignation at myself for not going over to Your law and Your covenant, O my God, where all my bones cried out that I should be,[102] extolling it to the skies. The way was not by ship or chariot or on foot:[103] it was not as far as I had gone when I went from the house to the place where we sat. For I had but to will to go, in order not merely to go but to arrive: I had only to will to go—but to will powerfully and wholly, not to turn and twist a will half-wounded this way and that, with the part that would rise struggling against the part that would keep to the earth.

(20) In the torment of my irresolution, I did many bodily acts. Now men sometimes will to do bodily acts but cannot, whether because they have not the limbs, or because their limbs are bound or weakened with illness or in some other way unable to act. If I tore my hair, if I beat my forehead, if I locked my fingers and clasped my knees, I did it because I willed to. But I might have willed and yet not done it, if my limbs had not had the pliability to do what I willed. Thus I did so many things where the will to do them was not at all the same thing as the power to do them: and I did not do what would have pleased me incomparably more to do—a thing too which I could have done as soon as I willed to, given that willing means willing *wholly*. For in that matter, the power was the same thing as the will, and the willing *was* the doing. Yet it was not done, and the body more readily obeyed the slightest wish of the mind, more readily moved its limbs at the mind's mere nod, than the mind obeyed itself in carrying out its own great will which could be achieved simply by willing.

IX

(21) Why this monstrousness? And what is the root of it? Let Your mercy enlighten me, that I may put the question: whether perhaps the answer lies in the mysterious punishment that has come upon men and some deeply hidden damage in the sons of Adam. Why this monstrousness? And what is the root of it? The mind gives the body an order, and is obeyed at once: the mind gives itself an order and is resisted. The mind commands the hand to move and there is such readiness that you can hardly distinguish the command from its execution. Yet the mind is mind, whereas the hand is body. The mind commands the mind to will, the mind is itself, but it does not do it. Why this monstrousness? And what is the root of it? The mind I say commands itself to will: it would not give the command unless it willed: yet it does not do what it commands. The trouble is that it does not totally will: therefore it does not totally command. It commands insofar as it wills; and it disobeys the command insofar as it does not will. The will is commanding itself to be a will—commanding itself, not some other. But it does not in its fullness give the command, so that what it commands is not done. For if the will were so in its fullness, it would not command itself to will, for it would already will. It is therefore no monstrousness, partly to will, partly not to will, but a sickness of the soul to be so weighted down by custom that it cannot wholly rise even with the support of truth. Thus there are two wills in us, because neither of them is entire: and what is lacking to the one is present in the other.

X

(22) Let them perish from Thy presence,[104] O God, as perish vain talkers and seducers of the soul,[105] who observing that there are two wills at issue in our coming to a decision proceed to assert [as the Manichees do] that there are two minds in us of different natures, one good, one evil. For they are evil themselves in holding such evil opinions; and they will become good only if they perceive truth and come to it as Your Apostle says to them, *You were heretofore darkness but now light in the Lord.*[106] But these men, though they want to be light, want to be light in themselves and not in the Lord, imagining the nature of the soul to be the same as God. Thus they become not light but deeper darkness, since in their abominable arrogance they have gone further from You, *the true Light that enlightens every man that comes into this world.*[107] Take heed what you say and blush for shame: *draw near unto Him and be enlightened, and your faces shall not be ashamed.*[108] When I was deliberating about serving the Lord my God,[109] as I had long meant to do, it was I who willed to do it, I who was unwilling. It was I. I did not wholly will, I was not wholly unwilling. Therefore I strove with myself and was distracted by myself. This distraction happened to me though I did not want it, and it showed me not the presence of some second mind, but the punishment of my own mind. Thus it was not I who

caused it but *the sin that dwells in me*,[110] the punishment of a sin more freely committed by Adam, whose son I am.[111]

(23) For if there be as many contrary natures in man as there are wills in conflict with one another, then there are not two natures in us but several. Take the case of a man trying to make up his mind whether he would go to the Manichees' meeting-house or to the theatre. The Manichees would say, "Here you have two natures, one good, bringing him to the meeting-house, the other evil, taking him away. How else could you have this wavering between two wills pulling against each other?" Now I say that both are bad, the will that would take him to the Manichees and the will that would take him to the theatre. But they hold that the will by which one comes to them is good. Very well! Supposing one of us is trying to decide and wavering between two wills in conflict, whether to go to the theatre or to *our* church, will not the Manichees be in some trouble about an answer? For either they must admit, which they do not want to, that a good will would take a man to our church as they think it is a good will that brings those who are receivers of their sacrament and belong to them to their church; or they must hold that there are two evil natures and two evil wills at conflict in one man, and what they are always saying will not be true— namely that there is one good will and one evil will. Otherwise, they must be converted to the truth and not deny that when a man is making a decision there is one soul drawn this way and that by diverse wills.

(24) Therefore, when they perceive that there are two wills in conflict in man, they must not say that there are two opposing minds in conflict, one good, one bad, from two opposing substances and two opposing principles. For You, O God of truth, refute them and disprove them and convict them of error: as in the case where both wills are bad, when, for instance, a man is deliberating whether he shall kill another man by poison or by dagger; whether he should seize this or that part of another man's property, when he cannot seize both; whether he should spend his money on lust or hoard his money through avarice; whether he should go to the Games or the theatre if they happen both to come on the same day. Let us add a third possibility to this last man, whether he should go and commit a theft from someone else's house, if the occasion should arise: and indeed a fourth, whether he should go and commit adultery, if the chance occurs at the same time. If all four things come together at the same point of time, and all are equally desired, yet all cannot be done, then they tear the mind by the conflicting pull of four wills—or even more, given the great mass of things which can be desired. Yet the Manichees do not hold such a multitude of different substances.

The same reasoning applies to wills that are good. For I ask them whether it is good to find delight in the reading of the Apostle, and good to find delight in the serenity of a psalm, and good to discuss the Gospel.[112]

To each of these they answer that it is good: but, if all these things attract us at the same moment, are not different wills tugging at the heart of man while we deliberate which we should choose? Thus they are all good, yet they are all in conflict until one is chosen, and then the whole will is at rest and at one, whereas it had been divided into many. Or again, when eternity attracts the higher faculties and the pleasure of some temporal good holds the lower, it is one same soul that wills both, but not either with its whole will; and it is therefore torn both ways and deeply troubled while truth shows the one way as better but habit keeps it to the other.

XI

(25) Thus I was sick at heart and in torment, accusing myself with a new intensity of bitterness, twisting and turning in my chain[113] in the hope that it might be utterly broken, for what held me was so small a thing! But it still held me. And You stood in the secret places of my soul, O Lord, in the harshness of Your mercy redoubling the scourges[114] of fear and shame lest I should give way again and that small slight tie which remained should not be broken but should grow again to full strength and bind me closer even than before. For I kept saying within myself, "Let it be now, let it be now," and by the mere words I had begun to move towards the resolution. I almost made it, yet I did not quite make it.[115] But I did not fall back into my original state, but as it were stood near to get my breath. And I tried again and I was almost there, and now I could all but touch it and hold it: yet I was not quite there, I did not touch it or hold it. I still shrank from dying unto death and living unto life. The lower condition which had grown habitual was more powerful than the better condition which I had not tried. The nearer the point of time came in which I was to become different, the more it struck me with horror; but it did not force me utterly back nor turn me utterly away, but held me there between the two.

(26) Those trifles of all trifles, and vanities of vanities,[116] my one-time mistresses,[117] held me back, plucking at my garment of flesh and murmuring softly: "Are you sending us away?" And, "From this moment shall we not be with you, now or forever?" And, "From this moment shall this or that not be allowed you, now or forever?" What were they suggesting to me in the phrase I have written, "this or that," what were they suggesting to me, O my God? May You in Your mercy keep from the soul of Your servant the vileness and uncleanness they were suggesting! And now I began to hear them not half so loud; they no longer stood against me face to face, but were softly muttering behind my back and, as I tried to depart, plucking stealthily at me to make me look behind. Yet even that was enough, so hesitating was I, to keep me from snatching myself free, from shaking them off and leaping upwards on the way I was called: for the strong force of habit said to me: "Do you think you can live without them?"

(27) But by this time its voice was growing fainter. In the direction towards which I had turned my face and was quivering in fear of going, I could see the austere beauty of Continence, serene and indeed joyous but not evilly, honourably soliciting me to come to her and not linger, stretching forth loving hands to receive and embrace me, hands full of multitudes of good examples. With her I saw such hosts of young men and maidens, a multitude of youth and of every age, gray widows and women grown old in virginity, and in them all Continence herself, not barren but the fruitful mother of children,[118] her joys, by You, Lord, her Spouse. And she smiled upon me and her smile gave courage as if she were saying: "Can you not do what these men have done, what these women have done? Or could men or women have done such in themselves, and not in the Lord their God? The Lord their God gave me to them. Why do you stand upon yourself and so not stand at all? Cast yourself upon Him and be not afraid; He will not draw away and let you fall. Cast yourself without fear. He will receive you and heal you."

Yet I was still ashamed, for I could still hear the murmuring of those vanities, and I still hung hesitant. And again it was as if she said: "Stop your ears against your unclean members,[119] that they may be mortified. They tell you of delights, but not of such delights as the law of the Lord your God tells."[120] This was the controversy raging in my heart, a controversy about myself against myself And Alypius stayed by my side and awaited in silence the issue of such agitation as he had never seen in me.

XII

(28) When my most searching scrutiny had drawn up all my vileness from the secret depths of my soul and heaped it in my heart's sight, a mighty storm arose in me, bringing a mighty rain of tears. That I might give way to my tears and lamentations, I rose from Alypius: for it struck me that solitude was more suited to the business of weeping. I went far enough from him to prevent his presence from being an embarrassment to me. So I felt, and he realised it. I suppose I had said something and the sound of my voice was heavy with tears. I arose, but he remained where we had been sitting, still in utter amazement. I flung myself down somehow under a certain fig tree[121] and no longer tried to check my tears, which poured forth from my eyes in a flood, *an acceptable sacrifice to Thee.*[122] And much I said not in these words but to this effect: *And Thou, O Lord, how long?*[123] *How long, Lord; wilt Thou be angry forever?*[124] *Remember not our former iniquities.*[125] For I felt that I was still bound by them. And I continued my miserable complaining: "How long, how long shall I go on saying tomorrow and again tomorrow?[126] Why not now, why not have an end to my uncleanness this very hour?"

(29) Such things I said, weeping in the most bitter sorrow of my heart.[127] And suddenly I heard a voice from some nearby house, a boy's voice or a girl's voice, I do not know: but it was a sort of sing-song, repeated again and again, "Take and read, take and read." I ceased weeping and immediately began to search my mind most carefully as to whether children were accustomed to chant these words in any kind of game, and I could not remember that I had ever heard any such thing. Damming back the flood of my tears I arose, interpreting the incident as quite certainly a divine command to open my book of Scripture and read the passage at which I should open. For it was part of what I had been told about Antony, that from the Gospel which he happened upon he had felt that he was being admonished, as though what was being read was being spoken directly to himself *Go, sell what thou hast and give to the poor, and thou shalt have treasure in heaven; and come follow Me.*[128] By this experience he had been in that instant converted to You. So I was moved to return to the place where Alypius was sitting, for I had put down the Apostle s book there when I arose. I snatched it up, opened it and in silence read the passage upon which my eyes first fell: *Not in rioting and drunkenness, not in chambering and impurities, not in contention and envy, but put ye on the Lord Jesus Christ and make not provision for the flesh in its concupiscences.*[129] I had no wish to read further, and no need. For in that instant, with the very ending of the sentence, it was as though a light of utter confidence shone in all my heart, and all the darkness of uncertainty vanished away.[130]

(30) Then leaving my finger in the place or marking it by some other sign, I closed the book and in complete calm told the whole thing to Alypius and he similarly told me what had been going on in himself, of which I knew nothing. He asked to see what I had read. I showed him, and he looked further than I had read. I had not known what followed. And this is what followed: *Now him that is weak in faith, take unto you.*[131] He applied this to himself and told me so. And he was confirmed by this message, and with no troubled wavering gave himself to God's good will and purpose—a purpose indeed most suited to his character, for in these matters he had been immeasurably better than I.

Then we went in to my mother and told her, to her great joy. We related how it had come about: she was filled with triumphant exultation, and praised You who are mighty beyond what we ask or conceive:[132] for she saw that You had given her more than with all her pitiful weeping she had ever asked. For You converted me to Yourself so that I no longer sought a wife nor any of this world's promises, but stood upon that same rule of faith in which You had shown me to her so many years before.[133] Thus You changed her mourning into joy,[134] a joy far richer than she had thought to wish, a joy much dearer and purer than she had thought to find in grandchildren of my flesh.

Notes

1. See Isa. 63:7.
2. Ps. 34(35):10.
3. Ps. 115(116):17.
4. See Jth. 13:24.
5. See Ps. 75:2(76:1), 8:2(1), resp.
6. See Isa. 29:2.
7. 1 Cor. 13:12. See X.5.7; XII.13.16; XIII.15.18.
8. See 1 Cor. 5:7–8.
9. See Matt. 7:14.
10. Literally, "it seemed good in my sight," a common biblical phrase. See I Kings (1 Sam.) 29:6; Ps. 15(16):8, 22(23):5, etc.
11. Simplicianus was the priest who baptized Ambrose in 374 and who became his mentor. Though advanced in years, Simplicianus would go on to succeed Ambrose as bishop of Milan in 397.
12. See 1 Cor. 7:7. In contrast to the Manichean sect, the Church consists of both the married and the celibate.
13. See Ps. 25(26):8.
14. 1 Cor. 7.
15. Matt. 19:12.
16. Wis. 13:1.
17. See John 1:1–3.
18. Rom. 1:21.
19. See Ps. 117:36(118:35), 62:9(63:8).
20. Job 28:28.
21. Ecclus.(Sir.) 7:5.
22. Rom. 1:22.
23. See Matt. 13:46.
24. See Col. 2:8.
25. See Matt. 11:25.
26. Marius Victorinus Afer (b. 281–291) was, like Augustine, a cultured African rhetor with philosophical leanings. He wrote several books on the liberal arts and translated some of the writings of Plotinus and Porphyry into Latin, translations that, as Augustine tells us here, initiated the intellectual conversion recounted in book seven.
27. According to St. Jerome, it was in Trajan's Forum.

28. Virgil, *Aeneid* 8.698–700.

29. Victorinus' enthusiasm for Egyptian polytheism yields to Israelite monotheism, a fitting metaphor for his exodus from bondage under sin to the liberation of baptism.

30. See Ecclus.(Sir.) 51:34; Jer. 27:12; Matt. 11:29.

31. See Gal. 5:11. The cross referenced here may be the sign of the cross made on the forehead during initiation into the catechumenate (see I.11.17).

32. Ps. 143:5.

33. See Isa. 14:4ff; Apoc.(Rev.) 17:9, etc.

34. See Ps. 28(29):5.

35. See Luke 12:8–9.

36. Or, "initiated into the first sacramentals of preparation," a reference to initiation into the catechumenate. See I.11.17, "Catechumenate," p. 327.

37. The "giving of the name" marked the second and more advanced stage of the catechumenate. See "Catechumenate," p. 327.

38. See Ps. 111(112): 10.

39. See Ps. 39:5(40:4).

40. The "profession of faith," or *redditio symboli*, was the public recital of the Apostles' Creed by the *competentes* after they had memorized it (see "Catechumenate," p. 327). Victorinus' *redditio symboli* on a raised platform recalls the wooden rule of Monica's dream and thus foreshadows Augustine's conversion (see note on 111.11.19).

41. Luke 15:7.

42. See Luke 15:4–6.

43. See Luke 15:8–9.

44. See Luke 15:24, 32 (the Parable of the Prodigal Son). Significantly, Augustine refers to this parable as being heard during the Liturgy of the Word.

45. See Ps. 101:28(102:27).

46. See Virgil, *Aeneid* 4.644.

47. Augustine coined a neologism, *salsiuncula*, to denote the "little salty things" tipplers munch on to increase their thirst, thus giving the West one of its first words for snack food.

48. See Luke 15:24, 32.

49. Literally, "what is this?" See Exod. 13:14, 16:15; Ecclus.(Sir.) 39:26.

50. See Matt. 24:31.

51. See Ps. 112(113):4–6.

52. See Isa. 33:5.

53. See Ps. 33:6(35:5).

54. See John 1:9,12.

55. 1 Cor. 1:27–28.

56. See Acts 13:7–12.

57. See Matt. 11:30.

58. See Virgil, *Aeneid* 6.853.

59. See 1 Cor. 15:9.

60. See Matt. 12:29.

61. 2 Tim. 2:21.

62. Julian the Apostate's edict was issued on June 17, 362.

63. See Wis. 10:21.

64. See Job 1:9 Old Latin.

65. See Eph. 4:22, 24; Col. 3:9–10.

66. See Rom. 7:14.

67. Gal. 5:17.

68. See Rom. 7:16–17.

69. See 2 Tim. 2:4.

70. See Ps. 62:7(63:6).

71. Eph. 5:14.

72. Rom. 7:22.

73. Rom. 7:24–25.

74. See Ps. 18:5(19:14).

75. See Ps. 53:8(54:6).

76. See note on VI.10.16.

77. A generous and relatively wealthy friend who lent his villa at Cassiciacum to Augustine and his friends (IX.3.5).

78. See Eph. 2:2.

79. Nothing is known of Ponticianus outside of what we are told here.

80. St Antony of Egypt (250–356), who withdrew into the solitude of the desert for a life of prayer and asceticism at the age of eighteen, was one of the first Christian hermits. He is said to be the father of Christian monasticism because he eventually instituted a monastic community under his direction.

81. Treves, or Trier, had been the capital of the Western empire under Diocletian before the court moved to Milan in 381. St. Athanasius, Bishop of Alexandria, had been exiled there from 335 to 337.

82. See Matt. 5:3.

83. *The Life of Antony* was written by St Athanasius, Bishop of Alexandria (d. 373). Latin translations of it were available from at least the early 370s.

84. *Agentes in rebus* were imperial inspectors whose duties ranged from secret police work to government communications.

85. See Ps. 4:5(4).

86. An unofficial title for favored holders of high office.

87. See Jas. 2:23; Jth. 8:22.

88. See Luke 14:28–33.

89. See Matt. 19:27; Luke 5:11, 28.

90. See Jer. 2:27.

91. See Ps. 49(50):21.

92. See Ps. 35:2–3.

93. See III.4.7.

94. The *Hortensius* most likely included an invitation to continence.

95. See Ecclus.(Sir.) 2:16.

96. See Ecclus.(Sir.) 5:8.

97. See Ps. 54:7(55:6).

98. See Matt. 6:6.

99. See Matt. 11:12.

100. See 1 Cor. 15:49–50.

101. Literally, "groaned in the spirit." See John 11:33.

102. See Ps. 34(35):10.

103. See I.18.28, where Augustine uses this image for the Prodigal Son.

104. See Ps. 67:3(68:2).

105. See Tit. 1:10.

106. Eph. 5:8.

107. John 1:9.

108. Ps. 33:6(34:5).

109. See Deut. 6:13; Jer. 30:9; Matt. 4:10.

110. Rom. 7:17, 20.

111. Adam, created without original sin, had greater freedom in not sinning than those born after him.

112. An epistle from the Apostle Raul, a psalm or *graduale*, and an excerpt from the Gospel comprised the essential components of the Liturgy of the Word as it was celebrated in Augustine's day.

113. See Persius, *Satire* 5.158–160.

114. See Virgil, *Aeneid* 5.547.

115. See Persius, *Satire* 5.157. Persius' fifth satire is about a man who tries to relinquish his mistress.

116. See Ecclus.(Sir.) 1:2.

117. That is, not his concubine(s) but his carnal vices. The personalization of his lusts foreshadows the appearance of Lady Continence (VIII.11.27).

118. See Ps. 112(113):9.

119. See Col. 3:5.

120. See Ps. 118(119):85.

121. For the biblical use of the fig tree, see Gen. 3:7, Matt 21:19, and especially John 1:48, which Augustine interprets to mean being "under the condition of the flesh" (*Explanations of the Psalms* 31.en.2.9).

122. Ps. 50(51): 19.

123. Ps. 6:4(3).

124. Ps. 78(79):5.

125. Ps. 78(79):8.

126. See Persius, *Satire* 5.66–69.

127. See Ps. 50:19(51:17).

128. Matt. 19:21. St. Antony walked into church just as these words were being read during the Gospel (Athanasius, *Life of Antony*, 2).

129. Rom. 13:13–14. In contrast to the animal skins of our mortality "put on" us by original sin (VII.18.24), Augustine construes this passage as a call to be baptized and to put on the robe given to a neophyte during the rite of baptism. See "Catechumenate," p. 327.

130. How does this central event differ from the *Sortes Vergilianae* that Augustine rejects in IV.3.5? The fact that the book of Raul's epistles had previously been lying on a gaming table (*Iusoria*, VIII.6.14) only amplifies the question. Augustine seems to be drawing our attention to the ostensibly minor but significant difference between a conscious attempt to divinize through chance events on the one hand, and an unscripted response to Cod's providential use of chance events in one's life. (Cf. Augustine's *Letter* 55.20.37, where Augustine frowns on a crude "Christianizing" of the *Sortes*.)

131. Rom. 14:1.

132. See Eph. 3:10.

133. See III.11.19.

134. See Ps. 29:12(30:11).

Book 9

I

(1) O LORD, I am Thy servant: I am Thy servant and the son of Thy hand-maid. Thou hast broken my bonds. I will sacrifice to Thee the sacrifice of praise.[1] Let my heart and my tongue praise Thee, and let all my bones say, O Lord, who is like to Thee?[2] Let them say and do Thou answer me and say to my soul: I am Thy salvation.[3] Who am I and what kind of man am I? What evil has there not been in my deeds, or if not in my deeds, in my words, or if not in my words, then in my will? But You, Lord, are good and merciful,[4] and Your right hand had regard to the profundity of my death and drew out the abyss of corruption that was in the bottom of my heart. By Your gift I had come totally not to will what I willed but to will what You willed.[5] But where in all that long time was my free will, and from what deep sunken hiding-place was it suddenly summoned forth in the moment in which I bowed my neck to Your easy yoke and my shoulders to Your light burden,[6] Christ Jesus,[7] my Helper and my Redeemer?[8] How lovely I suddenly found it to be free from the loveliness of those vanities, so that now it was a joy to renounce what I had been so afraid to lose. For You cast them out of me, O true and supreme Loveliness, You cast them out of me and took their place in me, You who are sweeter than all pleasure, yet not to flesh and blood; brighter than all light, yet deeper within than any secret; loftier than all honour, but not to those who are lofty to themselves. Now my mind was free from the cares that had gnawed it,[9] from aspiring and getting and weltering in filth and rubbing the scab of lust. And I talked with You as friends talk, my glory and my riches and my salvation, my Lord God.

II

(2) And I thought it would be good in Your sight if I did not dramatically snatch my tongue's service from the speech-market but quietly withdrew; but that in any event withdraw I must, so that youths—not students of Your law[10] or Your peace but of lying follies[11] and the conflicts of the law—should no longer buy at my mouth the tools of their madness.[12] Fortunately it happened that there were only a few days left before the Vintage Vacation;[13] and I decided to endure them so that I might leave with due deliberation, seeing that I had been redeemed by You and was not going to put myself up for sale again. Our purpose therefore was known to You, but not to men other than our own friends. We had agreed among ourselves not to spread the news abroad at all, although, in our ascent from *the valley of tears*[14] and our singing of the *song of degrees*,[15] You had given us *sharp arrows and burning coals against cunning tongues*[16] that might argue against us with pretended care for our interest, might destroy us saying that they loved us: as men consume food saying that they love it.

(3) You had pierced our hearts with the arrow of Your love, and our minds were pierced with the arrows of Your words. To burn away and utterly consume our slothfulness so that we might no more be sunk in its depths, we had the depths of our thought filled with the examples of Your servants whom You had changed from darkness to light and from death to life; and these inflamed us so powerfully that any false tongue of contradiction did not extinguish our flame but set us blazing more fiercely. But because for Your name, which You have sanctified throughout the earth,[17] our decision would find many to praise it, I was afraid that it would look like ostentation if I did not wait for the approaching vacation but immediately resigned from a profession which everyone knew I practised: for the faces of all about would be turned on my act, in that I had not chosen to wait for the vacation when it was so close, and it would be widely said that I had done it to make myself seem important. And what would it have profited me to have people discussing and arguing about my purpose and to have our good ill-spoken of?[18]

(4) Furthermore that very summer, under the too heavy labour of teaching, my lungs had begun to give way and I breathed with difficulty; the pain in my breast showed that they were affected and they no longer let me talk with any strength for too long at a time.[19] At first this had disturbed me, because it made it practically a matter of necessity that I should lay down the burden of teaching, or at least give it up for the time if I was to be cured and grow well again. But when the full purpose of giving myself leisure to meditate on how You are the Lord[20] arose in me and became a settled resolve—as you know, O my God—I actually found myself glad to have this perfectly truthful excuse to offer parents who might be offended and for their children's sake would never willingly have let me give up teaching. So I was full of joy, and I put up with the space of time that still had to ran—I fancy it was about twenty days. But to bear the time took considerable fortitude. Desire for money, which formerly had helped me to bear the heavy labour of teaching, was quite gone; so that I should have [had nothing to help me bear it and so] found it altogether crushing if patience had not taken the place of covetousness. Some of Your servants, my brethren, may think that I sinned in this, since having enrolled with all my heart in Your service, I allowed myself to sit for so much as an hour in the chair of untruthfulness. It may be so. But, most merciful Lord, have You not pardoned and remitted this sin, along with others most horrible and deadly,[21] in the holy water of baptism?

III

(5) Meanwhile Verecundus was worrying himself ill over the good that had come to us. He saw himself losing our company by reason of his own chains, which bound him very tight. He was not yet a Christian, though his wife was, and indeed she was the strongest obstacle of all in

the way of his setting out upon that journey on which we had started. For he said that he would not be a Christian in any other way than the way that was beyond his power. But he very generously offered that as long as we were in the country, we might stay in his house. You will reward him, O Lord, with the reward of the just,[22] for You have already given him the lot of the just.[23] At a time when we were away in Rome he was seized with some bodily illness, and in the course of it became a Christian and was baptised, and so departed this life. Thus you had mercy not only upon him, but upon us too: otherwise, thinking of the wonderful kindness our friend had shown us, we should have been tormented with unbearable sorrow if we had not been able to number him in Your flock. Thanks be to our God! We are Yours, as Your exhortations and consolations prove. You are faithful to Your promises, and you will repay Verecundus for his country house at Cassiciacum,[24] where we rested in You from the world's troubles, with the loveliness and eternal freshness of Your paradise: for You forgave him his sins upon earth in the mountain of abundance,[25] Your mountain, the mountain of richness.[26]

(6) At the time, however, Verecundus was very much perturbed; but Nebridius altogether joyful. For although before he was a Christian he had fallen into that same pit of deadly error and believed the true body of Your Son to be a phantasm, he had emerged from that error; and though he had not yet received any sacraments of Your Church, he was a most zealous seeker of the truth. Not long after our conversion and regeneration by Your baptism, You took him from this life, by then a baptised Catholic and serving You in Africa in perfect chastity among his own people, for he had made his whole family Christian. And now he lives in Abraham's bosom.[27] Whatever is meant by that bosom, there my Nebridius lives, my most beloved friend, Your son by adoption[28] and no longer a freed-man only. There he lives. For what other place is there for such a soul? There he lives, in the place of which he asked me, an ignorant poor creature, so many questions. He no longer puts his bodily ear to my lips, but the lips of his spirit to Your fountain, drinking his fill of wisdom, all that his thirst requires, happy without end. Nor do I think he is so intoxicated with the draught of that wisdom as to forget me since You, O Lord, of whom he drinks, are mindful of us.

There then we were, consoling the unhappy Verecundus, for our friendship was not impaired by conversion, and exhorting him to fidelity in his state, namely the married life. As for Nebridius, we were merely waiting for him to follow us. He was so close that he might well follow, and he was indeed on the point of doing so when at last those days of waiting for the vacation came to an end. For they seemed long and many to me, because of the longing I had for that freedom and leisure in which I might sing to You from the depths of my heart: *My heart hath said to Thee: I have sought Thy face. Thy face, O Lord, will I still seek.*[29]

IV

(7) And now the day was come on which I was to be set free from the teaching of Rhetoric in fact, as I was already free in mind. And so it came about. You delivered my tongue as You had already delivered my heart, and I rejoiced and praised You, and so went off with my friends to the country-house.[30] The amount of writing I did there—the writing was now in your service but during this breathing-space still smacked of the school of pride—my books exist to witness, with the record they give of discussions either with my friends there present or with Yourself when I was alone with You;[31] and there are my letters to show what correspondence I had with Nebridius while he was away.[32] But when shall I have the time to relate all Your great acts of goodness towards me, especially at that time, since I must hasten to tell of matters greater still?

For my memory reminds me, and pleasant it is, O Lord, to confess to You, what inner goads you used to tame me, and how you brought me low, *making low the mountains and hills* of my thoughts, *making straight what was crooked, and plain what was rough.*[33] And I remember too how You subdued my heart's brother Alypius to the name of Jesus Christ Your only-begotten Son, our Lord and Saviour, which at first he thought it would be in some sense lowering to put into my writings. For he would have had them redolent of the high cedars of the schools, which the Lord had now broken down,[34] rather than of the health-giving herbs of the Church which are of such avail against the bites of serpents.

(8) When I read the psalms of David, songs of faithfulness and devotion in which the spirit of pride has no entry, what cries did I utter to You, O my God, I but a novice in your true love, a catechumen keeping holiday in a country-house with that other catechumen Alypius: though my mother also was with us, a woman in sex, with the faith of a man, with the serenity of great age, the love of a mother, the piety of a Christian. What cries did I utter to You in those psalms and how was I inflamed towards You by them, and on fire to set them sounding through all the world, if I could, against the pride of man! But in truth they are already sung throughout the world and *there is none who can hide himself from Thy heat.*[35] I thought of the Manichees with indignation and a burning anguish of sorrow. I pitied them because they did not know our sacraments and our healing, but were insanely set against the medicine that would have cured their insanity. I wished that they might be somewhere close at hand—without my knowing that they were there—and could see my face and hear my words, when in that time of leisure I read the Fourth Psalm; and that they could see what that psalm did in me: *When I called upon Thee, Thou, God of my justice, didst hear me; when I was in distress, Thou hast enlarged me: have mercy on me, O Lord, and hear my prayer.*[36] Would that they could have heard me—without my knowing that they heard me, lest they might think it was

on their account I was speaking as I spoke when I recited these words: and indeed I would not have said those things or said them in the same way, if I had realised that I was being heard and seen by them: nor, if I *had* said them, would they have understood how I was speaking with myself and to myself in Your presence from the natural movement of my spirit.

(9) I was in fear and horror, and again I was on fire with hope and exultation in your mercy, O Father.[37] And all these emotions found expression in my eyes and in my voice when Your Holy Spirit turned to us and said: *O ye sons of men, how long will ye be dull of heart? Why do you love vanity so much and seek after lying?*[38] For I myself had loved vanity and sought after lying. *And Thou, Lord,* hadst already *made Thy holy one wonderful,*[39] raising Him from the dead and setting Him at Thy right hand,[40] whence He should send from on high His promise, the Paraclete, the Spirit of Truth.[41] And He had already sent Him,[42] though I knew it not. He had sent Him because already He was magnified and risen from the dead[43] and ascended into heaven. For till then the Spirit was not yet given, because Jesus was not yet glorified.[44] And the prophet cried aloud: *How long will you be dull of heart? Why do you love vanity and seek after lying? Know ye also that the Lord hath made His holy one wonderful?*[45] He cries out; "How long"; he cries out, "Know ye." And I so long was ignorant and loved vanity and sought after lying.

I heard these things and trembled to hear them, for they were spoken to such as I remembered myself to have been. For in those phantasms which I had taken for truth were vanity and lying. And I cried out many things strongly and earnestly in the grief I felt at what I remembered. If only those could have heard me who still loved vanity and sought after lying. Perchance they would have been troubled, and have vomited up their error; and You would have heard them when they cried to You:[46] for He who intercedes with You for us died for us with a true death of the body.

(10) I read, *Be angry and sin not.*[47] And by this I was much moved, O my God, for I had by then learned to be angry with myself for the past, that I might not sin in what remained of life:[48] and to be angry with good reason, because it was not some other nature of the race of darkness that had sinned in me [as the Manichees say]: and they are not angry at themselves, but treasure up to themselves wrath against the day of wrath and of the revelation of the just judgment of God.[49]

The good I now sought was not in things outside me, to be seen by the eye of flesh under the sun. For those that find their joy outside them easily fall into emptiness and are spilled out upon the things that are seen and the things of time,[50] and in their starved minds lick shadows. If only they could grow weary of their own hunger and say. *Who shall show us good things?*[51] And we should say and they should hear: *The light of Thy countenance is sealed upon us,*[52] O Lord. For we are not *the Light that enlightens every man*[53] but we are enlightened by Thee that *as we were heretofore darkness we are now light in Thee.*[54] If they could but see the Light interior and eternal: for now that I had known it,[55] I was frantic that I could not make them see it even were they to ask. *Who shall show us good things?*[56] For the heart they would bring me would be in their eyes, eyes that looked everywhere but at You. But there, where I had been angry with myself, in my own room where I had been pierced, where I had offered my sacrifice, slaying the self that I had been and, in the newly-taken purpose of newness of life,[57] hoping in You—there You began to make me feel Your love and to give *gladness in my heart.*[58] I cried out as I read this aloud and realised it within: and I no longer wished any increase of earthly goods, in which a man wastes time and is wasted by time, since in the simplicity of the Eternal I had other *corn and wine and oil.*[59]

(11) It was with a deep cry of my heart that I uttered the next verse: *O in peace! O in the Selfsame!* O how he has said, *I will sleep and I will rest.*[60] For who shall stand against *us when the saying that is written will come to pass: Death is swallowed up in victory?*[61] You supremely are that Selfsame,[62] for You are not changed and in You is that rest in which all cares are forgotten, since there is no other besides You, and we have not to seek other things which are not what You are: but You, Lord, alone have *made me dwell in hope.*[63] All these things I read and was on fire; nor could I find what could be done with those deaf dead, of whom indeed I had myself been one for I had been a scourge, a blind raging snarler against the Scriptures, which are all honeyed with the honey of heaven and all luminous with Your light:[64] and now I was fretting my heart out over the enemies of these same Scriptures.[65]

(12) When shall I recall and set down all that belongs to those days in the country? I have not forgotten, nor shall I pass in silence, the bite of Your scourge and the wonderful swiftness of Your mercy. During those days You sent me the torture of toothache, and when it had grown so agonising that I could not speak, it came into my heart[66] to ask all my friends there present to pray for me to You, the God of every kind of health.[67] I wrote this down on my tablet and gave it to them to read. As soon as we had gone on our knees in all simplicity, the pain went. But what was the pain or how did it go? I admit that I was terrified, O my Lord, my God,[68] for as far back as my earliest infancy I had never experienced any such thing. Thus in that depth I recognised the act of Your will, and I gave praise to Your name,[69] rejoicing in faith. But this faith would not let me feel safe about my past sins, since Your baptism had not yet come to remit them.

V

(13) When the Vintage Vacation was over I gave the people of Milan notice that they must find someone else to sell the art of words to their students, because I had chosen to serve You, and because owing to my difficulty in breathing and the pain in my lungs I could not continue my teaching. And in a letter I told Your bishop, the holy Ambrose, of my past errors and my present purpose, that he might advise me which of Your Scriptures I should especially read to prepare me and make me more fit to receive so great a grace. He told me to read Isaias the prophet, I imagine because he more clearly foretells the Gospel and the calling of the Gentiles than the other Old Testament writers; but I did not understand the first part of his book, and thinking that it would be all of the same kind, put it aside meaning to return to it when I should be more practised in the Lord's way of speech.[70]

VI

(14) When the time had come to give in my name for baptism,[71] we left the country and returned to Milan. Alypius had decided to be born again in You at the same time, for he was already endowed with the humility[72] that Your sacraments require, and had brought his body so powerfully under control that he could tread the icy soil of Italy with bare feet, which required unusual fortitude.[73] We also took with us the boy Adeodatus, carnally begotten by me in my sin. You had made him well. He was barely fifteen, yet he was more intelligent than many a grave and learned man. In this I am but acknowledging to You Your own gifts, O Lord my God, Creator of all[74] and powerful to reshape our shapelessness: for I had no part in that boy but the sin. That he had been brought up by us in Your way was because You had inspired us, no other. I do but acknowledge to You Your own gifts. There is a book of mine called *De Magistro*: it is a dialogue between him and me.[75] You know, O God, that all the ideas which are put into the mouth of the other party to the dialogue were truly his, though he was but sixteen. I had experience of many other remarkable qualities in him. His great intelligence filled me with a kind of awe: and who but You could be the maker of things so wonderful? But You took him early from this earth, and I think of him utterly without anxiety, for there is nothing in his boyhood or youth or anywhere in him to cause me to fear. We took him along with us, the same age as ourselves in Your grace, to be brought up in Your discipline: and we were baptised,[76] and all anxiety as to our past life fled away. The days were not long enough as I meditated, and found wonderful delight in meditating, upon the depth of Your design for the salvation of the human race.[77] I wept at the beauty of Your hymns and canticles, and was powerfully moved at the sweet sound of Your Church's

singing. Those sounds flowed into my ears, and the truth streamed into my heart: so that my feeling of devotion overflowed, and the tears ran from my eyes, and I was happy in them.

VII

(15) It was only a little while before that the church of Milan had begun to practise this kind of consolation and exultation, to the great joy of the brethren singing together with heart and voice. For it was only about a year, or not much more, since Justina, the mother of the boy Emperor Valentinian, was persecuting Your servant Ambrose in the interests of her own heresy: for she had been seduced by the Arians.[78] The devoted people had stayed day and night in the church, ready to die with their bishop. Your servant. And my mother, Your handmaid, bearing a great part of the trouble and vigil, had lived in prayer. I also, though still not warmed by the fire of Your Spirit, was stirred to excitement by the disturbed and wrought-up state of the city. It was at this time that the practice was instituted of singing hymns and psalms[79] after the manner of the Eastern churches, to keep the people from being altogether worn out with anxiety and want of sleep. The custom has been retained from that day to this, and has been imitated by many, indeed in almost all congregations throughout the world.[80]

(16) At this time You revealed to Your bishop Ambrose in a vision the place where the bodies of the martyrs Protasius and Gervasius[81] lay hid, which You had for so many years kept incorrupt in the treasury of Your secret knowledge that You might bring them forth at the proper moment to check a woman's fury—the woman being the ruler of the Empire! For when they were discovered and dug up and with due honour brought to Ambrose's basilica,[82] not only were people cured who had been tormented by evil spirits[83]—and the devils themselves forced to confess it—but also there was a man, a citizen well known to the city, who had been blind for many years: he asked what was the cause of the tumultuous joy of the people, and when he heard, he sprang up and asked his guide to lead him into the place. When he arrived there he asked to be allowed to touch with his handkerchief the place on which lay the saints,[84] whose death is precious in Your sight.[85] He did so, put the handkerchief to his eyes, and immediately they were opened.[86] The news spread abroad. Your praises glowed and shone, and if the mind of that angry woman was not brought to the sanity of belief, it was at least brought back from the madness of persecution. Thanks be to my God! From what and towards what have You led my memory, that it should confess to You these great things which I had altogether forgotten? Yet even then, *when the odour of Thy ointments was so sweet smelling*, I did not run *after Thee:*[87] and for this I wept all the

more now when I heard Your hymns and canticles, as one who had then sighed for You and now breathed in You, breathed so far as the air allows in this our house of grass.[88]

VIII

(17) You, Lord, who make men of one mind to dwell in one house,[89] brought to our company a young man of our own town, Evodius.[90] He had held office in the civil service, had been converted and baptised before us, had resigned from the state's service, and given himself to Yours. We kept together, meaning to live together in our devout purpose. We thought deeply as to the place in which we might serve You most usefully. As a result we started back for Africa. And when we had come as far as Ostia on the Tiber,[91] my mother died. I pass over many things, for I must make haste. Do You, O my God, accept my confessions and my gratitude for countless things of which I say nothing. But I will not omit anything my mind brings forth concerning her, Your servant, who brought me forth— brought me forth in the flesh to this temporal light, and in her heart to light eternal. Not of her gifts do I speak but of Your gifts in her. For she did not bring herself into the world or educate herself in the world: it was You who created her, nor did her father or mother know what kind of being was to come forth from them. It was the sceptre of Your Christ, the discipline of Your only-begotten, that brought her up in holy fear,[92] in a Catholic family which was a worthy member of Your Church. Yet it was not the devotion of her mother in her upbringing that she talked most of, but of a certain aged servant, who had indeed carried my mother's father on her back when he was a baby, as little ones are accustomed to be carried on the backs of older girls. Because of this, because also of her age and her admirable character, she was very much respected by her master and mistress in their Christian household. As a result she was given charge of her master's daughters. This charge she fulfilled most conscientiously, checking them sharply when necessary with holy severity and teaching them soberly and prudently. Thus, except at the times when they ate—and that most temperately—at their parents' table, she would not let them even drink water, no matter how tormenting their thirst. By this she prevented the forming of a bad habit, and she used to remark very sensibly:[93] "Now you drink water because you are not allowed to have wine; but when you are married, and thus mistresses of food-stores and wine-cellars, you will despise water, but the habit of drinking will still remain." By this kind of teaching and the authority of her commands she moderated the greediness that goes with childhood and brought the little girls' thirst to such a control that they no longer wanted what they ought not to have.

(18) Yet, as Your servant told me, her son, there did steal upon my mother an inclination to wine. For when, in the usual way, she was sent

by her parents, as a well-behaved child, to draw wine from the barrel, she would dip the cup in, but before pouring the wine from the cup into the flagon, she would sip a little with the very tip of her lips, only a little because she did not yet like the taste sufficiently to take more. Indeed she did it not out of any craving for wine, but rather from the excess of childhood's high spirits, which tend to boil over in absurdities, and are usually kept in check by the authority of elders. And so, adding to that daily drop a little more from day to day—for he that despises small things, falls little by little[94]—she fell into the habit, so that she would drink off greedily cups almost full of wine. Where then was that wise old woman with her forceful prohibitions? Could anything avail against the evil in us, unless Your healing, O Lord, watched over us? When our father and mother and nurses are absent, You are present, who created us, who call us, who can use those placed over us for some good unto the salvation of our souls. What did You do then, O my God? How did You cure her, and bring her to health? From another soul You drew a harsh and cutting sarcasm, as though bringing forth a surgeon's knife from Your secret store, and with one blow amputated that sore place. A maidservant with whom she was accustomed to go to the cellar, one day fell into a quarrel with her small mistress when no one else chanced to be about, and hurled at her the most biting insult possible, calling her a drunkard.[95] My mother was pierced to the quick, saw her fault in its true wickedness, and instantly condemned it and gave it up. Just as the flattery of a friend can pervert, so the insult of an enemy can sometimes correct. Nor do You, O God, reward men according to what You do by means of them, but according to what they themselves intended. For the girl being in a temper wanted to enrage her young mistress, not to amend her, for she did it when no one else was there, either because the time and place happened to be thus when the quarrel arose, or because she was afraid that elders would be angry because she had not told it sooner. But You, O Lord, Ruler of heavenly things and earthly, who turn to Your own purposes the very depths of rivers as they run and order the turbulence of the flow of time, did by the folly of one mind bring sanity to another; thus reminding us not to attribute it to our own power if another is amended by our word, even if we meant to amend him.

IX

(19) My mother, then, was modestly and soberly brought up, being rather made obedient to her parents by You than to You by her parents. When she reached the age for marriage,[96] and was bestowed upon a husband, she served him as her lord.[97] She used all her effort to win him to You, preaching You to him by her character,[98] by which You made her beautiful to her husband, respected and loved by him and admirable in his sight. For she bore his acts of unfaithfulness quietly, and never had any

jealous scene with her husband about them. She awaited Your mercy upon him,[99] that he might grow chaste through faith in You.[100] And as a matter of fact, though generous beyond measure, he had a very hot temper. But she knew that a woman must not resist a husband in anger, by deed or even by word. Only, when she saw him calm again and quiet, she would take the opportunity to give him an explanation of her actions, if it happened that he had been roused to anger unreasonably. The result was that whereas many matrons with much milder husbands carried the marks of blows to disfigure their faces, and would all get together to complain of the way their husbands behaved, my mother—talking lightly but meaning it seriously—advised them against their tongues, saying that from the day they heard the matrimonial contract[101] read to them they should regard it as an instrument by which they became servants; and from that time they should be mindful of their condition and not set themselves up against their masters. And they often expressed amazement—for they knew how violent a husband she had to live with—that it had never been heard, and there was no mark to show, that Patricius had beaten his wife or that there had been any family quarrel between them for so much as a single day. And when her friends asked her the reason, she taught them her rule, which was as I have just said. Those who followed it, found it good and thanked her; those who did not, went on being bullied and beaten.

(20) Her mother-in-law began by being angry with her because of the whispers of malicious servants. But my mother won her completely by the respect she showed, and her unfailing patience and mildness. She ended by going to her son, telling him of the tales the servants had bandied about to the destruction of peace in the family between herself and her daughter-in-law, and asking him to punish them for it. So he, out of obedience to his mother and in the interests of order in the household and peace among his womenfolk, had the servants beaten whose names he had been given, as she had asked when giving them. To which she added the promise that anyone must expect a similar reward from her own hands who should think to please her by speaking ill of her daughter-in-law. And as no one had the courage to do so, they lived together with the most notable degree of kindness and harmony.

(21) This great gift also, O my God, my Mercy,[102] You gave to Your good servant, in whose womb You created me, that she showed herself, wherever possible, a peacemaker between people quarreling and minds at discord. For swelling and undigested discord often belches forth bitter words when in the venom of intimate conversation with a present friend hatred at its rawest is breathed out upon an absent enemy. But when my mother heard bitter things said by each of the other, she never said anything to either about the other save what would help to reconcile them. This might seem a small virtue, if I had not had the sorrow of seeing for myself so many people who—as if by some horrible widespreading

infection of sin—not only tell angry people the things their enemies said in anger, but even add things that were never said at all. Whereas, on the contrary, ordinary humanity would seem to require not merely that we refrain from exciting or increasing wrath among men by evil speaking, but that we strive to extinguish wrath by kind speaking. Such a one was she: and You were the master who taught her most secretly in the school of her heart.

(22) The upshot was that towards the very end of his life she won her husband to You;[103] and once he was a Christian she no longer had to complain of the things she had had to bear with before he was a Christian. Further, she was a servant of Your servants.[104] Such of them as knew her praised and honoured and loved You, O God, in her; for they felt Your presence in her heart, showing itself in the fruit of her holy conversation.[105] She had been *the wife of one husband,*[106] *had requited her parents, had governed her house*[107] piously, *was well reported of for good works.*[108] She had *brought up her children*[109] being in labour of them[110] as often as she saw them swerving away from You. Finally of all of us Your servants, O Lord—since by Your gift You suffer us to speak—who before her death were living together after receiving the grace of baptism, she took as much care as if she had been the mother of us all, and served us as if she had been the daughter of us all.

X

(23) When the day was approaching on which she was to depart this life—a day that You knew though we did not—it came about, as I believe by Your secret arrangement, that she and I stood alone leaning in a window, which looked inwards to the garden within the house where we were staying, at Ostia on the Tiber; for there we were away from everybody, resting for the sea-voyage from the weariness of our long journey by land. There we talked together, she and I alone in deep joy; and *forgetting the things that were behind and looking forward to those that were before,*[111] we were discussing in the presence of Truth, which You are,[112] what the eternal life of the saints could be like, *which eye has not seen nor ear heard, nor has it entered into the heart of man.*[113] But with the mouth of our heart we panted for the high waters of Your fountain, the fountain of the life which is with You: that being sprinkled from that fountain according to our capacity, we might in some sense meditate upon so great a matter.

(24) And our conversation had brought us to this point, that any pleasure whatsoever of the bodily senses, in any brightness whatsoever of corporeal light, seemed to us not worthy of comparison with the pleasure of that eternal Light, not worthy even of mention. Rising as our love flamed upward towards that Selfsame,[114] we passed in review the various levels of bodily things, up to the heavens themselves, whence sun and

moon and stars shine upon this earth. And higher still we soared, thinking in our minds and speaking and marvelling at Your works: and so we came to our own souls, and went beyond them to come at last to that region of richness unending,[115] where You feed Israel[116] forever with the food of truth: and there life is that Wisdom by which all things are made,[117] both the things that have been and the things that are yet to be. But this Wisdom itself is not made: it is as it has ever been, and so it shall be forever: indeed "has ever been" and "shall be forever" have no place in it, but it simply is, for it is eternal: whereas "to have been" and "to be going to be" are not eternal. And while we were thus talking of His Wisdom and panting for it, with all the effort of our heart we did for one instant attain to touch it; then sighing, and leaving the first fruits of our spirit[118] bound to it, we returned to the sound of our own tongue, in which a word has both beginning and ending. For what is like to your Word, our Lord, who abides in Himself forever, yet grows not old and makes all things new![119]

(25) So we said: "If to any man the tumult of the flesh grew silent, silent the images of earth and sea and air: and if the heavens grew silent, and the very soul grew silent to herself and by not thinking of self mounted beyond self: if all dreams and imagined visions grew silent, and every tongue and every sign and whatsoever is transient—for indeed if any man could hear them, he should hear them saying with one voice, "We did not make ourselves,[120] but He made us who abides forever":[121] but if, having uttered this and so set us to listening to Him who made them, they all grew silent, and in their silence He alone spoke to us, not by them but by Himself: so that we should hear His word, not by any tongue of flesh nor the voice of an angel[122] nor the sound of thunder[123] nor in the darkness of a parable,[124] but that we should hear Himself whom in all these things we love, should hear Himself and not them: just as we two had but now reached forth and in a flash of the mind attained to touch the eternal Wisdom which abides over all: and if this could continue, and all other visions so different be quite taken away, and this one should so ravish and absorb and wrap the beholder in inward joys that his life should eternally be such as that one moment of understanding for which we had been sighing— would not this be: *Enter Thou into the joy of Thy Lord?*[125] But when shall it be? Shall it be when *we shall all rise again* and *shall not all he changed?*"[126]

(26) Such thoughts I uttered, though not in that order or in those actual words; but You know, O Lord, that on that day when we talked of these things the world with all its delights seemed cheap to us in comparison with what we talked of. And my mother said: "Son, for my own part I no longer find joy in anything in this world. What I am still to do here and why I am here I know not, now that I no longer hope for anything from this world. One thing there was, for which I desired to remain still a little longer in this life, that I should see you a Catholic Christian before I died.

This God has granted me in superabundance, in that I now see you His servant to the contempt of all worldly happiness. What then am I doing here?"[127]

XI

(27) What answer I made, I do not clearly remember; within five days or not much longer she fell into a fever. And in her sickness, she one day fainted away and for the moment lost consciousness. We ran to her but she quickly returned to consciousness, and seeing my brother[128] and me standing by her she said as one wondering: "Where was I?" Then looking closely upon us as we stood wordless in our grief, she said: "Here you will bury your mother." I stayed silent and checked my weeping. But my brother said something to the effect that he would be happier if she were to die in her own land and not in a strange country. But as she heard this she looked at him anxiously, restraining him with her eye because he savoured of earthly things, and then she looked at me and said: "See the way he talks." And then she said to us both: "Lay this body wherever it may be. Let no care of it disturb you. This only I ask of you: that you should remember me at the altar of the Lord wherever you may be." And when she had uttered this wish in such words as she could manage, she fell silent as her sickness took hold of her more strongly.

(28) But as I considered Your gifts, O unseen God,[129] which You send into the hearts of Your faithful to the springing up of such wonderful fruits, I was glad and gave thanks to You, remembering what I had previously known of the care as to her burial which had always troubled her: for she had arranged to be buried by the body of her husband. Because they had lived together in such harmony, she had wished—so little is the human mind capable of rising to the divine—that it should be granted her, as an addition to her happiness and as something to be spoken of among men, that after her pilgrimage beyond the sea the earthly part of man and wife should lie together under the same earth. Just when this vain desire had begun to vanish from her heart through the fullness of Your goodness, I did not know; but I was pleased and surprised that it had now so clearly vanished: though indeed in the conversation we had had together at the window, when she said: "What am I still doing here?" there had appeared no desire to die in her own land. Further I heard afterwards that in the time we were at Ostia, she had talked one day to some of my friends, as a mother talking to her children, of the contempt of this life and of the attraction of death. I was not there at the time. They marvelled at such courage in a woman—but it was You who had given it to her—and asked if she was not afraid to leave her body so far from her own city. But she said: "Nothing is far from God, and I have no fear that He will not know at

the end of the world from what place He is to raise me up." And so on the
ninth day of her illness, in the fifty-sixth year of her life and the thirty-third
of mine, that devout and holy soul was released from the body.

XII

(29) I closed her eyes; and an immeasurable sorrow flowed into my
heart and would have overflowed in tears. But my eyes under the mind's
strong constraint held back their flow and I stood dry-eyed. In that struggle it went very ill with me. As she breathed her last, the child Adeodatus
broke out into lamentation and we all checked him and brought him to
silence. But in this very fact the childish element in me, which was breaking out into tears, was checked and brought to silence by the manlier voice
of my mind. For we felt that it was not fitting[130] that her funeral should be
solemnised with moaning and weeping and lamentation, for so it is normal to weep when death is seen as sheer misery or as complete extinction.
But she had not died miserably, nor did she wholly die. Of this we were
sure by reason of her character and of her faith unfeigned.[131]

(30) What then was it that grieved my heart so deeply? Only the newness of the wound, in finding the custom I had so loved of living with her
suddenly snapped short. It was a joy to me to have this one testimony
from her: when her illness was close to its end, meeting with expressions
of endearment such services as I rendered, she called me a dutiful loving
son, and said in the great affection of her love that she had never heard
from my mouth any harsh or reproachful word addressed to herself. But
what possible comparison was there, O my God who made us,[132] between
the honour I showed her and the service she had rendered me? Because I
had now lost the great comfort of her, my soul was wounded and my very
life torn asunder, for it had been one life made of hers and mine together.

(31) When the boy had been quieted and ceased weeping, Evodius
took up the psalter and began to chant—with the whole house making the
responses—the psalm *Mercy and judgment I will sing to Thee, O Lord.*[133] And
when they heard what was being done, many of the brethren and religious
women came to us; those whose office it was were making arrangement
for the burial, while, in another part of the house where it could properly be done, I discoursed, with friends who did not wish to leave me by
myself, upon matters suitable for that time. Thus I used truth as a kind of
fomentation to bring relief to my torment, a torment known to You, but
not known to those others: so that listening closely to me they thought that
I lacked all feeling of grief. But in Your ears, where none of them could
hear, I accused the emotion in me as weakness; and I held in the flood
of my grief. It was for the moment a little diminished, but returned with
fresh violence, not with any pouring of tears or change of countenance: but
I knew what I was crushing down in my heart. I was very much ashamed

that these human emotions could have such power over me—though it belongs to the due order and the lot of our earthly condition that they should come to us—and I felt a new grief at my grief and so was afflicted with a twofold sorrow.

(32) When the body was taken to burial, I went and returned without tears. During the prayers which we poured forth to you when the sacrifice of our redemption was offered for her[134]—while the body, as the custom there is, lay by the grave[135] before it was actually buried—during those prayers I did not weep. Yet all that day I was heavy with grief within and in the trouble of my mind I begged of You in my own fashion to heal my pain; but You would not—I imagine because You meant to impress upon my memory by this proof how strongly the bond of habit holds the mind even when it no longer feeds upon deception. The idea came to me to go and bathe, for I had heard that the bath—which the Greeks call *bala-neion*—is so called because it drives anxiety from the mind.[136] And this also I acknowledge to Your mercy, O Father of orphans,[137] that I bathed and was the same man after as before. The bitterness of grief had not sweated out of my heart.[138] Then I fell asleep, and woke again to find my grief not a little relieved. And as I was in bed and no one about, I said over those true verses that Your servant Ambrose wrote of You:

> God, Creator of all things.
> Ruler of heaven, who robes the day
> With shimmering light, and makes the night
>
> For sleep's release:
> That quiet rest should give again
> To burdened bodies zest for work.
> And lift the weights from tired minds.
> Unravelling all anxious knots of grief.[139]

(33) And then little by little I began to recover my former feeling about Your handmaid, remembering how loving and devout was her conversation with You, how pleasant and considerate her conversation with me, of which I was thus suddenly deprived. And I found solace in weeping in Your sight both about her and for her, about myself and for myself. I no longer tried to check my tears, but let them flow as they would, making them a pillow for my heart: and it rested upon them, for it was Your ears that heard my weeping, and not the ears of a man, who would have misunderstood my tears and despised them. But now, O Lord, I confess it to You in writing, let him read it who will and interpret it as he will: and if he sees it as sin that for so small a portion of an hour I wept for my mother, now dead and departed from my sight, who had wept so many years for me that I should live ever in Your sight—let him not scorn me but rather, if he is a man of great charity, let him weep for my sins to You, the Father of all the brethren of Your Christ.

XIII

(34) Now that my heart is healed of that wound, in which there was perhaps too much of earthly affection, I pour forth to You, O our God, tears of a very different sort for Your handmaid–tears that flow from a spirit shaken by the thought of the perils there are for every soul that dies in Adam. For though she had been made alive in Christ,[140] and while still in the body had so lived that Your name was glorified in her faith and her character, yet I dare not say that from the moment of her regeneration in baptism[141] no word issued from her mouth contrary to Your command.[142] Your Son, who is Truth,[143] has said, *Whosoever shall say to his brother, Thou fool, shall be in danger of hell fire;*[144] and it would go ill with the most praise-worthy life lived by men, if You were to examine it with Your mercy laid aside![145] But because You do not enquire too fiercely into our sins, we have hope and confidence of a place with You. Yet if a man reckons up before You the merits he truly has, what is he reckoning except Your own gifts? If only men would know themselves to be but men, so that he that glories would glory in the Lord![146]

(35) Thus, my Glory[147] and my Life, God of my heart,[148] leaving aside for this time her good deeds, for which I give thanks to Thee in joy, I now pray to Thee for my mother's sins. Grant my prayer through the true Medicine of our wounds, who hung upon the cross[149] and who now sitting at Thy right hand makes intercession for us.[150] I know that she dealt mercifully, and from her heart forgave those who trespassed against her: do Thou also forgive such trespasses as she may have been guilty of[151] in all the years since her baptism, forgive them, Lord, forgive them, I beseech Thee:[152] enter not into judgment with her.[153] Let Thy mercy be exalted above Thy justice,[154] for Thy words are true and Thou hast promised that the merciful shall obtain mercy.[155] That they should be merciful is Thy gift who *hast mercy on whom Thou wilt,*[156] *and wilt have compassion on whom Thou wilt.*[157]

(36) And I believe that Thou hast already done what I am now asking; but be not offended, Lord, at the things my mouth would utter.[158] For on that day when her death was so close,[159] she was not concerned that her body should be sumptuously wrapped or embalmed with spices, nor with any thought of choosing a monument or even for burial in her own country. Of such things she gave us no command, but only desired to be remembered at Thy altar, which she had served without ever missing so much as a day, on which she knew that the holy Victim was offered, *by whom the handwriting is blotted out of the decree that was contrary to us,*[160] by which offering too the enemy was overcome who, reckoning our sins and seeking what may be laid to our charge, found nothing in Him,[161] in whom we are conquerors. Who shall restore to Him His innocent blood?[162] Who shall give Him back the price by which He purchased us[163] and so take us from Him? To this sacrament of our redemption Thy handmaid had

bound her soul by the bond of faith. Let none wrest her from Thy protection; let neither the lion nor the dragon[164] bar her way by force or craft. For she will not answer that she owes nothing, lest she should be contradicted and confuted by that cunning accuser: but she will answer that her debts have been remitted by Him, to whom no one can hand back the price which He paid for us, though He owed it not.

(37) So let her rest in peace, together with her husband, for she had no other before nor after him,[165] but served him, in patience bringing forth fruit for Thee,[166] and winning him likewise for Thee. And inspire, O my Lord my God,[167] inspire Thy servants my brethren, Thy sons my masters, whom I serve with heart and voice and pen, that as many of them as read this may remember at Thy altar Thy servant Monica, with Patricius, her husband, by whose bodies Thou didst bring me into this life, though how I know not. May they with loving mind remember these who were my parents in this transitory light, my brethren who serve Thee as our Father in our Catholic mother, and those who are to be fellow-citizens with me in the eternal Jerusalem, which Thy people sigh for[168] in their pilgrimage from birth until they come there: so that what my mother at her end asked of me may be fulfilled more richly in the prayers of so many gained for her by my Confessions than by my prayers alone.

Notes

1. Ps. 115:7–8(116:16–17).

2. Ps. 34(35):10.

3. Ps. 34(35):3.

4. See Ps. 85(86): 15.

5. See Matt. 26:39; Mark 14:36; John 5:30, 6:38.

6. See Matt. 11:30.

7. This is the only time in the *Confessions* that Christ is directly addressed by His proper name, perhaps because it follows so closely on Augustine's account of reading, "put ye on the Lord Jesus Christ."

8. See Ps. 18:15(19:14).

9. See Lucan 2.681; Horace, *Odes* 1.18.4.

10. Literally, "not meditating on Your law." See Ps. 118(119):77.

11. See Ps. 39:5(40:4).

12. See Virgil, *Aeneid* 1.150.

13. The vintage holidays, which last from August 23 to October 15, were for the purpose of avoiding the summer heat and helping with the autumn harvest

14. Ps. 83:7(84:6).

15. The title for Psalms 119(120) through 133(134). See XIII.9.10.

16. Ps. 119(120):3–4, the arrows signifying God's words and the coals are good examples of what to do (*Explanations of the Psalms* 119.5).

17. See Ezek. 36:23.

18. See Rom. 14:16.

19. The illness could have been any number of respiratory problems. Later, Augustine implicitly compares his difficulty in breathing to his lingering inflamed pride (IX.4.7).

20. Literally, "a full will of being still and seeing that you are the Lord." See Ps. 45:11(46:10).

21. Following 1 John 5:16–17, Augustine makes a distinction between mortal and venial sins, the former bringing "death" to the soul and the latter being lamentable but not deadly. Both are remitted by the sacrament of baptism.

22. See Luke 14:14.

23. See Ps. 124(125):3.

24. A village north of Milan, probably located near present-day Cassago, Italy.

25 See Ps. 67:16(68:15). Augustine's Old Latin text read "in the cheesy mountain," which he understood to signify the milky abundance of nourishing grace from Christ (see *Explanations of the Psalms* 67.22).

26. See Ps. 67:16(68:15).

27. See Luke 16:22.

28. See Gal. 4:5–7.

29. Ps. 26(27):8.

30. Augustine's companions included Monica, his brother Navigius, his son Adeodatus, Alypius, his pupils Licentius and Trygetius, and two cousins.

31. The dialogues are: *Against the Academics, On the Happy Life, On Order,* and the *Soliloquies.*

32. *Letters* 3 and 4.

33. Isa. 40:4. See Luke 3:4–5.

34. See Ps. 28(29):5. Literally, the cedars "of the gymnasia." Since the Cassiciacum dialogues include a prolonged disputation with Ciceronian thought, the reference is most likely to the two gymnasiums on Cicero's estates which served as a location for a number of his philosophical dialogues.

35. Ps. 18:7(19:6).

36. Ps. 4:2(1).

37. See Ps. 30:7–8(31:6–7).

38. Ps. 4:3(2).

39. Ps. 4:4(3).

40. See Mark 16:19.

41. See John 14:16–17; Luke 24:49.

42. See Acts 2:1–4.

43. See Rom. 6:9.

44. See John 7:39

45. Ps. 4:3–4(2–3).

46. See Ps. 4:4(3).

47. Ps. 4:5(4).

48. For Augustine, sinless anger occurs when one is angrier at one's own sins than at another's. See *Explanations of the Psalms* 4.6.

49. See Rom. 2:5.

50. That is, temporal goods. See 2 Cor. 4:18.

51. Ps. 4:6(5).

52. Ps. 4:7(6).

53. John 1:19.

54. Eph. 5:8.

55. Or, "I had tasted it." See Ps. 33:9(34:8).

56. Ps. 4:6(5).

57. Literally, "slaying my old [self] and beginning to meditate on my renewal," a reference to St. Paul's theology of the "old man" and the new (Eph. 4:22–24; Col. 3:9–10).

58. Ps. 4:8(7).

59. *Ibid.*

60. Ps. 4:9(8).

61. 1 Cor. 15:54.

62. The word *idipsum*, translated here as "selfsame," was for Augustine a mystical divine name comparable to the Tetragrammaton in Exod. 3:14. See VII.17.23, IX.10.24, XII.7.7; *Explanations of the Psalms* 121.5.

63. Ps. 4:10(8).

64. See Ps. 118(119):103.

65. See Ps. 138(139):21.

66. See 1 Cor. 2:9.

67. See Ps. 17:47(18:46), 37:23(38:22).

68. See John 20:28.

69. See Ps. 144(145):2; Ecclus.(Sir.) 51:15.

70. This entire incident is redolent of Acts 8:26–39.

71. That is, the beginning of Lent, Spring 387. See note on VIII.2.4.

72. Literally, "clothed with humility." See Col. 3:12.

73. Following the examples of Moses on Mount Sinai (Exod. 3:5) and Isaiah the prophet (Isa. 20:2–3), Christians sometimes went barefoot as a form of asceticism.

74. See 2 Macc. 1:24; Ambrose, *Hymn* 1.2.

75. *On the Teacher* was composed in Thagaste around the year 389.

76. By St. Ambrose during the Easter Vigil of April 24–25, 387. After entering the baptistery in Milan and being immersed three times in the inlaid font, Augustine was clothed in a white robe and led into the basilica, where he participated in the entire Eucharistic liturgy and received Holy Communion for the first time. Augustine may be circumspect about the details because of the discipline of the secret (see pp. 329–30).

77. Augustine may be referring to the "Octave of the Infants," the week following Easter Sunday when the neophytes, or "infants" in the faith, were given further instruction on the sacred mysteries (see "Catechumenate," p. 327).

78. The Empress Justina issued an edict in January 386 requiring Ambrose to surrender several of his churches to the Arian heretics. Ambrose defied the order and had the churches filled with Catholics to prevent their confiscation.

79. See Col. 3:16.

80. See Ambrose, *Letters* 20 and 21; Paulinus, *Life of Ambrose*. The incident took place in February 386.

81. Sts. Protasius and Gervasius were brothers who were martyred in Milan in the second century.

82. Their bodies may still be seen today in the crypt of the basilica S. Ambrogio.

83. See Luke 6:18.

84. See Acts 19:12. During the Roman persecutions, it had not been uncommon for the faithful to catch the immolated blood of the martyrs with their handkerchiefs.

85. See Ps. 115(116):16.

86. This took place around June 17–19, 386. According to Ambrose, the blind man was a butcher named Severus.

87. Cant.(Song) 1:3.

88. See Isa. 40:6.

89. See Ps. 67:7(68:6).

90. A native of Thagaste, Evodius went on to become bishop of Uzalis. He is Augustine's interlocutor in *On the Greatness of the Soul* and *On Free Choice of the Will*.

91. See Virgil, *Aeneid* 1.13. Ostia, located on the mouth of the Tiber, was the central port for the city of Rome.

92. See Ps. 22(23):4. Augustine interprets the Lord's scepter, or rod, as the discipline that ultimately consoles His flock (*Explanations of the Psalms* 22.4)

93. Literally, "adding a sound word." See Tim. 1:13; Tit. 2:8.

94. See Ecclus.(Sir.) 19:1.

95. The word *meribibulus/a*, or wine-bibber, does not appear in Latin literature prior to its use here, though this does not mean that the insult did not previously exist.

96. See Virgil, *Aeneid* 7.53.

97. See Eph. 5:22; 1 Pet. 3:6.

98. See 1 Pet. 3:1–2.

99. See Ps. 85(86): 13.

100. See 1 John 3:3. Chastity is not the complete absence of sexual activity but the well-ordered moderation of it.

101. Weddings in fourth-century North Africa involved a marriage contract, remotely similar, perhaps, to a Jewish *ketubah*.

102. See Ps. 58:18(59:17).

104. See Gen. 9:25.

105. See Tob. 14:17; 2 Pet. 3:11.

106. 1 Tim. 5:9.

107. 1 Tim. 5:4.

108. 1 Tim. 5:10.

109. 1 Tim. 5:10.

110. See Gal. 4:19. Monica bore at least three children, including a girl and a boy named Navigius.

111. Phil. 3:13.

112. See John 14:6;2 Pet. 1:12; Plotinus, *Enneads* 5.1.4.

113. 1 Cor. 2:9.

114. See note on IX.4.11.

115. See Ezek. 34:14.

116. See Ps. 79:2(80:1).

117. See John 1:3.

118. See Rom. 8:23.

119. See Wis. 7:27.

120. See Ps. 99(100):3.

121. See Ecclus.(Sir.) 18:1; Ps 32(33):11, etc.

122. See Gen. 22:11.

123. See Ps. 76:18(77:17); Exod. 19:19; John 12:29.

124. See 1 Cor. 13:12.

125. Matt. 25:21.

126. 1 Cor. 15:51. Augustine and Monica's ascent from outer to inner to upper (from external things to the mind to God) has Neoplatonic echoes, but with key differences. Because it is grounded in the incarnate Christ, its language is unabashedly sensuous; because it is centered on the Word and on faith, it employs auditory imagery as much as visual; unlike Plotinus' "flight of the alone to the Alone" (*Enneads* 6.9.11), it is communal from beginning to end; and unlike Augustine's intellectual conversion in VII.10.16–17.23, Augustine is able to linger in the experience thanks to his moral and religious conversions (VIII.12.29; IX.6.14, resp.). See "Neoplatonism," pp. 331–32.

127. According to Sr. Maria Boulding, there is a faint echo here of Aeneas' last meeting with his father, Anchises, the garden corresponding to the meadow of Hades (*Aeneid* 6.679, 703) and the name "Ostia" connoting the entrance to the underworld.

128. Navigius.

129. Literally, "invisible God," that is, incapable of being seen. See Col. 1:15.

130. See 1 Thess. 4:13.

131. See 1 Tim. 1:5.

132. See Ps. 99(100):3.

133. Ps. 100:1.

134. A likely reference to the Mass.

135. Monica was buried in Ostia, though her body was moved to San Agostino Church in Rome in 1430, where it still resides. The stone epitaph to her Ostian grave, erected in 431 by the consul, was rediscovered by youths erecting a basketball hoop in 1945.

136. Augustine had heard the somewhat fanciful theory that balaneion comes from *ballō* (drive) and *ania* (grief).

137. See Ps. 67:6(68:5).

138. Roman baths purged the pores by perspiration.

139. Ambrose, *Hymn* 1.

140. See 1 Cor. 15:22; Eph. 2:5

141. See Tit. 3:5.

142. See Matt. 12:36-37.

143. See John 14:6.

144. Matt. 5:22.

145. See Ps. 129(130):3.

146. See 1 Cor. 1:31; 2 Cor. 10:17.

147. See Ps. 117(118):14, 21:4, 26(22:3, 25), etc.

148. See Ps. 72(73):26.

149. Literally, wood or a tree. See Deut. 21:23; Gal. 3:13.

150. See Rom. 8:34.

151. See Matt. 6:12, 18:35.

152. See Num. 14:19.

153. See Ps. 142(143):2.

154. See Jas. 2:13.

155. See Matt. 5:7.

156. Rom. 9:15.

157. Exod. 33:19; see Rom. 9:15.

158. Literally, "approve the free offerings of my mouth." See Ps. 118(119):108.

159. Literally, on the day of her release or unfastening. See 2 Tim. 4:6.

160. Col. 2:14. Augustine is describing the sacrifice of the altar, or Mass, and its effects on sin.

161. See Luke 23:4; John 14:30, 18:38, 19:4.

162. See Matt. 27:4.

163. See 1 Cor. 6:20, 7:23.

164. See Ps. 90(91):13; VII.21.27.

165. See 1 Tim. 5:9.

166. See Luke 8:15.

167. See John 20:28.

168. See Heb. 11:10–14.

from Summa Contra Gentiles

Saint Thomas Aquinas

Chapter 3
On The Way in Which Divine Truth Is to Be Made Known

[1] The way of making truth known is not always the same, and, as the Philosopher has very well said, "it belongs to an educated man to seek such certitude in each thing as the nature of that thing allows."[1] The remark is also introduced by Boethius.[2] But, since such is the case, we must first show what way is open to us in order that we may make known the truth which is our object.

[2] There is a twofold mode of truth in what we profess about God. Some truths about God exceed all the ability of the human reason. Such is the truth that God is triune. But there are some truths which the natural reason also is able to reach. Such are that God exists, that He is one, and the like. In fact, such truths about God have been proved demonstratively by the philosophers, guided by the light of the natural reason.

[3] That there are certain truths about God that totally surpass man's ability appears with the greatest evidence. Since, indeed, the principle of all knowledge that the reason perceives about some thing is the understanding of the very substance of that being (for according to Aristotle "what a thing is" is the principle of demonstration),[3] it is necessary that the way in which we understand the substance of a thing determines the way in which we know what belongs to it. Hence, if the human intellect comprehends the substance of some thing, for example, that of a stone or of a triangle, no intelligible characteristic belonging to that thing surpasses the grasp of the human reason. But this does not happen to us in the case of God. For the human intellect is not able to reach a comprehension of the divine substance through its natural power. For, according to its manner of knowing in the present life, the intellect depends on the sense for the origin of knowledge; and so those things that do not fall under the senses cannot be grasped by the human intellect except in so far as the knowledge of them is gathered from sensible things. Now, sensible things cannot lead the human intellect to the point of seeing in them the nature of the divine substance; for sensible things are effects that fall short of the power of their cause. Yet, beginning with sensible things, our intellect is led to the point of knowing about God that He exists, and other such characteristics that

must be attributed to the First Principle. There are, consequently, some intelligible truths about God that are open to the human reason; but there are others that absolutely surpass its power.

[4] We may easily see the same point from the gradation of intellects. Consider the case of two persons of whom one has a more penetrating grasp of a thing by his intellect than does the other. He who has the superior intellect understands many things that the other cannot grasp at all. Such is the case with a very simple person who cannot at all grasp the subtle speculations of philosophy. But the intellect of an angel surpasses the human intellect much more than the intellect of the greatest philosopher surpasses the intellect of the most uncultivated simple person; for the distance between the best philosopher and a simple person is contained within the limits of the human species, which the angelic intellect surpasses. For the angel knows God on the basis of a more noble effect than does man; and this by as much as the substance of an angel, through which the angel in his natural knowledge is led to the knowledge of God, is nobler than sensible things and even than the soul itself, through which the human intellect mounts to the knowledge of God. The divine intellect surpasses the angelic intellect much more than the angelic surpasses the human. For the divine intellect is in its capacity equal to its substance, and therefore it understands fully what it is, including all its intelligible attributes. But by his natural knowledge the angel does not know what God is, since the substance itself of the angel, through which he is led to the knowledge of God, is an effect that is not equal to the power of its cause. Hence, the angel is not able, by means of his natural knowledge, to grasp all the things that God understands in Himself; nor is the human reason sufficient to grasp all the things that the angel understands through his own natural power. Just as, therefore, it would be the height of folly for a simple person to assert that what a philosopher proposes is false on the ground that he himself cannot understand it, so (and even more so) it is the acme of stupidity for a man to suspect as false what is divinely revealed through the ministry of the angels simply because it cannot be investigated by reason.

[5] The same thing, moreover, appears quite clearly from the defect that we experience every day in our knowledge of things. We do not know a great many of the properties of sensible things, and in most cases we are not able to discover fully the natures of those properties that we apprehend by the sense. Much more is it the case, therefore, that the human reason is not equal to the task of investigating all the intelligible characteristics of that most excellent substance.

[6] The remark of Aristotle likewise agrees with this conclusion. He says that "our intellect is related to the prime beings, which are most evident in their nature, as the eye of an owl is related to the sun."[4]

[7] Sacred Scripture also gives testimony to this truth. We read in Job: "Peradventure thou wilt comprehend the steps of God, and wilt find out the Almighty perfectly?" (11:7). And again: "Behold, God is great, exceeding our knowledge" (Job 36:26). And St. Paul: "We know in part" (I Cor. 13:9).

[8] We should not, therefore, immediately reject as false, following the opinion of the Manicheans and many unbelievers, everything that is said about God even though it cannot be investigated by reason.

Chapter 4
That the Truth about God to Which the Natural Reason Reaches Is Fittingly Proposed to Men for Belief

[1] Since, therefore, there exists a twofold truth concerning the divine being, one to which the inquiry of the reason can reach, the other which surpasses the whole ability of the human reason, it is fitting that both of these truths be proposed to man divinely for belief. This point must first be shown concerning the truth that is open to the inquiry of the reason; otherwise, it might perhaps seem to someone that, since such a truth can be known by the reason, it was uselessly given to men through a supernatural inspiration as an object of belief.

[2] Yet, if this truth were left solely as a matter of inquiry for the human reason, three awkward consequences would follow.

[3] The first is that few men would possess the knowledge of God. For there are three reasons why most men are cut off from the fruit of diligent inquiry which is the discovery of truth. Some do not have the physical disposition for such work. As a result, there are many who are naturally not fitted to pursue knowledge; and so, however much they tried, they would be unable to reach the highest level of human knowledge which consists in knowing God. Others are cut off from pursuing this truth by the necessities imposed upon them by their daily lives. For some men must devote themselves to taking care of temporal matters. Such men would not be able to give so much time to the leisure of contemplative inquiry as to reach the highest peak at which human investigation can arrive, namely, the knowledge of God. Finally, there are some who are cut off by indolence. In order to know the things that the reason can investigate concerning God, a knowledge of many things must already be possessed. For almost all of philosophy is directed towards the knowledge of God, and that is why metaphysics, which deals with divine things, is the last part of philosophy to be learned. This means that we are able to arrive at the inquiry concerning the aforementioned truth only on the basis of a great deal of labor spent in study. Now, those who wish to undergo such a labor for the mere love of knowledge are few, even though God has inserted into the minds of men a natural appetite for knowledge.

[4] The second awkward effect is that those who would come to discover the abovementioned truth would barely reach it after a great deal of time. The reasons are several. There is the profundity of this truth, which the human intellect is made capable of grasping by natural inquiry only after a long training. Then, there are many things that must be presupposed, as we have said. There is also the fact that, in youth, when the soul is swayed by the various movements of the passions, it is not in a suitable state for the knowledge of such lofty truth. On the contrary, "one becomes wise and knowing in repose," as it is said in the *Physics*.[5] The result is this. If the only way open to us for the knowledge of God were solely that of the reason, the human race would remain in the blackest shadows of ignorance. For then the knowledge of God, which especially renders men perfect and good, would come to be possessed only by a few, and these few would require a great deal of time in order to reach it.

[5] The third awkward effect is this. The investigation of the human reason for the most part has falsity present within it, and this is due partly to the weakness of our intellect in judgment, and partly to the admixture of images. The result is that many, remaining ignorant of the power of demonstration, would hold in doubt those things that have been most truly demonstrated. This would be particularly the case since they see that, among those who are reputed to be wise men, each one teaches his own brand of doctrine. Furthermore, with the many truths that are demonstrated, there sometimes is mingled something that is false, which is not demonstrated but rather asserted on the basis of some probable or sophistical argument, which yet has the credit of being a demonstration. That is why it was necessary that the unshakeable certitude and pure truth concerning divine things should be presented to men by way of faith.[6]

[6] Beneficially, therefore, did the divine Mercy provide that it should instruct us to hold by faith even those truths that the human reason is able to investigate. In this way, all men would easily be able to have a share in the knowledge of God, and this without uncertainty and error.

[7] Hence it is written: "Henceforward you walk not as also the Gentiles walk in the vanity of their mind, having their understanding darkened" (Eph. 4:17–18). And again: "All thy children shall be taught of the Lord" (Isa. 54:13).

Chapter 5

That the Truths the Human Reason Is Not Able to Investigate Are Fittingly Proposed to Men for Belief

[1] Now, perhaps some will think that men should not be asked to believe what the reason is not adequate to investigate, since the divine Wisdom provides in the case of each thing according to the mode of its nature.

We must therefore prove that it is necessary for man to receive from God as objects of belief even those truths that are above the human reason.

[2] No one tends with desire and zeal towards something that is not already known to him. But, as we shall examine later on in this work, men are ordained by the divine Providence towards a higher good than human fragility can experience in the present life.[7] That is why it was necessary for the human mind to be called to something higher than the human reason here and now can reach, so that it would thus learn to desire something and with zeal tend towards something that surpasses the whole state of the present life. This belongs especially to the Christian religion, which in a unique way promises spiritual and eternal goods. And so there are many things proposed to men in it that transcend human sense. The Old Law, on the other hand, whose promises were of a temporal character, contained very few proposals that transcended the inquiry of the human reason. Following this same direction, the philosophers themselves, in order that they might lead men from the pleasure of sensible things to virtue, were concerned to show that there were in existence other goods of a higher nature than these things of sense, and that those who gave themselves to the active or contemplative virtues would find much sweeter enjoyment in the taste of these higher goods.

[3] It is also necessary that such truth be proposed to men for belief so that they may have a truer knowledge of God. For then only do we know God truly when we believe Him to be above everything that it is possible for man to think about Him; for, as we have shown,[8] the divine substance surpasses the natural knowledge of which man is capable. Hence, by the fact that some things about God are proposed to man that surpass his reason, there is strengthened in man the view that God is something above what he can think.

[4] Another benefit that comes from the revelation to men of truths that exceed the reason is the curbing of presumption, which is the mother of error. For there are some who have such a presumptuous opinion of their own ability that they deem themselves able to measure the nature of everything; I mean to say that, in their estimation, everything is true that seems to them so, and everything is false that does not. So that the human mind, therefore, might be freed from this presumption and come to a humble inquiry after truth, it was necessary that some things should be proposed to man by God that would completely surpass his intellect.

[5] A still further benefit may also be seen in what Aristotle says in the *Ethics*.[9] There was a certain Simonides who exhorted people to put aside the knowledge of divine things and to apply their talents to human occupations. He said that "he who is a man should know human things, and he who is mortal, things that are mortal." Against Simonides Aristotle says that "man should draw himself towards what is immortal and divine

as much as he can." And so he says in the *De animalibus* that, although what we know of the higher substances is very little, yet that little is loved and desired more than all the knowledge that we have about less noble substances.[10] He also says in the *De caelo et mundo* that when questions about the heavenly bodies can be given even a modest and merely plausible solution, he who hears this experiences intense joy.[11] From all these considerations it is clear that even the most imperfect knowledge about the most noble realities brings the greatest perfection to the soul. Therefore, although the human reason cannot grasp fully the truths that are above it, yet, if it somehow holds these truths at least by faith, it acquires great perfection for itself.

[6] Therefore it is written: "For many things are shown to thee above the understanding of men" (Ecclus. 3:25). Again: "So the things that are of God no man knoweth but the Spirit of God, But to us God hath revealed them by His Spirit" (I Cor. 2:11, 10).

Chapter 6

That to Give Assent to the Truths of Faith Is Not Foolishness Even though They Are above Reason

[1] Those who place their faith in this truth, however, "for which the human reason offers no experimental evidence"[12] do not believe foolishly, as though "following artificial fables" (II Peter 1:16). For these "secrets of divine Wisdom" (Job 11:6) the divine Wisdom itself, which knows all things to the full, has deigned to reveal to men. It reveals its own presence, as well as the truth of its teaching and inspiration, by fitting arguments; and in order to confirm those truths that exceed natural knowledge, it gives visible manifestation to works that surpass the ability of all nature. Thus, there are the wonderful cures of illnesses, there is the raising of the dead, and the wonderful immutation in the heavenly bodies; and what is more wonderful, there is the inspiration given to human minds, so that simple and untutored persons, filled with the gift of the Holy Spirit, come to possess instantaneously the highest wisdom and the readiest eloquence. When these arguments were examined, through the efficacy of the abovementioned proof, and not the violent assault of arms or the promise of pleasures, and (what is most wonderful of all) in the midst of the tyranny of the persecutors, an innumerable throng of people, both simple and most learned, flocked to the Christian faith. In this faith there are truths preached that surpass every human intellect; the pleasures of the flesh are curbed; it is taught that the things of the world should be spurned. Now, for the minds of mortal men to assent to these things is the greatest of miracles, just as it is a manifest work of divine inspiration that, spurning visible things, men should seek only what is invisible. Now,

that this has happened neither without preparation nor by chance, but as a result of the disposition of God, is clear from the fact that through many pronouncements of the ancient prophets God had foretold that He would do this. The books of these prophets are held in veneration among us Christians, since they give witness to our faith.

[2] The manner of this confirmation is touched on by St. Paul: "Which," that is, human salvation, "having begun to be declared by the Lord, was confirmed unto us by them that hear Him: God also bearing them witness of signs, and wonders, and divers miracles, and distributions of the Holy Ghost" (Heb. 2:3–4).

[3] This wonderful conversion of the world to the Christian faith is the clearest witness of the signs given in the past; so that it is not necessary that they should be further repeated, since they appear most clearly in their effect. For it would be truly more wonderful than all signs if the world had been led by simple and humble men to believe such lofty truths, to accomplish such difficult actions, and to have such high hopes. Yet it is also a fact that, even in our own time, God does not cease to work miracles through His saints for the confirmation of the faith.

[4] On the other hand, those who founded sects committed to erroneous doctrines proceeded in a way that is opposite to this. The point is clear in the case of Mohammed. He seduced the people by promises of carnal pleasure to which the concupiscence of the flesh goads us. His teaching also contained precepts that were in conformity with his promises, and he gave free rein to carnal pleasure. In all this, as is not unexpected, he was obeyed by carnal men. As for proofs of the truth of his doctrine, he brought forward only such as could be grasped by the natural ability of anyone with a very modest wisdom. Indeed, the truths that he taught he mingled with many fables and with doctrines of the greatest falsity. He did not bring forth any signs produced in a supernatural way, which alone fittingly gives witness to divine inspiration; for a visible action that can be only divine reveals an invisibly inspired teacher of truth. On the contrary, Mohammed said that he was sent in the power of his arms—which are signs not lacking even to robbers and tyrants. What is more, no wise men, men trained in things divine and human, believed in him from the beginning. Those who believed in him were brutal men and desert wanderers, utterly ignorant of all divine teaching, through whose numbers Mohammed forced others to become his followers by the violence of his arms. Nor do divine pronouncements on the part of preceding prophets offer him any witness. On the contrary, he perverts almost all the testimonies of the Old and New Testaments by making them into fabrications of his own, as can be seen by anyone who examines his law. It was, therefore, a shrewd decision on his part to forbid his followers to read the Old and New Testaments, lest these books convict him of falsity. It is thus clear that those who place any faith in his words believe foolishly.

Chapter 7

That the Truth of Reason Is Not Opposed to the Truth of the Christian Faith

[1] Now, although the truth of the Christian faith which we have discussed surpasses the capacity of the reason, nevertheless that truth that the human reason is naturally endowed to know cannot be opposed to the truth of the Christian faith. For that with which the human reason is naturally endowed is clearly most true; so much so, that it is impossible for us to think of such truths as false. Nor is it permissible to believe as false that which we hold by faith, since this is confirmed in a way that is so clearly divine. Since, therefore, only the false is opposed to the true, as is clearly evident from an examination of their definitions, it is impossible that the truth of faith should be opposed to those principles that the human reason knows naturally.

[2] Furthermore, that which is introduced into the soul of the student by the teacher is contained in the knowledge of the teacher—unless his teaching is fictitious, which it is improper to say of God. Now, the knowledge of the principles that are known to us naturally has been implanted in us by God; for God is the Author of our nature. These principles, therefore, are also contained by the divine Wisdom. Hence, whatever is opposed to them is opposed to the divine Wisdom, and, therefore, cannot come from God. That which we hold by faith as divinely revealed, therefore, cannot be contrary to our natural knowledge.

[3] Again. In the presence of contrary arguments our intellect is chained, so that it cannot proceed to the knowledge of the truth. If, therefore, contrary knowledges were implanted in us by God, our intellect would be hindered from knowing truth by this very fact. Now, such an effect cannot come from God.

[4] And again. What is natural cannot change as long as nature does not. Now, it is impossible that contrary opinions should exist in the same knowing subject at the same time. No opinion or belief, therefore, is implanted in man by God which is contrary to man's natural knowledge.

[5] Therefore, the Apostle says: "The word is nigh thee, even in thy mouth and in thy heart. This is the word of faith, which we preach" (Rom. 10:8). But because it overcomes reason, there are some who think that it is opposed to it: which is impossible.

[6] The authority of St. Augustine also agrees with this. He writes as follows: "That which truth will reveal cannot in any way be opposed to the sacred books of the Old and the New Testament."[13]

[7] From this we evidently gather the following conclusion: whatever arguments are brought forward against the doctrines of faith are conclusions incorrectly derived from the first and self-evident principles

imbedded in nature. Such conclusions do not have the force of demonstration; they are arguments that are either probable or sophistical. And so, there exists the possibility to answer them.

Chapter 8
How the Human Reason Is Related to the Truth of Faith

[1] There is also a further consideration. Sensible things, from which the human reason takes the origin of its knowledge, retain within themselves some sort of trace of a likeness to God. This is so imperfect, however, that it is absolutely inadequate to manifest the substance of God. For effects bear within themselves, in their own way, the likeness of their causes, since an agent produces its like; yet an effect does not always reach to the full likeness of its cause. Now, the human reason is related to the knowledge of the truth of faith (a truth which can be most evident only to those who see the divine substance) in such a way that it can gather certain likenesses of it, which are yet not sufficient so that the truth of faith may be comprehended as being understood demonstratively or through itself. Yet it is useful for the human reason to exercise itself in such arguments, however weak they may be, provided only that there be present no presumption to comprehend or to demonstrate. For to be able to see something of the loftiest realities, however thin and weak the sight may be, is, as our previous remarks indicate, a cause of the greatest joy.

[2] The testimony of Hilary agrees with this. Speaking of this same truth, he writes as follows in his De Trinitate: "Enter these truths by believing, press forward, persevere. And though I may know that you will not arrive at an end, yet I will congratulate you in your progress. For, though he who pursues the infinite with reverence will never finally reach the end, yet he will always progress by pressing onward. But do not intrude yourself into the divine secret, do not, presuming to comprehend the sum total of intelligence, plunge yourself into the mystery of the unending nativity; rather, understand that these things are incomprehensible."[14]

Notes

1. Aristotle, *Nicomachean Ethics*, I, 3 (1094b 24).

2. Boethius, *De Trinitate*, II (PL, 64, col. 1250).

3. Aristotle, *Posterior Analytics*, II, 3 (90b 31).

4. Aristotle, *Metaphysics*, Ia, 1 (993b 9).

5. Aristotle, *Physics*, VII, 3 (247b 9).

6. Although St. Thomas does not name Maimonides or his *Guide for the Perplexed* (*Dux neutrorum*), there are evident points of contact between the Catholic and the Jewish theologian. On the reasons for revelation given here, on our

knowledge of God, on creation and the eternity of the world, and on Aristotelianism in general, St. Thomas has Maimonides in mind both to agree and to disagree with him. By way of background for *SCG*, I, the reader can usefully consult the references to Maimonides in E. Gilson, *History of Christian Philosophy in the Middle Ages* (New York, 1955), pp. 649–651.

7. *SCG*, III, ch. 48.

8. See above, ch. 3.

9. Aristotle, *Nicomachean Ethics*, X, 7 (1177b 31).

10. Aristotle, *De partibus animalium*, I, 5 (644b 32).

11. Aristotle, *De caelo et mundo*, II, 12 (291b 26).

12. St. Gregory, *Homiliae in evangelia*, II, hom. 26, i (PL, 76, col. 1197).

13. St. Augustine, *De genesi ad litteram*, II, c. 18 (PL, 34, col. 280).

14. St. Hilary, *De Trinitate*, II, io, ii (PL, 10, coll. 58–59).

from The Divine Comedy

Dante Alighieri

from The Inferno

Canto I

The Dark Wood of Error

Midway in his allotted threescore years and ten, Dante comes to himself with a start and realizes that he has strayed from the True Way into the Dark Wood of Error (Worldliness). As soon as he has realized his loss, Dante lifts his eyes and sees the first light of the sunrise (the Sun is the Symbol of Divine Illumination) lighting the shoulders of a little hill (The Mount of Joy). It is the Easter Season, the time of resurrection, and the sun is in its equinoctial rebirth. This juxtaposition of joyous symbols fills Dante with hope and he sets out at once to climb directly up the Mount of Joy, but almost immediately his way is blocked by the Three Beasts of Worldliness: THE LEOPARD OF MALICE AND FRAUD, THE LION OF VIOLENCE AND AMBITION, and THE SHE-WOLF OF INCONTINENCE. These beasts, and especially the She-Wolf drive him back despairing into the darkness of error. But just as all seems lost, a figure appears to him. It is the shade of VIRGIL, Dante's symbol of HUMAN REASON.

Virgil explains that he has been sent to lead Dante from error. There can, however, be no direct ascent past the beasts: the man who would escape them must go a longer and harder way. First he must descend through Hell (The Recognition of Sin), then he must ascend through Purgatory (The Renunciation of Sin), and only then may he reach the pinnacle of joy and come to the Light of God. Virgil offers to guide Dante, but only as far as Human Reason can go. Another guide (BEATRICE, symbol of DIVINE LOVE) must take over for the final ascent, for Human Reason is self-limited. Dante submits himself joyously to Virgil's guidance and they move off.

> Midway in our life's journey, I went astray
>   from the straight road and woke to find myself
>   alone in a dark wood. How shall I say
>
> what wood that was! I never saw so drear,
>   so rank, so arduous a wilderness!   5
>   Its very memory gives a shape to fear.

Death could scarce be more bitter than that place!
    But since it came to good, I will recount
    all that I found revealed there by God's grace.

How I came to it I cannot rightly say,   10
    so drugged and loose with sleep had I become
    when I first wandered there from the True Way.

But at the far end of that valley of evil
    whose maze had sapped my very heart with fear!
    I found myself before a little hill   15

and lifted up my eyes. Its shoulders glowed
    already with the sweet rays of that planet
    whose virtue leads men straight on every road,

and the shining strengthened me against the fright
    whose agony had wracked the lake of my heart   20
    through all the terrors of that piteous night.

Just as a swimmer, who with his last breath
    flounders ashore from perilous seas, might turn
    to memorize the wide water of his death—

so did I turn, my soul still fugitive   25
    from death's surviving image, to stare down
    that pass that none had ever left alive.

And there I lay to rest from my heart's race
    till calm and breath returned to me. Then rose
    and pushed up that dead slope at such a pace   30

each footfall rose above the last. And lo!
    almost at the beginning of the rise
    I faced a spotted Leopard, all tremor and flow

and gaudy pelt. And it would not pass, but stood
    so blocking my every turn that time and again   35
    I was on the verge of turning back to the wood.

This fell at the first widening of the dawn
    as the sun was climbing Aries with those stars
    that rode with him to light the new creation.

Thus the holy hour and the sweet season   40
    of commemoration did much to arm my fear
    of that bright murderous beast with their good omen.

Yet not so much but what I shook with dread
    at sight of a great Lion that broke upon me
    raging with hunger, its enormous head   45

held high as if to strike a mortal terror
    into the very air. And down his track,
    a She-Wolf drove upon me, a starved horror

ravening and wasted beyond all belief.
    She seemed a rack for avarice, gaunt and craving.   50
    Oh many the souls she has brought to endless grief!

She brought such heaviness upon my spirit
    at sight of her savagery and desperation,
    I died from every hope of that high summit.

And like a miser—eager in acquisition   55
    but desperate in self-reproach when Fortune's wheel
    turns to the hour of his loss—all tears and attrition

I wavered back; and still the beast pursued,
    forcing herself against me bit by bit
    till I slid back into the sunless wood.   60

And as I fell to my soul's ruin, a presence
    gathered before me on the discolored air,
    the figure of one who seemed hoarse from long silence.

At sight of him in that friendless waste I cried:
    "Have pity on me, whatever thing you are,   65
    whether shade or living man." And it replied:

"Not man, though man I once was, and my blood
    was Lombard, both my parents Mantuan.
    I was born, though late, *sub Julio*, and bred

in Rome under Augustus in the noon   70
    of the false and lying gods. I was a poet
    and sang of old Anchises' noble son

who came to Rome after the burning of Troy.
    But you—why do *you* return to these distresses
    instead of climbing that shining Mount of Joy   75

which is the seat and first cause of man's bliss?"
    "And are you then that Virgil and that fountain
    of purest speech?" My voice grew tremulous:

"Glory and light of poets! now may that zeal
    and love's apprenticeship that I poured out   80
    on your heroic verses serve me well!

For you are my true master and first author,
    the sole maker from whom I drew the breath
    of that sweet style whose measures have brought me honor.

See there, immortal sage, the beast I flee.   85
    For my soul's salvation, I beg you, guard me from her,
    for she has struck a mortal tremor through me."

And he replied, seeing my soul in tears:
    "He must go by another way who would escape
    this wilderness, for that mad beast that fleers   90

before you there, suffers no man to pass.
    She tracks down all, kills all, and knows no glut,
    but, feeding, she grows hungrier than she was.

She mates with any beast, and will mate with more
    before the Greyhound comes to hunt her down.   95
    He will not feed on lands nor loot, but honor

and love and wisdom will make straight his way.
    He will rise between Feltro and Feltro, and in him
    shall be the resurrection and new day

of that sad Italy for which Nisus died,   100
    and Turnus, and Euryalus, and the maid Camilla.
    He shall hunt her through every nation of sick pride

till she is driven back forever to Hell
    whence Envy first released her on the world.
    Therefore, for your own. good, I think it well   105

you follow me and I will be your guide
    and lead you forth through an eternal place.
    There you shall see the ancient spirits tried

in endless pain, and hear their lamentation
    as each bemoans the second death of souls.   110
    Next you shall see upon a burning mountain

souls in fire and yet content in fire,
    knowing that whensoever it may be
    they yet will mount into the blessed choir.

To which, if it is still your wish to climb,   115
    a worthier spirit shall be sent to guide you.
    With her shall I leave you, for the King of Time,

who reigns on high, forbids me to come there
    since, living, I rebelled against his law.
    He rules the waters and the land and air   120

and there holds court, his city and his throne.
    Oh blessed are they he chooses!" And I to him:
    "Poet, by that God to you unknown,

lead me this way. Beyond this present ill
    and worse to dread, lead me to Peter's gate   125
    and be my guide through the sad halls of Hell."

And he then: "Follow." And he moved ahead
in silence, and I followed where he led.

Notes

1. *Midway in our life's journey:* The Biblical life span is threescore years and ten. The action opens in Dante's thirty-fifth year, i.e., a.d. 1300.

17. *that planet:* The Sun. Ptolemaic astronomers considered it a planet. It is also symbolic of God as He who lights man's way.

31. *each footfall rose above the last:* The literal rendering would be: "So that the fixed foot was ever the lower." "Fixed" has often been translated "right" and an ingenious reasoning can support that reading, but a simpler explanation offers itself and seems more competent: Dante is saying that he climbed with such zeal and haste that every footfall carried him above the last despite the steepness of the climb. At a slow pace, on the other hand, the rear foot might be brought up only as far as the forward foot. This device of selecting a minute but exactly

centered detail to convey the whole of a larger action is one of the central characteristics of Dante's style.

THE THREE BEASTS. These three beasts undoubtedly are taken from *Jeremiah*, v, 6. Many additional and incidental interpretations have been advanced for them, but the central interpretation must remain as noted. They foreshadow the three divisions of Hell (incontinence, violence, and fraud) which Virgil explains at length in Canto XI, 16–111. I am not at all sure but what the She-Wolf is better interpreted as Fraud and the Leopard as Incontinence. Good arguments can be offered either way.

38–39. *Aries . . . that rode with him to light the new creation:* The medieval tradition had it that the sun was in Aries at the time of the Creation. The significance of the astronomical and religious conjunction is an important part of Dante's intended allegory. It is just before dawn of Good Friday A.D. 1300 when he awakens in the Dark Wood. Thus his new life begins under Aries, the sign of creation, at dawn (rebirth) and in the Easter season (resurrection). Moreover the moon is full and the sun is in the equinox, conditions that did not fall together on any Friday of 1300. Dante is obviously constructing poetically the perfect Easter as a symbol of his new awakening.

69. *sub Julio:* In the reign of Julius Caesar.

95. *The Greyhound . . . Feltro and Feltro:* Almost certainly refers to Can Grande della Scala (1290–1329), great Italian leader born in Verona, which lies between the towns of Feltre and Montefeltro.

100–101. *Nisus, Turnus, Euryalus, Camilla:* All were killed in the war between the Trojans and the Latians when, according to legend, Aeneas led the survivors of Troy into Italy. Nisus and Euryalus (*Aeneid*, IX) were Trojan comrades-in-arms who died together. Camilla (*Aeneid*, XI) was the daughter of the Latian king and one of the warrior women. She was killed in a horse charge against the Trojans after displaying great gallantry. Turnus (*Aeneid*, XII) was killed by Aeneas in a duel.

110. *the second death:* Damnation. "This is the second death, even the lake of fire." [*Revelation*, xx, 14)

118. *forbids me to come there since, living, etc.:* Salvation is only through Christ in Dante's theology. Virgil lived and died before the establishment of Christ's teachings in Rome, and cannot therefore enter Heaven.

125. *Peter's gate:* The gate of Purgatory. (See *Purgatorio*, IX, 76 ff.) The gate is guarded by an angel with a gleaming sword. The angel is Peter's vicar (Peter, the first Pope, symbolized all Popes; i.e., Christ's vicar on earth) and is entrusted with the two great keys.

Some commentators argue that this is the gate of Paradise, but Dante mentions no gate beyond this one in his ascent to Heaven. It should be remembered, too, that those who pass the gate of Purgatory have effectively entered Heaven.

The three great gates that figure in the entire journey are: the gate of Hell (Canto III, 1–11), the gate of Dis (Canto VIII, 79–113, and Canto IX, 86–87), and the gate of Purgatory, as above.

Canto II

The Descent

It is evening of the first day (Friday). Dante is following Virgil and finds himself tired and despairing. How can he be worthy of such a vision as Virgil has described? He hesitates and seems about to abandon his first purpose.

To comfort him Virgil explains how Beatrice descended to him in Limbo and told him of her concern for Dante. It is she, the symbol of Divine Love, who sends Virgil to lead Dante from error. She has come into Hell itself on this errand, for Dante cannot come to Divine Love unaided; Reason must lead him. Moreover Beatrice has been sent with the prayers of the Virgin Mary (COMPASSION), and of Saint Lucia (DIVINE LIGHT). Rachel (THE CONTEMPLATIVE LIFE) also figures in the heavenly scene which Virgil recounts.

Virgil explains all this and reproaches Dante: how can he hesitate longer when such heavenly powers are concerned for him, and Virgil himself has prom- ised to lead him safely?

Dante understands at once that such forces cannot fail him, and his spirits rise in joyous anticipation.

The light was departing. The brown air drew down
    all the earth's creatures, calling them to rest
    from their day-roving, as I, one man alone,

prepared myself to face the double war
    of the journey and the pity, which memory   5
    shall here set down, nor hesitate, nor err.

O Muses! O High Genius! Be my aid!
    O Memory, recorder of the vision,
    here shall your true nobility be displayed!

Thus I began: "Poet, you who must guide me,   10
    before you trust me to that arduous passage,
    look to me and look through me—can I be worthy?

You sang how the father of Sylvius, while still
    in corruptible flesh won to that other world,
    crossing with mortal sense the immortal sill.   15

But if the Adversary of all Evil
    weighing his consequence and who and what
    should issue from him, treated him so well—

that cannot seem unfitting to thinking men,
    since he was chosen father of Mother Rome   20
    and of her Empire by God's will and token.

Both, to speak strictly, were founded and foreknown
    as the established Seat of Holiness
    for the successors of Great Peter's throne.

In that quest, which your verses celebrate,   25
    he learned those mysteries from which arose
    his victory and Rome's apostolate.

There later came the chosen vessel, Paul,
    bearing the confirmation of that Faith
    which is the one true door to life eternal.   30

But I—how should I dare? By whose permission?
    I am not Aeneas. *I* am not Paul.
    Who could believe me worthy of the vision?

How, then, may I presume to this high quest
    and not fear my own brashness? You are wise   35
    and will grasp what my poor words can but suggest."

As one who unwills what he wills, will stay
    strong purposes with feeble second thoughts
    until he spells all his first zeal away—

so I hung back and balked on that dim coast   40
    till thinking had worn out my enterprise,
    so stout at starting and so early lost.

"I understand from your words and the look in your eyes,"
    that shadow of magnificence answered me,
    "your soul is sunken in that cowardice   45

that bears down many men, turning their course
    and resolution by imagined perils,
    as his own shadow turns the frightened horse.

To free you of this dread I will tell you all
    of why I came to you and what I heard   50
    when first I pitied you. I was a soul

among the souls of Limbo, when a Lady
    so blessed and so beautiful, I prayed her
    to order and command my will, called to me.

Her eyes were kindled from the lamps of Heaven.   55
    Her voice reached through me, tender, sweet, and low.
    An angel's voice, a music of its own:

'O gracious Mantuan whose melodies
    live in earth's memory and shall live on
    till the last motion ceases in the skies,   60

my dearest friend, and fortune's foe, has strayed
    onto a friendless shore and stands beset
    by such distresses that he turns afraid

from the True Way, and news of him in Heaven
    rumors my dread he is already lost.   65
    I come, afraid that I am too-late risen.

Fly to him and with your high counsel, pity,
    and with whatever need be for his good
    and soul's salvation, help him, and solace me.

It is I, Beatrice, who send you to him.   70
    I come from the blessed height for which I yearn.
    Love called me here. When amid Seraphim

I stand again before my Lord, your praises
    shall sound in Heaven. She paused, and I began:
    'O Lady of that only grace that raises   75

feeble mankind within its mortal cycle
    above all other works God's will has placed
    within the heaven of the smallest circle;

so welcome is your command that to my sense,
    were it already fulfilled, it would yet seem tardy.   80
    I understand, and am all obedience.

But tell me how you dare to venture thus
    so far from the wide heaven of your joy
    to which your thoughts yearn back from this abyss.'

'Since what you ask,' she answered me, 'probes near   85
    the root of all, I will say briefly only
    how I have come through Hell's pit without fear.

Know then, O waiting and compassionate soul,
    that is to fear which has the power to harm,
    and nothing else is fearful even in Hell.   90

I am so made by God's all-seeing mercy
    your anguish does not touch me, and the flame
    of this great burning has no power upon me.

There is a Lady in Heaven so concerned
    for him I send you to, that for her sake   95
    the strict decree is broken. She has turned

and called Lucia to her wish and mercy
    saying: "Thy faithful one is sorely pressed;
    in his distresses I commend him to thee."

Lucia, that soul of light and foe of all   100
    cruelty, rose and came to me at once
    where I was sitting with the ancient Rachel,

saying to me: "Beatrice, true praise of God,
    why dost thou not help him who loved thee so
    that for thy sake he left the vulgar crowd?   105

Dost thou not hear his cries? Canst thou not see
    the death he wrestles with beside that river
    no ocean can surpass for rage and fury?"

No soul of earth was ever as rapt to seek
    its good or flee its injury as I was—   110
    when I had heard my sweet Lucia speak—

to descend from Heaven and my blessed seat
    to you, laying my trust in that high speech
    that honors you and all who honor it.'

She spoke and turned away to hide a tear   115
    that, shining, urged me faster. So I came
    and freed you from the beast that drove you there,

blocking the near way to the Heavenly Height.
　　And now what ails you? Why do you lag? Why
　　this heartsick hesitation and pale fright　　　　　　　　120

when three such blessed Ladies lean from Heaven
　　in their concern for you and my own pledge
　　of the great good that waits you has been given?"

As flowerlets drooped and puckered in the night
　　turn up to the returning sun and spread　　　　　　　　125
　　their petals wide on his new warmth and light—

just so my wilted spirits rose again
　　and such a heat of zeal surged through my veins
　　that I was born anew. Thus I began:

"Blesséd be that Lady of infinite pity,　　　　　　　　　130
　　and blessed be thy taxed and courteous spirit
　　that came so promptly on the word she gave thee.

Thy words have moved my heart to its first purpose.
　　My Guide! My Lord! My Master! Now lead on:
　　one will shall serve the two of us in this."　　　　　　135

He turned when I had spoken, and at his back
I entered on that hard and perilous track.

Notes

13–30. AENEAS AND THE FOUNDING OF ROME.

Here is a fair example of the way in which Dante absorbed pagan themes into his Catholicism.

According to Virgil, Aeneas is the son of mortal Anchises and of Venus. Venus, in her son's interest, secures a prophecy and a promise from Jove to the effect that Aeneas is to found a royal line that shall rule the world. After the burning of Troy, Aeneas is directed by various signs to sail for the Latian lands (Italy) where his destiny awaits him. After many misadventures, he is compelled (like Dante) to descend to the underworld of the dead. There he finds his father's shade; and there he is shown the shades of the great kings that are to stem from him. (*Aeneid*, VI, 921 ff.) Among them are Romulus, Julius Caesar, and Augustus Caesar. The full glory of the Roman Empire is also foreshadowed to him.

Dante, however, continues the Virgilian theme and includes in the predestination not only the Roman Empire but the Holy Roman Empire and its Church.

Thus what Virgil presented as an arrangement of Jove, a concession to the son of Venus, becomes part of the divine scheme of the Catholic God, and Aeneas is cast as a direct forerunner of Peter and Paul.

13. *father of Sylvius:* Aeneas.

51–52. *I was a soul among the souls of Limbo:* See Canto IV, lines 31–45, where Virgil explains his state in Hell.

78. *the heaven of the smallest circle:* The Moon. "Heaven" here is used in its astronomical sense. All within that circle is the earth. According to the Ptolemaic system the earth was the center of creation and was surrounded by nine heavenly spheres (nine heavens) concentrically placed around it. The Moon was the first of these, and therefore the smallest. A cross section of this universe could be represented by drawing nine concentric circles (at varying distances about the earth as a center). Going outward from the center these circles would indicate, in order, the spheres of

> The Moon
> Mercury
> Venus
> The Sun
> Mars
> Jupiter
> Saturn
> The Fixed Stars
> The Primum Mobile

Beyond the Primum Mobile lies the Empyrean.

97. *Lucia* (Loo-TCHEE-yah): Allegorically she represents Divine Light. Her name in Italian inevitably suggests "luce" (light), and she is the patron saint of eyesight. By a process quite common in medieval religion, the special powers attributed to Lucia seem to have been suggested by her name rather than her history. (In France, by a similar process, St. Clair is the patroness of sight.)

102. *Rachel:* Represents the Contemplative Life.

A note on "thee" and "thou": except for the quotations from the souls in Heaven, and for Dante's fervent declamation to Virgil, I have insisted on "you" as the preferable pronoun form. I have used "thee" and "thou" in these cases with the idea that they might help to indicate the extraordinary elevation of the speakers and of the persons addressed.

Canto III

THE VESTIBULE OF HELL   *The Opportunists*

The Poets pass the Gate of Hell and are immediately assailed by cries of anguish. Dante sees the first of the souls in torment. They are THE OPPOR-TUNISTS, those souls who in life were neither for good nor evil but only for themselves. Mixed with them are those outcasts who took no sides in the Rebellion of the Angels. They are neither in Hell nor out of it. Eternally unclassified, they race round and round pursuing a wavering banner that runs forever before them through the dirty air; and as they run they are pursued by swarms of wasps and hornets, who sting them and produce a constant flow of blood and putrid matter which trickles down the bodies of the sinners and is feasted upon by loathsome worms and maggots who coat the ground.

The law of Dante's Hell is the law of symbolic retribution. As they sinned so are they punished. They took no sides, therefore they are given no place. As they pursued the ever-shifting illusion of their own advantage, changing their courses with every changing wind, so they pursue eternally an elusive, ever-shifting ban-ner. As their sin was a darkness, so they move in darkness. As their own guilty conscience pursued them, so they are pursued by swarms of wasps and hornets. And as their actions were a moral filth, so they run eternally through the filth of worms and maggots which they themselves feed.

Dante recognizes several, among them POPE CELESTINE V, but without delaying to speak to any of these souls, the Poets move on to ACHERON, the first of the rivers of Hell. Here the newly-arrived souls of the damned gather and wait for monstrous CHARON to ferry them over to punishment. Charon recognizes Dante as a living man and angrily refuses him passage. Virgil forces Charon to serve them, but Dante swoons with terror, and does not reawaken until he is on the other side.

I AM THE WAY INTO THE CITY OF WOE.
I AM THE WAY TO A FORSAKEN PEOPLE.
I AM THE WAY INTO ETERNAL SORROW.

SACRED JUSTICE MOVED MY ARCHITECT.
I WAS RAISED HERE BY DIVINE OMNIPOTENCE,   5
PRIMORDIAL LOVE AND ULTIMATE INTELLECT.

ONLY THOSE ELEMENTS TIME CANNOT WEAR
WERE MADE BEFORE ME, AND BEYOND TIME I STAND.
ABANDON ALL HOPE YE WHO ENTER HERE.

These mysteries I read cut into stone   10
    above a gate. And turning I said: "Master,
    what is the meaning of this harsh inscription?"

And he then as initiate to novice:
    "Here must you put by all division of spirit
    and gather your soul against all cowardice.   15

This is the place I told you to expect.
    Here you shall pass among the fallen people,
    souls who have lost the good of intellect."

So saying, he put forth his hand to me,
    and with a gentle and encouraging smile   20
    he led me through the gate of mystery.

Here sighs and cries and wails coiled and recoiled
    on the starless air, spilling my soul to tears.
    A confusion of tongues and monstrous accents toiled

in pain and anger. Voices hoarse and shrill   25
    and sounds of blows, all intermingled, raised
    tumult and pandemonium that still

whirls on the air forever dirty with it
    as if a whirlwind sucked at sand. And I,
    holding my head in horror, cried: "Sweet Spirit,   30

what souls are these who run through this black haze?"
    And he to me: "These are the nearly soulless
    whose lives concluded neither blame nor praise.

They are mixed here with that despicable corps
    of angels who were neither for God nor Satan,   35
    but only for themselves. The High Creator

scourged them from Heaven for its perfect beauty,
    and Hell will not receive them since the wicked
    might feel some glory over them." And I:

"Master, what gnaws at them so hideously   40
    their lamentation stuns the very air?"
    "They have no hope of death," he answered me,

"and in their blind and unattaining state
  their miserable lives have sunk so low
  that they must envy every other fate.   45

No word of them survives their living season.
  Mercy and Justice deny them even a name.
  Let us not speak of them: look, and pass on."

I saw a banner there upon the mist.
  Circling and circling, it seemed to scorn all pause.   50
  So it ran on, and still behind it pressed

a never-ending rout of souls in pain.
  I had not thought death had undone so many
  as passed before me in that mournful train.

And some I knew among them; last of all   55
  I recognized the shadow of that soul
  who, in his cowardice, made the Great Denial.

At once I understood for certain: these
  were of that retrograde and faithless crew
  hateful to God and to His enemies.   60

These wretches never born and never dead
  ran naked in a swarm of wasps and hornets
  that goaded them the more the more they fled,

and made their faces stream with bloody gouts
  of pus and tears that dribbled to their feet   65
  to be swallowed there by loathsome worms and
                              maggots.

Then looking onward I made out a throng
  assembled on the beach of a wide river,
  whereupon I turned to him: "Master, I long

to know what souls these are, and what strange usage   70
  makes them as eager to cross as they seem to be
  in this infected light." At which the Sage:

"All this shall be made known to you when we stand
  on the joyless beach of Acheron." And I
  cast down my eyes, sensing a reprimand   75

in what he said, and so walked at his side
    in silence and ashamed until we came
    through the dead cavern to that sunless tide.

There, steering toward us in an ancient ferry
    came an old man with a white bush of hair,   80
    bellowing: "Woe to you depraved souls! Bury

here and forever all hope of Paradise:
    I come to lead you to the other shore,
    into eternal dark, into fire and ice.

And you who are living yet, I say begone   85
    from these who are dead." But when he saw me stand
    against his violence he began again:

"By other windings and by other steerage
    shall you cross to that other shore. Not here! Not here!
    A lighter craft than mine must give you passage."   90

And my Guide to him: "Charon, bite back your spleen:
    this has been willed where what is willed must be,
    and is not yours to ask what it may mean."

The steersman of that marsh of ruined souls,
    who wore a wheel of flame around each eye,   95
    stifled the rage that shook his woolly jowls.

But those unmanned and naked spirits there
    turned pale with fear and their teeth began to chatter
    at sound of his crude bellow. In despair

they blasphemed God, their parents, their time on earth,   100
    the race of Adam, and the day and the hour
    and the place and the seed and the womb that gave them birth.

But all together they drew to that grim shore
    where all must come who lose the fear of God.
    Weeping and cursing they come for evermore,   105
and demon Charon with eyes like burning coals
    herds them in, and with a whistling oar
    flails on the stragglers to his wake of souls.

As leaves in autumn loosen and stream down
    until the branch stands bare above its tatters   110
    spread on the rustling ground, so one by one

the evil seed of Adam in its Fall
    cast themselves, at his signal, from the shore
    and streamed away like birds who hear their call.

So they are gone over that shadowy water,   115
    and always before they reach the other shore
    a new noise stirs on this, and new throngs gather.

"My son," the courteous Master said to me,
    "all who die in the shadow of God's wrath
    converge to this from every clime and country.   120

And all pass over eagerly, for here
    Divine Justice transforms and spurs them so
    their dread turns wish: they yearn for what they fear.

No soul in Grace comes ever to this crossing;
    therefore if Charon rages at your presence   125
    you will understand the reason for his cursing."

When he had spoken, all the twilight country
    shook so violently, the terror of it
    bathes me with sweat even in memory:

the tear-soaked ground gave out a sigh of wind   130
    that spewed itself in flame on a red sky,
    and all my shattered senses left me. Blind,

like one whom sleep comes over in a swoon,
I stumbled into darkness and went down.

Notes

7–8. *Only those elements time cannot wear*: The Angels, the Empyrean, and the
First Matter are the elements time cannot wear, for they will last to all time.
Man, however, in his mortal state, is not eternal. The Gate of Hell, therefore, was
created before man. The theological point is worth attention. The doctrine of
Original Sin is, of course, one familiar to many creeds. Here, however, it would
seem that the preparation for damnation predates Original Sin. True, in one
interpretation, Hell was created for the punishment of the Rebellious Angels

and not for man. Had man not sinned, he would never have known Hell. But on the other hand, Dante's God was one who knew all, and knew therefore that man would indeed sin. The theological problem is an extremely delicate one.

It is significant, however, that having sinned, man lives out his days on the rind of Hell, and that damnation is forever below his feet. This central concept of man's sinfulness, and, opposed to it, the doctrine of Christ's ever-abounding mercy, are central to all of Dante's theology. Only as man surrenders himself to Divine Love may he hope for salvation, and salvation is open to all who will surrender themselves.

8. *and beyond time I stand:* So odious is sin to God that there can be no end to its just punishment.

9. *Abandon all hope ye who enter here:* The admonition, of course, is to the damned and not to those who come on Heaven-sent errands. The Harrowing of Hell (see Canto IV, note to 1. 53) provided the only exemption from this decree, and that only through the direct intercession of Christ.

57. *who, in his cowardice, made the Great Denial:* This is almost certainly intended to be Celestine V, who became Pope in 1294. He was a man of saintly life, but allowed himself to be convinced by a priest named Benedetto that his soul was in danger since no man could live in the world without being damned. In fear for his soul he withdrew from all worldly affairs and renounced the Papacy. Benedetto promptly assumed the mantle himself and became Boniface VIII, a Pope who became for Dante a symbol of all the worst corruptions of the Church. Dante also blamed Boniface and his intrigues for many of the evils that befell Florence. We shall learn in Canto XIX that the fires of Hell are waiting for Boniface in the pit of the Simoniacs, and we shall be given further evidence of his corruption in Canto XXVII. Celestine's great guilt is that his cowardice (in selfish terror for his own welfare) served as the door through which so much evil entered the Church.

80. *an old man:* Charon. He is the ferryman of dead souls across the Acheron in all classical mythology.

88–90. *By other windings:* Charon recognizes Dante not only as a living man but as a soul in grace, and knows, therefore, that the Infernal Ferry was not intended for him. He is probably referring to the fact that souls destined for Purgatory and Heaven assemble not at his ferry point, but on the banks of the Tiber, from which they are transported by an Angel.

100. *they blasphemed God:* The souls of the damned are not permitted to repent, for repentance is a divine grace.

123. *they yearn for what they fear:* Hell (allegorically Sin) is what the souls of the damned really wish for. Hell is their actual and deliberate choice, for divine grace is denied to none who wish for it in their hearts. The damned must, in fact, deliberately harden their hearts to God in order to become damned. Christ's grace is sufficient to save all who wish for it.

133–134. DANTE'S SWOON. This device (repeated at the end of Canto V) serves a double purpose. The first is technical: Dante uses it to cover a transition. We are never told how he crossed Acheron, for that would involve certain narrative matters he can better deal with when he crosses Styx in Canto VII. The second is to provide a point of departure for a theme that is carried through the entire descent: the theme of Dante's emotional reaction to Hell. These two swoons early in the descent show him most susceptible to the grief about him. As he descends, pity leaves him, and he even goes so far as to add to the torments of one sinner. The allegory is clear: we must harden ourselves against every sympathy for sin.

Canto IV

CIRCLE ONE: LIMBO   *The Virtuous Pagans*

Dante wakes to find himself across Acheron. The Poets are now on the brink of Hell itself, which Dante conceives as a great funnel-shaped cave lying below the northern hemisphere with its bottom point at the earth's center. Around this great circular depression runs a series of ledges, each of which Dante calls a CIRCLE. Each circle is assigned to the punishment of one category of sin.

As soon as Dante's strength returns, the Poets begin to cross the FIRST CIR-CLE. Here they find the VIRTUOUS PAGANS. They were born without the light of Christ's revelation, and, therefore, they cannot come into the light of God, but they are not tormented. Their only pain is that they have no hope.

Ahead of them Dante sights a great dome of light, and a voice trumpets through the darkness welcoming Virgil back, for this is his eternal place in Hell. Immediately the great Poets of all time appear—HOMER, HORACE, OVID, and LUCAN. They greet Virgil, and they make Dante a sixth in their company.

With them Dante enters the Citadel of Human Reason and sees before his eyes the Master Souls of Pagan Antiquity gathered on a green, and illuminated by the radiance of Human Reason. This is the highest state man can achieve without God, and the glory of it dazzles Dante, but he knows also that it is nothing compared to the glory of God.

A monstrous clap of thunder broke apart
    the swoon that stuffed my head; like one awakened
    by violent hands, I leaped up with a start.

And having risen; rested and renewed,
    I studied out the landmarks of the gloom   5
    to find my bearings there as best I could.

And I found I stood on the very brink of the valley
    called the Dolorous Abyss, the desolate chasm
    where rolls the thunder of Hell's eternal cry,

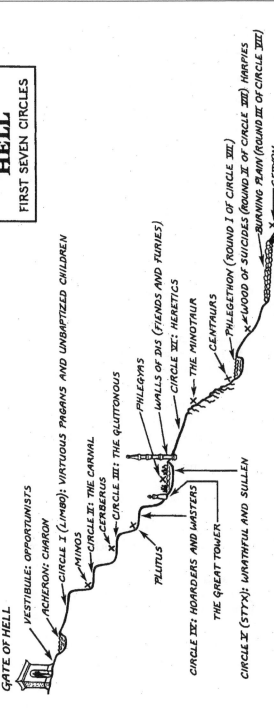

HELL
FIRST SEVEN CIRCLES

GATE OF HELL

VESTIBULE: OPPORTUNISTS

ACHERON: CHARON

CIRCLE I (LIMBO): VIRTUOUS PAGANS AND UNBAPTIZED CHILDREN

MINOS

CIRCLE II: THE CARNAL

CERBERUS

CIRCLE III: THE GLUTTONOUS

PLUTUS

CIRCLE IV: HOARDERS AND WASTERS

THE GREAT TOWER

CIRCLE V (STYX): WRATHFUL AND SULLEN

PHLEGYAS

WALLS OF DIS (FIENDS AND FURIES)

CIRCLE VI: HERETICS

THE MINOTAUR

CENTAURS

PHLEGETHON (ROUND I OF CIRCLE VII)

WOOD OF SUICIDES (ROUND II OF CIRCLE VII) HARPIES

BURNING PLAIN (ROUND III OF CIRCLE VII)

GERYON

WATERFALL

X INDICATES STATIONS OF MONSTERS

so depthless-deep and nebulous and dim 10
    that stare as I might into its frightful pit
    it gave me back no feature and no bottom.

Death-pale, the Poet spoke: "Now let us go
    into the blind world waiting here below us.
    I will lead the way and you shall follow." 15

And I, sick with alarm at his new pallor,
    cried out, "How can I go this way when you
    who are my strength in doubt turn pale with terror?"

And he: "The pain of these below us here,
    drains the color from my face for pity, 20
    and leaves this pallor you mistake for fear.

Now let us go, for a long road awaits us."
    So he entered and so he led me in
    to the first circle and ledge of the abyss.

No tortured wailing rose to greet us here 25
    but sounds of sighing rose from every side,
    sending a tremor through the timeless air,

a grief breathed out of untormented sadness,
    the passive state of those who dwelled apart,
    men, women, children—a dim and endless congress. 30

And the Master said to me: "You do not question
    what souls these are that suffer here before you?
    I wish you to know before you travel on

that these were sinless. And still their merits fail,
    for they lacked Baptism's grace, which is the door 35
    of the true faith *you* were born to. Their birth fell
before the age of the Christian mysteries,
    and so they did not worship God's Trinity
    in fullest duty. I am one of these.

For such defects are we lost, though spared the fire 40
    and suffering Hell in one affliction only:
    that without hope we live on in desire."

I thought how many worthy souls there were
    suspended in that Limbo, and a weight
    closed on my heart for what the noblest suffer. 45

"Instruct me, Master and most noble Sir,"
    I prayed him then, "better to understand
    the perfect creed that conquers every error:

has any, by his own or another's merit,
    gone ever from this place to blessedness?" 50
    He sensed my inner question and answered it:

"I was still new to this estate of tears
    when a Mighty One descended here among us,
    crowned with the sign of His victorious years.

He took from us the shade of our first parent, 55
    of Abel, his pure son, of ancient Noah,
    of Moses, the bringer of law, the obedient.

Father Abraham, David the King,
    Israel with his father and his children,
    Rachel, the holy vessel of His blessing, 60

and many more He chose for elevation
    among the elect. And before these, you must know,
    no human soul had ever won salvation."

We had not paused as he spoke, but held our road
    and passed meanwhile beyond a press of souls 65
    crowded about like trees in a thick wood.

And we had not traveled far from where I woke
    when I made out a radiance before us
    that struck away a hemisphere of dark.
We were still some distance back in the long night, 70
    yet near enough that I half-saw, half-sensed,
    what quality of souls lived in that light.

"O ornament of Wisdom and of art,
    what souls are these whose merit lights their way
    even in Hell: What joy sets them apart?" 75

And he to me: "The signature of honor
     they left on earth is recognized in Heaven
     and wins them ease in Hell out of God's favor."

And as he spoke a voice rang on the air:
     "Honor the Prince of Poets; the soul and glory   80
     that went from us returns. He is here! He is here!"

The cry ceased and the echo passed from hearing;
     I saw four mighty presences come toward us
     with neither joy nor sorrow in their bearing.

"Note well," my Master said as they came on,   85
     "that soul that leads the rest with sword in hand
     as if he were their captain and champion.

It is Homer, singing master of the earth.
     Next after him is Horace, the satirist,
     Ovid is third, and Lucan is the fourth.   90

Since all of these have part in the high name
     the voice proclaimed, calling me Prince of Poets,
     the honor that they do me honors them."

So I saw gathered at the edge of light
     the masters of that highest school whose song   95
     outsoars all others like an eagle's flight.

And after they had talked together a while,
     they turned and welcomed me most graciously,
     at which I saw my approving Master smile.

And they honored me far beyond courtesy,   100
     for they included me in their own number,
     making me sixth in that high company.
So we moved toward the light, and as we passed
     we spoke of things as well omitted here
     as it was sweet to touch on there. At last   105

we reached the base of a great Citadel
     circled by seven towering battlements
     and by a sweet brook flowing round them all.

This we passed over as if it were firm ground.
    Through seven gates I entered with those sages   110
    and came to a green meadow blooming round.

There with a solemn and majestic poise
    stood many people gathered in the light,
    speaking infrequently and with muted voice.

Past that enameled green we six withdrew   115
    into a luminous and open height
    from which each soul among them stood in view.

And there directly before me on the green
    the master souls of time were shown to me.
    I glory in the glory I have seen!   120

Electra stood in a great company
    among whom I saw Hector and Aeneas
    and Caesar in armor with his falcon's eye.

I saw Camilla, and the Queen Amazon
    across the field. I saw the Latian King   125
    seated there with his daughter by his throne.

And the good Brutus who overthrew the Tarquin:
    Lucrezia, Julia, Marcia, and Cornelia;
    and, by himself apart, the Saladin.

And raising my eyes a little I saw on high   130
    Aristotle, the master of those who know,
    ringed by the great souls of philosophy.

All wait upon him for their honor and his.
    I saw Socrates and Plato at his side
    before all others there. Democritus   135

who ascribes the world to chance, Diogenes,
    and with him there Thales, Anaxagoras,
    Zeno, Heraclitus, Empedocles.

And I saw the wise collector and analyst—
    Dioscorides I mean. I saw Orpheus there,   140
    Tully, Linus, Seneca the moralist,

Euclid the geometer, and Ptolemy,
    Hippocrates, Galen, Avicenna,
    and Averroës of the Great Commentary.

I cannot count so much nobility;   145
    my longer theme pursues me so that often
    the word falls short of the reality.

The company of six is reduced by four.
    My Master leads me by another road
    out of that serenity to the roar   150

and trembling air of Hell. I pass from light
into the kingdom of eternal night.

Notes

13 ff. *death-pale:* Virgil is most likely affected here by the return to his own place in Hell. "The pain of these below" then (line 19) would be the pain of his own group in Limbo (the Virtuous Pagans) rather than the total of Hell's suffering.

31 ff. *You do not question:* A master touch of characterization. Virgil's *amour propre* is a bit piqued at Dante's lack of curiosity about the position in Hell of Virgil's own kind. And it may possibly be, by allegorical extension, that Human Reason must urge the soul to question the place of reason. The allegorical point is conjectural, but such conjecture is certainly one of the effects inherent in the use of allegory; when well used, the central symbols of the allegory continue indefinitely to suggest new interpretations and shades of meaning.

53. *a Mighty One:* Christ. His name is never directly uttered in Hell.

53. *descended here:* The legend of the Harrowing of Hell is Apocryphal. It is based on I *Peter*, iii, 19: "He went and preached unto the spirits in prison." The legend is that Christ in the glory of His resurrection descended into Limbo and took with Him to Heaven the first human souls to be saved. The event would, accordingly, have occurred in A.D. 33 or 34. Virgil died in 19 B.C.

102. *making me sixth in that high company:* Merit and self-awareness of merit may well be a higher thing than modesty. An additional point Dante may well have had in mind, however, is the fact that he saw himself as one pledged to continue in his own times the classic tradition represented by these poets.

103–105. These lines amount to a stylistic note. It is good style (*'l tacere è bello* where *bello* equals "good style") to omit this discussion, since it would digress from the subject and, moreover, his point is already made. Every great narrator tends to tell his story from climax to climax. There are times on the other hand when Dante delights in digression. (See General Note to Canto XX.)

106. A GREAT CITADEL. The most likely allegory is that the Citadel represents philosophy (that is, human reason without the light of God) surrounded by seven walls which represent the seven liberal arts, or the seven sciences, or the seven virtues. Note that Human Reason makes a light of its own, but that it is a light in darkness and forever separated from the glory of God's light. The *sweet brook flowing* round them all has been interpreted in many ways. Clearly fundamental, however, is the fact that it divides those in the Citadel (those who wish to know) from those in the outer darkness.

109. *as if it were firm ground*: Since Dante still has his body, and since all others in Hell are incorporeal shades, there is a recurring narrative problem in the *Inferno* (and through the rest of the *Commedia*): how does flesh act in contact with spirit? In the *Purgatorio* Dante attempts to embrace the spirit of Casella and his arms pass through him as if he were empty air. In the Third Circle, below (Canto VI, 34–36), Dante steps on some of the spirits lying in the slush and his foot passes right through them. (The original lines offer several possible readings of which I have preferred this one.) And at other times Virgil, also a spirit, picks Dante up and carries him bodily.

It is clear, too, that Dante means the spirits of Hell to be weightless. When Virgil steps into Phlegyas' bark (Canto VIII) it does not settle into the water, but it does when Dante's living body steps aboard. There is no narrative reason why Dante should not sink into the waters of this stream and Dante follows no fixed rule in dealing with such phenomena, often suiting the physical action to the allegorical need. Here, the moat probably symbolizes some requirement (The Will to Know) which he and the other poets meet without difficulty.

THE INHABITANTS OF THE CITADEL. They fall into three main groups:

1. *The heroes and heroines:* All of these it must be noted were associated with the Trojans and their Roman descendants. (See note on AENEAS AND THE FOUNDING OF ROME, Canto II.) The Electra Dante mentions here is not the sister of Orestes (see Euripides' *Electra*) but the daughter of Atlas and the mother of Dardanus, the founder of Troy.

2. *The philosophers:* Most of this group is made up of philosophers whose teachings were, at least in part, acceptable to Church scholarship. Democritus, however, "who ascribes the world to chance," would clearly be an exception. The group is best interpreted, therefore, as representing the highest achievements of Human Reason unaided by Divine Love. *Plato and Aristotle:* Through a considerable part of the Middle Ages Plato was held to be the fountainhead of all scholarship, but in Dante's time practically all learning was based on Aristotelian theory as interpreted through the many commentaries. *Linus:* the Italian is "Lino" and for it some commentators read "Livio" (Livy).

3. *The naturalists:* They are less well known today. In Dante's time their place in scholarship more or less corresponded to the role of the theoretician and historian of science in our universities. *Avicenna* (his major work was in the eleventh century) and *Averroës* (twelfth century) were Arabian philosophers and physicians especially famous in Dante's time for their commentaries on Aristotle. *Great Commentary:* has the force of a title, i.e., The Great Commentary as distinguished from many lesser commentaries.

The Saladin: This is the famous Saladin who was defeated by Richard the Lion-Heart, and whose great qualities as a ruler became a legend in medieval Europe.

Canto V

CIRCLE TWO   *The Carnal*

The Poets leave Limbo and enter the SECOND CIRCLE. Here begin the torments of Hell proper, and here, blocking the way, sits MINOS, the dread and semi-bestial judge of the damned who assigns to each soul its eternal torment. He orders the Poets back; but Virgil silences him as he earlier silenced Charon, and the Poets move on.

They find themselves on a dark ledge swept by a great whirlwind, which spins within it the souls of the CARNAL, those who betrayed reason to their appetites. Their sin was to abandon themselves to the tempest of their passions; so they are swept forever in the tempest of Hell, forever denied the light of reason and of God. Virgil identifies many among them. SEMIRAMIS is there, and DIDO, CLEO-PATRA, HELEN, ACHILLES, PARIS, and TRISTAN. Dante sees PAOLO and FRANCESCA swept together, and in the name of love he calls to them to tell their sad story. They pause from their eternal flight to come to him, and Francesca tells their history while Paolo weeps at her side. Dante is so stricken by compassion at their tragic tale that he swoons once again.

So we went down to the second ledge alone;
    a smaller circle of so much greater pain
    the voice of the damned rose in a bestial moan.

There Minos sits, grinning, grotesque, and hale.
    He examines each lost soul as it arrives   5
    and delivers his verdict with his coiling tail.

That is to say, when the ill-fated soul
    appears before him it confesses all,
    and that grim sorter of the dark and foul
decides which place in Hell shall be its end,   10
    then wraps his twitching tail about himself
    one coil for each degree it must descend.

The soul descends and others take its place:
    each crowds in its turn to judgment, each confesses,
    each hears its doom and falls away through space.   15

"O you who come into this camp of woe,"
    cried Minos when he saw me turn away
    without awaiting his judgment, "watch where you go

once you have entered here, and to whom you turn!
    Do not be misled by that wide and easy passage!"   20
    And my Guide to him: "That is not your concern;

it is his fate to enter every door.
    This has been willed where what is willed must be,
    and is not yours to question. Say no more."

Now the choir of anguish, like a wound,   25
    strikes through the tortured air. Now I have come to
    Hell's full lamentation, sound beyond sound.

I came to a place stripped bare of every light
    and roaring on the naked dark like seas
    wracked by a war of winds. Their hellish flight   30

of storm and counterstorm through time foregone,
    sweeps the souls of the damned before its charge.
    Whirling and battering it drives them on,

and when they pass the ruined gap of Hell
    through which we had come, their shrieks begin anew.   35
    There they blaspheme the power of God eternal.

And this, I learned, was the never-ending flight
    of those who sinned in the flesh, the carnal and lusty
    who betrayed reason to their appetite.

As the wings of wintering starlings bear them on   40
    in their great wheeling flights, just so the blast
    wherries these evil souls through time foregone.
Here, there, up, down, they whirl and, whirling, strain
    with never a hope of hope to comfort them,
    not of release, but even of less pain.   45

As cranes go over sounding their harsh cry,
    leaving the long streak of their flight in air,
    so come these spirits, wailing as they fly.

And watching their shadows lashed by wind, I cried:
    "Master, what souls are these the very air   50
    lashes with its black whips from side to side?"

"The first of these whose history you would know,"
    he answered me, "was Empress of many tongues.
    Mad sensuality corrupted her so

that to hide the guilt of her debauchery   55
    she licensed all depravity alike,
    and lust and law were one in her decree.

She is Semiramis of whom the tale is told
    how she married Ninus and succeeded him
    to the throne of that wide land the Sultans hold.   60

The other is Dido; faithless to the ashes
    of Sichaeus, she killed herself for love.
    The next whom the eternal tempest lashes

is sense-drugged Cleopatra. See Helen there,
    from whom such ill arose. And great Achilles,   65
    who fought at last with love in the house of prayer.

And Paris. And Tristan." As they whirled above
    he pointed out more than a thousand shades
    of those torn from the mortal life by love.

I stood there while my Teacher one by one   70
    named the great knights and ladies of dim time;
    and I was swept by pity and confusion.

At last I spoke: "Poet, I should be glad
    to speak a word with those two swept together
    so lightly on the wind and still so sad."   75
And he to me: "Watch them. When next they pass,
    call to them in the name of love that drives
    and damns them here. In that name they will pause."

Thus, as soon as the wind in its wild course
    brought them around, I called: "O wearied souls!   80
    if none forbid it, pause and speak to us."

As mating doves that love calls to their nest
    glide through the air with motionless raised wings,
    borne by the sweet desire that fills each breast—

Just so those spirits turned on the torn sky   85
    from the band where Dido whirls across the air;
    such was the power of pity in my cry.

"O living creature, gracious, kind, and good,
    going this pilgrimage through the sick night,
    visiting us who stained the earth with blood,   90

were the King of Time our friend, we would pray His peace
    on you who have pitied us. As long as the wind
    will let us pause, ask of us what you please.

The town where I was born lies by the shore
    where the Po descends into its ocean rest   95
    with its attendant, streams in one long murmur.

Love, which in gentlest hearts will soonest bloom
    seized my lover with passion for that sweet body
    from which I was torn unshriven to my doom.

Love, which permits no loved one not to love,   100
    took me so strongly with delight in him
    that we are one in Hell, as we were above.

Love led us to one death. In the depths of Hell
    Caïna waits for him who took our lives."
    This was the piteous tale they stopped to tell.   105

And when I had heard those world-offended lovers
    I bowed my head. At last the Poet spoke:
    "What painful thoughts are these your lowered brow covers?"
When at length I answered, I began: "Alas!
    What sweetest thoughts, what green and young desire   110
    led these two lovers to this sorry pass."

Then turning to those spirits once again,
    I said: "Francesca, what you suffer here
    melts me to tears of pity and of pain.

But tell me: in the time of your sweet sighs   115
    by what appearances found love the way
    to lure you to his perilous paradise?"

And she: "The double grief of a lost bliss
    is to recall its happy hour in pain.
    Your Guide and Teacher knows the truth of this.   120

But if there is indeed a soul in Hell
    to ask of the beginning of our love
    out of his pity, I will weep and tell:

On a day for dalliance we read the rhyme
    of Lancelot, how love had mastered him.   125
    We were alone with innocence and dim time.

Pause after pause that high old story drew
    our eyes together while we blushed and paled;
    but it was one soft passage overthrew

our caution and our hearts. For when we read   130
    how her fond smile was kissed by such a lover,
    he who is one with me alive and dead

breathed on my lips the tremor of his kiss.
    That book, and he who wrote it, was a pander.
    That day we read no further." As she said this,   135

the other spirit, who stood by her, wept
    so piteously, I felt my senses reel
    and faint away with anguish. I was swept

by such a swoon as death is, and I fell,
    as a corpse might fall, to the dead floor of Hell.   140

Notes

2. *a smaller circle:* The pit of Hell tapers like a funnel. The circles of ledges accordingly grow smaller as they descend.

4. *Minos:* Like all the monsters Dante assigns to the various offices of Hell, Minos is drawn from classical mythology. He was the son of Europa and of Zeus who descended to her in the form of a bull. Minos became a mythological king of Crete, so famous for his wisdom and justice that after death his soul was

made judge of the dead. Virgil presents him fulfilling the same office at Aeneas' descent to the underworld. Dante, however, transforms him into an irate and hideous monster with a tail. The transformation may have been suggested by the form Zeus assumed for the rape of Europa—the monster is certainly bullish enough here—but the obvious purpose of the brutalization is to present a figure symbolic of the guilty conscience of the wretches who come before it to make their confessions. Dante freely reshapes his materials to his own purposes.

8. *it confesses all*: Just as the souls appeared eager to cross Acheron, so they are eager to confess even while they dread. Dante is once again making the point that sinners elect their Hell by an act of their own will.

27. *Hell's full lamentation:* It is with the second circle that the real tortures of Hell begin.

34. *the ruined gap of Hell:* See note to Canto IV, 53. At the time of the Harrowing of Hell a great earthquake shook the underworld shattering rocks and cliffs. Ruins resulting from the same shock are noted in Canto XII, 34, and Canto XXI, 112 ff. At the beginning of Canto XXIV, the Poets leave the *bolgia* of the Hypocrites by climbing the ruined slabs of a bridge that was shattered by this earthquake.

THE SINNERS OF THE SECOND CIRCLE (THE CARNAL): Here begin the punishments for the various sins of Incontinence (The sins of the She-Wolf). In the second circle are punished those who sinned by excess of sexual passion. Since this is the most natural sin and the sin most nearly associated with love, its punishment is the lightest of all to be found in Hell proper. The Carnal are whirled and buffeted endlessly through the murky air (symbolic of the beclouding of their reason by passion) by a great gale (symbolic of their lust).

53. *Empress of many tongues:* Semiramis, a legendary queen of Assyria who assumed full power at the death of her husband, Ninus.

61. *Dido:* Queen and founder of Carthage. She had vowed to remain faithful to her husband, Sichaeus, but she fell in love with Aeneas. When Aeneas abandoned her she stabbed herself on a funeral pyre she had had prepared.

According to Dante's own system of punishment, she should be in the Seventh Circle (Canto XIII) with the suicides. The only clue Dante gives to the tempering of her punishment is his statement that, "she killed herself for love." Dante always seems readiest to forgive in that name.

65. *Achilles*: He is placed among this company because of his passion for Polyxena, the daughter of Priam. For love of her, he agreed to desert the Greeks and to join the Trojans, but when he went to the temple for the wedding (according to the legend Dante has followed) he was killed by Paris.

74. *those two swept together:* Paolo and Francesca (PAH-oe-loe; Frahn-CHAY-ska). Dante's treatment of these two lovers is certainly the tenderest and most sympathetic accorded any of the sinners in Hell, and legends immediately began to grow about this pair.

The facts are these. In 1275 Giovanni Malatesta (Djoe-VAH-nee Mahl-ah-TEH-stah) of Rimini, called Giovanni the Lame, a somewhat deformed but brave and powerful warrior, made a political marriage with Francesca, daughter of

Guido da Polenta of Ravenna. Francesca came to Rimini and there an amour grew between her and Giovanni's younger brother Paolo. Despite the fact that Paolo had married in 1269 and had become the father of two daughters by 1275, his affair with Francesca continued for many years. It was sometime between 1283 and 1286 that Giovanni surprised them in Francesca's bedroom and killed both of them.

Around these facts the legend has grown that Paolo was sent by Giovanni as his proxy to the marriage, that Francesca thought he was her real bridegroom and accordingly gave him her heart irrevocably at first sight. The legend obviously increases the pathos, but nothing in Dante gives it support.

102. *that we are one in Hell, as we were above:* At many points of the *Inferno* Dante makes clear the principle that the souls of the damned are locked so blindly into their own guilt that none can feel sympathy for another, or find any pleasure in the presence of another. The temptation of many readers is to interpret this line romantically: i.e., that the love of Paolo and Francesca survives Hell itself. The more Dantean interpretation, however, is that they add to one another's anguish (a) as mutual reminders of their sin, and (b) as insubstantial shades of the bodies for which they once felt such great passion.

104. *Caïna waits for him:* Giovanni Malatesta was still alive at the writing. His fate is already decided, however, and upon his death, his soul will fall to Caïna, the first ring of the last circle (Canto XXXII), where lie those who performed acts of treachery against their kin.

124–125. *the rhyme of Lancelot:* The story exists in many forms. The details Dante makes use of are from an Old French version.

126. *dim time:* The original simply reads "We were alone, suspecting nothing." "Dim time" is rhyme-forced, but not wholly outside the legitimate implications of the original, I hope. The old courtly romance may well be thought of as happening in the dim ancient days. The apology, of course, comes after the fact: one does the possible then argues for justification, and there probably is none.

134. *that book, and he who wrote it, was a pander:* "Galeotto," the Italian word for "pander," is also the Italian rendering of the name of Gallehault, who, in the French Romance Dante refers to here, urged Lancelot and Guinevere on to love.

from **Purgatorio**

Canto XXX

THE EARTHLY PARADISE   *Beatrice*

Virgil Vanishes

The procession halts and the Prophets turn to the chariot and sing "Come, my bride, from Lebanon." They are summoning BEATRICE, who appears on the left side of the chariot, half-hidden from view by showers of blossoms poured from above by A HUNDRED ANGELS. Dante, stirred by the sight, turns to Virgil to express his overflowing emotions, and discovers that VIRGIL HAS VANISHED.

Because he bursts into tears at losing Virgil DANTE IS REPRIMANDED BY BEATRICE. The Angel Choir overhead immediately breaks into a Psalm of Compassion, but Beatrice, still severe, answers by detailing Dante's offenses in not making proper use of his great gifts. It would violate the ordering of the Divine Decree, she argues, to let Dante drink the waters of Lethe, thereby washing all memory of sin from his soul, before he had shed the tears of a real repentance.

When the Septentrion of the First Heaven,
    which does not rise nor set, and which has never
    been veiled from sight by any mist but sin,

and which made every soul in that high court
    know its true course (just as the lower Seven   5
    direct the helmsman to his earthly port),

had stopped; the holy prophets, who till then
    had walked between the Griffon and those lights,
    turned to the car like souls who cry "Amen."

And one among them who seemed sent from Heaven   10
    clarioned: "*Veni, sponsa, de Libano,*"
    three times, with all the others joining in.

As, at the last trump every saint shall rise
    out of the grave, ready with voice new-fleshed
    to carol *Alleluliah* to the skies;   15

just so, above the chariot, at the voice
    of such an elder, rose a hundred Powers
    and Principals of the Eternal Joys,

all saying together: *"Benedictus qui venis"*;
    then, scattering flowers about on every side: 20
    "Manibus o date lilia plenis."

Time and again at daybreak I have seen
    the eastern sky glow with a wash of rose
    while all the rest hung limpid and serene,

and the Sun's face rise tempered from its rest   25
    so veiled by vapors that the naked eye
    could look at it for minutes undistressed.

Exactly so, within a cloud of flowers
    that rose like fountains from the angels' hands
    and fell about the chariot in showers,   30

a lady came in view: an olive crown
    wreathed her immaculate veil, her cloak was green,
    the colors of live flame played on her gown.

My soul—such years had passed since last it saw
    that lady and stood trembling in her presence,   35
    stupefied by the power of holy awe—

now, by some power that shone from her above
    the reach and witness of my mortal eyes,
    felt the full mastery of enduring love.

The instant I was smitten by the force,   40
    which had already once transfixed my soul
    before my boyhood years had run their course,

I turned left with the same assured belief
    that makes a child run to its mother's arms
    when it is frightened or has come to grief,   45

to say to Virgil: "There is not within me
    one drop of blood unstirred. I recognize
    the tokens of the ancient flame." But he,

he had taken his light from us. He had gone.
    Virgil had gone. Virgil, the gentle Father   50
    to whom I gave my soul for its salvation!

Not all that sight of Eden lost to view
    by our First Mother could hold back the tears
    that stained my cheeks so lately washed with dew.

"Dante, do not weep yet, though Virgil goes.   55
    Do not weep yet, for soon another wound
    shall make you weep far hotter tears than those!"

As an admiral takes his place at stern or bow
    to observe the handling of his other ships
    and spur all hands to do their best—so now,   60

on the chariot's left side, I saw appear
    when I turned at the sound of my own name
    (which, necessarily, is recorded here),

that lady who had been half-veiled from view
    by the flowers of the angel-revels. Now her eyes   65
    fixed me across the stream, piercing me through.

And though the veil she still wore, held in place
    by the wreathed flowers of wise Minerva's leaves,
    let me see only glimpses of her face,

her stern and regal bearing made me dread   70
    her next words, for she spoke as one who saves
    the heaviest charge till all the rest are read.

"Look at me well. I am she. I am Beatrice.
    How dared you make your way to this high mountain?
    Did you not know that here man lives in bliss?"   75

I lowered my head and looked down at the stream.
    But when I saw myself reflected there,
    I fixed my eyes upon the grass for shame.

I shrank as a wayward child in his distress
    shrinks from his mother's sternness, for the taste   80
    of love grown wrathful is a bitterness.

She paused. At once the angel chorus sang
    the blessed psalm: *"In te, Domine, speravi."*
    As far as *"pedes meos"* their voices rang.

As on the spine of Italy the snow   85
    lies frozen hard among the living rafters
    in winter when the northeast tempests blow;

then, melting if so much as a breath stir
    from the land of shadowless noon, flows through itself
    like hot wax trickling down a lighted taper—   90

just so I froze, too cold for sighs or tears
    until I heard that choir whose notes are tuned
    to the eternal music of the spheres.

But when I heard the voice of their compassion
    plead for me more than if they had cried out: 95
    "Lady, why do you treat him in this fashion?";

the ice, which hard about my heart had pressed,
    turned into breath and water, and flowed out
    through eyes and throat in anguish from my breast.

Still standing at the chariot's left side,   100
    she turned to those compassionate essences
    whose song had sought to move her, and replied:

"You keep your vigil in the Eternal Day
    where neither night nor sleep obscures from you
    a single step the world takes on its way;   105

but I must speak with greater care that he
    who weeps on that far bank may understand
    and feel a grief to match his guilt. Not only

by the workings of the spheres that bring each seed
    to its fit end according to the stars   110
    that ride above it, but by gifts decreed

in the largesse of overflowing Grace,
    whose rain has such high vapors for its source
    our eyes cannot mount to their dwelling place;

this man, potentially was so endowed   115
    from early youth that marvelous increase
    should have come forth from every good he sowed.

But richest soil the soonest will grow wild
    with bad seed and neglect. For a while I stayed him
    with glimpses of my face. Turning my mild   120

and youthful eyes into his very soul,
    I let him see their shining, and I led him
    by the straight way, his face to the right goal.

The instant I had come upon the sill
    of my second age, and crossed and changed my life,   125
    he left me and let others shape his will.

When I rose from the flesh into the spirit,
    to greater beauty and to greater virtue,
    he found less pleasure in me and less merit.

He turned his steps aside from the True Way,   130
    pursuing the false images of good
    that promise what they never wholly pay.

Not all the inspiration I won by prayer
    and brought to him in dreams and meditations
    could call him back, so little did he care.   135

He fell so far from every hope of bliss
    that every means of saving him had failed
    except to let him see the damned. For this

I visited the portals of the dead
    and poured my tears and prayers before that spirit   140
    by whom his steps have, up to now, been led.

The seal Almighty God's decree has placed
    on the rounds of His creation would be broken
    were he to come past Lethe and to taste

the water that wipes out the guilty years   145
without some scot of penitential tears!"

Notes

1. *the Septentrion of the First Heaven:* The Septentrion is the seven stars of the Big Dipper. Here Dante means the seven candelabra. They are the Septentrion of the First Heaven (the Empyrean) as distinct from the seven stars of the dipper which occur lower down in the Sphere of the Fixed Stars.

2. *which does not rise nor set:* The North Star does not rise or set north of the equator, but the Septentrion, revolving around the North Star, does go below the horizon in the lower latitudes. This Septentrion of the First Heaven, however, partaking of the perfection and constancy of Heaven, neither rises nor sets but is a constant light to mankind. So these unchanging lights guide the souls of man on high, as the "lower Seven" (line 5), in their less perfect way, guide the earthly helmsmen to their earthly ports.

7. *the holy prophets:* The twenty-four elders who represent the books of the Old Testament. (See XXIX, 64, note.)

10. *one among them: The Song of Solomon.*

11. *Veni, sponsa, de Libano:* "Come [with me] from Lebanon, my spouse." *Song of Solomon,* iv, 8. This cry, re-echoed by choirs of angels, summons Beatrice, who may be taken here as revelation, faith, divine love, hence as the bride of the spirit, to Dante (man's redeemed soul).

17–18. *a hundred Powers and Principals:* Angels.

19. *Benedictus qui venis:* "Blessed is he who cometh." (*Matthew,* xxi, 9.)

21. *Manibus o date lilia plenis:* "Oh, give lilies with full hands." These are the words of Anchises in honor of Marcellus. (*Aeneid,* VI, 883.) Thus they are not only apt to the occasion but their choice is a sweetly conceived last literary compliment to Virgil before he vanishes.

31. *a lady:* Beatrice. She is dressed in the colors of Faith (white), Hope (green), and Caritas (red).

34. *since last it saw:* Beatrice died in 1290. Thus Dante has passed ten years without sight of her.

36. *stupefied:* Dante describes the stupor of his soul at the sight of the living Beatrice in *La Vita Nuova,* XIV, and XXIV. Then, however, it was mortal love; here it is eternal, and the effect accordingly greater.

54. washed with dew: By Virgil. 1, 124.

55. Dante: This is the only point in the *Commedia* at which Dante mentions his own name. Its usage here suggests many allegorical possibilities. Central to all of them, however, must be the fact that Dante, in ending one life (of the mind) and beginning a new one (of faith), hears his name. The suggestion of a second baptism is inevitable. And just as a child being baptized is struck by the priest, so Beatrice is about to strike him with her tongue before he may proceed to the holy water.

64. *that lady:* There are thirty-four Cantos in the *Inferno* and this is the thirtieth of the *Purgatorio*, hence the sixty-fourth Canto of the *Commedia*. This is the sixty-fourth line of the sixty-fourth Canto. In Dante's numerology such correspondences are always meaningful. Six plus four equals ten and ten equals the sum of the square of trinity and unity. Obviously there can be no conclusive way of establishing intent in such a structure of mystic numbering, but it certainly is worth noting that the line begins with "that lady." The Italian text, in fact, begins with *vidi la donna*, i.e., I saw the lady [who represents the sum of the square of trinity plus unity?]. The lady, of course, is Beatrice.

68. *wise Minerva's leaves:* The olive crown.

80. *his mother's sternness:* Beatrice appears in the pageant as the figure of the Church Triumphant. The Church is the mother of the devout and though she is stern, as law decrees, her sternness is that of a loving mother.

83–84. *In te, Domine, speravi . . . pedes meos:* In mercy the Angel chorus sings Psalm XXXI, 1–8, beginning "In thee, O Lord, do I put my trust" and continuing as far as "thou hast set my feet in a large room."

85–90. *the spine of Italy:* The Apennines, *the living rafters:* The trees, *the land of shadowless noon:* Africa. In equatorial regions the noonday sun is at the zenith over each point twice a year. Its rays then fall straight down and objects cast no shadows.

101. *compassionate essences:* The Angel chorus.

106. *greater care:* For his understanding than for your intercession.

109–11. *the workings of the spheres . . . :* The influence of the stars in their courses which incline men at birth to good or evil ends according to the astrological virtue of their conjunctions.

114. *our eyes:* Beatrice is still replying to the plea of the Angel choir. Hence "our eyes" must refer not to mortal eyes, but to the eyes of the blessed. Not even such more-than-human eyes may mount to the high place of those vapors, for that place is nothing less than the Supreme Height, since Grace flows from God Himself.

124–126. *my second age:* Beatrice's womanhood. When she had reached the full bloom of youth Dante turned from her and wrote to his *donna gentile*. Allegorically, he turned from divine "sciences" to an overreliance upon philosophy (the human "sciences"). For this sin he must suffer.

144–145. *were he to come past Lethe:* In passing Lethe and drinking its waters, the soul loses all memory of guilt. This, therefore, is Dante's last opportunity to do penance.

Canto XXXI

THE EARTHLY PARADISE   *Lethe*
Beatrice, Matilda

Beatrice continues her reprimand, forcing Dante to confess his faults until he swoons with grief and pain at the thought of his sin. He wakes to find himself in Lethe, held in the arms of Matilda, who leads him to the other side of the stream and there immerses him that he may drink the waters that wipe out all memory of sin.

Matilda then leads him to THE FOUR CARDINAL VIRTUES, who dance about him and lead him before THE GRIFFON where he may look into THE EYES OF BEATRICE. In them Dante sees, in a FIRST BEATIFIC VISION, the radiant reflection of the Griffon, who appears now in his human and now in his godly nature.

THE THREE THEOLOGICAL VIRTUES now approach and beg that Dante may behold THE SMILE OF BEATRICE. Beatrice removes her veil, and in a SECOND BEATIFIC VISION, Dante beholds the splendor of the unveiled shining of Divine Love.

"You, there, who stand upon the other side—"
    (turning to me now, who had thought the edge
    of her discourse was sharp, the point) she cried

without pause in her flow of eloquence,
    "Speak up! Speak up! Is it true? To such a charge
    your own confession must give evidence."   5

I stood as if my spirit had turned numb:
    the organ of my speech moved, but my voice
    died in my throat before a word could come.

Briefly she paused, then cried impatiently: 10
    "What are you thinking? Speak up, for the waters
    have yet to purge sin from your memory."

Confusion joined to terror forced a broken
    "yes" from my throat, so weak that only one
    who read my lips would know that I had spoken.   15

As an arbalest will snap when string and bow
    are drawn too tight by the bowman, and the bolt
    will strike the target a diminished blow—

so did I shatter, strengthless and unstrung,
    under her charge, pouring out floods of tears,   20
    while my voice died in me on the way to my tongue.

And she: "Filled as you were with the desire
    I taught you for That Good beyond which nothing
    exists on earth to which man may aspire,

what yawning moats or what stretched chain-lengths lay   25
    across your path to force you to abandon
    all hope of pressing further on your way?

What increase or allurement seemed to show
    in the brows of others that you walked before them
    as a lover walks below his lady's window?"   30

My breath dragged from me in a bitter sigh;
    I barely found a voice to answer with;
    my lips had trouble forming a reply.

In tears I said: "The things of the world's day,
    false pleasures and enticements, turned my steps   35
    as soon as you had ceased to light my way."

And she: "Had you been silent, or denied
    what you confess, your guilt would still be known
    to Him from Whom no guilt may hope to hide.

But here, before our court, when souls upbraid   40
    themselves for their own guilt in true remorse,
    the grindstone is turned back against the blade.

In any case that you may know your crime
    truly and with true shame and so be stronger
    against the Siren's song another time,   45

control your tears and listen with your soul
    to learn how my departure from the flesh
    ought to have spurred you to the higher goal.

Nothing in Art or Nature could call forth
    such joy from you, as sight of that fair body   50
    which clothed me once and now sifts back to earth.

And if my dying turned that highest pleasure
    to very dust, what joy could still remain
    in mortal things for you to seek and treasure?

At the first blow you took from such vain things   55
    your every thought should have been raised to follow
    my flight above decay. Nor should your wings

have been weighed down by any joy below—
    love of a maid, or any other fleeting
    and useless thing—to wait a second blow.   60

The fledgling waits a second shaft, a third;
    but nets are spread and the arrow sped in vain
    in sight or hearing of the full-grown bird."

As a scolded child, tongue-tied for shame, will stand
    and recognize his fault, and weep for it,   65
    bowing his head to a just reprimand,

so did I stand. And she said: "If to hear me
    grieves you, now raise your beard and let your eyes
    show you a greater cause for misery."

The blast that blows from Libya's hot sand,   70
    or the Alpine gale, overcomes less resistance
    uprooting oaks than I, at her command,

overcame then in lifting up my face;
    for when she had referred to it as my "beard"
    I sensed too well the venom of her phrase.   75

When I had raised my eyes with so much pain,
    I saw those Primal Beings, now at rest,
    who had strewn blossoms round her thick as rain;

and with my tear-blurred and uncertain vision
    I saw Her turned to face that beast which is   80
    one person in two natures without division.

Even veiled and across the river from me
    her face outshone its first-self by as much
    as she outshone all mortals formerly.

And the thorns of my repentance pricked me so 85
    that all the use and substance of the world
    I most had loved, now most appeared my foe.

Such guilty recognition gnawed my heart
    I swooned for pain; and what I then became
    she best knows who most gave me cause to smart. 90

When I returned to consciousness at last
    I found the lady who had walked alone
    bent over me. "Hold fast!" she said, "Hold fast!"

She had drawn me into the stream up to my throat,
    and pulling me behind her, she sped on 95
    over the water, light as any boat.

Nearing the sacred bank, I heard her say
    in tones so sweet I cannot call them back,
    much less describe them here: *"Asperges me."*

Then the sweet lady took my head between 100
    her open arms, and embracing me, she dipped me
    and made me drink the waters that make clean.

Then raising me in my new purity
    she led me to the dance of the Four Maidens;
    each raised an arm and so joined hands above me. 105

"Here we are nymphs; stars are we in the skies.
    Ere Beatrice went to earth we were ordained
    her handmaids. We will lead you to her eyes;

but that your own may see what joyous light
    shines in them, yonder Three, who see more deeply, 110
    will sharpen and instruct your mortal sight."

Thus they sang, then led me to the Griffon.
    Behind him, Beatrice waited. And when I stood
    at the Griffon's breast, they said in unison:

"Look deep, look well, however your eyes may smart. 115
    We have led you now before those emeralds
    from which Love shot his arrows through your heart."

A thousand burning passions, every one
    hotter than any flame, held my eyes fixed
    to the lucent eyes she held fixed on the Griffon.   120

Like sunlight in a glass the twofold creature
    shone from the deep reflection of her eyes,
    now in the one, now in the other nature.

Judge, reader, if I found it passing strange
    to see the thing unaltered in itself   125
    yet in its image working change on change.

And while my soul in wonder and delight
    was savoring that food which in itself
    both satisfies and quickens appetite,

the other Three, whose bearing made it clear   130
    they were of higher rank, came toward me dancing
    to the measure of their own angelic air.

"Turn, Beatrice, oh turn the eyes of grace,"
    was their refrain, "upon your faithful one
    who comes so far to look upon your face.   135

Grant us this favor of your grace: reveal
    your mouth to him, and let his eyes behold
    the Second Beauty, which your veils conceal."

O splendor of the eternal living light!
    who that has drunk deep of Parnassus' waters,   140
    or grown pale in the shadow of its height,

would not, still, feel his burdened genius fail
    attempting to describe in any tongue
    how you appeared when you put by your veil

in that free air open to heaven and earth   145
whose harmony is your shining shadowed forth!

Notes

1. *the other side*: Of Lethe. But also the other side of the immortal life, *i.e.*, still living.

2–3. *edge . . . point*: The image of the sword (of Justice) is carried over from lines 56–57 of the preceding Canto. It is continued in line 42, below. So far the sword has only cut, now it pierces.

11. *the waters*: Of Lethe.

16 ff. *arbalest . . . snap . . . diminished blow*: The figure is a bit confusing. Dante seems to say that the bolt (corresponding to an arrow) of a crossbow strikes the target with less force when the bow snaps. He does not stop to consider that the bolt may miss the target entirely. Nevertheless, the intent of his figure is clear enough.

25. *moats . . . chain-lengths*: These were, of course, defensive military measures. The moats guarded castles. The chains were strung to block roads, bridges, and gates. Both measures imply great labor forces. Thus the point of Beatrice's question: "What enormous forces blocked your way?" The block was, of course, within Dante himself.

42. *the grindstone is turned back against the blade*: Turning the grindstone away from the blade sharpens it. Turning it back against the blade dulls it. Thus Beatrice is saying that when a soul openly confesses in true repentance what could not in any case be hidden from God, the sword of Justice is blunted, *i.e.*, no longer cuts as deeply.

49–60. DANTE'S FOLLY. If the beauty of her earthly body was Dante's supreme joy and still decayed to mere dust, says Beatrice, how could Dante have placed his trust in any other earthly thing? *love of a maid*: Dante mentions another maiden in some of his songs but in an indefinite way. No specific reference can be attached to these words.

62. *nets*: Were sometimes used for trapping birds.

68–75. *your beard*: Beatrice means "your face," but the word choice is especially cutting. She has been accusing Dante of acting like a child or a fledgling bird. To refer to his beard, therefore, is a sarcastic way of reminding him that he is, presumably, a full-grown man. *a greater cause for misery*: The sight of her accompanied by the guilty knowledge that he had turned away from so much beauty and perfection.

80–81. *that beast which is one person in two natures*: The Griffon. He is the masque of Christ and represents His two aspects as man and God.

83. *first-self*: Her mortal self.

92. *the lady who had walked alone*: Matilda.

94. *She had drawn me into the stream*: Dante wakens to find Matilda bending over him. She has already pulled Dante into Lethe and he is in the water up to his throat, but Matilda walks upon the water. The fact that this particular miracle is attributed specifically to Christ cannot fail to suggest an allegorical meaning.

97. *the sacred bank:* The far bank, the other side. One bank of Lethe is nearer the world, the other nearer Heaven. The sacred bank, moreover, lies the other side of the absolution of Lethe's water. On the near side sin may still be said to exist; on the sacred side, even the memory of sin has been washed away. Contrast Beatrice's words in line 1.

99. *Asperges me: Asperges me hyssopo, et mundabor; lavabis me, et super nivem dealbabor.* ("Purge me with hyssop, and I shall be clean; wash me, and I shall be whiter than snow.") Psalms, li, 7. These are the words the priest utters when he sprinkles holy water over the confessed sinner to absolve him. Matilda, that is to say, is performing the office of absolution. Her action, therefore, must be seen as being directly connected with Dante's confession and repentance, for nothing else could prepare him for absolution.

104. *the Four Maidens:* The Four Cardinal Virtues: Justice, Prudence, Fortitude, and Temperance. In their present manifestation they are nymphs. In another manifestation they are the four stars Dante saw above him when he arrived at the base of the mountain. (I, 23, note.) As the Cardinal Virtues (*i.e.*, the best man can achieve without the revelation of Christ's Church) they cannot themselves bring the soul to the Second Vision (of Divine Love receiving the soul) but they can lead to the First Vision (of the Two I Natures of Christ), and thence to the Three Theological Virtues, through which the Second Vision may be received.

Since Beatrice, in one of her present manifestations, represents the Authority of the Church, lines 107–108 must mean that the Four Cardinal Virtues were ordained to be the handmaidens of the Church even before it was founded, working in the virtuous pagans, and in all men, to prepare the way for the triumph of the Church.

110. *yonder Three:* The Theological Virtues: Faith, Hope, and Charity (*i.e.*, *Caritas*).

116. *those emeralds:* The eyes of Beatrice. Dante may have intended to describe them as green (hazel) but more likely his choice of words here is meant only to signify "jewel bright." Green is, of course, the color of Hope, and an allegorical significance may be implied in that.

118–126. THE EYES OF BEATRICE. Led by the Four Cardinal Virtues, Dante takes his place before the Griffon and receives a first beatific vision of its nature, seeing now the lion (the human) and now the eagle (the divine); now one, now the other, constantly shifting, though the Griffon itself remains immovable (*i.e.*, constant, perfect). He does not, however, see the two natures as one. For that revelation he must wait till he reaches the top of Paradiso.

Note that Dante does not achieve his revelation by looking at the Griffon itself, but rather by looking at its reflection in the eyes of Beatrice (as the Church). Thus he achieves here the first fruits of Faith, seeing as much of the nature of God as is perceivable in the first life. The final revelation can happen only in Heaven, in the rapturous presence of God.

129. *both satisfies and quickens appetite:* "They that eat me shall yet be hungry, and they that drink me shall yet be thirsty." (Ecclesiasticus, xxiv, 21.)

138. *the Second Beauty:* The smile of Beatrice (Divine Love). Dante was led to the First Beauty by the Four Cardinal Virtues. Now the Three Theological Virtues, as higher beings, lead him to the second, and higher, beauty, which is the joy of Divine Love in receiving the purified soul.

140. *Parnassus' waters:* The fountain of Castalia. To drink from it is to receive poetic gifts. To grow pale in the shadow of Parnassus signifies to labor at mastering the art of poetry. Note that Dante makes no effort to describe the smile of Divine Love, but only his rapture at beholding it.

145–146. *that free air:* Dante has earlier made the point that the Earthly Paradise possesses an atmosphere that is entirely unconstrained by earthly influences, but moves only in perfect harmony with the primal motion. That harmony is, however, no more than the shadow of the shining of Perfect Love.

Canto XXXII

THE EARTHLY PARADISE   *Beatrice Unveiled*

Departure of the Heavenly Pageant
Transformation of the Chariot

Beatrice unveils and for the first time in ten years Dante looks upon her face. When he recovers from that blinding sight, Dante finds the Heavenly Pageant has wheeled about and is heading east. Dante and Statius follow the Chariot to THE TREE OF GOOD AND EVIL, which rises to vast heights but bears neither leaves nor flowers. The Griffon ties the pole of the Chariot to the Tree, and the Tree immediately breaks into leaf and flower. The Heavenly Pageant greets this wonder with a hymn unknown to mortals. Overpowered by the singing DANTE SLEEPS.

He awakens to find himself, as he believes at first, alone with Matilda. The Heavenly Pageant has, in fact, departed, but as Dante soon learns, Beatrice has remained behind to guard the chariot and the Seven Nymphs have remained to attend her. She is seated upon the ground, on the roots of the tree and under its shade.

Dante then witnesses an allegorical masque of THE CORRUPTION OF THE CHURCH THROUGH WEALTH. First AN EAGLE (the Roman Empire) attacks the tree and the chariot. Then A FOX (heresy). Then the Eagle returns and covers the chariot with its feathers. Immediately A DRAGON (Satan) rips at the chariot's foundation. The chariot then covers itself with the feathers (riches) and is converted into A MONSTROUS BEAST on which rides A HARLOT (the corrupted Papacy) attended by A GIANT (the French Monarchy) that beats the harlot and drags the monster into the woods and out of sight.

My eyes were fixed with such intensity
    on quenching, at long last, their ten years' thirst
    that every sense but sight abandoned me.

Tranced by the holy smile that drew me there
    into the old nets, I forgot all else—   5
    my eyes wore blinders, and I could not care.

When suddenly my gaze was wrenched away
    and forced to turn left to those goddesses:
    "He stares too fixedly" I heard them say.

And as a man is blinded by the light   10
    when he has looked directly at the sun,
    just so I found that I had lost my sight.

When I could make out lesser (I mean, of course,
    "less sensible objects") as compared to the greater
    from which I had been called away by force,   15

I saw the legion of those souls in grace
    had turned right-wheel-about, and marched back now
    with the sun and the seven torches in its face.

As forward troops when they are giving ground
    turn under their shields, and their standards face about   20
    before the rest of the column has turned round—

just so the vanguard of that heavenly force
    had all gone by before the chariot
    had swung its pole around to the new course.

Then to their wheels the ladies turned together,   25
    and the Griffon once more pulled the sacred car,
    not ruffling so much as a single feather.

Statius and I followed across that park
    with the lady who had led me through the ford,
    behind the wheel that turned the lesser arc.   30

We marched across the sacred wood which she
    who heeded a forked tongue had left deserted,
    our steps timed by angelic melody.

We had moved on, I think, about as far
    as three good bowshots, end to end, might reach,   35
    when Beatrice descended from the car.

"Adam!" I heard all murmur, censuring him.
    Then they all formed a circle round a tree
    that bore no leaf nor flower on any limb.

It soared so high that even in woods like those   40
    the Indians know it would have seemed a wonder;
    and the crown spread out the more the more it rose.

"Blessed art thou, Griffon, whose beak hath rent
    no morsel of the sweet wood of this tree,
    for it grips the belly with a raging torment!"   45

—So shouted all the others as they stood
    about the tree. And the two-natured being:
    "Thus is preserved the seed of every good!"

Then he drew up before the widowed mast
    the chariot's pole, and what came from the tree   50;
    he gave it back, and tied the two stems fast.

As in the spring on earth, when the great light
    falls mingled with the rays of those sweet stars
    that follow Pisces into Heaven's height,

the trees begin to swell, then burgeon full,   55
    each one in its own hue, before the Sun
    harnesses his team beneath the Bull—

just so the boughs that had been bare before
    took color, turning something less than rose
    and more than violet as they bloomed once more.   60

The hymn I heard those blessed souls sing then
    is not sung here, nor did I understand it;
    nor did I hear it through to the Amen.

Could I portray the eyes of Argus here,
    lulled one by one by drowsy tales of Syrinx,   65
    that time their pitiless watch cost him so dear.

as a painter paints his model, I would try
  to show exactly how I fell asleep.
  But who can image drowsiness? Not I.

Therefore, I pass to my waking, and declare   70
  a radiance tore the veil of sleep; a voice
  cried out: "Arise! What are you doing there?"

When they were shown the flowering of that Tree
  that makes the angels hungry for Its fruit
  and sets a feast in Heaven eternally,   75

Peter, John, and James, awe-stricken, fell
  into a sleep from which they were recalled
  by the same word that broke a greater spell;

and saw their company reduced, as both
  Moses and Elijah vanished from them;   80
  and saw the Master's robe change back to cloth.

Just so did I awaken from my dream
  to find, bent over me, the compassionate lady
  who had conducted me along the stream.

Fearful I cried out, "Beatrice! Where is she?"   85
  And the lady: "She is seated on the roots
  of the new foliage, as you can see,

encircled by the seven shining Graces.
  The others mount to Heaven behind the Griffon,
  intoning sweeter and profounder praises."   90

If she said more, her words were lost on me,
  for now my eyes were fixed once more on Beatrice,
  my senses closed to all that was not she.

She sat on the bare earth alone, left there
  to guard the chariot that the Biformed Beast   95
  had fastened to the tree with such great care.

A living cloister ringing her about,
  the Seven Nymphs stood, holding in their hands
  those candles no wind ever shall blow out.

"Here briefly in this forest shall you dwell; 100
    and evermore, with me, be of that Rome
    in which Christ is a Roman. Hence, look well

there at the great car, and that you may be
    a light to the dark world, when you return
    set down exactly all that you shall see." 105

Thus Beatrice; and I, devoutly bent
    at the feet of her commands, turned mind and eye
    as she had willed, in all obedient.

No flash from densest clouds when the rains fall
    from the remotest reaches of the sky 110
    ever shot down as fast out of the squall

as did the bird of Jove that I saw break
    down through the tree, ripping the flowers, the leaves,
    even the bark, with its fierce claws and beak.

He struck the chariot a tremendous blow ,115
    at which it lurched like a storm-battered ship,
    now rolled to port, now starboard, to and fro.

Next came a fox, so gaunt and angular
    it seemed to know no fit food; and it pounced
    upon the cab of the triumphal car. 120

But threatening all its filthy sins with woe
    my lady sent it reeling back from there
    as fast as such a bag of bones could go.

Then, through the tree, I saw the bird descend
    once more into the car, and shed its plumes 125
    to feather it in gold from end to end.

And from the sky, as if a heart let slip
    all of its grief in one sound, a voice cried:
    "Oh what a load you bear, my little ship!"

Then, as I watched, I saw a fissure split 130
    the earth between the two wheels, and a dragon
    rise to the car and sink its tail in it.

Much as an angry wasp draws back its stinger,
　　it drew its tail back, ripping the car's floor,
　　and wandered off as if it meant to linger.　　　　　135

Like rich soil left to weeds, what then remained
　　covered itself with feathers, which no doubt
　　had been intended to burnish what they stained.

And both the wheels and the pole were overgrown,
　　and all the car to the last part, and all　　　　　140
　　in less time than the lips part for a moan.

So changed, the holy ark began to sprout
　　heads from its various parts: three from the pole,
　　one from each corner. Seven in all grew out.

The three were horned like oxen, but the four　　　145
　　were each armed with a single evil horn.
　　No one had seen the monster's like before.

Secure as a great fortress on a crag,
　　an ungirt harlot rode the beast, her eyes
　　darting with avarice. Beside that hag,　　　　　150

and ready to risk all to keep her his,
　　a giant strode erect, and as they passed,
　　from time to time the two exchanged a kiss.

But when she turned her hungry eyes on me,
　　her savage lover in a bestial rage　　　　　155
　　whipped her from head to foot unmercifully.

Then in a jealous fit the brute untied
　　the monster from the tree, and dragged it off
　　into the woods, far toward the other side,

until between me and that doxie queen　　　　　160
on her weird beast, he made the trees a screen.

Notes

1–9. DANTE'S RAPTURE ADMONISHED. Beatrice had died in 1290. Dante has not, therefore, seen her for ten years, and the sight of her unveiled face so draws him into the old nets (of love) that he loses track of all else until he is brought to his senses by overhearing the Three Maidens charge him with overdoing. For it is immoderate [*non è bello, i.e.*, it is not an Aristotelian mean of good conduct) to stare so intensely, even at the vision of eternal beauty, if in so doing a man loses sight of the other gifts of God. Bear in mind, too, that Dante is staring with his earthly memory of the other Beatrice. The Heavenly Beatrice has not yet been truly revealed to him. That revelation will take place in the next Canto.

16–18. The Heavenly Pageant came originally from the east. It passed Dante, executed a right-wheel-about, and is now returning, face to the east. Accordingly, it now has in its face the light of the Sun as well as that of the candelabra.

20. *under their shields:* Troops turning in retreat within range of the enemy held their shields over their heads for protection.

22. *the vanguard of that heavenly force:* The twenty-four elders.

30. *the wheel that turned the lesser arc:* The right. In making a right turn, it would swing through the lesser arc. The Poets, therefore, are walking behind the Three Theological Virtues.

36. *when Beatrice descended:* In this masque, Beatrice has entered in a chariot that represents the Church Triumphant. The procession is now moving to the tree that represents the Civil Authority of the Holy Roman Empire. Her descent in order to approach on foot signifies the humility the Church should display before civil authority, as commanded by Paul (*Romans*, xiii, 1): "Let every soul be subject unto the higher powers. For there is no power but of God: the powers that be are ordained of God." To this, as Dante's image of the ideal Church, contrast his lament for the evils that befell the Church when it grew rich and arrogant (*Inferno*, XIX, 109–111, and note), and the final allegory of the present Canto.

37–60. THE TREE OF GOOD AND EVIL. This passage contains an elaborate conception, difficult in itself, and made more difficult by much of Dante's phrasing in what is certainly his least attractive style.

The tree, to begin with, is instantly recognizable, by its resemblance to its offshoot on the ledge below, as the original Tree of Good and Evil. It is for this reason that all souls murmur against Adam at sight of it.

Then, in a second symbolism, the tree is made to represent the Holy Roman Empire, towering so high (and spreading wider as it soars) that no tree in the Indian forests (the comparison is from Virgil) could equal it. (The comparison to Indian forests implies, of course, the superiority of the Christian empire.) But though enormous, the tree is, by itself, barren.

When Christ (the Griffon) approaches the tree, all praise Him for not having eaten (peculiar diet) the sweet-tasting wood (the material riches of the Empire), for by His holy poverty in this world He escaped the bellyache of corruption (with which the Church has been plagued ever since it grew rich). The Griffon replies that only so (in holy poverty) can the seed of goodness be preserved.

To understand the Griffon's next action, it is necessary to know that the true cross, according to legend, had been cut from the Tree of Good and Evil. The Griffon draws the Chariot (the Church) to the tree and binds fast to the tree "what came from it," i.e., the pole of the chariot. Thus one may understand that the pole the Griffon has been pulling (and what draws the Church forward) is the true cross. This interpretation is disputed but does have the virtue of being coherent.

Now with the Church securely bound to the Empire by the true cross, the tree that had been barren breaks into bloom, turning (lines 59–60) something less than rose and more than violet (*i.e.*, the Imperial purple).

For good measure, Dante throws in a legendary reference and several astrological ones. Sense of lines 52–57: "As in the spring on earth when the great light falls mingled with the rays of those sweet stars [of Aries, the sign in which the Sun rides from March 21 to April 19] that follow Pisces [the zodiacal sign immediately preceding Aries] the trees begin to swell, then burgeon full. . . before the Sun [Apollo, the charioteer of the Sun] harnesses his team [to bear the Sun across the sky] beneath the Bull [Taurus, the sign the Sun enters on April 20]."

64–65. *Argus . . . Syrinx:* Argus (called Panoptes or "the all-seeing") had a hundred eyes all over his body. When Jupiter was smitten by Io, Juno changed the girl into a cow and sent Argus to keep watch over her. Jupiter, in his turn, sent Mercury to lull Argus to sleep either by the magic of his flute or, in the version Dante follows, by a kind of Arabian Nights series of tales about Syrinx, who was loved by Pan, and who was changed into a reed by her sisters to save her from Pan's pursuit. His watch cost him dear because Mercury, after lulling him to sleep, cut off his head. Juno set the eyes of her dead gamekeeper into the tail of the peacock, the bird sacred to her. (See XXIX, 95, note.)

70 ff. DANTE'S DREAM AND AWAKENING. The strains of the heavenly hymn lull Dante into a blissful sleep, which may be taken as symbolizing the serenity of the Kingdom. A radiance reaches through his closed eyes and he awakens to hear a voice cry "Arise!" This is the word with which Christ called Lazarus, among others, from the "greater spell" of death. Obviously, therefore, Dante's awakening symbolizes one more release from mortal error into eternal life. Opening his eyes, Dante finds Matilda bending over him. It was she who cried to him, and at first Dante thinks that all the others have left and that he is alone with her.

Dante then compares his experience to that of Peter, John, and James at the Transfiguration. "And after six days Jesus taketh with him Peter, and James, and John his brother, and bringeth them up into a high mountain apart, and he was transfigured before them: and his face did shine as the sun, and his garments became white as the light . . . they fell on their face, and were sore afraid. And Jesus came and touched them and said, Arise, and be not afraid. And lifting up their eyes, they saw no one, save Jesus only." (*Matthew*, xvii, 1–8.) And see also *Luke*, ix, 28–36, especially, "Now Peter and they that were with him were heavy with sleep: but when they were fully awake, they saw his glory, and the two men that stood with him."

Basing his account on these two passages, Dante adds his own allegory. The vision that is shown to the disciples becomes a vision of Christ as the Mystic

Tree of Heaven (which is, of course, another aspect of the Tree of Good and Evil). The vision, however, is not of the fruit of the tree but of its flowers (line 73). It is, therefore, the vision of the flowering promise of Christ, from which will follow the fruit of eternal rejoicing. The vision is especially apt since, during Dante's sleep, Christ (the Griffon) has reascended to Heaven with most of the Heavenly Procession. There Dante shall follow him in the Paradiso, and there the fruit of felicity awaits.

73. *that Tree*: Christ.

81. *and saw the Master's robe change back to cloth*: I.e., back to its mortal state, as it was before the Transfiguration.

83. *the compassionate lady*: Matilda.

85. *Fearful*: Seeing only Matilda by him, Dante is afraid that Beatrice has left.

86–90. *She is seated on the roots of the new foliage*: As Christ, after his Transfiguration, resumed his earthly appearance, so Beatrice, having entered as the figure of revelation aboard the triumphal chariot, is now seated upon the ground.

Beatrice is seated *on* the ground and *under* the new foliage (that sprang from the touch of Christ—the Griffon). Let the tree in this aspect symbolize the Holy Roman Empire, and the roots Rome. The chariot, of course, represents the Church. It rests on the roots (Rome) and is tied to the tree (the Empire). Beatrice (Divine Love) is left on earth to guard the chariot under the protective shade of the tree, while the Griffon (Christ) ascends to Heaven followed by the rest of the Heavenly Train, which is singing a hymn that is sweeter and profounder than earth can understand. Beatrice is left on earth encircled and attended by the Seven Nymphs (the Three Theological Virtues and the Four Cardinal Virtues).

109–111. Dante's meteorological figure here is based on the belief that the highest reaches of the sky are the domain of fire. The highest clouds, therefore, being closest to the sphere of fire would be especially subject to fiery influences and would give forth the most powerful lightning flashes.

112. *the bird of Jove*: The eagle. See *Ezekiel*, xvii, the Parable of the Eagles and the Cedar. There, the eagle represents the Babylonian persecution of the Jews. Here, Dante clearly enough intends its attack to symbolize the Roman persecution of the early Christians.

118. *a fox*: Is most usually taken to represent the heresies that threatened the early Church and that were repelled by the divine wisdom of the Church Fathers.

124–129. THE GIFT OF THE EAGLE. The Eagle of Imperial Rome returns and covers the car (the Church) with its feathers (riches) and a voice from Heaven cries out in grief. The grief is clearly for the evils that descended upon the Church when it grew rich. Dante must certainly have had the Donation of Constantine (see *Inferno*, XIX, 109–111, and note) in mind in the first feathering of the car. The second gift of the eagle would then symbolize the whole process whereby the temporal wealth of the Empire passed so largely into the hands of the Church.

131. *a dragon:* Satan.

135. *as if it meant to linger:* Having broken the floor of the car (the foundation of the Church, once it has been weakened by wealth), Satan would certainly not run away, but rather remain to see what other mischief he could do, wandering off only very slowly.

142–147. THE CAR TRANSFORMS ITSELF INTO A SEVEN-HEADED MONSTER. "And I saw a woman sitting upon a scarlet-colored beast full of the names of blasphemy, having seven heads and ten horns." (*Revelation*, xvii, 3.)

The Seven Heads have been interpreted in endless ingenious ways. Let them be taken as representing the Seven Deadly Sins. They thus took root in the Church as soon as it covered itself with wealth. The first three of the seven are Pride, Wrath, and Avarice. Being the worst sins, they sprout from the pole (*i.e.,* they come before the others). And since they represent offenses against both God and one's neighbors, they are represented as having two horns. The four lesser sins (Acedia, Envy, Gluttony and Lust) offend God but not necessarily one's neighbors and they are, therefore, represented as having single horns. Thus the total of ten horns.

149–150. *an ungirt harlot:* She represents the Papacy as it existed under Boniface VIII and Clement V, the two Popes Dante most charges with corruption. (See *Inferno*, XIX, and note to 77–79.) "Ungirt" (Dante uses *sciolta*, "untied, unbound") should be understood to imply both lewdness (immodesty of dress) and lack of restraint (knowing no bounds), *her eyes darting with avarice:* looking everywhere for plunder.

152. *a giant:* The French monarchy, and especially Philip the Fair (Philip IV, 1268–1314, crowned in 1285), who made the Papacy his puppet.

154. *But when she turned her hungry eyes on me:* The question here is why the giant beats the harlot for looking at Dante. Again, many answers have been suggested, but two seem most to the point.

If Dante is taken here as representing Italy, the whipping can only refer to Philip's humiliation of Boniface VIII (see Canto XX, 85–93, note), and the harlot's covetous glance at Dante-as-Italy would represent Boniface's intrigues with various rulers. It was these intrigues that put him most at odds with Philip.

On the other hand, Dante may be taken to represent the typical Christian who looks to the Church for guidance. The allegory would then be saying that every time the corrupt Church is stirred by a wish to return to its true pastoral mission, the French kings whip her and drag her back to sin.

158. *and dragged it off:* In 1304 Philip engineered the election of Clement V and transferred the Papal Seat (dragged it off) to Avignon.

Canto XXXIII

THE EARTHLY PARADISE   *Eunoë*

Dante's Purification Completed

The Seven Nymphs sing a hymn of sorrow for the grief of the Church, and Beatrice answers with Christ's words announcing his resurrection. All then move onward, Beatrice summoning Dante to her side as they walk on.

Beatrice begins her discourse with an obscurely worded prophecy of the Deliverance of the Church. In much simpler language, she then utters her FINAL REPROACH TO DANTE for having so lost sight of the truth.

Just as she finishes, the train halts before THE GREAT SPRING from which flow the waters of both Lethe and Eunoë. At Beatrice's command, the Seven Nymphs lead Dante forward and he DRINKS THE WATERS OF EUNOË. By drinking the waters of Lethe, Dante has already forgotten all sin and error; now every good is strengthened in him. Thus is his FINAL PURIFICATION completed, and Dante rises "perfect, pure, and ready for the stars."

"*Deus, venerunt gentes*"—the Holy Seven,
    in alternating chorus through their tears,
    first three, then four, raised a sweet chant to Heaven;

and Beatrice, when she heard them mourn such loss
    sighed with a grief so deep that even Mary   5
    could not have changed more at the foot of the cross.

But when the other virgins in their choir
    fell still for her reply, she rose erect
    in holy zeal, and said, as if afire:

"*Modicum et non videbitis me;*   10
    et iterum, dearly beloved sisters,
    modicum, et vos videbitis me.

Then placing the Seven before her, she moved ahead
    with a nod to me, to the Lady, and to the Sage
    that had remained, to follow where she led.   15

So she strolled on, and she had not yet laid
    her tenth step on the sward, when she turned round
    and struck my eyes with her eyes as she said

with a serene tranquillity: "Draw near,
    that you may, if I wish to speak to you   20
    as we move on, be better placed to hear."

When I was, as I should be, at her side,
    she said: "Dear brother, why are you not moved
    to question me as we move on?"—Tongue-tied,

like one who knows his station is beneath   25
    that of the presences in which he stands,
    and cannot drag his voice across his teeth,

so did I, with a voice almost choked through,
    manage to say: "My Lady, all my need
    and all that is my good is known to you."   30

And she to me: "My wish is that you break
    the grip of fear and shame, and from now on
    no longer speak like one but half awake.

The cart the dragon broke was, and is not;
    let him whose fault that is believe God's wrath   35
    will not be calmed by soup, however hot.

The eagle you saw shed its plumes back there
    to make the cart a monster and a prey,
    will not remain forever without heir;

for certain as my words, my eyes foresee,   40
    already nearing, the unstayable stars
    that bring the time in which, by God's decree,

five hundred, ten, and five shall be the sign
    of one who comes to hunt down and destroy
    the giant and his thievish concubine.   45

My prophecy, being obscure as those
    of Themis and the Sphinx, may fail to move you,
    since all such words hide what they should disclose;

but soon now, like an Oedipus reborn,
    events themselves shall solve the dark enigma,   50
    and without loss of either sheep or corn.

Note my words well, and when you give them breath,
    repeat them as I said them, to the living
    whose life is no more than a race toward death.

And when you come to write them down, make clear 55
    what you have seen of the Tree, now twice-despoiled
    since all-creating God first raised it here.

All those who rob or break those boughs commit
    a blasphemy-in-deed, offending God
    who sacred to Himself created it. 60

For just one bite, the First Soul's tears were spilt
    five thousand years and more, yearning for Him
    who suffered in His own flesh for that guilt.

Your wits must be asleep not to have known
    that a particular reason must account 65
    for its great height and its inverted crown.

Had not your idle thoughts been to your brain
    an Elsan water, and your pleasure in them
    a Pyramus to the mulberry's new stain,

those two facts surely should have made you see 70
    the justice of God's interdict shine forth
    as the moral meaning of the form of the Tree.

It is my wish—because I see your mind
    turned into stone, and like a stone, so darkened
    that the light of what I tell you strikes it blind— 75

that you bear back, if not in writing, then
    in outline, what I say, as pilgrims wreathe
    their staffs with palm to show where they have been."

And I to her: "As pressed wax will retain
    a faithful imprint of the signet ring, 80
    so is your seal imprinted on my brain.
But why do your desired words fly so high
    above my power to follow their intent
    that I see less and less the more I try?"

"They fly so high," she said, "that you may know   85
    what school you followed, and how far behind
    the truth I speak its feeble doctrines go;

and see that man's ways, even at his best,
    are far from God's as earth is from the heaven
    whose swiftest wheel turns above all the rest."   90

"But," I replied, "I have no recollection
    of ever having been estranged from you.
    Conscience does not accuse me of defection."

And she then with a smile: "If, as you say
    you lack that memory, then call to mind   95
    how you drank Lethe's waters here today.

As certainly as smoke betrays the fire,
    this new forgetfulness of your wish to stray
    betrays the sinfulness of that desire.

But I assure you that I shall select   100
    the simplest words that need be from now on
    to make things clear to your dull intellect."

Now with a brighter flame and slower pace
    the sun was holding its meridian height,
    which varies round the world from place to place,   105

when suddenly—as one who leads a line
    of travelers as their escort will stop short
    at a strange sight or an unusual sign—

so stopped the Seven at an edge of shade
    pale as a shadow cast by a cold peak   110
    on a cold stream deep in an Alpine glade.

And there ahead of them, in a single flow,
    Tigris and Euphrates seemed to rise
    and part as friends who linger as they go.
"O light and glory of mankind," I cried,   115
    "what is this flood that pours forth from one source
    and then parts from itself to either side?"

In answer to that prayer I heard the name
    "Matilda" and "ask her." Who spoke up then
    as one does who absolves himself of blame: 120

"This, and much more, I have this very day
    explained to him, and Lethe certainly
    could not have washed that memory away."

And Beatrice: "Perhaps a greater care,
    as often happens, dims his memory   125
    and his mind's eye. But see Eunoë there—

lead him, as is your custom, to the brim
    of that sweet stream, and with its holy waters
    revive the powers that faint and die in him."

Then as a sweet soul gladly shapes its own   130
    good will to the will of others, without protest,
    as soon as any sign has made it known,

so the sweet maid, taking me by the hand
    and saying in a modest voice to Statius,
    "Come you with him," obeyed the good command.   135

Reader, had I the space to write at will,
    I should, if only briefly, sing a praise
    of that sweet draught. Would I were drinking still!

But I have filled all of the pages planned
    for this, my second, canticle, and Art   140
    pulls at its iron bit with iron hand.

I came back from those holiest waters new,
    remade, reborn, like a sun-wakened tree
    that spreads new foliage to the Spring dew

in sweetest freshness, healed of Winter's scars;   145
perfect, pure, and ready for the Stars.

Notes

1. *Deus, venerunt gentes:* Psalm LXXIX, the lamentation for the destruction of Jerusalem. "O God, the heathen are come into thine inheritance; thy holy temple have they defiled; they have laid Jerusalem on heaps." So have the later unbelievers despoiled and defiled the Church.

3. *first three, then four:* The Seven Nymphs sing the psalm antiphonally, the Three Theological Virtues singing first (they being higher in the scale of things), and then the Four Cardinal Virtues.

5–6. *even Mary could not have changed more:* The comparison is not a hyperbole. Beatrice, mourning for the crucifixion of the Church, would endure the same grief Mary suffered at the crucifixion of her son, Christ and the Church being one.

10–12. *Modicum et non videbitis me . . . :* "A little while and ye shall not see me; and again a little while, and ye shall see me [because I go to the Father]." (*John,* xvi, 16.) These are Christ's words to his disciples, announcing his resurrection. Beatrice speaks them afire with her holy zeal in reply to the mournful psalm. She is saying, in effect, that the triumph of the True Faith shall be seen again. On one level her words may be taken to mean that the pure in heart shall rise above the corruption of the Church to see Christ again in Heaven. More likely, Dante meant that the Church shall be purged until Christ is once more truly visible in its workings.

14–15. *the Lady:* Matilda. *the Sage that had remained:* Statius. The other Sage, Virgil, has departed.

17. *her tenth step:* Every number mentioned by Dante invites allegorical conjecture, and many have taken the "ten" here to refer to the Ten Commandments. The interpretation seems doubtful, however, especially since the actual steps taken were not yet ten.

18. *struck my eyes with her eyes:* Dante takes this forceful way of emphasizing the power of her eyes. (The Lamps of Heaven?)

19. *serene tranquillity:* The change in Beatrice is not a matter of feminine mood. When Dante still had upon himself a stain of neglect, Beatrice berated him for it. But he has now done fit penance and the stain has been removed, thereby removing all cause for anger.

22. *When I was, as I should be, at her side:* Dante's whole progress up to this time has been, as it should be the object of every soul, to stand beside Divine Love.

27. *and cannot drag his voice across his teeth:* It is characteristic of Dante that a certain pungency should creep into his phrasing even at such sublime moments.

31–33. *like one but half awake:* Dante has achieved purification, and all memory of sin has been washed from him by the waters of Lethe. He must yet drink of the waters of Eunoë, which will strengthen every good memory in him. Because he has not yet been so strengthened, he still speaks, partly, with the habituated fears and confusions of his former ways. It is these fears and confusions Beatrice is telling him to put by.

34–36. Beatrice now refers to the allegory that concluded Canto XXXII, assuring Dante, as in her answer to the psalm, that a dawn of righteousness is approaching. *was, and is not:* These are the words of John, *Revelation,* xvii, 8: "The beast thou sawest was, and is not." *soup:* In some parts of ancient Greece a murderer could protect himself from all vengeance if for nine successive days he ate soup on the grave of his victim. In Florence it became a custom to stand guard for nine days over the grave of a murdered man to see that no one ate soup upon it. The reference is a strange one, but Dante's intent is, clearly, that no such simple rite will ward off the vengeance of God.

37–39. *the eagle . . . will not remain forever without heir:* The eagle is, of course, the Roman Empire. The true heir of the Caesars, who will restore order and goodness, will come at last. Dante thought of Frederick II as the last real heir of the Caesars.

41. *the unstayable stars:* Nothing can stay the stars in their courses. Beatrice foresees propitious stars already near at hand. (God's wrath will not be stayed: cf. lines 35–36)

43. *five hundred, ten, and five:* As Beatrice says in the next tercet, she is speaking in the veiled tongue of prophecy, and her words hide what they should disclose. Whatever the numerological significance Dante intended by the number, it cannot be identified. Since Dante could make himself clear enough when he wanted to, and since he goes on to have Beatrice say that her meaning is hidden, it follows, as a fair guess, that Dante deliberately kept his reference vague.

46–51. The basic sense of this passage is: "Though my way of speaking is obscure, events themselves will soon make clear my meaning." It is the mythological references that may confuse the modern reader. *Themis:* Daughter of Gaea (Earth) and Uranus (Heaven). She was the second wife of Zeus, and later, no longer as his wife, became his Goddess of Law and Order. She was noted for the obscurity of her oracles. *the Sphinx:* A monster with the head of an innocent maiden and the body of a savage beast. One of the oracles of Themis. She waited for travelers on a rock near Thebes and killed them when they failed to solve her famous riddle: "What walks on four legs in the morning, on two at noon, and on three at night?" *Oedipus:* The ill-fated King of Thebes answered properly that the riddle meant a man in the three stages of his life (for he crawls on all fours as an infant, walks on two legs in the middle of his life, and totters on two legs and a cane thereafter). The Sphinx was so enraged on hearing the right answer that she killed herself. (Dante's text reads not "Oedipus" but "the Naiads." The Naiads had no connection with the riddle. Dante's error follows a corrupt text of Ovid's *Metamorphoses,* VII, 759, which reads "Naiades"—the Naiads—for "Laiades"—son of Laius, i.e., Oedipus.) *without loss of either sheep or corn:* Themis, to avenge her oracle, sent a monstrous beast to ravage the flocks and fields of Thebes.

52. *and when you give them breath:* This phrase is my own invention, forced upon the text by the, to me, clear necessity to render line 54 with "death" as the rhyme. I hope the rendering will seem at least approximately Dantean: since the words thus far have been spoken only by Beatrice, a spirit, they have not yet been given breath, as they will be when Dante repeats them with his mortal voice.

56. *twice-despoiled:* Dante probably meant the Fall as the first despoilment of the tree, and the corruption of the Church as the second.

59. *blasphemy-in-deed:* As distinct from blasphemy-in-word and blasphemy-in-thought.

61. *the First Soul's:* Adam's.

62. *five thousand years and more:* According to *Genesis,* v, 5, Adam lived 930 years on earth. According to *Paradiso,* XXVI, 118, he then waited in Limbo for 4,302 years. Dante follows, in this, the chronology of the ecclesiastical historian Eusebius, who set Christ's birth in the year 5200 since the Creation. Christ's death, therefore (and the Harrowing of Hell, for which see *Inferno,* IV, 53, note), would have occurred in the year 5232.

65. *particular reason:* The tree is enormously tall and broadens toward the crown (hence "inverted"). The "particular reason" for such a form must have been to make the fruit inaccessible to man. The story of *Genesis,* however, indicates that Eve certainly had no trouble getting her apple. It must follow that the tree has grown since *Genesis.* According to the chronology of Eusebius, the year 1300 would be the year 6500 since Creation— time enough for the knowledge of good and evil to show some substantial growth rings.

68–69. *an Elsan water:* The Elsa, a river of Tuscany, is so rich in lime that at some points along its course objects left in its waters will either petrify or become coated. So Dante's idle thoughts (seemingly flowing around his brain more than through it) have petrified his intellect. *a Pyramus to the mulberry's new stain:* The blood of Pyramus (and Thisbe) stained the mulberry red. (See XXVII, 37 ff., note.) So Dante's delight in his idle thoughts has stained his intellect. Lines 73–75, below, further explain Dante's meaning here.

72. *the moral meaning:* The form of the tree symbolizes its essential nature. Interpreted in the moral sense (as distinct, for example, from the allegorical narrative, or anagogical senses) the two main facts of the tree's form (its great height and inverted crown) express how far above and beyond man is the final understanding of Good and Evil. Hence the justice of God's interdict in forbidding man what lies beyond his grasp.

74. *turned into stone:* As if by Elsan waters, *so darkened:* As was the mulberry.

77–78. *as pilgrims wreathe their staffs with palm:* The palm grows in the Holy Land. Returning pilgrims wreathed their staffs with palm to prove they had been there.

86. *what school you followed:* The school of philosophy, whose error lies in placing its dependence on reason as an end, and which cannot, therefore, comprehend the mysteries of faith.

89–90. *the heaven whose swiftest wheel. . . .* The Primum Mobile, uppermost of the nine spheres. Since all the spheres turn together, the outermost must move most swiftly.

91–102. BEATRICE'S LAST REPROACH. Dante protests that he has no recollection of ever having been estranged from Beatrice, despite the fact that he had relied more heavily on human philosophy than on divine love. Beatrice, smiling, points out that he has just drunk the waters of Lethe, whose powers wipe away all memory of sin. Since they have wiped out the memory of his estrangement, it follows that the estrangement was sinful.

But Beatrice cannot mean that he sinned in following Virgil, for she herself sent him to Dante. Dante's sinful estrangement must have happened before he met Virgil. And since it was from the three beasts of worldliness that Virgil rescued Dante, setting him on the road to the mysteries of faith, worldliness (or the overexaltation of philosophy as his guide) must be the sin that estranged Dante from Beatrice. (See note to XXX, 124–126.)

103. *brighter flame and slower pace:* To an observer the sun seems brightest at its noon height and seems to move most slowly then. (Its slowness is an illusion, as is the speed with which it seems to set once it has touched the horizon, but its brightness can be accounted for by the fact that its rays travel a vertical, and hence shortest, course through the atmosphere at noon.)

105. *varies round the world from place to place:* In one sense, the sun is always at the meridian: it is always noon somewhere on the earth.

113. *Tigris and Euphrates:* The Tigris flows through Turkey and Iraq (ancient Chaldea) to join the Euphrates, which rises in Armenia and flows into the Persian Gulf. *Genesis*, ii, 10 ff:, identifies the Euphrates as one of the four rivers of Eden, all of which rise from the same source. The rivers of Dante's Earthly Paradise are Lethe and Eunoë. They "seem to rise" as if they were Tigris and Euphrates rising from a single spring.

117. *parts from itself to either side:* The two rivers flow off in opposite directions, just as their powers, rising from one source, work in opposite ways to achieve one good.

122–123. *Lethe certainly could not have washed that memory away:* There being nothing sinful in it.

142–146. Dante ends each canticle with the word "stars," a fixed architectural device, and one that any rendition must preserve at whatever cost. Unfortunately for English renditions, the cost of forcing a rhyme for "stars" is great, and I have had to take considerable liberties. More closely rendered, these lines read: "I came back from that holiest wave [flood] made new like new trees renewed with new foliage, pure and prepared to mount to the stars."

from **Paradiso**

Canto XXXIII

Prayer to the Virgin
The Vision of God

ST. BERNARD offers a lofty PRAYER TO THE VIRGIN, asking her to intercede in Dante's behalf, and in answer Dante feels his soul swell with new power and grow calm in rapture as his eyes are permitted the DIRECT VISION OF GOD.

There can be no measure of how long the vision endures. It passes, and Dante is once more mortal and fallible. Raised by God's presence, he had looked into the Mystery and had begun to understand its power and majesty. Returned to himself, there is no power in him capable of speaking the truth of what he saw. Yet the impress of the truth is stamped upon his soul, which he now knows will return to be one with God's Love.

"Virgin Mother, daughter of thy son;
    humble beyond all creatures and more exalted;
    predestined turning point of God's intention;

thy merit so ennobled human nature
    that its divine Creator did not scorn   5
    to make Himself the creature of His creature.

The Love that was rekindled in Thy womb
    sends forth the warmth of the eternal peace
    within whose ray this flower has come to bloom.

Here, to us, thou art the noon and scope   10
    of Love revealed; and among mortal men,
    the living fountain of eternal hope.

Lady, thou art so near God's reckonings
    that who seeks grace and does not first seek thee
    would have his wish fly upward without wings.   15

Not only does thy sweet benignity
    flow out to all who beg, but oftentimes
    thy charity arrives before the plea.

In thee is pity, in thee munificence,
    in thee the tenderest heart, in thee unites   20
    all that creation knows of excellence!

Now comes this man who from the final pit
    of the universe up to this height has seen,
    one by one, the three lives of the spirit.

He prays to thee in fervent supplication   25
    for grace and strength, that he may raise his eyes
    to the all-healing final revelation.

And I, who never more desired to see
    the vision myself than I do that he may see It,
    add my own prayer, and pray that it may be   30

enough to move you to dispel the trace
    of every mortal shadow by thy prayers
    and let him see revealed the Sum of Grace.

I pray thee further, all-persuading Queen,
    keep whole the natural bent of his affections   35
    and of his powers after his eyes have seen.

Protect him from the stirrings of man's clay;
    see how Beatrice and the blessed host
    clasp reverent hands to join me as I pray."

The eyes that God reveres and loves the best   40
    glowed on the speaker, making clear the joy
    with which true prayer is heard by the most blest.

Those eyes turned then to the Eternal Ray,
    through which, we must indeed believe, the eyes
    of others do not find such ready way.   45

And I, who neared the goal of all my nature,
    felt my soul, at the climax of its yearning,
    suddenly, as it ought, grow calm with rapture.
Bernard then, smiling sweetly, gestured to me
    to look up, but I had already become   50
    within myself all he would have me be.

Little by little as my vision grew
    it penetrated further through the aura
    of the high lamp which in Itself is true.

What then I saw is more than tongue can say.   55
    Our human speech is dark before the vision.
    The ravished memory swoons and falls away.

As one who sees in dreams and wakes to find
    the emotional impression of his vision
    still powerful while its parts fade from his mind—   60

just such am I, having lost nearly all
    the vision itself, while in my heart I feel
    the sweetness of it yet distill and fall.

So, in the sun, the footprints fade from snow.
    On the wild wind that bore the tumbling leaves   65
    the Sybil's oracles were scattered so.

O Light Supreme who doth Thyself withdraw
    so far above man's mortal understanding,
    lend me again some glimpse of what I saw;

make Thou my tongue so eloquent it may   70
    of all Thy glory speak a single clue
    to those who follow me in the world's day;

for by returning to my memory
    somewhat, and somewhat sounding in these verses,
    Thou shalt show man more of Thy victory.   75

So dazzling was the splendor of that Ray,
    that I must certainly have lost my senses
    had I, but for an instant, turned away.

And so it was, as I recall, I could
    the better bear to look, until at last   80
    my vision made one with the Eternal Good.
Oh grace abounding that had made me fit
    to fix my eyes on the eternal light
    until my vision was consumed in it!

I saw within Its depth how It conceives   85
    all things in a single volume bound by Love,
    of which the universe is the scattered leaves;

substance, accident, and their relation
    so fused that all I say could do no more
    than yield a glimpse of that bright revelation.   90

I think I saw the universal form
    that binds these things, for as I speak these words
    I feel my joy swell and my spirits warm.

Twenty-five centuries since Neptune saw
    the *Argo's* keel have not moved all mankind,   95
    recalling that adventure, to such awe

as I felt in an instant. My tranced being
    stared fixed and motionless upon that vision,
    ever more fervent to see in the act of seeing.

Experiencing that Radiance, the spirit   100
    is so indrawn it is impossible
    even to think of ever turning from It.

For the good which is the will's ultimate object
    is all subsumed in It; and, being removed,
    all is defective which in It is perfect.   105

Now in my recollection of the rest
    I have less power to speak than any infant
    wetting its tongue yet at its mother's breast;

and not because that Living Radiance bore
    more than one semblance, for It is unchanging   110
    and is forever as it was before;

rather, as I grew worthier to see,
    the more I looked, the more unchanging semblance
    appeared to change with every change in me.
Within the depthless deep and clear existence   115
    of that abyss of light three circles shone—
    three in color, one in circumference:

the second from the first, rainbow from rainbow;
    the third, an exhalation of pure fire
    equally breathed forth by the other two.   120

But oh how much my words miss my conception,
    which is itself so far from what I saw
    that to call it feeble would be rank deception!

O Light Eternal fixed in Itself alone,
    by Itself alone understood, which from Itself   125
    loves and glows, self-knowing and self-known;

that second aureole which shone forth in Thee,
    conceived as a reflection of the first—
    or which appeared so to my scrutiny—

seemed in Itself of Its own coloration   130
    to be painted with man's image. I fixed my eyes
    on that alone in rapturous contemplation.

Like a geometer wholly dedicated
    to squaring the circle, but who cannot find,
    think as he may, the principle indicated—   135

so did I study the supernal face.
    I yearned to know just how our image merges
    into that circle, and how it there finds place;

but mine were not the wings for such a flight.
    Yet, as I wished, the truth I wished for came   140
    cleaving my mind in a great flash of light.

Here my powers rest from their high fantasy,
    but already I could feel my being turned—
    instinct and intellect balanced equally

as in a wheel whose motion nothing jars—   145
by the Love that moves the Sun and the other stars.

Notes

1–39. ST. BERNARD'S PRAYER TO THE VIRGIN MARY. No reader who has come this far will need a lengthy gloss of Bernard's prayer. It can certainly be taken as a summarizing statement of the special place of Mary in Catholic faith. For the rest only a few turns of phrase need underlining. 3. *predestined turning point of God's intention:* All-foreseeing God built his whole scheme for mankind with Mary as its pivot, for through her He would become man. 7. *The Love that was rekindled in thy womb:* God. In a sense he withdrew from man when Adam and Eve sinned. In Mary He returned and Himself became man. 35. *keep whole the natural bent of his affections:* Bernard is asking Mary to protect Dante lest the intensity of the vision overpower his faculties. 37. *Protect him from the stirrings of man's clay:* Protect him from the stirrings of base human impulse, especially from pride, for Dante is about to receive a grace never before granted to any man and the thought of such glory might well move a mere mortal to an hubris that would turn glory to sinfulness.

40. *the eyes:* Of Mary.

50. *but I had already become:* I.e., "But I had already fixed my entire attention upon the vision of God." But if so, how could Dante have seen Bernard's smile and gesture? Eager students like to believe they catch Dante in a contradiction here. Let them bear in mind that Dante is looking directly at God, as do the souls of Heaven, who thereby acquire—insofar as they are able to contain it—God's own knowledge. As a first stirring of that heavenly power, therefore, Dante is sharing God's knowledge of St. Bernard.

54. *which in Itself is true:* The light of God is the one light whose source is Itself. All others are a reflection of this.

65–66. *tumbling leaves . . . oracles:* The Cumean Sybil (Virgil describes her in *Aeneid*, III, 441 ff.) wrote her oracles on leaves, one letter to a leaf, then sent her message scattering on the wind. Presumably, the truth was all contained in that strew, could one only gather all the leaves and put the letters in the right order.

76–81. How can a light be so dazzling that the beholder would swoon if he looked away for an instant? Would it not be, rather, in looking at, not away from, the overpowering vision that the viewer's senses would be overcome? So it would be on earth. But now Dante, with the help of all heaven's prayers, is in the presence of God and strengthened by all he sees. It is by being so strengthened that he can see yet more. So the passage becomes a parable of grace. Stylistically it once more illustrates Dante's genius: even at this height of concept, the poet can still summon and invent new perceptions, subtlety exfoliating from subtlety.

The simultaneous metaphoric statement, of course, is that no man can lose his good in the vision of God, but only in looking away from it.

85–87. The idea here is Platonic: the essence of all things (form) exists in the mind of God. All other things exist as exempla.

88. *substance:* Matter, all that exists in itself, *accident:* All that exists as a phase of matter.

92. *these things:* Substance and accident.

109–114. In the presence of God the soul grows ever more capable of perceiving God. Thus, the worthy soul's experience of God is a constant expansion of awareness. God appears to change as He is better seen. Being perfect, He is changeless within Himself, for any change would be away from perfection.

130–144. The central metaphor of the entire *Comedy* is the image of God and the final triumphant in-Godding of the elected soul returning to its Maker. On the mystery of that image, the metaphoric symphony of the *Comedy* comes to rest.

In the second aspect of Trinal-unity, in the circle reflected from the first, Dante thinks he sees the image of mankind woven into the very substance and coloration of God. He turns the entire attention of his soul to that mystery, as a geometer might seek to shut out every other thought and dedicate himself to squaring the circle. In *Il Convivio*, II, 14, Dante asserted that the circle could not be squared, but that impossibility had not yet been firmly demonstrated in Dante's time and mathematicians still worked at the problem. Note, however, that Dante assumes the impossibility of squaring the circle as a weak mortal example of mortal impossibility. How much more impossible, he implies, to resolve the mystery of God, study as man will.

The mystery remains beyond Dante's mortal power. Yet, there in Heaven, in a moment of grace, God revealed the truth to him in a flash of light—revealed it, that is, to the God-enlarged power of Dante's emparadised soul. On Dante's return to the mortal life, the details of that revelation vanished from his mind but the force of the revelation survives in its power on Dante's feelings.

So ends the vision of the *Comedy*, and yet the vision endures, for ever since that revelation, Dante tells us, he feels his soul turning ever as one with the perfect motion of God's love.